DICTIONARY OF
ESSENTIAL
SYNONYMS
AND ANTONYMS

Mohd Masood Ishaq is a faculty in a reputed college in Hyderabad, and has more than eighteen years' teaching experience. He teaches general English, soft skills and spoken English to adults at Global English Academy, Hyderabad, and coaches students preparing for competitive examinations at CEDM, Nizam College, Hyderabad. Previously, he taught spoken English at Rama Krishna Math, Hyderabad. He is also an academic consultant for the distance education students of Maulana Azad National Urdu University, Hyderabad. Besides teaching, he is a freelance content developer for English and general books and prepares language material for students of competitive examinations in Hyderabad. He has authored a bestselling academic book *Effective Spoken English and Grammar* and a thought-provoking play *An Interview @ Tiger International School: A Comic Play on Fancy School Education*.

DICTIONARY OF
ESSENTIAL SYNONYMS AND ANTONYMS

For All Competitive Examinations

MOHD MASOOD ISHAQ

RUPA

Published by
Rupa Publications India Pvt. Ltd 2021
7/16, Ansari Road, Daryaganj
New Delhi 110002

Sales centres:
Allahabad Bengaluru Chennai
Hyderabad Jaipur Kathmandu
Kolkata Mumbai

ISBN: 978-93-90547-08-1

First impression 2021

10 9 8 7 6 5 4 3 2 1

Printed at Nutech Print Services, Faridabad

*Dedicated to my
brothers and sisters*

Preface

This *Dictionary of Essential Synonyms and Antonyms: For All Competitive Examinations* provides a clear and comprehensive selection of thousands of words and their closest synonyms and antonyms. Though primarily written for students appearing for competitive and entrance examinations, this dictionary is essential for everyone who wants to use language well, whether speaking or writing, at work, at home or for fun. The reader will also find this dictionary a useful resource for crossword puzzles and other word games.

Since a book of this size cannot possibly list all words of the English language, some simple words were deliberately left out. Yet it contains hundreds of selective primary words that are useful for cracking competitive examinations. Not just this, it also provides a broad selection of words that are common in everyday usage.

This innovative dictionary is designed especially to meet the day-to-day needs of those who want a compact and handy book on synonyms and antonyms. It is also an ideal companion for school and college students for their academic examinations. It will help students as well as lay persons to expand their vocabulary and improve verbal skills.

All entries are listed in an alphabetical order and parts of speech labels are given to all the headwords. They are abbreviated as follows:

n (noun)
v (verb)
adv (adverb)
adj (adjective)
prep (preposition)
conj (conjunction)

Also, some headwords are labelled with the words *informal*, *humorous*, *literary*, *law*, *old use*, *old-fashioned* that express a particular attitude or appropriateness in a particular situation.

You have in your hand the perfect resourceful dictionary for all your examinations and general communication. I hope you will enjoy using it in all your best endeavours. Use it and see your English improve.

I earnestly hope that the book would find proper response from teachers and learners of English. I will be thankful to have constructive suggestions, new ideas and new techniques for the improvement of this book. You can write to me at masoodenglish@gmail.com

I wish you a happy and successful journey through the book.

Aa

abandon (v)
syn. desert, leave, ditch, quit, discard, abdicate, renounce
ant. keep, stay, continue

abase (v)
syn. degrade, disgrace, demean, malign, humiliate, debase, depress
ant. honour, elevate, exalt

abashed (adj)
syn. ashamed, bewildered, discouraged, humiliated, shamefaced, cowed
ant. unabashed, composed, audacious

abate (v)
syn. subside, decrease, fade, alleviate, diminish, weaken
ant. intensify, increase, strengthen

abbreviate (v)
syn. shorten, condense, reduce, abridge, precis, summarize
ant. expand, lengthen

abdicate (v)
syn. quit, renounce, abandon, give up, abjure, surrender
ant. retain, hold, maintain

aberration (n)
syn. defect, eccentricity, abnormality, freak, illusion, peculiarity, rouge
ant. conformity, regularity

abet (v)
syn. assist, aid, help, encourage, promote, succour, uphold
ant. discourage, block, hinder

abeyance (n)
syn. inactivity, discontinuation, recess, lull, waiting, suspension
ant. activity, continuation, revival

abhor (v)
syn. hate, despise, detest, loathe, abominate, execrate
ant. admire, love, adore

abide (v)
syn. continue, accept, remain, submit, tolerate
ant. dispute, quit

ability (n)
syn. capability, capacity, potential, talent
ant. inability, incompetence

abject (adj)
syn. contemptible, mean, degraded, miserable, deplorable, forlorn, hopeless
ant. honourable, exalted

abjure (v)
syn. abandon, deny, discard, disown, reject, relinquish, renounce
ant. assent, agree, support

able (adj)
syn. talented, skilled, intelligent, adept, competent, expert
ant. incompetent, incapable

abnormal (adj)
syn. strange, freak, odd, peculiar, unusual, eccentric
ant. normal

abolish (v)
syn. remove, ban, dissolve, cancel, nullify, revoke
ant. continue, retain

abominable (adj)
syn. hateful, repellent, loathsome, disgusting, unpleasant, horrible, obnoxious
ant. admirable, good, delightful, lovable

aborigine (n)
syn. aboriginal, native
ant. immigrant

abortive (adj)
syn. vain, unsuccessful, futile, failed, idle, useless
ant. successful, productive

abrasive (adj)
syn. harsh, rough, coarse, annoying, hurtful, biting
ant. gentle, compassionate

abridge (v)
syn. condense, shorten, edit, summarize, concise, reduce, cut
ant. extend, expand, amplify

abrogate (v)
syn. cancel, abolish, annul, dissolve, end, nullify, recall, repeal
ant. establish, institute

abrupt (adj)
syn. blunt, brisk, curt, discourteous, hasty, hurried, impolite, short
ant. leisurely, ceremonious, expansive
absolute (adj)
syn. perfect, complete, sheer, unlimited, actual, definite
ant. partial, limited, conditional
absolve (v)
syn. discharge, excuse, acquit, forgive, let off, redeem, vindicate
ant. charge, condemn
absorbing (adj)
syn. interesting, fascinating, engrossing, captivating, enthralling
ant. boring, dull
abstemious (adj)
syn. disciplined, moderate, self-denying, sober, abstinent, ascetic, teetotal
ant. intemperate, gluttonous, luxurious, greedy
abstinence (n)
syn. self-restraint, sobriety, self-denial, frugality
ant. self-indulgence
abstract (n)
syn. synopsis, summary, outline, epitome, precise, essence
ant. expansion, amplification, enlargement
absurd (adj)
syn. illogical, pointless, irrational, ridiculous, stupid, silly, crazy
ant. sensible, logical, rational
abundance (n)
syn. plenty, plethora, profusion, bonanza, riches, bounty
ant. scarcity, dearth
abusive (adj)
syn. rude, offensive, insulting, violent, derisive, derogatory
ant. polite, complimentary
accede (v)
syn. agree, accept, assume, concede, endorse, inherit
ant. object, demur
accelerate (v)
syn. speed up, hurry, hasten, crank up
ant. delay
acceptance (n)
syn. acknowledgement, consent, agreement

ant. refusal, dissent
accessible (adj)
syn. approachable, reachable, available
ant. inaccessible
accidental (adj)
syn. coincidental, unexpected, incidental, chance, unplanned
ant. intentional
acclaim (n)
syn. praise, tributes, admiration, approval
ant. criticism
accolade (n)
syn. praise, laurels, award, kudos, honour
ant. criticism, blame
accomplished (adj)
syn. expert, skilled, gifted, polished, talented, ace
ant. inexpert, unskilled
accord (n)
syn. agreement, deal, treaty, pact, consensus
ant. disagreement, discord
accredited (adj)
syn. approved, authorized, certified
ant. unauthorized
accumulate (v)
syn. amass, gather, stash, increase, collect, store, grow
ant. disperse, disseminate, diffuse
accursed (adj)
syn. bewitched, cursed, condemned, ill-fated
ant. blessed
accuse (v)
syn. blame, allege, charge, inculpate, impute, incriminate, indict
ant. exonerate, exculpable, defend
ace (adj)
syn. champion, brilliant, great, matchless, expert, excellent, first-class, star
ant. amateur, inept, unskilled
acerbity (n)
syn. bitterness, sourness, sarcasm, acrimony, trenchancy
ant. mildness, sweetness

acknowledge (v)
syn. accept, concede, admit, allow, recognize, answer, respond to
ant. deny, ignore
acolyte (n)
syn. admirer, follower, slave, assistant
ant. opponent, rival
acquiescence (n)
syn. agreement, assent, compliance, conformity, consent, acceptance, approval
ant. disagreement, rebelliousness
acquire (v)
syn. gain, get, obtain, procure, collect, bag
ant. lose, relinquish
acquisition (n)
syn. achievement, gain, possession, attainment, procurement, take-over
ant. loss, lack, dearth
acquit (v)
syn. clear, absolve, free, exonerate, exculpate, pardon
ant. convict, condemn
acrid (adj)
syn. acrimonious, bitter, harsh, acid, nasty, venomous, malicious
ant. delicious, complimentary
acrimonious (adj)
syn. abusive, ill-tempered, peevish, harsh, nasty, ill-natured
ant. kindly, peaceable
acting (adj)
syn. interim, temporary, provisional
ant. permanent
actual (adj)
syn. genuine, real, authentic, absolute, factual
ant. imaginary, false
acumen (n)
syn. cleverness, insight, intuition, quickness, shrewdness, intelligence, perception
ant. obtuseness, stupidity
acute (adj)
syn. serious, sharp, perceptive, astute, keen, shrewd, intelligent, canny
ant. dull, mild

adamant (adj)
syn. resolute, unshakeable, rigid, determined
ant. flexible, pliant

adapt (v)
syn. modify, change, adjust, tailor, remodel, accommodate
ant. differ, dislocate, misfit

add (v)
syn. affix, attach, include
ant. subtract

adept (adj)
syn. skilful, expert, ace, masterly, proficient, accomplished
ant. inept, incompetent

adequate (adj)
syn. enough, sufficient, reasonable, tolerable
ant. inadequate, insufficient

adherent (n)
syn. follower, advocate, supporter, fan, devotee
ant. opponent, cynic

adjourn (v)
syn. suspend, discontinue, putt off, postpone, hold over
ant. convene, complete

adjunct (n)
syn. accessory, addition, extension, auxiliary, supplement, appendix
ant. lessening, subtraction

admirable (adj)
syn. praiseworthy, sterling, commendable, good, worthy, excellent
ant. deplorable, despicable

admiration (n)
syn. respect, appreciation, esteem, liking, awe, regard
ant. contempt, scorn, mockery, ridicule

admire (v)
syn. adore, respect, love, worship, esteem
ant. despise, hate

admirer (n)
syn. devotee, fan, follower, disciple
ant. critic

admit (v)
syn. acknowledge, confess, accept, disclose, receive

ant. deny, exclude
admittance (n)
syn. entry, entrance, admission, access, acceptance, reception
ant. exclusion
admonish (v)
syn. advise, chide, caution, rebuke, scold, warn, censure, tell off
ant. praise, applaud, commend
adolescent (n)
syn. teenager, juvenile, teen, youth
ant. adult, oldie
adopt (v)
syn. endorse, embrace, choose, approve
ant. abandon, disown
adore (v)
syn. love, admire, revere, worship, venerate, esteem
ant. hate, abhor, despise
adorn (v)
syn. beautify, decorate, ornament, embellish, trim, array, enrich
ant. disfigure, strip
adrift (adj)
syn. aimless, anchorless, goalless, purposeless, insecure, amiss, lost, at sea
ant. stable, anchored, secure
adroit (adj)
syn. adept, clever, able, apt, expert, ingenious, nimble, skilled
ant. inept, clumsy, maladroit
adulation (n)
syn. bootlicking, flattery, blandishment, fawning, sycophancy, worship, idolatry
ant. obloquy, censure, abuse
adult (adj)
syn. mature, grown-up, of age
ant. immature
adulterate (v)
syn. contaminate, corrupt, bastardise, devalue, pollute, infect
ant. refine, cleanse, purify
advance (v)
syn. attack, press on, proceed, strengthen, support
ant. retreat, retard

advent (n)
syn. arrival, dawn, inception, appearance, introduction, approach
ant. end, departure
adventurous (adj)
syn. bold, daring, impetuous, perilous, risky, venturesome, audacious, rash
ant. timid, prudent, cautious, chary
adversary (n)
syn. rival, enemy, opponent, antagonist, competitor, foe
ant. ally, supporter, friend
adversity (n)
syn. distress, hardship, misery, bad luck, affliction, catastrophe, suffering
ant. prosperity
affable (adj)
syn. amiable, amicable, agreeable, cordial, mild, kindly, gracious, sociable, urbane
ant. unfriendly, reserved, cool, reticent
affectation (n)
syn. mannerism, pose, theatricality, fakery, artificiality, act, insincerity, pretence, show
ant. ingenuousness, artlessness
affinity (n)
syn. sympathy, harmony, understanding, closeness, bond, empathy, chemistry
ant. aversion, antipathy
afflict (v)
syn. burden, trouble, beset, distress, harass, torment
ant. comfort, solace
agile (adj)
syn. adroit, alert, clever, acute, lively, nimble, sharp, alert, active
ant. stiff, clumsy, torpid
agitation (n)
syn. clamour, alarm, anxiety, disquiet, disturbance, outcry, turmoil
ant. calm, tranquillity
agog (adj)
syn. curious, excited, avid, eager, keen, enthralled
ant. incurious, laid-back

agony (n)
syn. suffering, pain, torture, anguish, torment, misery
ant. ecstasy, comfort, relief
aid (n)
syn. assistance, help, backing, support, helper, assistant, ally
ant. hindrance, opponent
ailing (adj)
syn. ill, sickly, weak, unwell, suffering, in poor/bad health, fragile
ant. healthy, flourishing
aimless (adj)
syn. undirected, purposeless, random, useless
ant. purposeful
akin (adj)
syn. close, related, similar, alike, analogous
ant. unlike, unrelated
alacrity (n)
syn. avidity, alertness, cheerfulness, gaiety, liveliness, quickness, zeal
ant. disinclination, reluctance, apathy
alien (adj)
syn. foreign, unknown, unfamiliar, exotic
ant. native, familiar
alienate (v)
syn. isolate, estrange, distance, cut off, divorce, antagonize, separate
ant. conciliate, friendly
affluent (adj)
syn. wealthy, moneyed, rich, well off, prosperous, well-to-do, opulent
ant. poor, penniless, impoverished, impecunious
affront (v)
syn. annoy, abuse, anger, displease, insult, snub, provoke, offend, outrage
ant. appease, compliment
afraid (adj)
syn. apprehensive, fearful, frightened, reluctant, shy, unwilling, hesitant
ant. unafraid, confident, brave
aggravate (v)
syn. inflame, worsen, annoy, irritate, provoke, vex, magnify
ant. alleviate, appease, improve
aggressive (adj)
syn. violent, combative, antagonistic, warlike, bellicose, forceful

ant. peaceable, peaceful, submissive
aggrieved (adj)
syn. distressed, hurt, afflicted, insulted, pained, offended, unhappy
ant. pleased, contented
aghast (adj)
syn. astonished, frightened, shocked, amazed, terrified
ant. calm, unaffected, unsurprised
alike (adj)
syn. akin, equal, identical, similar, the same
ant. unlike, different
allay (v)
syn. appease, calm, alleviate, lull, pacify, reduce
ant. intensify, exacerbate
alleged (adj)
syn. reported, claimed, unproven, supposed
ant. confirmed
allegiance (n)
syn. faithfulness, adherence, devotion, obedience, loyalty
ant. enmity, disloyalty, treachery
alleviate (v)
syn. allay, ease, relieve, reduce, lessen, soothe
ant. aggravate, intensify
alliance (n)
syn. union, association, league, syndicate, coalition, marriage
ant. estrangement, hostility, divorce
allied (adj)
syn. united, associated, linked, combined, in league
ant. unrelated, independent
allure (n)
syn. appeal, charm, lure, attraction, enticement, glamour
ant. repulsion
ally (n)
syn. associate, friend, accomplice, colleague, supporter
ant. enemy, antagonist, opponent
aloof (adj)
syn. remote, distant, unfriendly, reserved, detached
ant. friendly, amicable

altercation (n)
syn. disagreement, argument, discord, quarrel, row, contention
ant. agreement, concord, harmony
altruism (n)
syn. generosity, philanthropy, unselfishness, humanity, public, spirit
ant. selfishness
amalgamate (v)
syn. unite, mix, combine, blend, join
ant. separate
amass (v)
syn. gather, assemble, collect, accumulate, stockpile
ant. scatter, disperse
amateur (n)
syn. layman, non-professional, dabbler
ant. expert, professional
ambiguity (n)
syn. obscurity, uncertainty, vagueness, confusion, enigma, ambivalence
ant. clarity, certainty
ambivalence (n)
syn. ambiguity, confusion, hesitancy, uncertainty, irresolution, clash
ant. certainty, clarity
ameliorate (v)
syn. elevate, advance, enhance, improve, reform, promote
ant. exacerbate, worsen
amenable (adj)
syn. agreeable, docile, responsible, open, submissive, tractable, accountable
ant. defiant, intractable, obstinate
amenity (n)
syn. convenience, attraction, charm, beauty, comfort, facility
ant. inconvenience, eyesore
amiable (adj)
syn. cordial, friendly, amicable, likeable, pleasant, nice
ant. unfriendly, disagreeable
amicable (adj)
syn. amiable, friendly, sociable, congenial, harmonious, polite
ant. hostile, unfriendly

amity (n)
syn. friendship, accord, cordiality, harmony, fellowship, good will, understanding
ant. enmity, hostility

amorous (adj)
syn. affectionate, attached, erotic, lovesick, passionate, impassioned, lustful
ant. cold, indifferent

amorphous (adj)
syn. vague, chaotic, undefined, irregular, characterless, indistinct, confused
ant. definite, distinctive, ordered

ample (adj)
syn. considerable, abundant, plenty, big, sufficient, liberal, large, enough
ant. meagre, insufficient

amusement (n)
syn. delight, entertainment, glee, mirth, pastime, recreation
ant. bore, boredom

anaemic (adj)
syn. bloodless, colourless, dull, feeble, sickly, insipid
ant. ruddy, full-blooded

analogy (n)
syn. comparison, similarity, relation, likeness, resemblance, parallel
ant. difference, dissimilarity

anarchy (n)
syn. pandemonium, chaos, lawlessness, riot, disorder, revolution
ant. rule, order, peace

ancestor (n)
syn. forefather, predecessor, progenitor, grandparent
ant. descendant

ancient (adj)
syn. archaic, age-old, olden, early, bygone
ant. modern, contemporary, recent

angelic (adj)
syn. beautiful, heavenly, saintly, virtuous, adorable, divine
ant. devilish, fiendish

angry (adj)
syn. vexed, furious, irked, enraged, displeased, annoyed
ant. pleased, calm

anguish (n)
syn. suffering, pain, agony, woe, distress, sorrow, heartache
ant. happiness, solace
animated (adj)
syn. energetic, excited, lively, enthusiastic, spirited, full of life, vigorous, quick, elated, gay
ant. inert, lethargic, lifeless, sluggish, dull
animosity (n)
syn. enmity, antipathy, hostility, hatred, loathing, animus, malice
ant. friendship, goodwill, love
annihilate (v)
syn. eradicate, destroy, wipe out, abolish, eliminate, nullify
ant. create, preserve
annoy (v)
syn. anger, irritate, vex, irk, antagonize, harass
ant. soothe, please
annulment (n)
syn. abolition, cancellation, invalidation, recall, repeal, retraction, nullification
ant. restoration, enactment
anonymous (adj)
syn. unknown, unnamed, nameless, unacknowledged
ant. identifiable, named
antagonize (v)
syn. provoke, anger, irritate, annoy, anger, alienate, intimidate
ant. pacify, disarm
antagonism (n)
syn. animosity, conflict, hostility, ill-feeling, discord, antipathy, contention
ant. amity, sympathy, rapport
anterior (adj)
syn. earlier, former, previous, preceding, antecedent, introductory
ant. subsequent
antidote (n)
syn. cure, remedy, solution, antitoxin
ant. poison
antipathy (n)
syn. antagonism, dislike, hostility, hatred, loathing, abhorrence, animosity
ant. sympathy, affinity, liking

antiquated (adj)
syn. outdated, outworn, old-fashioned, antique, archaic
ant. modern
antiquity (n)
syn. antique, old age, ancient times, olden days, elderliness
ant. modernity, novelty
anxiety (n)
syn. worry, fear, stress, apprehension, disquiet
ant. composure, tranquillity
anxious (adj)
syn. apprehensive, fearful, worried, nervous, tense, afraid, eager, desperate, impatient
ant. unconcerned, composed, calm
apathetic (adj)
syn. lethargic, indifferent, unfeeling, uninterested, uninvolved, unresponsive
ant. enthusiastic, responsive
apathy (n)
syn. coldness, indifference, inertia, lethargy, phlegm, unfeelingness, unconcern
ant. enthusiasm, concern, warmth
apex (n)
syn. acme, climax, top, height, peak, high point, zenith, pinnacle
ant. nadir, base, bottom
aplomb (n)
syn. calmness, composure, self-confidence, balance, equanimity
ant. discomposure, agitation
apocryphal (adj)
syn. doubtful, fabricated, imaginary, mythical, fictitious, legendary, unauthentic
ant. true, authentic
appease (v)
syn. pacify, placate, reconcile, sweeten, satisfy, lull
ant. provoke, aggravate
appeasement (n)
syn. concession, mollification, softening, compromise, pacification
ant. aggravation, resistance

applaud (v)
syn. praise, welcome, congratulate, celebrate, clap, compliment
ant. criticize, boo, censure
appreciation (n)
syn. acknowledgement, admiration, enjoyment, gratitude, knowledge, praise, thanks, increase, recognition
ant. depreciation, ingratitude, scorn
apprehension (n)
syn. fear, anxiety, nervousness, concern, unease, misgiving, arrest
ant. confidence, composure
approximately (adv)
syn. almost, close to, about, more or less, roughly, nearly
ant. exactly, precisely
apt (adj)
syn. suitable, likely, sharp, clever, talented, genius, appropriate
ant. inapt, inappropriate
aptitude (n)
syn. flair, skill, talent, potential, ability, intelligence, competence
ant. inaptitude, incompetence
arbitrary (adj)
syn. discretionary, absolute, high-handed, fanciful, optional, tyrannical, summary, unreasoned
ant. rational, circumspect, reasoned
arcane (adj)
syn. enigmatic, cryptic, hidden, mystical, profound, obscure, secret, mysterious
ant. commonplace, normal
archaic (adj)
syn. old, ancient, antique, outdated, obsolete, bygone
ant. modern
ardent (adj)
syn. zealous, committed, passionate, keen, wholehearted, avid, zealous
ant. apathetic, dispassionate, cool
ardour (n)
syn. devotion, animation, avidity, enthusiasm, passion, zeal, zest, spirit, fervour
ant. apathy, coolness, indifference

arduous (adj)
syn. hard, tough, difficult, challenging, killing
ant. easy
argumentative (adj)
syn. contentious, combative, belligerent, perverse, quarrelsome, polemical
ant. complaisant, agreeable, obliging
arid (adj)
syn. barren, dry, waterless, infertile, boring, uninteresting
ant. fertile, wet, lively
aristocrat (n)
syn. nobleman, noblewoman, noble, lord, patrician, lady
ant. commoner, plebeian
aroma (n)
syn. fragrance, scent, smell, odour, perfume
ant. stink
arrival (n)
syn. coming, entry, appearance
ant. departure
arrogance (n)
syn. conceit, contempt, haughtiness, loftiness, pretension, pride, scorn
ant. humility, modesty
arrogant (adj)
syn. proud, haughty, insolent, conceited, self-important
ant. humble, modest, meek
artful (adj)
syn. canny, cunning, clever, ingenious, resourceful, skilful, shrewd, smart
ant. artless, ingenuous, naïve
artistry (n)
syn. craft, art, brilliance, expertise, mastery, skill, accomplishment
ant. ineptitude, incompetence
ascendancy (n)
syn. control, authority, domination, leadership, power, superiority, command, supremacy
ant. subordination, decline, servitude
asceticism (n)
syn. celibacy, puritanism, self-control, self-denial, frugality, abstinence
ant. voluptuousness

ashamed (adj)
syn. abashed, guilty, blushing, sorry, shame-faced, sheepish, apologetic, bad
ant. unashamed, unabashed, shameless, proud

asinine (adj)
syn. brainless, idiotic, goofy, senseless, witless, stupid, silly, foolish, half-witted
ant. sensible, intelligent, clever

aspersion (n)
syn. abuse, defamation, derogation, censure, mud-slinging, calumny
ant. compliment, commendation, praise

assent (v)
syn. agree, accept, approve, allow, comply, accede, consent
ant. dissent, disagree

assertive (adj)
syn. bold, determined, confident, strong-willed, positive
ant. timid, hesitant

assiduous (adj)
syn. devoted, attentive, diligent, studious, hard-working, untiring, industrious
ant. indolent, negligent

assimilate (v)
syn. adapt, absorb, blend, accept, digest, imbibe, take in, incorporate
ant. reject

associated (adj)
syn. related, linked, accompanying, connected
ant. unassociated, unrelated

assorted (adj)
syn. mixed, various, different, sundry, miscellaneous, heterogeneous
ant. uniform, homogeneous

assuage (v)
syn. alleviate, lessen, appease, lighten, pacify, reduce, calm, soften
ant. exacerbate

assumed (adj)
syn. fake, false, invented, phoney
ant. genuine

assured (adj)
syn. self-assured, poised, confident, certain, guaranteed, sure

ant. nervous, uncertain, doubtful
astonishing (adj)
syn. surprising, amazing, remarkable, incredible, mind-boggling
ant. unremarkable, ordinary
astounding (adj)
syn. surprising, amazing, incredible, remarkable, unbelievable, mind-boggling
ant. unremarkable, ordinary
astute (adj)
syn. clever, intelligent, shrewd, smart, acute, sharp
ant. slow, stupid
atheistic (adj)
syn. irreligious, sceptical, unbelieving, rationalistic, ungodly, unreligious
ant. religious, spiritual
attentive (adj)
syn. alert, considerate, heedful, observant, thoughtful, vigilant
ant. inattentive, heedless, inconsiderate
atrocious (adj)
syn. inhuman, cruel, wicked, terrible, barbaric, shocking, awful
ant. superb, admirable
attract (v)
syn. fascinate, charm, tempt, draw, entice
ant. repel, disgust
attraction (n)
syn. appeal, enchantment, magnetism, charm, enticement, allure, fascination
ant. repulsion, disgust
audacious (adj)
syn. adventurous, bold, brazen, courageous, daring, shameless, rude
ant. cautious, timid, reserved
audacity (n)
syn. adventurousness, boldness, bravery, shamelessness, rudeness
ant. caution, timidity, reserve
audible (adj)
syn. perceptible, clear, detectable, distinct
ant. inaudible, faint
augment (v)
syn. enhance, boost, increase, expand, hike up

ant. decrease, reduce

auspicious (adj)

syn. favourable, timely, promising, good, advantageous, cheerful, fortunate, happy

ant. inauspicious, unfavourable, ominous

austere (adj)

syn. harsh, severe, cold, unfriendly, ascetic, spartan, simple, strict

ant. easy-going, extravagant, genial

austerity (n)

syn. strictness, harshness, abstinence, self-denial, asceticism, sobriety, chastity

ant. leniency, geniality, luxury

authentic (adj)

syn. real, genuine, factual, reliable, trustworthy

ant. unreliable, fake

autocracy (n)

syn. dictatorship, fascism, absolution, despotism, Hitlerism

ant. democracy

autonomy (n)

syn. self-rule, independence, self-government, freedom

ant. dependence

avarice (n)

syn. greed, rapacity, meanness, miserliness, parsimony

ant. generosity, liberality

averse (adj)

syn. antagonistic, hostile, opposed, loath, unwilling, unfavourable, inimical, anti

ant. keen, willing, sympathetic

aversion (n)

syn. hostility, dislike, hatred, antipathy, loathing, abhorrence

ant. love, liking, sympathy

avid (adj)

syn. keen, ardent, devoted, eager, enthusiastic

ant. apathetic, indifferent

aware (adj)

syn. familiar, knowledgeable, knowing, conscious, alert

ant. unaware, ignorant

awareness (n)
syn. perception, consciousness, familiarity, knowledge, understanding
ant. ignorance, insensitivity
awe (n)
syn. wonder, reverence, admiration, respect, fear, veneration, amazement
ant. contempt, disdain, scorn, ridicule
awesome (adj)
syn. amazing, stunning, mind-blowing, brilliant, breathtaking, magnificent, fearsome
ant. unimpressive, contemptible
awful (adj)
(informal)
syn. horrible, disgusting, foul, terrible, lamentable, pathetic, unwell, sick, poorly
ant. wonderful, delightful, excellent, well
awkward (adj)
syn. difficult, unhelpful, unreasonable, inconvenient, uncomfortable, embarrassing, humiliating, inelegant, clumsy
ant. easy, agreeable, convenient, elegant

Bb

baffle (v)
syn. amaze, puzzle, confuse, bewilder, perplex, astound
ant. enlighten, explain

balanced (adj)
syn. fair, impartial, sensible, calm, unprejudiced, unbiased
ant. prejudiced, biased

bald (adj)
syn. hairless, shaven, bare, plain, stark, blunt
ant. hairy

balderdash (n)
(old-fashioned)
syn. nonsense, rubbish, trash, rot, verbiage, humbug
ant. wisdom, sanity

baleful (adj)
(literary)
syn. destructive, deadly, harmful, menacing, ominous, venomous, sad, woeful
ant. auspicious, favourable

banal (adj)
syn. unoriginal, commonplace, boring, unimaginative, overused, tried, old hat
ant. original

bane (n)
syn. adversity, curse, misery, evil, woe, affliction
ant. blessing, delight

banish (v)
syn. debar, discard, ban, dismiss, expel, deport
ant. welcome, recall

bankrupt (adj)
syn. ruined, failed, depleted, insolvent, broke, bust, in debt
ant. solvent, wealthy, affluent

barbaric (adj)
syn. brutal, inhuman, cruel, uncultured, savage

ant. civilized, humane
bark (v)
syn. yell, growl, shout, roar
ant. whisper
barmy (adj)
syn. foolish, insane, mad, idiotic, balmy, crazy, stupid, silly, loony
ant. sane, sensible, rational
baroque (adj)
syn. bold, extravagant, fantastic, florid, fanciful, flamboyant, grotesque, elaborate
ant. plain, ordinary
barren (adj)
syn. infertile, unproductive, sterile, lifeless, useless, ineffectual
ant. fertile, productive, useful
baseless (adj)
syn. groundless, unconfirmed, unjustified, unsupported, unjustifiable
ant. justifiable, reasonable
bashful (adj)
syn. timid, reserved, shy, nervous, shamefaced, sheepish
ant. confident, bold
bawdy (adj)
(old-fashioned)
syn. dirty, indecent, erotic, blue, lewd, coarse, obscene, pornographic, vulgar
ant. clean, chaste, decorous
beautiful (adj)
syn. pretty, handsome, elegant, glamorous, lovely, ravishing
ant. ugly, unattractive, plain
beautify (v)
syn. decorate, prettify, adorn, glamorize, embellish, decorate
ant. spoil, disfigure
bedeck (v)
syn. beautify, embellish, adorn, decorate, trim, garnish, ornament
ant. strip, spoil, disfigure
bedlam (n)
syn. chaos, anarchy, furore, commotion, pandemonium, uproar, clamour, turmoil
ant. calm, quiet, peace

bedraggled (adj)
syn. disordered, unkempt, dishevelled, untidy, dirty, messy, mussed
ant. neat, tidy
befitting (adj)
syn. suitable, appropriate, correct, right, proper, fitting
ant. unbecoming, improper
beguile (v)
syn. charm, deceive, amuse, mislead, fool, delight
ant. repel, dissuade
belated (adj)
syn. late, delayed, overdue, unpunctual, tardy
ant. early, punctual, timely
believer (n)
syn. follower, devotee, worshipper, disciple, adherent, convert
ant. unbeliever, infidel, apostate, sceptic
bellicose (adj)
syn. aggressive, combative, hostile, antagonistic, argumentative, warlike, quarrelsome, jingoistic
ant. genial, easy-going, calm, composed
belligerent (adj)
syn. aggressive, bellicose, hostile, combative, argumentative, warlike
ant. peaceful, easy-going, genial, calm
bemoan (v)
syn. lament, deplore, bewail, mourn, regret, weep for
ant. gloat, rejoice
bemused (adj)
syn. confused, distracted, bewildered, stunned, absent-minded, stupefied
ant. clear-headed, clear, lucid
benediction (n)
syn. favour, blessing, thanksgiving, prayer, grace, beatitude
ant. curse, execration, anathema
benefactor (n)
syn. contributor, friend, philanthropist, patron, promoter, sponsor, supporter, well-wisher
ant. opponent, persecutor
beneficial (adj)
syn. advantageous, useful, helpful, wholesome, healthy, profitable
ant. disadvantageous, unwholesome

benevolence (n)
syn. altruism, charity, fellow-feeling, compassion, goodwill, goodness, kindness, generosity, sympathy
ant. malevolence, meanness
benevolent (adj)
syn. kind, kind-hearted, compassionate, caring, benign, altruistic, humane, goodwill, loving
ant. malevolent, unkind
benign (adj)
syn. benevolent, amiable, advantageous, favourable, genial, gentle, kind, mild, sympathetic, friendly
ant. hostile, harmful, malignant, unkind
berate (v)
syn. chastise, criticize, chide, rebuke, scold, reprimand
ant. commend, praise
besmirch (v)
syn. dirty, slander, stain, dishonour, defame, tarnish
ant. enhance, honour, respect
besotted (adj)
syn. confused, bewitched, intoxicated, obsessed, infatuated, hypnotized
ant. sober, indifferent
bestial (adj)
syn. barbaric, brutal, savage, sensual, beastly, animal, sordid, vile, subhuman
ant. civilized, humane
bestir (v)
syn. arouse, incite, motivate, activate, animate, rouse, stimulate
ant. lull, calm, quell
betrayal (n)
syn. treachery, deception, disloyalty
ant. loyalty
bewail (v)
syn. bemoan, cry, moan, repent, regret, deplore
ant. gloat, glory
bewildered (adj)
syn. confused, perplexed, surprised, uncertain, baffled, stunned
ant. unperturbed, collected, clear

bewitch (v)
syn. enchant, charm, delight, captivate, fascinate, beguile
ant. disenchant, disgust, repel
bias (n)
syn. partiality, prejudice, unfairness, bent, predilection
ant. impartiality
biased (adj)
syn. partial, bigoted, prejudiced, discriminatory, one-sided, partisan
ant. impartial, fair
bigot (n)
syn. fanatic, racist, zealot, chauvinist, sectarian, dogmatist, sexist
ant. liberal, humanitarian
bigoted (adj)
syn. biased, partial, prejudiced, narrow-minded, intolerant, dogmatic
ant. open-minded, liberal, tolerant
bigotry (n)
syn. chauvinism, fanaticism, bias, intolerance, prejudice, jingoism, discrimination, sexism, injustice
ant. moderation, impartiality, fairness, tolerance
bigwig (n)
(informal)
syn. big shot, big gun, celebrity, notable, somebody, VIP
ant. nobody
bitchy (adj)
syn. malicious, spiteful, cruel, venomous, vindictive, nasty, vicious
ant. kind, benevolent
bizarre (adj)
syn. odd, funny, peculiar, strange, curious
ant. normal
blab (v)
syn. reveal, disclose, leak, tell, gossip
ant. suppress, hide
blame (v)
syn. accuse, hold responsible, charge, accountable, pin, condemn, criticize, chide
ant. exonerate, absolve, praise
blasphemy (n)
syn. irreligion, profanity, sacrilege, impiety

ant. reverence

blatant (adj)

syn. conspicuous, glaring, open-flagrant, shameless, unashamed, outright, harsh, noisy

ant. concealed, inconspicuous, discreet

bleak (adj)

syn. exposed, bare, empty, unpromising, gloomy, disheartening, grim, depressing, hopeless, sombre

ant. promising, lush, cheerful, congenial

blemish (n)

syn. flaw, fault, imperfection, defect, stain, mark

ant. strength

blend (v)

syn. combine, compound, fuse, harmonize, unite, synthesize

ant. separate

blessed (adj)

syn. contented, favoured, joyful, sanctified, fortunate

ant. cursed, ill-fated, bewitched

blight (n)

syn. depression, bane, affliction, pollution, curse, contamination, woe

ant. boon, blessing

bliss (n)

syn. happiness, pleasure, joy, ecstasy, delight

ant. misery, distress, damnation

blissful (adj)

syn. delighted, enchanted, joyful, ecstatic, joyous, happy

ant. wretched, miserable, distressing

blithe (adj)

syn. cheerful, cheery, happy, animated, gay, carefree, careless, thoughtless

ant. morose, dejected, depressed

bloom (v)

syn. blossom, develop, flower, prosper, mature, open, flourish

ant. wither, decline

blossom (v)

syn. develop, mature, flower, flourish, progress, bloom

ant. wither, decline

blues (n)
syn. depression, gloominess, miseries, dejection, melancholy, moodiness, despondency
ant. euphoria, ecstasy, joy, bliss, happiness
blurred (adj)
syn. clouded, dim, confused, fuzzy, misty, indistinct, ill-defined, foggy, unclear, vague
ant. distinct, clear
blushing (adj)
syn. embarrassed, confused, rosy, suffused, red, glowing
ant. composed, pale
blustery (adj)
syn. blowy, stormy, wild, gusty, windy
ant. calm, quiet
boastful (adj)
syn. bragging, cocky, arrogant, swanky
ant. modest, humble
boasting (n)
syn. conceit, swank, bluster, bragging, windiness
ant. modesty, humility
bogus (adj)
syn. counterfeit, fake, false, artificial
ant. genuine, real
boisterous (adj)
syn. spirited, animated, lively, wild, rough, riotous, unruly, noisy, exuberant
ant. restrained, calm, quiet
bold (adj)
syn. intrepid, brave, daring, heroic, fearless, insolent, striking
ant. timid, faint
bolster (v)
syn. boost, buttress, increase, strengthen, support, help
ant. undermine, weaken
bona fide (adj)
syn. actual, legal, true, genuine, valid, authentic
ant. bogus, fake
bondage (n)
syn. imprisonment, captivity, servitude, slavery, enthralment
ant. freedom, independence

bookish (adj)
syn. intellectual, cultured, scholarly, academic, lettered, erudite
ant. illiterate, unlettered, lowbrow
boom (n)
syn. development, growth, advance, improvement, increase
ant. collapse, failure
boon (n)
syn. benefit, favour, advantage, gratification
ant. disadvantage, blight
boorish (adj)
syn. rude, coarse, vulgar, uncivilized, awkward, uncouth, ill-bred
ant. refined, cultured, polite
boost (n)
syn. advancement, help, enhancement, increase, supplement, praise
ant. blow, setback
boot licking (n)
syn. flattery, fawning, sycophancy, crawling, ingratiation, servility
ant. criticism
boredom (n)
syn. dullness, apathy, weariness
ant. interest, excitement
bossy (adj)
syn. despotic, arrogant, oppressive, authoritarian, dictatorial, insistent
ant. unassertive, submissive, meek
bountiful (adj)
syn. boundless, abundant, lavish, plentiful, prolific, profuse, generous, magnanimous
ant. mean, meagre, sparse, miserly
boycott (v)
syn. disallow, ban, reject, prohibit, outlaw
ant. support, encourage
bragging (n)
syn. boastfulness, bluster, boasting, exaggeration, talk, showing off
ant. modesty, unobtrusiveness
brainy (adj)
(informal)
syn. brilliant, intelligent, smart, bright, clever
ant. dull, stupid

brash (adj)
syn. heedless, impetuous, assured, incautious, rash, assuming, rude, insolent, arrogant, showy
ant. cautious, reserved, meek, modest
bravado (n)
syn. boast, bragging, boastfulness, show, swank, talk, pretence
ant. restraint, modesty, humility
brave (adj)
syn. courageous, audacious, gallant, stalwart, bold
ant. timid, cowardly
bravery (n)
syn. courage, audacity, daring, gallantry, heroism
ant. timidity, cowardice
brawny (adj)
syn. strong, powerful, sturdy, muscular, well built
ant. weak, puny, frail
brazen (adj)
syn. bold, audacious, immodest, shameless, unashamed, blatant, impudent
ant. shamefaced, humble, shy
breakthrough (n)
syn. development, success, advance, innovation, step forward, revolution
ant. setback
brevity (n)
syn. conciseness, shortness, briefness, economy, crispness
ant. longevity, verbosity, prolixity
brief (adj)
syn. short, compact, concise, quick, crisp, cursory
ant. long, verbose
bright (adj)
syn. dazzling, shining, glowing, sunny, intelligent, clever, canny, brainy, astute
ant. dull, dark, stupid
brilliance (n)
syn. glitter, brightness, luminosity, intelligence, genius, prowess, aptitude, intellect, wisdom
ant. dullness, mediocrity, stupidity
brilliant (adj)
syn. shining, dazzling, bright, clever, intelligent, smart, superb, excellent, talented.

ant. dim, mediocre, stupid, undistinguished.

brisk (adj)

syn. fast, speedy, rapid, sharp

ant. leisurely

brittle (adj)

syn. crisp, breakable, delicate, fragile, nervous, short, tense, crumbling, irritable

ant. resilient, durable, sturdy, flexible

broad (adj)

syn. wide, expansive, great, comprehensive, general, rough

ant. narrow, limited

broad-minded (adj)

syn. tolerant, progressive, liberal, unbiased, unprejudiced

ant. narrow-minded, intolerant

broken-hearted (adj)

syn. desolate, miserable, heartbroken, forlorn, inconsolable, woeful

ant. overjoyed, delighted, euphoric

brotherly (adj)

syn. caring, friendly, sympathetic, amicable, affectionate, loving

ant. callous, unkind

browbeat (v)

syn. pressure, bully, coerce, terrorize, force, threaten

ant. coax, praise

brusque (adj)

syn. blunt, curt, brisk, discourteous, rude, impolite, sharp, short, undiplomatic

ant. polite, courteous, tactful

brutal (adj)

syn. cruel, wicked, savage, barbaric, violent, ruthless, inhuman, callous

ant. gentle, humane, kindly

brutality (n)

syn. barbarism, coarseness, ruthlessness, atrocity, callousness, inhumanity, cruelty, savagery

ant. humanity, gentleness, kindness

brute (n)

syn. barbarian, beast, animal, devil, sadist, swine

ant. gentleman, saint

budding (adj)

syn. developing, hopeful, growing, promising, potential

ant. experienced
bumbling (adj)
syn. bungling, awkward, clumsy, inept, incompetent, inefficient, stumbling
ant. efficient, competent
bumptious (adj)
syn. conceited, arrogant, impudent, boastful, pompous, overconfident, showy
ant. modest, humble, meek, lowly
buoyant (adj)
syn. floating, weightless, happy, cheerful, joyful, cheery, light-hearted, sunny
ant. heavy, gloomy, depressed
burlesque (n)
syn. mockery, satire, parody, ridicule, mock, caricature, travesty, irony, sarcasm
ant. seriousness, tragedy
bury (v)
syn. lay to rest, inter, conceal, cover
ant. exhume
bustling (adj)
syn. busy, buzzing, lively, crowded, hectic
ant. quiet
busy (adj)
syn. brisk, active, diligent, assiduous, hectic, lively, restless, working
ant. idle, free
buttress (v)
syn. reinforce, support, strengthen, defend, uphold, bolster, back up
ant. weaken
bygone (adj)
syn. ancient, olden, departed, past, erstwhile
ant. modern, future

Cc

cacophony (n)
syn. discord, disharmony, stridency, clamour, noise
ant. harmony, concord

cajole (v)
syn. coax, entice, beguile, flatter, seduce, dupe, sweet-talk
ant. bully, force

calamity (n)
syn. misfortune, disaster, adversity, catastrophe, hardship, trouble
ant. blessing, godsend

calculated (adj)
syn. considered, intended, planned, deliberate, purposeful
ant. unplanned, unintended, unintentional

calculating (adj)
syn. cunning, devious, cautious, canny, manipulate, shrewd, sharp, Machiavellian
ant. open, naïve, artless, direct

calibre (n)
syn. ability, capacity, talent, capability, competence, gauge
ant. inability, incompetence

callous (adj)
syn. uncaring, heartless, unsympathetic, cold, unfeeling, insensitive
ant. kind, compassionate, sympathetic

callow (adj)
syn. inexperienced, immature, raw, unsophisticated
ant. experienced, sophisticated

calm (adj)
syn. serene, relaxed, quiet, composed, unexcited
ant. nervous, excited

candid (adj)
syn. truthful, outspoken, frank, open, fair, straightforward, naive
ant. guarded, devious, deceitful

candour (n)
syn. frankness, honesty, openness, artlessness, sincerity, truthfulness

ant. deviousness, evasiveness, dishonesty
canny (adj)
syn. sharp, shrewd, wise, clever, judicious, prudent
ant. foolish, imprudent
canonical (adj)
syn. approved, accepted, authoritative, regular, recognized, orthodox
ant. uncanonical, unorthodox
capability (n)
syn. ability, potential, flair, aptitude
ant. incapability, inability
capitulate (v)
syn. surrender, concede, submit, give in
ant. resist
capricious (adj)
syn. changeable, fickle, unreliable, uncertain, fanciful, whimsical
ant. firm, consistent, steady
captivate (v)
syn. attract, charm, enthral, delight, enchant, allure
ant. bore, repel
captivity (n)
syn. imprisonment, detention, custody, bondage
ant. freedom
care (n)
syn. protection, custody, charge, attention, regard, anxiety, worry, stress
ant. neglect, carelessness, indifference
carefree (adj)
syn. relaxed, unworried, untroubled, easy-going, cheerful
ant. troubled, anxious
careful (adj)
syn. alert, cautious, attentive, discreet, mindful, prudent, thoughtful
ant. careless, thoughtless, inattentive
carelessness (n)
syn. inattention, irresponsibility, absent-mindedness, neglect, thoughtlessness
ant. care, thoughtfulness
carnal (adj)
syn. erotic, impure, bodily, animal, lustful, profane, sexual, sensuous, sensual, physical, unchaste

ant. spiritual, pure, chaste

carp (v)
syn. complain, nag, criticize, reproach, whine, find fault, bitch
ant. praise

casual (adj)
syn. uncaring, spontaneous, unthinking, accidental, unexpected, informal, apathetic, easy-going
ant. serious, deliberate, formal

catastrophe (n)
syn. disaster, affliction, adversity, calamity, tragedy, fiasco, trouble, misfortune
ant. prosperity, fortune, success, triumph

caustic (adj)
syn. acrimonious, acidulous, bitter, burning, biting, pungent, severe, cutting, sarcastic
ant. soothing, mild

cautious (adj)
syn. judicious, attentive, careful, prudent
ant. rash, reckless

celebrated (adj)
syn. admired, great, acclaimed, esteemed, distinguished, notable, renowned
ant. unsung, unknown

celebrity (n)
syn. star, VIP, big shot, personality, fame, repute, stardom, distinction
ant. nobody, obscurity, ignominy

celerity (n)
syn. haste, dispatch, quickness, speed, promptness, swiftness
ant. slowness, sloth

censorious (adj)
syn. carping, critical, severe, disapproving, fault-finding, carping
ant. complimentary, approving, appreciative

censure (n)
syn. condemnation, blame, admonition, rebuke, disapproval, reprimand, criticism
ant. approval, praise

centralize (v)
syn. condense, amalgamate, converge, incorporate, unify
ant. decentralize

certainty (n)
syn. assurance, confidence, positiveness, sureness
ant. uncertainty, doubt

cessation (n)
syn. end, halt, finish, termination, suspension, break, discontinuation
ant. commencement, start, resumption

chagrin (n)
syn. displeasure, annoyance, dissatisfaction, humiliation, embarrassment, irritation
ant. pleasure, delight

chaos (n)
syn. disorder, bedlam, pandemonium, confusion
ant. order, calm

charisma (n)
syn. charm, magnetism, allure, appeal, attractiveness, strength of character, glamour
ant. repulsion, revulsion, repugnance

charismatic (adj)
syn. charming, attractive, appealing, alluring, inspiring, glamorous, mesmerizing
ant. repellent, repulsive, disgusting

charming (adj)
syn. pleasing, lovely, delightful, appealing, attractive, bewitching, captivating, good-looking, enchanting
ant. ugly, unattractive, repulsive

chary (adj)
syn. heedful, cautious, careful, prudent, guarded, uneasy, unwilling, reluctant
ant. heedless, reckless

chaste (adj)
(old-fashioned)
syn. pure, decorous, innocent, elegant, modest, simple, virginal, neat, refined, decent
ant. unchaste, corrupt, indecorous, lewd

chastity (n)
syn. purity, innocence, virtue, celibacy, self-restraint, virginity, modesty
ant. immorality, impurity, corruption

cheap (adj)
syn. low-cost, inexpensive, affordable, worthless, mean, contemptible
ant. expensive, superior

cheeky (adj)
(informal)
syn. rude, disrespectful, impudent, insolent
ant. polite, respectful

cheer (v)
syn. applaud, animate, clap, please, encourage, exhilarate, hearten
ant. boo, depress, jeer, dishearten

cheerful (adj)
syn. animated, happy, sunny, jolly, joyful, buoyant, pleasant
ant. sad, gloomy

cheerfulness (n)
syn. buoyancy, geniality, cheeriness, happiness, joy
ant. sadness, dejection

cheering (adj)
syn. bright, inspiring, auspicious, promising, comforting
ant. disheartening, depressing

chic (adj)
syn. smart, fashionable, stylish, elegant, sophisticated, trendy
ant. unfashionable

chide (v)
syn. admonish, censure, blame, criticize, rebuke, scold, reprimand
ant. commend, praise

childish (adj)
syn. boyish, girlish, foolish, silly, immature
ant. mature, sensible

childlike (adj)
syn. youthful, artless, naive, natural, trusting, unsophisticated
ant. adult

chill (n)
syn. coldness, shiver, coolness, frigidity
ant. warmth

chirpy (adj)
syn. cheerful, bright, gay, merry, happy, sunny, blithe
ant. sad, downcast

chivalrous (adj)
syn. courageous, gallant, bold, courteous, polite, heroic, respectful
ant. cowardly, ungallant, rude
choppy (adj)
syn. turbulent, rough, stormy, heavy
ant. calm
chronic (adj)
syn. incurable, persistent, constant, continuing, severe, compulsive
ant. temporary
chum (n)
(informal, old-fashioned)
syn. friend, companion, crony, comrade, pal, mate, buddy
ant. enemy
churlish (adj)
syn. impolite, rude, discourteous, uncouth, rough
ant. polite, urbane
circumspect (adj)
syn. canny, cautious, attentive, careful, discreet, guarded, judicious,
vigilant
ant. unguarded, unwary
civilization (n)
syn. advancement, progress, human development, refinement, culture,
enlightenment, society
ant. barbarity, primitiveness
civilized (adj)
syn. sophisticated, developed, advanced, cultured, polished, polite
ant. unsophisticated, rude
civility (n)
syn. amenity, affability, courteousness, politeness, courtesy, urbanity
ant. uncouthness, rudeness
clamour (n)
syn. uproar, noise, agitation, commotion, hue and cry, outcry,
shouting, row
ant. silence, quiet, calm, peace
clannish (adj)
syn. close, narrow, sectarian, unfriendly, insular
ant. friendly, open

clarity (n)
syn. intelligibility, explicitness, lucidity, precision, comprehensibility, transparency
ant. obscurity, vagueness
cleanse (v)
syn. clean, absolve, rinse, purify, wash, clear
ant. dirty, defile
clement (adj)
syn. calm, mild, compassionate, generous, humane, forgiving, merciful, magnanimous, kind-hearted
ant. inclement, harsh, ruthless, heartless, merciless, cruel
cleverness (n)
syn. astuteness, ability, intelligence, smartness, cunning, sense
ant. foolishness, senselessness, naivety
cloistered (adj)
syn. confined, insulated, enclosed, restricted, secluded, shielded, withdrawn
ant. open, urbane
clumsy (adj)
syn. awkward, graceless, inept, unskilful, crude, heavy, inexpert, ungraceful, uncoordinated
ant. adroit, skilful, graceful
cloudy (adj)
syn. black, sunless, overcast, gloomy, dirty, murky, indistinct
ant. clear, sunny, bright
coarse (adj)
syn. rough, unrefined, impure, rude, vulgar, lewd, impolite, uncivil, uncouth
ant. fine, polite, courteous, refined
coax (v)
syn. beguile, entice, cajole, allure, flatter, sweet-talk, soft-soap
ant. coerce, force
cocky (adj)
(informal)
syn. arrogant, overconfident, brash, conceited, swollen-headed, boastful
ant. modest
coerce (v)
syn. bully, compel, press, pressure, browbeat, threaten
ant. coax, persuade

coercion (n)
syn. bullying, browbeating, force, threats, pressure, compulsion
ant. coaxing, persuasion

cogent (adj)
syn. effective, convincing, forceful, persuasive, sound, lucid, logical, influential, compelling
ant. ineffective, unsound, weak

cognate (adj)
syn. connected, affiliated, allied, alike, related, associated, akin
ant. unconnected, unrelated

cognisant (adj)
syn. conscious, familiar, aware, acquainted, versed, knowledgeable, informed
ant. ignorant, unaware

coherent (adj)
syn. clear, logical, lucid, intelligible, rational, sound, connected
ant. incoherent, muddled

coincide (v)
syn. coexist, happen together, accord, tally, match up, correspond
ant. differ, clash

coincidental (adj)
syn. chance, accidental, unplanned, unintentional
ant. deliberate, planned

cold (adj)
syn. chilly, cool, unfriendly, stiff, apathetic, aloof, distant
ant. hot, warm, friendly

cold-blooded (adj)
syn. brutal, cruel, barbaric, dispassionate, heartless, inhuman, ruthless, uncompassionate
ant. merciful, humane, sympathetic, compassionate

cold-hearted (adj)
syn. cold, frigid, heartless, insensitive, uncaring, inhuman, uncompassionate, unsympathetic, unkind
ant. warm-hearted, kind-hearted, compassionate, sympathetic

collected (adj)
syn. calm, self-controlled, self-possessed, cool, composed, efficient, placid, serene, relaxed, confident
ant. excited, worried, disorganized

collective (adj)
syn. combined, common, mutual, united, cooperative
ant. individual
colloquial (adj)
syn. informal, familiar, casual, vernacular, idiomatic
ant. formal
collusion (n)
syn. conspiracy, complicity, deceit, artifice, connivance, intrigue, plot
ant. estrangement, discord, separation
colossal (adj)
syn. enormous, huge, giant, massive, vast, gigantic, immense, titanic
ant. tiny, small, little
comatose (adj)
syn. drowsy, sleepy, cataleptic, lethargic, unconscious, insensible, stupefied
ant. conscious, lively
combative (adj)
syn. aggressive, bellicose, argumentative, antagonistic, quarrelsome
ant. conciliatory, peaceful, pacific
comedy (n)
syn. jokes, fun, humour, satire, farce
ant. tragedy
comely (adj)
syn. beautiful, attractive, blooming, decent, fitting, handsome, pleasing,
lovely, suitable, wholesome
ant. ugly, unattractive, unlovely
comfort (n)
syn. repose, luxury, ease, relief, consolation, reassurance
ant. discomfort, distress
comforting (adj)
syn. cheering, soothing, reassuring, encouraging, heart-warming,
heartening, consoling
ant. upsetting, worrying
comic (adj)
syn. funny, humorous, witty, amusing, joking, farcical
ant. serious, tragic, unfunny
commence (v)
syn. start, open, begin, inaugurate, get going, kick off
ant. conclude, end

commend (v)
syn. honour, praise, congratulate, applaud, compliment, support
ant. censure, criticize
commendable (adj)
syn. admirable, deserving, excellent, laudable, praiseworthy, noble, worthy
ant. deplorable, reprehensible, blameworthy
commensurate (adj)
syn. acceptable, appropriate, consistent, due, fitting, proportionate, sufficient
ant. incommensurate, inappropriate
committed (adj)
syn. active, devoted, motivated, dedicated, driven, firm, faithful, ardent, passionate
ant. apathetic, indifferent, sluggish, dull
commonplace (adj)
syn. common, everyday, ordinary, customary, stale, uninteresting, widespread
ant. rare, distinctive, exceptional
common sense (n)
syn. good judgment, good sense, prudence, wisdom, intelligence, gumption
ant. folly, stupidity
commotion (n)
syn. pandemonium, uproar, disturbance, rumpus, disorder, fuss, chaos, hue and cry
ant. calm, peace, serenity
communicative (adj)
syn. extrovert, friendly, sociable, candid, talkative, chatty
ant. reticent, reserved
commute (v)
syn. decrease, alter, adjust, lighten, reduce, curtail
ant. increase, extend
compact (adj)
syn. compressed, dense, solid, neat, handy, small, portable, concise, brief, condensed, short and sweet
ant. lengthy, loose, bulky
compact (n)
syn. accord, treaty, deal, agreement, pact, settlement

ant. disagreement, breach, quarrel
compassion (n)
syn. pity, care, sympathy, empathy, mercy, kindness
ant. indifference, cruelty
compassionate (adj)
syn. caring, sympathetic, pitying, loving, soft-hearted, merciful, kind
ant. indifferent, unsympathetic, harsh
compatibility (n)
syn. agreement, affinity, accord, empathy, harmony, rapport, sympathy,
unity, understanding
ant. incompatibility, antagonism, antipathy
compatible (adj)
syn. agreeable, congenial, adaptable, harmonious, sympathetic,
like-minded
ant. incompatible, antipathetic, conflicting, opposite
compel (v)
syn. bully, coerce, browbeat, force, drive, impel, pressurize, urge
ant. coax, persuade
compelling (adj)
syn. coercing, cogent, forceful, powerful, convincing, enthralling, gripping,
mesmerizing, enchanting
ant. weak, boring
competence (n)
syn. ability, proficiency, expertise, skill, capability, mastery, efficiency, power
ant. incompetence, inefficiency
competent (adj)
syn. able, capable, efficient, fit, well-qualified, expert, skilled, empowered
ant. incompetent, inept, inefficient
competitive (adj)
syn. aggressive, combative, keen, ambitious, zealous
ant. unambitious, sluggish
compile (v)
syn. assemble, compose, gather, accumulate, organize, arrange
ant. disassemble, disperse, scatter
complacent (adj)
syn. pleased, contented, smug, self-satisfied, gloating, satisfied,
self-assured, self-congratulatory
ant. discontented, diffident, uneasy

complexity (n)
syn. complication, entanglement, variety, intricacy
ant. simplicity
compliance (n)
syn. agreement, consent, obedience, submission, co-operation, assent
ant. disobedience, resistance, defiance
complicity (n)
syn. agreement, collusion, involvement, knowledge, collaboration, approval, connivance
ant. innocence, ignorance
compliment (n)
syn. accolade, tribute, praise, congratulations, flattery, kudos, admiration
ant. criticism, insult, abuse
complimentary (adj)
syn. congratulatory, flattering, admiring, appreciative
ant. critical, insulting
comply (v)
syn. obey, accord, agree, abide by, follow, respect, observe, submit
ant. disobey, refuse, resist
composed (adj)
syn. calm, relaxed, collected, cool, complacent, placid, at ease, serene, chilled
ant. agitated, ruffled, nervous
comprehend (v)
syn. understand, know, perceive, grasp, follow, conceive
ant. misunderstand
comprehensible (adj)
syn. intelligible, coherent, understandable, lucid, knowable, explicit, straightforward
ant. incomprehensible, unintelligible, unclear
comprehension (n)
syn. mastery, grasp, knowledge, conception, perception, sense, intelligence
ant. incomprehension, ignorance
comprehensive (adj)
syn. complete, inclusive, thorough, detailed, broad, extensive, wide, general
ant. limited, incomplete, selective

compromise (n)
syn. agreement, concession, settlement, cooperation
ant. disagreement
compulsion (n)
syn. pressure, obligation, need, urge, obsession
ant. freedom, liberty
comrade (n)
syn. associate, friend, brother, companion, colleague, fellow, crony, mate, ally
ant. enemy, adversary, rival, opponent
conceal (v)
syn. cover, bury, hide, veil, obscure, keep secret
ant. reveal, confess
concede (v)
syn. admit, accept, agree, acknowledge, recognize, confess
ant. deny, dispute
conceit (n)
syn. arrogance, vanity, self-admiration, pride, self-love, narcissism, fancy
ant. humility, modesty
conceivable (adj)
syn. believable, likely, probable, possible, imaginable, thinkable
ant. inconceivable, unimaginable, unthinkable
conceive (v)
syn. imagine, think, understand, comprehend, fancy, think up, create
ant. misunderstand
concentration (n)
syn. attentiveness, absorption, close attention, focus
ant. inattention, distraction
concerted (adj)
syn. collective, organized, collaborative, joint, united, planned, shared, strenuous, intensive
ant. separate, disorganized, uncoordinated
conciliation (n)
syn. pacification, appeasement, satisfaction, placation, peace-making, reconciliation
ant. antagonization, alienation
concise (adj)
syn. brief, abridged, condensed, compact

ant. lengthy
conclude (v)
syn. end, finish, finalize, settle, surmise, decide
ant. begin, introduce
concluding (adj)
syn. final, closing, ultimate, last, terminal
ant. beginning, introductory
conclusion (n)
syn. finish, end, settlement, judgement, outcome
ant. beginning, introduction
concord (n)
syn. accord, compact, agreement, consensus, peace, treaty, harmony
ant. discord, disharmony
concur (v)
syn. accord, assent, comply, agree, combine, unite, harmonize, cooperate
ant. dissent, disagree
concurrence (n)
syn. agreement, assent, community, association, co-existence, unity, harmony
ant. dissent, disagreement, difference
condemn (v)
syn. criticize, deplore, denounce, censure, damn
ant. commend, praise
condense (v)
syn. abbreviate, abridge, summarize, compact, shorten, edit, précis
ant. expand, amplify
condescending (adj)
syn. patronizing, disdainful, superior, lofty, lordly, unbending, gracious, stooping
ant. humble, approachable
condolence (n)
syn. compassion, sympathy, pity, consolation, support
ant. congratulation
condone (v)
syn. excuse, disregard, forgive, pardon, ignore, tolerate, overlook, allow, accept
ant. condemn, censure, disallow, punish

conducive (adj)
syn. advantageous, favourable, promising, helpful, encouraging, good, beneficial
ant. unfavourable, adverse

confess (v)
syn. reveal, admit, disclose, profess, concede, acknowledge, assert
ant. deny, conceal

confession (n)
syn. revelation, admission, disclosure, profession, acknowledgement, assertion
ant. denial, concealment

confide (v)
syn. disclose, reveal, tell, declare, confess, impart, admit
ant. hide, suppress

confidence (n)
syn. faith, trust, credence, conviction, self-possession, self-assurance
ant. distrust, doubt, diffidence

confident (adj)
syn. sure, satisfied, certain, self-assured, convinced, positive
ant. diffident, sceptical, doubtful

confine (v)
syn. bind, bound, imprison, cage, hold, captive, restrict, keep
ant. free, release

confirm (v)
syn. justify, prove, corroborate, affirm, assert, approve
ant. deny, contradict

confiscate (v)
syn. seize, take, appropriate, remove, impound, commandeer
ant. restore, establish

conflict (n)
syn. disagreement, quarrel, clash, dispute, discord, antagonism, struggle, war, fighting, agony, contention
ant. agreement, concord, harmony, peace

conflicting (adj)
syn. incompatible, contradictory, inconsistent, opposite, opposing, clashing, antagonistic, discordant
ant. compatible, harmonious, agreeable

conform (n)
syn. accord, agree, comply, obey, harmonize, adapt, suit, follow, fit in
ant. differ, flout, rebel
confound (v)
syn. bewilder, confuse, baffle, amaze, destroy, surprise, stupefy, upset
ant. enlighten, clear
confront (v)
syn. challenge, meet, face, oppose, tackle, address
ant. evade, elude
confused (adj)
syn. bewildered, mystified, puzzled, unclear, chaotic, disorderly
ant. lucid, clear
confusion (n)
syn. uncertainty, bewilderment, disorder, muddle, mess, chaos
ant. enlightenment, clarity, order
confute (v)
syn. annihilate, disprove, confound, nullify, refute, overturn, rebut, overthrow
ant. prove, confirm
congenial (adj)
syn. friendly, agreeable, amicable, nice, pleasant, favourable, sympathetic
ant. unfriendly, disagreeable, unpleasant
congested (adj)
syn. crowded, blocked, jammed, packed, clogged, snarled up
ant. clear
conglomerate (v)
syn. aggregate, assemble, collect, amass, gather, congregate, agglomerate
ant. separate, disperse
congratulations (n)
syn. compliments, greetings, felicitations, kudos
ant. condolences, commiserations
congregate (v)
syn. conglomerate, assemble, convene, come together, gather, group
ant. disperse, dismiss
conjectural (adj)
syn. hypothetical, academic, supposed, postulated, theoretical, surmised, assumed, tentative
ant. real, factual, true, proven

conjecture (n)
syn. hypothesis, assumption, guess, inference, surmise, presumption, theory
ant. reality, fact, truth, proof
connive (v)
syn. conspire, plot, collude, scheme, ignore, disregard, overlook.
ant. disagree, part.
conniving (adj)
syn. cunning, devious, scheming, wily, deceitful, Machiavellian, manipulate, artful
ant. honest, ethical, truthful
connoisseur (n)
syn. expert, buff, authority, devotee, judge, specialist
ant. dimwit, ignoramus, moron, tyro
conquer (v)
syn. annex, defeat, overcome, capture, overrun, control, rise above
ant. surrender, yield
conscience-stricken (adj)
syn. regretful, ashamed, repentant, guilty, disturbed, sorry
ant. unrepentant, unashamed
conscientious (adj)
syn. diligent, careful, faithful, honest, moral, meticulous, responsible, straightforward, scrupulous, hard-working
ant. irresponsible, careless, casual
conscious (adj)
syn. alert, aware, awake, knowing, deliberate, wilful, considered, rational, intentional
ant. unconscious, unaware, unintentional
consecutive (adj)
syn. chronological, successive, running, in a row, succeeding, sequential, uninterrupted
ant. discontinuous, intermittent, sporadic
consensus (n)
syn. harmony, agreement, unity, accord, consent, unanimity
ant. disagreement, dissension
consent (n)
syn. agreement, acceptance, assent, approval, accordance, compliance, go-ahead, OK

ant. dissent, refusal, opposition

consequence (n)

syn. outcome, result, effect, ramification, repercussion, importance, significance

ant. cause, unimportance

conservation (n)

syn. protection, preservation, husbandry, maintenance, upkeep, saving

ant. destruction, abolition

conservative (adj)

syn. reactionary, traditional, right-wing, sober, modest, die-hard, conventional, old-fashioned

ant. socialist, radical, left-wing, liberal

conservative (n)

syn. right-winger, traditionalist, reactionary, moderate, stick-in-the-mud

ant. radical, left-winger

conserve (v)

syn. protect, preserve, keep, save, safeguard, sustain

ant. squander, waste, use

consider (v)

syn. think, examine, believe, discuss, respect, ponder

ant. ignore

considerable (adj)

syn. substantial, plentiful, sizeable, abundant, ample, comfortable, big

ant. paltry, insignificant, slight

considerate (adj)

syn. thoughtful, attentive, solicitous, caring, unselfish, kind, sensitive, polite

ant. inconsiderate, thoughtless, selfish

consideration (n)

syn. thought, attention, examination, deliberation, issue, factor, aspect, attentiveness, solicitude, understanding

ant. disregard, disdain, thoughtlessness

consistency (n)

syn. accordance, coherence, agreement, constancy, regularity, sameness, harmony, uniformity, steadiness, compatibility

ant. inconsistency, incompatibility, antagonism

consistent (adj)

syn. accordant, coherent, agreeing, constant, regular, uniform, steady,

unchanging, compatible
ant. inconsistent, erratic, irregular
consolation (n)
syn. comfort, sympathy, solace, relief, encouragement, cheer, support
ant. distress, discouragement
console (v)
syn. comfort, support, sympathize with, encourage
ant. upset
conspicuous (adj)
syn. apparent, obvious, noticeable, blatant, evident, clear
ant. inconspicuous, hidden
conspiracy (n)
syn. plot, collusion, plan, scheme, intrigue, fix
ant. loyalty, faith
constant (adj)
syn. persistent, continuous, perpetual, eternal, non-stop, consistent,
uniform, regular, loyal, fast
ant. occasional, irregular, fickle
constantly (adv)
syn. continuously, continually, always, non-stop, relentlessly, endlessly
ant. occasionally
consternation (n)
syn. anxiety, dismay, alarm, distress, fear, discomposure, awe, panic,
amazement
ant. composure, relief
constrained (adj)
syn. forced, embarrassed, stiff, uneasy, reticent, unnatural
ant. relaxed, free
constraint (n)
syn. restriction, curb, limitation, control, uneasiness, embarrassment,
awkwardness, coercion, hindrance
ant. freedom, ease
constriction (n)
syn. restriction, tightness, constraint, pressure, limitation, narrowing
ant. expansion
constructive (adj)
syn. productive, advantageous, useful, helpful, positive, practical,
worthwhile

ant. destructive, unhelpful, negative
construe (v)
syn. explain, interpret, analyse, decipher, translate, expound
ant. obfuscate, obscure
consummate (v)
syn. accomplish, achieve, complete, effectuate, finish, fulfil, perfect, end, perform, compass
ant. abort, fail
consummate (adj)
syn. accomplished, finished, absolute, matchless, skilled, superb, supreme, ultimate, perfect
ant. imperfect, superficial
contaminate (v)
syn. poison, pollute, adulterate, tarnish, defile
ant. purify, cleanse
contemplate (v)
syn. consider, examine, think, study, meditate, ponder, regard
ant. ignore
contemporary (adj)
syn. coexisting, current, modern, present, recent, trendy, fashionable
ant. old-fashioned, former, ancient
contempt (n)
syn. disrespect, scorn, disdain, dishonour, disregard, derision, loathing
ant. admiration, respect, regard
contemptible (adj)
syn. loathsome, shameful, despicable, contempt, deplorable, disgraceful, unspeakable, cheap, worthless
ant. admirable, honourable, noble
contemptuous (adj)
syn. cynical, haughty, arrogant, insolent, scornful, insulting
ant. humble, respectful, polite
content (v)
syn. satisfy, please, appease, pacify, delight, gladden
ant. displease, annoy, upset
contention (n)
syn. allegation, belief, claim, controversy, dispute, enmity, hostility, debate, rivalry, struggle
ant. cooperation, amity, peace, friendship

contentious (adj)
syn. controversial, disputed, vexed, debatable, antagonistic, hostile, peevish, quarrelsome
ant. cooperative, uncontroversial, peaceable

contentment (n)
syn. content, satisfaction, happiness, contentedness, pleasure, comfort, cheerfulness
ant. discontent, dissatisfaction

continual (adj)
syn. regular, frequent, constant, non-stop, chronic, perpetual, continuous
ant. occasional, temporary, intermittent

contort (v)
syn. deform, distort, disfigure, misshape, twist, wriggle
ant. beautify, shape

contraction (n)
syn. constriction, shortening, abbreviation, elision, tightening
ant. expansion, growth

contradiction (n)
syn. disagreement, clash, conflict, rebuttal
ant. agreement, harmony

contradictory (adj)
syn. inconsistent, opposed, contrary, antagonistic, conflicting, incompatible
ant. consistent, compatible, affirmative

contravene (v)
syn. contradict, break, disobey, interfere, refute, oppose, violate, cross
ant. uphold, consent, endorse

contribute (v)
syn. afford, help, give, add, donate, provide
ant. withhold, subtract

contrition (n)
syn. penitence, sorrow, remorse, humiliation, repentance, compunction, shame
ant. impenitence, pride, honour

contrive (v)
syn. create, devise, construct, manufacture, hatch, find a way, manage
ant. fail, flop

contrived (adj)
syn. unnatural, forced, laboured, false, artificial

ant. natural, spontaneous
controversial (adj)
syn. contentious, disputable, debatable, disputed, attacking, polemical, questionable
ant. uncontroversial, indisputable, peaceable, cooperative
controversy (n)
syn. contention, dispute, argument, disagreement, quarrel, debate, row, polemic, alteration, strife
ant. agreement, accord
convalescence (n)
syn. rehabilitation, recovery, restoration, improvement, recuperation
ant. damage, weakening, removal
convene (v)
syn. gather, assemble, summon, call, congregate, meet, collect
ant. disperse, disband
convenient (adj)
syn. suitable, advantageous, favourable, timely, accessible, nearby, handy
ant. inconvenient, awkward
conventional (adj)
syn. traditional, orthodox, accepted, customary, conservative, old-fashioned, routine, unoriginal, prosaic
ant. unconventional, unorthodox, exotic, original
converge (v)
syn. connect, meet, merge, intersect, link up, mingle, join, gather
ant. diverge, disperse
convict (v)
syn. sentence, find, guilty, penalize, punish, condemn
ant. acquit, release
conviction (n)
syn. views, beliefs, stance, opinions, confidence, assurance
ant. diffidence, doubt
convincing (adj)
syn. cogent, persuasive, probable, impressive, telling, plausible
ant. unconvincing, improbable
convivial (adj)
syn. genial, friendly, cheerful, jolly, merry, jovial, gay, sociable
ant. taciturn, uncommunicative, gloomy

convoluted (adj)
syn. complicated, complex, meandering, twisting, tangled
ant. straightforward

convulsion (n)
syn. commotion, disturbance, furore, disturbance, outburst, turbulence, agitation, upheaval
ant. calm, serenity, peace

cool (adj)
syn. chilly, cold, chill, fresh, unenthusiastic, indifferent, apathetic, unfriendly, aloof, composed, calm, relaxed
ant. warm, friendly, enthusiastic

copious (adj)
syn. plentiful, abundant, extensive, ample, lavish, generous, many, liberal, galore
ant. sparse, scanty, meagre, paltry

cordial (adj)
syn. affectionate, friendly, heartfelt, sociable, affable, warm, hearty, warm-hearted
ant. cool, aloof, hostile, distant

corny (adj)
syn. commonplace, banal, dull, old-fashioned, stale, stereotyped, sentimental
ant. new, original

corporal (adj)
syn. physical, bodily, material, tangible, concrete, anatomical
ant. spiritual

corporeal (adj)
syn. bodily, physical, human, actual, material, substantial, mortal, tangible
ant. spiritual, religious

corpulent (adj)
syn. fat, obese, beefy, large, plump, pot-bellied, stout
ant. thin, slim, lean, skinny

correlation (n)
syn. correspondence, interaction, relationship, link, equivalence, interchange
ant. divergence, independence

correspondence (n)
syn. communication, agreement, coincidence, analogy, congruity,

correlation, harmony, equivalence, writing, relation
ant. divergence, incongruity, difference
corroborate (v)
syn. ratify, endorse, authenticate, confirm, support, substantiate, prove
ant. invalidate, contradict
corrosive (adj)
syn. acrid, acid, abrasive, cutting, biting, virulent, sarcastic, venomous, trenchant
ant. kindly, peaceable, mild
corrupt (adj)
syn. illegal, dishonest, unlawful, immoral, perverted, debauched, impure, tainted
ant. honest, moral, pure
corrupt (v)
syn. contaminate, adulterate, bribe, pollute, defile, sully, pervert, demoralize
ant. purify, clean, cleanse, moralize
corruption (n)
syn. bribery, bribing, adulteration, demoralization, extortion, fraud, perversion, immorality, dishonesty
ant. honesty, morality, purification, virtue
cosmetic (adj)
syn. superficial, outward, non-essential, surface, external
ant. essential, fundamental
cosmopolitan (adj)
syn. international, global, multicultural, cultured, sophisticated, urbane, multiracial
ant. insular, rustic, parochial
cosy (adj)
syn. snug, comfortable, warm, homely, homelike, secure
ant. uncomfortable, cold
counterfeit (adj)
syn. bogus, fake, forged, pirate, fraudulent
ant. genuine
courage (n)
syn. valour, bravery, daring, heroism
ant. cowardice
courteous (adj)
syn. polite, well behaved, respectful, urbane, well-mannered, affable

ant. discourteous, rude, impolite
courtesy (n)
syn. politeness, civility, grace, respect, good manners, benevolence, affability, elegance
ant. discourtesy, rudeness, impoliteness
covert (adj)
syn. secret, concealed, hidden, clandestine, stealthy, underground, hush-hush
ant. overt, open
covet (v)
syn. desire, crave, fancy, long for, yearn for, thirst for, want, envy
ant. abjure, despise, dislike
covetous (adj)
syn. acquisitive, envious, jealous, greedy, yearning, mercenary
ant. generous, temperate
coward (n)
syn. faint-heart, chicken, sneak, mouse, baby
ant. hero
cowardice (n)
syn. cravenness, funk, timidity, unmanliness
ant. bravery, courage
cowardly (adj)
syn. chicken-hearted, craven, faint-hearted, fearful, spineless, gutless, lily-livered, timid
ant. brave, bold, courageous, daring, gallant, gutsy
coy (adj)
syn. shy, demure, diffident, modest, bashful, timid, reserved, self-effacing
ant. brazen, sober, impudent, forward
cracked (adj)
syn. batty, broken, crazy, defective, eccentric, loony, insane, flawed, imperfect
ant. perfect, sane, flawless
crafty (adj)
syn. cunning, tricky, sly, wily, dishonest, canny, deceitful, devious, scheming, shrewd
ant. honest, open, naive, artless
craggy (adj)
syn. broken, jagged, rough, rocky, rugged, stony
ant. smooth, pleasant

cramped (adj)
syn. uncomfortable, poky, confined, constricted, congested, small, tight, illegible, unreadable
ant. spacious, roomy, huge

cranky (adj)
(informal)
syn. eccentric, idiosyncratic, odd, irritable, peculiar, funny, bizarre, crabbed
ant. sensible, normal, placid

crave (v)
syn. desire, ask, fancy, long for, seek, thirst for, want, yearn for
ant. spurn, dislike

craven (adj)
syn. cowardly, fearful, chicken hearted, lily-livered, scared, weak
ant. courageous, brave, bold

craving (n)
syn. desire, longing, hunger, appetite, thirst, yearning
ant. dislike, distaste

crazy (adj)
(informal)
syn. insane, mad, lunatic, stupid, silly, foolish, absurd, passionate, fanatical
ant. sane, sensible, rational, normal

creation (n)
syn. formation, foundation, establishment, production, invention
ant. destruction, abolition

creative (adj)
syn. innovative, inventive, imaginative, visionary, artistic, ingenious, talented
ant. unimaginative, dull

creativity (n)
syn. imagination, talent, inventiveness, vision, artistry, ingenuity
ant. unimaginativeness, dullness

credibility (n)
syn. integrity, reliability, trustworthiness, plausibility, credence
ant. implausibility, unreliability

credible (adj)
syn. believable, conceivable, plausible, convincing, reasonable, reliable, trusty, trustworthy
ant. incredible, implausible, unreliable

creditable (adj)
syn. excellent, admirable, good, commendable, laudable, exemplary, worthy, praiseworthy, sterling
ant. shameful, blameworthy

credulous (adj)
syn. unsuspicious, gullible, naive, innocent, trusting, impressionable
ant. suspicious, sceptical

creepy (adj)
syn. awful, frightening, horrible, menacing, scary, spooky, unpleasant, terrifying
ant. normal, pleasant

crestfallen (adj)
syn. disappointed, downhearted, discouraged, dejected, sad, melancholy, despondent
ant. cheerful, elated, delighted, happy

criminal (n)
syn. culprit, felon, lawbreaker, malefactor, wrongdoer, miscreant, offender
ant. saint, gentleman, worthy

crisis (n)
syn. catastrophe, trouble, calamity, impasse, dilemma, plight, emergency
ant. prosperity, fortune, success

crisp (adj)
syn. crunchy, firm, fresh, brisk, invigorating, brief, short
ant. flexible, sultry, lengthy

critical (adj)
syn. fault-finding, unfavourable, disapproving, serious, precarious, vital, crucial, essential
ant. complimentary, flattering, unimportant

criticism (n)
syn. fault-finding, disapproval, censure, appraisal, evaluation, analysis, assessment
ant. commendation, praise

crony (n)
syn. associate, chum, friend, comrade, henchman, accomplice
ant. enemy, rival

crook (n)
(informal)
syn. criminal, rogue, cheat, swindler, robber, shark

ant. saint, gentleman, worthy

cross (adj)

syn. angry, irritated, vexed, annoyed, displeased, peevish, opposed, in a bad mood

ant. pleased, calm, placid

crotchety (adj)

syn. awkward, cross, contrary, bad-tempered, disagreeable, irritable, peevish

ant. placid, calm, pleasant

crowded (adj)

syn. full, swarming, packed, busy, jam-packed

ant. deserted

crucial (adj)

syn. key, pivotal, all-important, essential, critical, vital

ant. unimportant, insignificant, trivial

crude (adj)

syn. coarse, unrefined, natural, simple, rude, dirty, vulgar, indecent, uncouth

ant. refined, cultured, decent

cruel (adj)

syn. brutal, inhuman, harsh, callous, painful, savage, ruthless

ant. compassionate, humane, merciful

cruelty (n)

syn. brutality, barbarity, ferocity, inhumanity, ruthlessness, sadism

ant. mercy, compassion, kindness

crumble (v)

syn. decay, break up, decompose, deteriorate, perish, grind, crush, collapse, crumple

ant. flourish, thrive, grow

crummy (adj)

(informal)

syn. inferior, cheap, poor, rotten, miserable, grotty, pathetic, trashy, weak, useless, worthless

ant. excellent, superb, wonderful

cryptic (adj)

syn. ambiguous, bizarre, enigmatic, dark, hidden, obscure, mysterious, puzzling, vague, strange

ant. obvious, clear, straightforward

culminate (v)
syn. conclude, climax, peak, consummate, finish
ant. begin, start
culmination (n)
syn. climax, acme, peak, high point, apex, zenith, conclusion, finale, perfection
ant. beginning, start
culpable (adj)
syn. guilty, to blame, at fault, accountable, sinful, blameworthy
ant. inculpable, innocent, blameless
cult (n)
syn. admiration, craze, devotion, idolization, worship, veneration, faith, following, religion
ant. vilification, negligence
cultivate (v)
syn. work, farm, plough, till, grow, raise, woo, improve, refine, enrich, develop, educate
ant. neglect, ignore, omit
cultured (adj)
syn. civilized, learned, cultivated, enlightened, refined, urbane, erudite
ant. uncultured, barbarous, ignorant
cumbersome (adj)
syn. clumsy, awkward, burdensome, heavy, bulky, onerous, unmanageable
ant. light, convenient, manageable
cunning (adj)
syn. crafty, Machiavellian, artful, sly, wily, dishonest, canny, clever, shrewd, creative
ant. honest, artless, stupid
cunning (n)
syn. craftiness, art, astuteness, cleverness, skill, shrewdness, wiliness, slyness, guile
ant. openness, artlessness, simplicity
curb (v)
syn. control, bridle, hinder, constrain, repress, restrict
ant. encourage, foster
curious (adj)
syn. eager, intrigued, interested, peculiar, strange, funny, weird, bizarre, abnormal

ant. incurious, uninterested, normal

current (adj)
syn. modern, contemporary, present-day, common, accepted, prevalent, popular, valid, incumbent
ant. obsolete, old-fashioned, past

curse (n)
syn. malediction, jinx, anathema, misery, ordeal, affliction, profanity, expletive, dirty word
ant. blessing, advantage

cursory (adj)
syn. hasty, quick, rapid, casual, superficial
ant. thorough

curtail (v)
syn. shorten, cut, reduce, decrease, restrict, curb, slash, abridge
ant. increase, extend, prolong

customary (adj)
syn. traditional, usual, common, normal, habitual, routine, conventional
ant. unusual, uncommon, unconventional

cute (adj)
(informal)
syn. lovely, pretty, endearing, sweet, delightful, charming, shrewd, clever
ant. ugly, horrible, repulsive, dull

cutting (adj)
syn. acrimonious, acid, hurtful, malicious, bitter, trenchant, sarcastic, scathing, cruel
ant. soothing, kindly, mild

cynic (n)
syn. doubter, septic, doubting Thomas, pessimist
ant. optimist, idealist

cynical (adj)
syn. doubtful, sceptical, pessimistic, suspicious, disillusioned, unbelieving
ant. optimistic, idealistic

Dd

daft (adj)
syn. foolish, silly, ridiculous, absurd, crazy
ant. sensible, wise

dainty (adj)
syn. elegant, delicate, graceful, exquisite, fussy, fastidious, finicky, particular, neat, pretty, refined
ant. unwieldy, clumsy, gross

damn (v)
(informal)
syn. criticize, condemn, denounce, attack, blaspheme, slam
ant. praise, bless

damp (adj)
syn. moist, sweaty, humid, wet, rainy, misty, clammy
ant. dry, arid

damp (n)
syn. moisture, humidity, wet, clamminess
ant. dryness

dampen (v)
syn. check, decrease, depress, moisten, wet, dishearten, dismay
ant. dry, encourage

danger (n)
syn. risk, peril, threat
ant. safety

dangerous (adj)
syn. threatening, menacing, risky, hazardous, insecure
ant. safe, harmless, secure

dapper (adj)
syn. debonair, elegant, smart, well-dressed, dainty, well-groomed, stylish
ant. scruffy, shabby, dishevelled

daring (adj)
syn. fearless, bold, brave, courageous, adventurous, intrepid
ant. timorous, cowardly, timid

dark (adj)
syn. gloomy, black, dingy, ebony, fatalistic, grim, negative, angry, moody, ominous, evil, bad, crooked, obscure
ant. bright, happy, lucid

darken (v)
syn. blacken, cloud, depress, deepen, dim, deject, sadden, obscure
ant. brighten, lighten

dashing (adj)
(old-fashioned)
syn. debonair, stylish, flamboyant, debonair, bold, smart, elegant, spirited
ant. drab, modest, unstylish

dastardly (adj)
syn. cowardly, contemptible, lily-livered, sneaky, craven, spiritless
ant. heroic, noble

dated (adj)
syn. outdated, unfashionable, old-fashioned
ant. modern

daunt (v)
syn. dishearten, discourage, demoralize, awe, scare, put off, terrify
ant. hearten, encourage

daunted (adj)
syn. disheartened, discouraged, demoralized, frightened, alarmed, disillusioned
ant. heartened, encouraged

dauntless (adj)
syn. courageous, bold, fearless, resolute, heroic, lion-hearted, brave
ant. disheartened, discouraged, cowardly

daydream (n)
syn. fantasy, musing, dream, phantasm, wish, imagining, vision
ant. realism

daze (n)
syn. confusion, trance, stupor, muddle, shock
ant. clarity, composure

dazzling (adj)
syn. brilliant, glittering, glaring, sensational, splendid, sublime, stunning
ant. dull, drab, ordinary

deaden (v)
syn. dull, numb, alleviate, reduce, muffle, mute, soften, damp

ant. intensify, amplify
deafening (adj)
syn. booming, ear-splitting, crashing, resounding, roaring, thunderous
ant. quiet, low, soft
dearth (n)
syn. lack, shorten, scarcity, absence, insufficiency, inadequacy, poverty, need, famine
ant. excess, abundance, surfeit
debacle (n)
syn. failure, fiasco, disaster, catastrophe, havoc, downfall, defeat, collapse, fail
ant. success, triumph
debar (v)
syn. bar, deny, expel, obstruct, prevent, stop
ant. admit
debase (v)
syn. degrade, abase, cheapen, adulterate, demean, disgrace, humiliate, dishonour, shame
ant. elevate, upgrade, enhance
debate (n)
syn. discussion, talks, argument, dispute
ant. agreement
debauch (v)
syn. deprave, corrupt, pollute, violate, ravish, seduce, demoralize, ruin
ant. cleanse, purify, purge
debauched (adj)
syn. corrupted, abandoned, depraved, immoral, dissolute, licentious, degraded, lecherous
ant. pure, virtuous, decent, ascetic
debauchery (n)
syn. dissoluteness, depravity, immorality, gluttony, licentiousness, lust, lewdness
ant. decency, modesty, temperance, restraint
debilitate (v)
syn. devitalize, weaken, undermine, relax, exhaust, enfeeble
ant. strengthen, energize

debonair (adj)
(old-fashioned)
syn. charming, dashing, urbane, buoyant, affable, courteous, cheerful, refined, elegant
ant. depressed

debt (n)
syn. arrears, debit, claim, obligation, liability, sin
ant. credit, asset

decadence (n)
syn. decay, corruption, deterioration, dissolution, perversion, fall, debasement
ant. rise, flourishing

decadent (adj)
syn. corrupt, debauched, declining, depraved, immoral, dissolute, decaying, debased
ant. moral, ethical, principled, virtuous

decamp (v)
syn. escape, abscond, flee, run away, make off
ant. stay, stand

decay (v)
syn. decline, crumble, deteriorate, perish, rot, wane, spoil
ant. flourish, ripen, grow

deceit (n)
syn. fraud, deception, cheating, wiles, falsehood
ant. honesty, integrity, sincerity

deceive (v)
syn. cheat, trick, delude, betray, fool, swindle, abuse, mislead
ant. enlighten

decency (n)
syn. civility, courtesy, decorum, modesty, etiquette
ant. indecency, discourtesy

decent (adj)
syn. decorous, correct, modest, satisfactory, fair, courteous, pleasant, amiable
ant. indecent, improper, poor

deception (n)
syn. deceit, fraud, treachery, cheating, bluff, trick, ruse, hoax, swindle, scam, con, illusion
ant. openness, artlessness, honesty, sincerity

deceptive (adj)
syn. illusory, misleading, ambiguous, confusing, fake, dishonest, unreliable
ant. open, genuine, artless, sincere, honest
decipher (v)
syn. crack, figure out, decode, interpret, solve, understood, unravel, unfold, explain
ant. encode
decisive (adj)
syn. resolute, strong-willed, firm, strong-minded, determined, deciding, critical, determining, crucial
ant. indecisive, insignificant
decline (v)
syn. reject, dismiss, turn down, decrease, collapse, worsen
ant. accept, increase, improve
decode (v)
syn. interpret, solve, decipher, translate
ant. encode
decompose (v)
syn. perish, rot, decay, deteriorate, go off, spoil
ant. combine, unite
decorous (adj)
syn. comely, decent, correct, appropriate, modest, well-behaved, dignified
ant. indecorous, unseemly
decorum (n)
syn. decency, propriety, politeness, custom, etiquette, good manners, respectability, dignity
ant. indecorum, impropriety, indecency, immodesty
decrease (v)
syn. reduce, lessen, drop, subside
ant. increase
decrease (n)
syn. decline, cut, reduction, drop
ant. increase
decrepit (adj)
syn. crippled, dilapidated, feeble, weak, battered, broken-down, frail
ant. fit, youthful, strong
decry (v)
syn. blame, criticize, condemn, denounce, undervalue, devalue, derogate, abuse

ant. praise, appreciate, value

dedicated (adj)

syn. committed, devoted, faithful, enthusiastic, whole-hearted, zealous, specialized

ant. apathetic, uncommitted, half-hearted

deduct (v)

syn. take off, subtract, debit, knock off

ant. add

deface (v)

syn. blemish, disfigure, damage, spoil, vandalize

ant. repair

defamation (n)

syn. derogation, aspersion, vilification, slander, libel, smear, slur

ant. commendation, praise

defamatory (adj)

syn. derogatory, insulting, abusive, vilifying, slanderous

ant. complimentary, appreciative

defective (adj)

syn. imperfect, faulty, broken, lacking, flawed

ant. perfect

deference (n)

syn. civility, compliance, courtesy, obedience, respect, politeness, reverence, submissiveness, honour, esteem

ant. disrespect, insolence, incivility

deferential (adj)

syn. courteous, civil, obedient, regardful, polite, submissive, complaisant

ant. immodest, arrogant, defiant

defiance (n)

syn. rebellion, resistance, disregard, contempt, confrontation

ant. compliance, obedience

deficient (adj)

syn. imperfect, defective, meagre, scarce, unsatisfactory, weak

ant. excessive, superfluous

deficit (n)

syn. shortage, shortfall, arrears, loss

ant. surplus

defile (v)

syn. abuse, debase, corrupt, disgrace, rape, molest, violate, tarnish, dirty, contaminate

ant. cleanse, purify
defy (v)
syn. disregard, violate, disobey, breach, break, challenge, confront, despise
ant. obey, comply, follow, flinch
degenerate (adj)
syn. corrupt, dissolute, immoral, fallen, degraded, mean, perverted, base
ant. virtuous, moral, upright
degrade (v)
syn. demean, humiliate, dehumanize, disgrace, defame, demote
ant. dignify, exalt, praise
dejected (adj)
syn. disheartened, depressed, downcast, crestfallen, despondent, sad, melancholy
ant. cheerful, delighted, sunny, happy
dejection (n)
syn. depression, gloom, sadness, despair, melancholy, unhappiness, sorrow
ant. happiness, cheerfulness, ecstasy, bliss
delay (v)
syn. make late, hamper, drag, linger, postpone, defer, put off, retard
ant. hurry, advance, accelerate, expedite
delectable (adj)
syn. agreeable, delightful, adorable, enjoyable, pleasant, enticing, yummy
ant. unpleasant, horrid, repulsive
delectation (n)
syn. contentment, delight, enjoyment, amusement, pleasure, comfort, happiness, entertainment
ant. distaste, discontentment, loathing
deleterious (adj)
syn. destructive, harmful, injurious, bad, prejudicial
ant. helpful, enhancing
deliberate (adj)
syn. intentional, intended, careful, methodical, meticulous, purposeful
ant. accidental, hasty, unintentional
deliberately (adj)
syn. consciously, wilfully, intentionally, knowingly
ant. unintentionally, accidentally
delicacy (n)
syn. fragility, fineness, thinness, difficulty, sensitivity, awkwardness, care,

tact, treat, titbit
ant. indelicacy, tactlessness
delicate (adj)
syn. soft, graceful, light, fragile, weak, difficult, sensitive, awkward, tactful, discreet
ant. strong, coarse, robust
delicious (adj)
syn. mouth-watering, tasty, flavoursome, finger-licking, yummy
ant. unpalatable, unpleasant
delight (v)
syn. enchant, thrill, charm, amuse, ravish, cheer, please
ant. disappoint, disgust, dismay, displease
delighted (adj)
syn. happy, pleased, thrilled, overjoyed, elated, jubilant, ecstatic, captivated
ant. disappointed, dismayed, displeased, disillusioned
delightful (adj)
syn. amusing, lovely, pleasant, charming, captivating, appealing, cute, thrilling
ant. horrible, awful
delinquent (adj)
syn. careless, neglectful, culpable, negligent, guilty
ant. blameless, careful
delirious (adj)
syn. crazy, ecstatic, frantic, hysterical, mad, insane, excited, frenzied
ant. sane, rational, sober
delirium (n)
syn. frenzy, fever, hysteria, lunacy, insanity, madness, ecstasy
ant. sanity, calm, composure
delude (v)
syn. cheat, dupe, beguile, deceive, misguide, mislead, hoax, trick, fool, con
ant. enlighten, elucidate
delusion (n)
syn. deception, misconception, illusion, false, impression, misapprehension, fancy, mistake, fantasy
ant. reality, actuality
demean (v)
syn. abase, degrade, debase, lower, humble, stoop
ant. enhance, elevate, exalt

demented (adj)
syn. crazy, distraught, foolish, insane, lunatic, idiotic, unbalanced, mad
ant. sane, rational, normal

demise (n)
syn. death, end, fall
ant. birth

demoralization (n)
syn. debasement, corruption, perversion, depression, despondency, vitiation
ant. encouragement

demote (v)
syn. reduce, declass, downgrade, degrade
ant. promote, upgrade

demure (adj)
syn. decent, modest, shy, proper, reserved, prudish, sober, reticent, decorous
ant. brazen, wanton, forward, bold

denigration (n)
syn. defamation, aspersion, scandal, backbiting, vilification, derogation, slander
ant. commendation, praise

denounce (v)
syn. censure, condemn, decry, damn, revile, attack, expose, implicate, accuse, vilify
ant. commend, praise, eulogize

denunciation (n)
syn. censure, accusation, criticism, condemnation, denouncement, incrimination, obloquy, reproof
ant. commendation, praise, compliment, eulogy

deny (v)
syn. refute, contradict, challenge, reject, veto, turn down
ant. confirm, accept

deplete (v)
syn. reduce, diminish, decrease, expend, empty, consume
ant. augment, enhance

depletion (n)
syn. reduction, decrease, expenditure, deficiency, lessening
ant. increase, supply

deplore (v)
syn. regret, disapprove of, condemn, abhor, lament
ant. extol, applaud

deport (v)
syn. banish, repatriate, expel
ant. admit

depraved (adj)
syn. corrupt, base, debased, dissolute, immoral, lewd, licentious, shameless, perverted, wicked, sinful
ant. upright, virtuous, moral, ethical

depravity (n)
syn. corruption, baseness, debasement, debauchery, dissoluteness, immorality, licence, perversion, vice
ant. uprightness, morality, chastity

deprecate (v)
syn. condemn, disapprove of, reject, deplore, protest, depreciate
ant. commend, praise, approve

deprecation (n)
syn. decline, slump, derogation, underestimation, disparagement
ant. appreciation, commendation, praise

depressed (adj)
syn. unhappy, dejected, sad, inactive, poor, needy, distressed
ant. cheerful, happy, affluent

depression (n)
syn. dejection, downheartedness, blues, hard times, melancholy, hopelessness, inactivity, sadness, slump
ant. elation, cheerfulness, ecstasy, bliss, prosperity

deprivation (n)
syn. hardship, poverty, dispossession, distress
ant. prosperity

deprive (v)
syn. strip, dispossess, rob, deny
ant. bestow, give

deprived (adj)
syn. disadvantaged, poor, poverty-stricken, needy, unprivileged, impoverished, depressed
ant. prosperous, privileged, fortunate

deranged (adj)
syn. confused, delirious, disturbed, berserk, insane, mad, lunatic, irrational, crazed, unbalanced
ant. sane, rational, calm

dereliction (n)
syn. abdication, faithlessness, negligence, failure, remissness, betrayal, abandonment, desertion, renunciation
ant. devotion, faithfulness, fulfilment

derision (n)
syn. ridicule, mockery, taunts, jeers, insults, disparagement, scorn, contempt, satire, laughter, disrespect
ant. praise, respect, admiration, appreciation

derogatory (adj)
syn. disrespectful, critical, unfavourable, insulting, defamatory, abusive
ant. flattering, complimentary

desecrate (v)
syn. blaspheme, defile, abuse, debase, insult, dishonour, contaminate, violate, profane
ant. consecrate, praise, honour, sanctify

desecration (n)
syn. blasphemy, impiety, defilement, insult, profanation, violation, abuse
ant. consecration, reverence

deserted (adj)
syn. marooned, abandoned, forlorn, empty, unoccupied, lonely, desolate
ant. populous

desolate (adj)
syn. bleak, grim, miserable, depressed, unhappy, broken-hearted, dismal, inhospitable, deserted, abandoned
ant. cheerful, happy, delighted, populous

despair (n)
syn. hopelessness, unhappiness, misery, depression, dejection, anguish
ant. hope, joy, euphoria, delight

despicable (adj)
syn. abhorrent, base, degrading, contemptible, hateful, disgraceful, infamous, shameful, worthless
ant. laudable, admirable, noble

despise (v)
syn. loathe, detest, scorn, deplore, revile, shun, condemn, dislike

ant. adore, respect, appreciate
despoil (v)
syn. denude, destroy, loot, plunder, rob, vandalize
ant. enrich, adorn
despondent (adj)
syn. blue, dejected, depressed, broken-hearted, disheartened, downcast, gloomy, hopeless, miserable, melancholy, sorrowful
ant. cheerful, hopeful, delighted, sunny, happy
despot (n)
syn. boss, autocrat, Hitler, absolutist, dictator, oppressor
ant. liberal, democrat, egalitarian
despotic (adj)
syn. bossy, autocratic, absolute, oppressive, arbitrary, absolutist, tyrannical, dictatorial, authoritarian
ant. liberal, democratic, tolerant, egalitarian
despotism (n)
syn. absolutism, dictatorship, oppression, totalitarianism, autocracy, tyranny
ant. liberalism, tolerance, democracy, egalitarianism
destitute (adj)
syn. poor, penniless, poverty-stricken, impoverished
ant. rich, affluent, wealthy
destruction (n)
syn. annihilation, demolition, bane, elimination, end, massacre, overthrow
ant. creation, preservation
desultory (adj)
syn. disorderly, inconstant, aimless, loose, undirected, inconsistent, capricious, inexact
ant. methodical, systematic
detach (v)
syn. isolate, loose, disconnect, remove, cut off
ant. attach, join
detailed (adj)
syn. comprehensive, elaborate, full, specific, thorough, meticulous
ant. cursory, brief, perfunctory
detain (v)
syn. confine, hold up, arrest, restrain, impede, stop
ant. release, free

detention (n)
syn. confinement, custody, imprisonment, duress
ant. release, freedom
deteriorate (v)
syn. fail, decline, worsen, debase
ant. improve
determination (n)
syn. resolution, dedication, tenacity, resolve, perseverance, guts
ant. irresolution
deterrent (n)
syn. curb, discouragement, obstruction, difficulty, bar, check, barrier
ant. incentive, encouragement
detest (v)
syn. hate, despise, loathe, abhor, dislike, deplore
ant. love, adore
detraction (n)
syn. defamation, derogation, slander, revilement, abuse, insinuation
ant. praise, appreciation, flattery
detrimental (adj)
syn. injurious, harmful, destructive, damaging, adverse
ant. beneficial, advantageous, favourable
deviation (n)
syn. abnormality, change, divergence, shift, fluctuation
ant. conformity
devious (adj)
syn. dishonest, cunning, underhand, crafty, crooked, meandering, indirect, treacherous
ant. honest, candid, direct
devotion (n)
syn. commitment, fondness, zeal, fidelity, loyalty, piety, spirituality
ant. apathy, negligence, inconstancy
devout (adj)
syn. devoted, loyal, pious, dedicated, god-fearing, fervent, committed
ant. uncommitted, insincere
dexterity (n)
syn. mastery, ability, aptitude, expertise, proficiency, skill, ingenuity, art
ant. ineptitude, clumsiness

dictator (n)
syn. tyrant, autocrat, supreme, despot
ant. democrat

diehard (adj)
syn. hard-line, hardcore, inflexible, stubborn, reactionary, rigid, uncompromising, ultra-conservative
ant. progressive, flexible, enlightened

differ (v)
syn. conflict, clash, disagree, oppose, argue
ant. agree, confirm

diffident (adj)
syn. shy, unconfident, insecure, timid, bashful, reserved, sheepish
ant. confident, bold

dignify (v)
syn. honour, ennoble, glorify, adorn
ant. degrade, demean

dilapidated (adj)
syn. decayed, ruined, ramshackle, battered, run down, shabby
ant. renovated, restored

dilate (v)
syn. increase, expand, amplify, widen, broaden, elaborate
ant. curtail, abbreviate

dilatory (adj)
syn. slow, backward, delaying, slothful, sluggish, lingering, loitering
ant. diligent, prompt

dilemma (n)
syn. predicament, conflict, quandary, mess, plight, fix
ant. ease, comfort

diligent (adj)
syn. hard-working, careful, industrious, meticulous
ant. lazy, idle, indolent

diminish (v)
syn. decrease, abate, lessen, reduce, subside
ant. increase, enhance

din (n)
syn. cacophony, uproar, noise, pandemonium, commotion, ruckus, rumpus, outcry, row
ant. silence, calm, quiet

dingy (adj)
syn. dirty, shabby, discoloured, faded, worn, sombre
ant. clean, bright
diplomatic (adj)
syn. discreet, tactful, judicious, sagacious, prudent, polite, subtle
ant. tactless, rude, thoughtless
dire (adj)
syn. alarming, catastrophic, terrible, sore, serious, appalling, awful
ant. delightful, splendid
disadvantaged (adj)
syn. impoverished, deprived, underprivileged, handicapped
ant. privileged
disappointed (adj)
syn. displeased, upset, downhearted, crestfallen, disheartened, gutted
ant. delighted, cheerful, happy
disappointment (n)
syn. displeasure, regret, sadness, dismay, let-down
ant. delight, satisfaction, ecstasy
disaster (n)
syn. tragedy, calamity, catastrophe, mishap, misfortune, fiasco, failure,
affliction
ant. success, triumph, blessing
discard (v)
syn. reject, get rid of, ditch, trash, dump, abandon, throw away
ant. keep, adopt, embrace, retain
discernible (adj)
syn. perceptible, noticeable, clear, obvious, visible, apparent, detectable,
plain
ant. imperceptible, invisible
discernment (n)
syn. cleverness, insight, acumen, intelligence, sagacity, sharpness, wisdom,
perception
ant. obtuseness, slowness, dullness
disclose (v)
syn. tell, pass on, reveal, make public
ant. conceal
disconsolate (adj)
syn. dejected, forlorn, heartbroken, hopeless, miserable, sad, desolate,

wretched, inconsolable
ant. joyful, cheerful, cheery, delighted
discontented (adj)
syn. dissatisfied, resentful, displeased, frustrated, disgruntled, aggrieved
ant. contented, satisfied, happy
discord (n)
syn. din, dispute, cacophony, conflict, incompatibility, wrangling, disharmony, disunity, opposition
ant. concord, agreement, harmony
discordant (adj)
syn. cacophonous, harsh, inharmonious, strident, contradictory, disagreeing, shrill
ant. harmonious, concordant
discovery (n)
syn. breakthrough, innovation, finding, disclosure
ant. concealment
discreet (n)
syn. diplomatic, careful, tactful, sensitive, strategic, judicious, circumspect, thoughtful
ant. indiscreet, tactless, careless
discrepancy (n)
syn. disparity, disagreement, mismatch, difference
ant. correspondence
discretion (n)
syn. diplomacy, prudence, tact, acumen, responsibility, choice, preference, will, wisdom
ant. indiscretion, rashness
discrimination (n)
syn. intolerance, prejudice, bigotry, bias
ant. impartiality
disdain (n)
syn. disrespect, contempt, haughtiness, derision, scorn, arrogance
ant. respect, admiration
disfigure (v)
syn. damage, distort, spoil, deface, blemish
ant. adorn
disgrace (n)
syn. shame, stigma, dishonour, scandal, blemish, reproach

ant. honour, esteem, respect
disgraceful (adj)
syn. blameworthy, shameful, dishonourable, scandalous, bad
ant. admirable, honourable
disgruntled (adj)
syn. discontented, displeased, dissatisfied, fed up, annoyed, cheesed off
ant. contented, pleased
disguise (v)
syn. conceal, cover up, hide, muffle, mask
ant. expose, reveal
disgust (adj)
syn. displease, offend, repel, revolt, horrify
ant. delight, gratify
disgusting (adj)
syn. loathsome, abominable, repulsive, objectionable, horrifying, appalling
ant. delightful, attractive, pleasant
dishearten (v)
syn. depress, dampen, discourage, deject, dismay, weary
ant. hearten, encourage
disheartened (adj)
syn. depressed, crestfallen, disappointed, dismayed, weary, dejected, discouraged
ant. heartened, encouraged, delighted
dishevelled (adj)
syn. disordered, rumpled, untidy, bedraggled, disarranged, unkempt
ant. neat, tidy
dishonesty (n)
syn. insincerity, cheating, craft, corruption, deceit, falsity, wiliness
ant. honesty, truthfulness
disinterested (adj)
syn. candid, unbiased, impartial, unselfish, unprejudiced, neutral, honest
ant. biased, prejudiced, dishonest
dismal (adj)
syn. dejected, morose, gloomy, forlorn, dim, dull, dingy
ant. bright, cheerful, happy
dismantle (v)
syn. demolish, break up, raze, strike

ant. assemble, build
dismay (n)
syn. distress, alarm, anxiety, apprehension, disappointment, upset
ant. relief, pleasure, boldness
disparage (v)
syn. criticize, defame, disdain, malign, slander, scorn, degrade, vilify
ant. praise, admire, respect
dispensable (adj)
syn. inessential, useless, disposable, unnecessary, superfluous
ant. indispensable, essential
disperse (n)
syn. disband, disappear, dissolve, drive off, scatter, dissipate
ant. gather, assemble
dispirited (adj)
syn. crestfallen, depressed, disheartened, gloomy, dejected, morose, discouraged
ant. encouraged, high-spirited
displeased (adj)
syn. annoyed, peeved, angry, irritated, furious, put out, upset, disappointed
ant. pleased, contented, satisfied, delighted
disproportionate (adj)
syn. inappropriate, unequal, excessive, unbalanced, unreasonable
ant. appropriate, balanced
dispute (n)
syn. argument, conflict, discord, feud, disagreement, quarrel
ant. agreement, concord, harmony
disregard (v)
syn. overlook, ignore, neglect, disobey
ant. heed
dissemble (v)
syn. conceal, disguise, affect, fake, hide, falsify, sham, pretend
ant. admit, disclose
dissension (n)
syn. discord, difference, contention, disagreement, quarrel, conflict, strife
ant. peace, agreement, harmony
dissident (n)
syn. rebel, dissenter, protester, objector, agitator
ant. conformist, assenter

dissimulation (n)
syn. deception, hypocrisy, act, sham, pretence, deceit, affectation, double-dealing, wiles
ant. openness, honesty

dissipate (v)
syn. disperse, consume, disappear, deplete, dispel, expend, scatter, spend, vanish
ant. accumulate, concentrate

dissolute (adj)
syn. corrupt, dissipated, lewd, immoral, loose, abandoned, vicious, licentious, debauched
ant. virtuous, austere, moral, ethical

dissoluteness (n)
syn. corruption, immorality, dissipation, vice, depravity
ant. virtue, morality

dissolution (n)
syn. break-up, decay, demise, disappearance, dismissal, divorce, overthrow, resolution, end
ant. unification

dissonant (adj)
syn. cacophonous, disagreeing, discordant, disharmonious, congruous, differing, unmelodious, irreconcilable
ant. harmonious, compatible

dissuade (v)
syn. deter, put off, disincline, discourage
ant. persuade, urge

distinctive (adj)
syn. peculiar, unique, special, exclusive, notable, remarkable
ant. common, unremarkable

distinguished (adj)
syn. famous, eminent, great, prominent, celebrated
ant. unknown, obscure

distracted (adj)
syn. inattentive, worried, preoccupied, vague, confused
ant. attentive, composed

distraught (adj)
syn. anxious, distracted, distressed, overwrought, crazy, frantic, mad, hysterical

ant. calm, composed, untroubled
distress (n)
syn. heartbreak, unhappiness, anguish, sorrow, suffering, peril, danger, trouble, adversity
ant. joy, happiness, ease, relief
ditch (v)
(informal)
syn. discard, abandon, jettison, dump, scrap
ant. adopt, embrace
diverge (v)
syn. divide, separate, bifurcate, disagree, clash, differ, be different
ant. converge, agree, join
diverse (adj)
syn. sundry, different, various, unlike, mixed, miscellaneous, divergent
ant. similar, identical
diversity (n)
syn. miscellany, difference, variety, mix, assortment
ant. uniformity, similarity, sameness
divine (adj)
syn. holy, angelic, sacred, godly, celestial, exalted, spiritual, splendid, supreme
ant. earthly, unholy, mortal
divulge (v)
syn. reveal, pass on, disclose, communicate, tell
ant. conceal, hide
dizzy (adj)
syn. giddy, unsteady, faint, muzzy, light-headed, reeling, shaky, foolish, confused
ant. sober, sensible, clear-headed
docile (adj)
syn. submissive, compliant, obedient, yielding, meek, manageable, amenable
ant. obstinate, disobedient, wilful
doctrinaire (adj)
syn. dogmatic, inflexible, biased, ideological, rigid, theoretical, fanatical, unrealistic, hypothetical
ant. undoctrinaire, flexible, realistic

doddery (adj)
syn. aged, shaky, weak, rambling, unsteady, senile, feeble
ant. hale, youthful
dodgy (adj)
syn. difficult, uncertain, unsafe, unreliable, dangerous
ant. easy, safe
doff (v)
(old-fashioned)
syn. remove, undress, shed, lift, throw off, discard
ant. don, wear
dogged (adj)
syn. resolute, persistent, tenacious, persevering, determined, stubborn
ant. irresolute, half-hearted, apathetic
dogmatic (adj)
syn. adamant, doctrinaire, dictatorial, emphatic, uncompromising, opinionated, authoritarian, arbitrary
ant. tolerant, egalitarian, liberal, amenable
doldrums (n)
syn. apathy, dullness, gloom, blues, inertia, tedium, depression, boredom
ant. interest, liveliness
doleful (adj)
syn. cheerless, gloomy, mournful, blue, forlorn, melancholy, sombre, dolorous
ant. happy, cheerful, joyful, rapturous
dolorous (adj)
syn. distressing, melancholy, miserable, sad, sombre, anguished
ant. happy, cheerful, joyful, ecstatic
dolour (n)
(literary)
syn. sorrow, misery, anguish, grief, heartbreak, mourning, great sadness
ant. beatitude, happiness, joy
domineering (adj)
syn. bossy, dictatorial, arrogant, oppressive, despotic, tyrannical, coercive
ant. meek, servile
don (v)
syn. put on, assume, dress in, change into
ant. creation

donor (n)
syn. contributor, giver, sponsor, patron, benefactor
ant. beneficiary, recipient
doom (n)
syn. nemesis, destruction, ruin, annihilation, downfall
ant. creation
dormant (adj)
syn. hibernating, latent, inactive, slumbering, unrealized, inert, sleeping, undeveloped
ant. active
dotty (adj)
(old-fashioned, informal)
syn. eccentric, peculiar, crazy, touched, feeble-minded
ant. sensible
doughty (adj)
(old-fashioned)
syn. bold, daring, heroic, brave, resolute, gallant, fearless
ant. timorous, cowardly, weak
dowdy (adj)
syn. shabby, unsmart, dingy, unfashionable, ill-dressed, tatty
ant. smart, dressy, fashionable
downcast (adj)
syn. depressed, disappointed, cheerless, dispirited, sad, crestfallen, miserable
ant. happy, cheerful
downhearted (adj)
syn. crestfallen, dismayed, sad, disheartened, depressed, dejected
ant. happy, cheerful, enthusiastic
down-to-earth (adj)
syn. sensible, mundane, unsentimental, realistic, sane
ant. impractical, fantastic
drab (adj)
syn. dull, dingy, gloomy, cheerless, sombre, dismal, uninteresting, boring
ant. bright, interesting
drastic (adj)
syn. harsh, severe, dire, extreme, radical, intensive
ant. mild, moderate

drawback (n)
syn. defect, disadvantage, block, handicap, obstacle
ant. advantage, benefit
dreadful (adj)
syn. awful, horrible, shocking, fearful, terrible, appalling, alarming
ant. wonderful, excellent
dream (n)
syn. trance, daydream, ambition, hope, wish
ant. nightmare
dreary (adj)
syn. boring, monotonous, dull, tedious, unexciting, uninteresting, cheerless, lifeless, forlorn
ant. exciting, interesting
droll (adj)
syn. comic, humorous, farcical, amusing, laughable, ridiculous, witty
ant. serious, unamusing
droop (v)
syn. dangle, drop, bend, decline, fall down, sink, fade, weaken
ant. rise, straighten, flourish
drowsy (adj)
syn. sleepy, torpid, lethargic, dozy, restful
ant. awake, alert
drudgery (n)
syn. labour, chore, sweat, donkey-work, toil, slavery, sweated labour
ant. rest, leisure, ease
drunk (adj)
syn. inebriated, drunken, intoxicated, legless, loaded
ant. sober
drunkard (n)
(old-fashioned)
syn. drinker, alcoholic, dipsomaniac, drunk, carouser, rummy
ant. teetotaller
drunken (adj)
syn. boozy, boozing, intoxicated, drunk, spongy, dissipated
ant. sober
dry (adj)
syn. waterless, arid, dull, boring, uninteresting, dreary, cynical, subtle, sarcastic

ant. wet, interesting, sweet
dual (adj)
syn. twin, double, paired
ant. single
dubious (adj)
syn. sceptical, doubtful, suspicious, unreliable, ambiguous, unclear, unsure, undecided, uncertain, iffy, dodgy
ant. certain, reliable, trustworthy
dull (adj)
syn. boring, uninteresting, gloomy, dismal, drab, stupid, unintelligent, slow, half-witted
ant. interesting, exciting, sharp, bright, alert
dumb (adj)
syn. speechless, silent, mute, stupid, unintelligent, dim
ant. talkative, clever, intelligent
dummy (n)
syn. fool, blockhead, dunce, dimwit, copy, counterfeit, sham, copy, counterfeit
ant. genius, brain, original
dunce (n)
(old-fashioned)
syn. blockhead, dimwit, duffer, moron, donkey, dullard, loon, half-wit
ant. intellectual, brain, genius
durability (n)
syn. endurance, longevity, stability, constancy, strength
ant. fragility, weakness, impermanence
durable (adj)
syn. long-lasting, sturdy, hard-wearing, strong, long-term, permanent, enduring, tough
ant. short-lived, delicate, weak, fragile
dusk (n)
syn. sunset, evening, twilight, nightfall
ant. dawn
dusky (adj)
syn. dark, cloudy, dim, shady, twilight, obscure, murky
ant. light, bright
dwindle (v)
syn. decrease, lessen, diminish, wane, reduce, shrink, decline, fade

ant. increase
dying (adj)
syn. declining, waning, fading, ebbing, sinking, at death's door
ant. reviving, coming
dynamic (adj)
syn. active, spirited, lively, energetic, enterprising, high-powered, zippy
ant. lethargic, apathetic, inactive, slow
dynamism (n)
syn. energy, initiative, vigour, liveliness, enterprise
ant. apathy, slowness

Ee

eager (adj)
syn. zealous, enthusiastic, anxious, impatient, desirous, keen
ant. apathetic, unenthusiastic, indifferent

eagerly (adv)
syn. keenly, avidly, enthusiastically, ardently
ant. apathetically

eagerness (n)
syn. keenness, avidity, enthusiasm, longing, yearning, thirst
ant. apathy, disinterest

earn (v)
syn. gain, procure, receive, deserve, win
ant. lose, spend

earnest (adj)
syn. sober, serious, intense, grave, heartfelt, sincere, fervent, devout, wholehearted
ant. apathetic, half-hearted, frivolous

earnings (n)
syn. income, emoluments, profits, revenue, salary, pay
ant. expenses, outgoings

earthly (adj)
(literary)
syn. worldly, material, carnal, physical, temporal, sensual, profane, base, sordid
ant. heavenly, spiritual

earthy (adj)
syn. simple, unsophisticated, down-to-earth, natural, coarse, bawdy, indecent, vulgar
ant. refined, cultured

ease (n)
syn. simplicity, effortlessness, informality, composure, prosperity, wealth, comfort, luxury
ant. difficulty, discomfort

easy-going (adj)
syn. carefree, relaxed, patient, tolerant, calm, flexible
ant. strict, intolerant, fussy

ebb (v)
syn. diminish, wane, decline, recede, decrease, lessen, retreat, fall back, subside
ant. increase, rise

ebullient (adj)
syn. cheerful, sparkling, jolly, enthusiastic, vivacious, elated
ant. depressed, dull, lethargic

eccentric (adj)
syn. strange, unconventional, odd, abnormal, cranky, idiosyncratic, bizarre
ant. conventional, sane, normal

economical (adj)
syn. low-cost, cheap, thrifty, prudent
ant. expensive, spendthrift

economy (n)
syn. wealth, prudence, saving, thrift, frugality, careful, budgeting
ant. extravagance, improvidence

ecstasy (n)
syn. joy, elation, euphoria, delight, rapture, exaltation
ant. misery, torment

ecstatic (adj)
syn. elated, joyful, enraptured, blissful, over the moon, on cloud nine
ant. downcast, indifferent, dejected

edgy (adj)
(informal)
syn. irritable, tense, anxious, uneasy, nervous, apprehensive, wired
ant. placid, calm

edify (v)
syn. educate, guide, train, elevate, improve, enlighten, enhance
ant. debase, deprave, corrupt

eerie (adj)
syn. awesome, mysterious, creepy, ghostly, scary, spooky, uncanny, unnatural, fearful
ant. natural, ordinary

effective (adj)
syn. powerful, valuable, successful, potent, strong, convincing, cogent,

practical
ant. ineffective, useless
effeminate (adj)
syn. delicate, soft, unmanly, womanish, feminine, womanlike, weak
ant. virile, manly
effervescent (adj)
syn. lively, excited, vivacious, buoyant, enthusiastic, animated, fizzy, merry
ant. apathetic, dull
efficacy (n)
syn. competence, efficiency, ability, force, potency, strength, capability, virtue
ant. inefficacy, uselessness, ineffectiveness
efficiency (n)
syn. order, productivity, competence, skill, expertise, ability
ant. inefficiency, incompetence
efficient (adj)
syn. adept, skilful, productive, economic, methodical, skilled, competent, effective, capable
ant. inefficient, incompetent
effrontery (n)
syn. arrogance, audacity, brazenness, insolence, shamelessness, incivility, disrespect, imprudence
ant. shyness, modesty, humility, propriety
effusive (adj)
syn. talkative, enthusiastic, profuse, wordy, extravagant, unreserved, unrestrained
ant. quiet, restrained
egotism (n)
syn. egoism, conceitedness, self-importance, vanity, narcissism, superiority, self-love
ant. humility, lowliness, modesty, altruism
egotistic (adj)
syn. egoistic, conceited, self-important, vain, boasting, opinionated, swollen-headed
ant. humble, meek, modest
egregious (adj)
syn. glaring, arrant, intolerable, infamous, notorious, shocking, heinous, outrageous, scandalous

ant. slight, inoffensive, concealed
elated (adj)
syn. thrilled, overjoyed, jubilant, delighted, rapturous, delighted, rapturous, on cloud nine
ant. miserable, downcast, dejected
elation (n)
syn. joy, ecstasy, euphoria, glee, jubilation, delight, happiness
ant. depression, dejection
elderly (adj)
syn. old, aged, senile, over the hill
ant. young, youthful
elegance (n)
syn. sophistication, dignity, style, aptness, neatness, chic, politeness, propriety
ant. inelegance, rudeness, crudeness, coarseness
elegant (adj)
syn. sophisticated, stylish, chic, polished, smart, simple, refined, polite
ant. inelegant, crude, rough
elegy (n)
syn. lament, dirge, plaint, moan, groan, wailing, complaint
ant. joy, elation, revelry
elevate (v)
syn. raise, boost, hoist, upgrade, promote, increase, uplift
ant. lessen, lower, demote
elevation (n)
syn. rise, promotion, exaltation, sublimity, grandeur, uplift, upgrading
ant. baseness, demotion, informality
eligible (adj)
syn. qualified, suitable, worthy, fit
ant. ineligible
eliminate (v)
syn. annihilate, remove, end, destroy, rule out, delete
ant. accept
elite (n)
syn. best, gentry, nobility, aristocracy, cream, ruling class, high society
ant. dregs, rabble
eloquence (n)
syn. oratory, expression, rhetoric, expressiveness, forcefulness, fluency

ant. inarticulateness

eloquent (adj)

syn. fluent, expressive, lucid, articulate, vivid, well-expressed

ant. inarticulate, tongue-tied

elucidate (v)

syn. explain, illustrate, annotate, unfold, clarify, interpret

ant. obscure, confuse

elusive (adj)

syn. fallacious, deceptive, indefinable, ambiguous, intangible, evasive, misleading, unanalysable, illusory

ant. comprehensible, upright

emaciated (adj)

syn. bony, thin, wasted, skinny, withered, shrunken, skeletal, meagre

ant. fat, plump, well-fed, obese

emancipation (n)

syn. freedom, liberty, unbinding, release, deliverance, liberation

ant. enslavement

embargo (n)

syn. ban, blockage, hindrance, proscription, stoppage, bar, prohibition

ant. permission, licence

embarrassment (n)

syn. discomfort, humiliation, shamefacedness, awkwardness, mess, difficulty, predicament, shame

ant. ease, assurance, imperturbability

embellish (v)

syn. beautify, dress up, adorn, decorate, garnish, enrich, trim

ant. simplify, denude, disfigure

embittered (adj)

syn. disaffected, sour, bitter, disillusioned

ant. pacified

embody (v)

syn. combine, comprise, collect, personify, organize, represent, express

ant. disembody

embolden (v)

syn. cheer, inspire, encourage, strengthen, hearten

ant. dishearten, discourage

embryonic (adj)

syn. underdeveloped, early, beginning, immature, rudimentary, insipient,

primary, inchoate
ant. developed, advanced
emerge (v)
syn. arise, rise, appear, turn up, crop up
ant. disappear, fade
emergence (n)
syn. rise, coming, appearance, dawn, advent
ant. disappearance, decline
emergent (adj)
syn. developing, coming, rising, emerging, budding
ant. disappearing, declining
emigrate (v)
syn. migrate, move, abroad, relocate, leave your country
ant. immigrate
eminent (adj)
syn. renowned, noted, great, distinguished, prominent, famous
ant. unknown
emit (v)
syn. release, eject, discharge, belch, produce, utter, let out
ant. absorb
emotional (adj)
syn. ardent, passionate, temperamental, poignant, touching, hot-blooded, sentimental
ant. cold, calm, unemotional, detached
empathy (n)
syn. sympathy, accord, fellow feeling, rapport, understanding, compatibility, compassion
ant. cruelty, enmity, animosity
emphatic (v)
syn. energetic, explicit, forceful, unconditional, definite, insistent
ant. unemphatic, understated, quiet
empower (v)
syn. authorize, enable, liberate, license
ant. forbid, disqualify
emulation (n)
syn. rivalry, contest, challenge, jealousy, competition, strife
ant. co-operation

en masse (adv)
(French word)
syn. altogether, all at once, as a whole, together
ant. separately
enable (v)
syn. permit, let, allow, empower
ant. prevent
enact (v)
syn. approve, make law, authorize, validate, ratify, present
ant. repeal, abrogate, cancel
enamoured (adj)
syn. fascinated, charmed, smitten, enchanted, captivated, fond
ant. disenchanted, bored
encapsulate (v)
syn. condense, summarize, abridge, precis, exemplify, epitomize, sum up
ant. expand, dilute
enchanting (adj)
syn. charming, lovely, captivating, delightful, fascinating, wonderful, bewitching, attractive
ant. boring, repellent
enclosed (adj)
syn. included, contained, imprisoned, confined, bound
ant. unenclosed, open
encouragement (n)
syn. support, inspiration, coaxing, persuasion, backing, nurture
ant. discouragement, disapproval
encouraging (adj)
syn. hopeful, favourable, promising, welcome, supportive, positive, helpful
ant. discouraging
encroach (v)
syn. trespass, intrude, overstep, invade, intervene, interfere
ant. ignore, avoid, pass over
encumbrance (n)
syn. onus, burden, load, obstacle, embarrassment, obstruction
ant. aid, assistance
encyclopaedic (adj)
syn. vast, complete, thorough, broad, comprehensive, all-inclusive, compendious

ant. narrow, incomplete
end (n)
syn. annihilation, conclusion, limit, aim, wish, boundary, finale, death
ant. beginning, start, opening
endanger (v)
syn. hazard, put in danger, risk, threaten, imperil
ant. safeguard, protect
endearing (adj)
syn. attractive, charming, enchanting, lovely, delightful, appealing
ant. boring, repellent
endeavour (n)
syn. attempt, bid, try, effort, venture, act, undertaking, action
ant. laziness, ease
endorse (v)
syn. back, agree with, sign, support, recommend, ratify, approve, authorize
ant. denounce, oppose, disapprove
endorsement (n)
syn. agreement, advocacy, support, patronage, backing, recommendation, OK, ratification, sanction
ant. denouncement, disapproval
endow (v)
syn. sponsor, finance, fund, furnish, provide, bless, favour, grace
ant. divest, strip, spoil
endurance (n)
syn. tolerance, patience, stoicism, toughness, stamina, resistance, strength
ant. intolerance, bigotry, prejudice
enduring (adj)
syn. durable, continuing, lasting, permanent, immortal, steady, persisting
ant. changeable, unstable, inconstant
enemy (n)
syn. foe, antagonist, rival, adversary, competitor, opponent
ant. friend, ally
energetic (adj)
syn. lively, enthusiastic, active, tough
ant. lethargic, lazy
energy (n)
syn. stamina, strength, vitality, zest, spirit, force, ardour
ant. inertia, weakness, lethargy

enervate (v)
syn. weaken, fatigue, tire, deplete, paralyse, exhaust, devitalize
ant. energize, activate

enfeeble (v)
syn. deplete, exhaust, reduce, weaken, diminish, devitalize, undermine
ant. strengthen, fortify, boost

enforce (v)
syn. force, coerce, carry out, impose, implement, execute
ant. ignore, disregard

engaging (adj)
syn. attractive, pleasant, charming, agreeable, lovable, likeable, appealing, sweet
ant. loathsome, boring, unappealing

engrossed (adj)
syn. interested, immersed, absorbed, captivated, fascinated, enthralled, involved
ant. disinterested, bored, detached, uninterested

enhance (v)
syn. boost, improve, increase
ant. diminish, minimize

enigmatic (adj)
syn. doubtful, mysterious, ambiguous, incomprehensible, strange, obscure, unintelligible, riddling
ant. straightforward, simple, plain

enjoy (v)
syn. appreciate, like, relish, adore, rejoice in
ant. abhor, dislike

enjoyable (adj)
syn. pleasant, entertaining, delightful, agreeable, convivial, fun
ant. unpleasant, disagreeable

enjoyment (n)
syn. pleasure, recreation, happiness, entertainment, joy, liking, advantage, delight
ant. displeasure, dissatisfaction, abhorrence

enlarge (v)
syn. expand, augment, extend, swell, bulge, develop, increase
ant. reduce, shrink, decrease

enlighten (v)
syn. civilize, counsel, educate, tell, instruct
ant. confuse, puzzle

enlightenment (n)
syn. knowledge, insight, awakening, civilization, education, refinement, understanding
ant. confusion, ignorance

enlist (v)
syn. enrol, register, join up, recruit, mobilize, get, win
ant. discharge, demobilize

enmity (n)
syn. animosity, feud, antagonism, malice, bad blood, ill-will, rancour, antipathy, hostility
ant. amity, friendship, empathy

enormous (adj)
syn. immense, huge, mighty, vast, massive, tremendous
ant. tiny, small

enough (adj)
syn. ample, sufficient, adequate
ant. insufficient

enrich (adj)
syn. better, enhance, refine, improve, develop, develop
ant. impoverish

enslavement (n)
syn. slavery, oppression, bondage, enthralment, servitude, repression, captivity, duress
ant. emancipation, freedom, deliverance

entangle (v)
syn. confuse, complicate, implicate, bewilder, jumble, puzzle, ravel
ant. disentangle, extricate, clear

enterprise (n)
syn. venture, undertaking, activity, business, scheme, project, imagination, initiative, creativity, operation, zeal, adventure
ant. apathy, inertia, laziness, lethargy

enterprising (adj)
syn. venturesome, active, ambitious, dashing, imaginative, resourceful, creative, entrepreneurial, zealous, adventurous
ant. unenterprising, lethargic, unadventurous

entertain (v)
syn. cheer, amuse, charm, please, receive, feed, treat, consider, think of
ant. bore, reject
enthralling (adj)
syn. delightful, fascinating, enchanting, exciting
ant. boring
enthusiasm (n)
syn. zeal, passion, keenness, interest, mania, fervour, gusto, devotion, zest
ant. apathy, indifference, lethargy
enthusiast (n)
syn. admirer, fan, lover, follower, supporter, buff
ant. detractor, knocker
enthusiastic (adj)
syn. ardent, keen, passionate, avid, devoted, zealous, committed, fanatical
ant. apathetic, reluctant, unenthusiastic
entice (v)
syn. attract, coax, tempt, woo, beguile, appeal, seduce, allure, sweet-talk, induce
ant. scare, repulse, disgust
envious (adj)
syn. grudging, jealous, resentful, desirous, green-eyed, malicious, spiteful
ant. generous, kind, uninterested, tolerant
envy (n)
syn. grudge, jealousy, resentment, spite, ill-will, malice, hatred
ant. generosity, kindness, tolerance
ephemeral (adj)
syn. short-lived, brief, transitory, temporary, short-term, momentary, transient
ant. permanent, perpetual, enduring
epilogue (n)
syn. conclusion, afterword, postscript, coda, ending
ant. prologue, preface
epitome (n)
syn. model, summary, abstract, essence, précis, compendium, synopsis
ant. amplification, expansion
equanimity (n)
syn. calm, serenity, composure, cool
ant. anxiety

equilibrium (n)
syn. balance, harmony, symmetry, poise, stability, cool
ant. imbalance
equitable (adj)
syn. disinterested, honest, reasonable, uprightness, ethical, proportionate, impartial, rightful, fair, unbiased
ant. inequitable, unfair
equity (n)
syn. honesty, fair, rectitude, impartiality, justice, integrity, uprightness
ant. inequity, injustice
equivalent (adj)
syn. similar, comparable, analogous, corresponding, parallel, equal, correlative
ant. dissimilar, unlike
equivocal (adj)
syn. vague, unclear, ambiguous, inexact, indefinite, hazy, doubtful, misleading
ant. unequivocal, definite, clear
equivocation (n)
syn. ambiguity, waffle, doubtfulness, confusion, evasion, shuffling
ant. directness, explicitness
eradicate (v)
syn. remove, destroy, eliminate, annihilate, wipe out, suppress, obliterate
ant. establish, instil, generate, restore
erect (v)
syn. create, build, construct, raise, put up, fabricate, assemble
ant. demolish, destroy, dismantle
erosion (n)
syn. deterioration, abrasion, destruction, weathering, disintegration
ant. creation, preservation
erotic (adj)
syn. pornographic, amorous, carnal, voluptuous, lustful, seductive, sensual, blue
ant. ascetic, austere, self-denying
erratic (adj)
syn. inconsistent, varying, changeable, unstable, unreliable
ant. consistent

erroneous (adj)
syn. false, mistaken, incorrect, illogical, fallacious, wrong
ant. correct
erudite (adj)
syn. educated, learned, academic, literate, highbrow, cultured
ant. unlettered, illiterate
escalate (v)
syn. shoot up, increase, develop, intensify, expand, grow
ant. plunge, subside
escape (v)
syn. run away, abscond, avoid, decamp, break free, skip
ant. return, stay, pursue, stand
eschew (v)
syn. avoid, abandon, abjure, give up, renounce
ant. embrace
esoteric (adj)
syn. hidden, mystic, abstruse, obscure, confidential, secret
ant. exoteric, popular, familiar
espouse (v)
syn. advocate, back, defend, support, betroth, embrace, patronize
ant. abandon, reject, repudiate, deny
essential (adj)
syn. vital, all-important, crucial, indispensable, fundamental, basic, characteristic
ant. inessential, unimportant, incidental
established (adj)
syn. standard, accepted, common, traditional, conventional, official, respected, settled
ant. unreliable, impermanent
esteem (n)
syn. admiration, honour, good opinion, respect, veneration, regard, reverence, love
ant. abomination, hate, antipathy, disgrace, contempt
estimable (adj)
syn. admirable, esteemed, praiseworthy, respectable, honourable, respected
ant. unworthy, insignificant, despicable
estrangement (n)
syn. alienation, divorce, break-up, separation, breach, parting, split

ant. reconciliation, appeasement

eternal (adj)

syn. endless, immortal, everlasting, permanent, perpetual, continuous, non-stop, undying, never-ending

ant. temporary, changeable, ephemeral, mortal

eternity (n)

syn. endlessness, ever, heaven, all time, perpetuity, forever, infinity, immortality

ant. impermanence, ephemerality, transience

ethical (adj)

syn. principled, fair, moral, honourable, virtuous, honest, decent, upright

ant. unethical, nefarious, immoral

eulogy (n)

syn. praise, glorification, commendation, compliment, accolade, tribute, laud, exaltation

ant. obloquy, condemnation, vilification, slander

euphony (n)

syn. melody, melodiousness, harmony, mellifluousness, sweetness

ant. cacophony, din

euphoria (n)

syn. joy, elation, delight, excitement, bliss, exhilaration, jubilation

ant. despondency, depression, misery

evade (v)

syn. avoid, leave behind, elude, bypass, shun, escape (from), flee

ant. face, confront

evanescent (adj)

syn. temporary, brief, ephemeral, transient, short-lived, vanishing, momentary

ant. permanent

evasive (adj)

syn. ambiguous, unclear, equivocal, elusive, misleading, secretive, cunning, tricky

ant. frank, direct, candid, straightforward

even-tempered (adj)

syn. calm, cool, peaceable, composed, peaceful, unexcitable, placid, cool-headed

ant. excitable

eventful (adj)
syn. busy, active, lively, hectic, remarkable, interesting, action-packed, exciting
ant. uneventful, dull, ordinary
everlasting (adj)
syn. never-ending, infinite, eternal, undying, endless
ant. transient, occasional
evil (adj)
syn. bad, immoral, vile, wicked, demonic, harmful, nasty, unpleasant
ant. good, virtuous, noble
evince (v)
syn. declare, exhibit, attest, display, confess, indicate, reveal, manifest
ant. suppress, conceal
evoke (v)
syn. invoke, arouse, activate, raise, stimulate, excite, conjure
ant. suppress, quell
exacerbate (v)
syn. increase, magnify, aggravate, worsen, inflame, provoke, excite, vex
ant. soothe, reduce
exacting (adj)
syn. laborious, arduous, hard, demanding, challenging, tough, severe, difficult, painstaking
ant. easy, easy-going, tolerant
exaggeration (n)
syn. hyperbole, excess, amplification, parody, overstatement, overestimation, burlesque
ant. understatement
exalt (v)
syn. applaud, elevate, honour, praise, glorify, inspire, raise, promote
ant. debase, demean, degrade
exasperate (v)
syn. aggravate, annoy, infuriate, irk, provoke, anger, vex
ant. calm, soothe, appease
excel (v)
syn. outstrip, shine, beat, top, better, outperform, be excellent
ant. trail, drag
excellence (n)
syn. greatness, distinction, calibre, brilliance, eminence, virtue

ant. inferiority, fault, blemish, mediocrity

excellent (adj)

syn. superb, fantastic, marvellous, exceptional, A1, exemplary, remarkable, wonderful

ant. inferior, average, mediocre, poor

exceptional (adj)

syn. abnormal, unexpected, unusual, special, remarkable, outstanding, superior, strange

ant. unexceptional, normal, average, mediocre

excess (n)

syn. surplus, disproportionate, exorbitant, over-abundance, extravagance, overindulgence

ant. dearth, lack, restraint, deficiency

excessive (adj)

syn. disproportionate, immoderate, uncontrolled, extravagant, unreasonable, exorbitant

ant. insufficient, meagre, deficient, moderate

excitable (adj)

syn. emotional, sensitive, temperamental, hot-headed, passionate

ant. calm, placid

excited (adj)

syn. elated, enthusiastic, frenzied, thrilled, frantic, impassioned

ant. apathetic, bored

excitement (n)

syn. elation, enthusiasm, pleasure, thrill, joy, delight, buzz, passion, action, commotion

ant. apathy, calm, calmness

exciting (adj)

syn. enthralling, thrilling, intoxicating, compelling, inspiring

ant. unexciting, boring

exclusion (n)

syn. ban, boycott, elimination, eviction, omission, proscription, removal, refusal

ant. inclusion, allowance, admittance

excruciating (adj)

syn. agonising, painful, bitter, savage, unbearable, torturing, harrowing, atrocious

ant. painless, heartening, comfortable, soothing

exculpate (v)
syn. absolve, excuse, forgive, exonerate, vindicate, acquit, pardon, condone
ant. inculpate, charge, condemn, blame
excusable (adj)
syn. forgivable, ignorable, defensible, explicable, slight
ant. blameworthy
excuse (v)
syn. forgive, pardon, disregard, tolerate, absolve, let off
ant. punish, condemn
execrable (adj)
syn. deplorable, hateful, loathsome, shocking, abhorrent, appalling, horrible, repulsive
ant. admirable, delightful
execrate (v)
syn. condemn, damn, abhor, hate, loathe, deplore, vilify, curse, denounce
ant. commend, praise, eulogize, admire
exemplary (adj)
syn. model, perfect, impeccable, ideal, excellent, worthy, commendable
ant. deplorable, imperfect, unworthy
exemplify (v)
syn. exhibit, display, demonstrate, show, illustrate, depict, represent, manifest
ant. hide, cover
exemption (n)
syn. privilege, discharge, exclusion, freedom, exoneration, exception
ant. liability, accountability, burden
exertion (n)
syn. effort, action, exercise, labour, pains, struggle, work, toil
ant. inertia, rest, idleness, relaxation
exhalation (n)
syn. breath, air, emission, smoke respiration, discharge
ant. inhalation
exhausted (adj)
syn. dissipated, fatigued, weak, consumed, enervated, prostrated, spent, weary
ant. vigorous, active, fresh
exhaustion (n)
syn. tiredness, fatigue, prostration, feebleness, weariness

ant. freshness
exhilarate (v)
syn. cheer, elate, excite, delight, hearten, invigorate, animate, thrill
ant. depress, discourage, bore
exhilarating (adj)
syn. cheering, exciting, thrilling, mind-blowing, breath-taking, electrifying
ant. depressing, discouraging, boring
exhort (v)
syn. encourage, urge, press, advise, counsel, persuade
ant. discourage, block
exodus (n)
syn. migration, flight, long march, departure, evacuation, exit
ant. influx, immigration
exonerate (v)
syn. acquit, discharge, clear, absolve, vindicate, excuse
ant. convict, charge
exorbitant (adj)
syn. excessive, unreasonable, extortionate, extreme, immodest, enormous.
ant. cheap, fair, reasonable
exotic (adj)
syn. eye-catching, striking, extravagant, colourful, foreign, distant, different
ant. ordinary, native, indigenous
expansion (n)
syn. stretching, enlargement, development, growth, spread, extension, increase
ant. contraction, decrease
expansive (adj)
syn. expanding, broad, comprehensive, extensive, friendly, genial, garrulous, open, sociable, outgoing, talkative
ant. cold, reserved, reticent, withdrawn
expedite (v)
syn. quicken, hurry, accelerate, speed, advance, hasten, promote
ant. delay
expel (v)
syn. banish, dismiss, ban, belch, evict, deport, drive out, chuck out
ant. admit

expenditure (n)
syn. expense, payment, consumption, spending
ant. savings, profit

expensive (adj)
syn. costly, exorbitant, dear, overpriced, high-priced
ant. inexpensive, cheap

experience (n)
syn. knowledge, familiarity, skill, acquaintance, happening, incident, episode
ant. inexperience

expert (n)
syn. master, specialist, connoisseur, professional, ace
ant. amateur, novice, layman

expertise (n)
syn. competence, aptitude, prowess, skill, knowledge, capability, ability, command
ant. inexpertise, incompetence

expiry (n)
syn. end, close, demise, death, termination, cease
ant. beginning, continuation

explanatory (adj)
syn. demonstrative, illustrative, descriptive, interpretive
ant. confusing, baffling

explicit (adj)
syn. clear, accurate, plain, precise, outspoken, straightforward, candid, unreserved, absolute
ant. inexplicit, vague, unclear, ambiguous

exploit (v)
syn. abuse, utilize, misuse, treat unfairly, ill-treat, bleed, fleece
ant. respect, honour

exponent (n)
syn. defender, supporter, advocate, promoter, backer, player, proponent, spokesperson
ant. opponent, antagonist, enemy

expose (v)
syn. disclose, exhibit, reveal, uncover, manifest, show, unveil, bring to light, unfold
ant. cover, protect, shield, guard

expound (v)
syn. explain, describe, interpret, explicate, elucidate, unfold, illustrate
ant. confuse, obscure, baffle

expulsion (n)
syn. eviction, removal, dismissal, elimination, banishment
ant. admission, welcome

expunge (v)
syn. annihilate, delete, abolish, destroy, remove, eradicate, wipeout, annual, erase, exterminate
ant. retain, save, establish, preserve

exquisite (adj)
syn. lovely, fine, beautiful, fragile, attractive, comely, delicious, excellent, matchless, refined, sensitive, impeccable, superb
ant. poor, flawed, imperfect, faulty, ugly

extemporary (adj)
syn. unprepared, extempore, spontaneous, improvized, unplanned, unrehearsed
ant. planned

extensive (adj)
syn. comprehensive, broad, thorough, great, large, substantial, vast, wide
ant. narrow, limited, restricted, small

extenuate (v)
syn. diminish, lessen, decrease, reduce, modify, excuse, weaken, moderate
ant. enhance, increase, exaggerate

exterior (n)
syn. external, outside, outward, façade, surface
ant. interior, inherent

exterminate (v)
syn. abolish, eradicate, destroy, annihilate, wipeout, eliminate, finish off
ant. establish, save, retain, preserve

external (adj)
syn. outward, outer, exterior, outside, exotic, foreign
ant. internal, inherent

extinct (adj)
syn. dead, vanished, defunct, abolished, lost, destroyed, wiped out, gone
ant. living, active, dormant, existing

extinction (n)
syn. destruction, abolition, extermination, annihilation, disappearance, vanishing
ant. retention, preservation, survival

extirpate (v)
syn. destroy, abolish, eliminate, annihilate, eradicate, uproot, remove, wipe out
ant. retain, preserve, save, establish

extol (v)
syn. applaud, praise, eulogize, laud, commend, glorify, exalt
ant. decry, criticize, blame

extortionate (adj)
syn. outrageous, excessive, blood-sucking, exorbitant, unreasonable, harsh, oppressive, immoderate, daylight robbery
ant. reasonable, fair, moderate

extract (v)
syn. derive, draw out, uproot, obtain, elicit, cite, take out, release, extort
ant. insert

extraordinary (adj)
syn. exceptional, remarkable, sensational, amazing, enormous, tremendous, very great, noteworthy, outstanding
ant. ordinary, unremarkable, commonplace

extravagance (n)
syn. excess, lavishness, absurdity, unthrift, profusion, immoderation, waste, wastage, dissipation, recklessness
ant. thrift, moderation, frugality, economy

extremely (adv)
syn. immensely, very, supremely, highly
ant. slightly

extremist (n)
syn. militant, fanatic, radical
ant. moderate

extricate (v)
syn. liberate, free, clear, remove, relieve, withdraw, deliver, rescue, untie
ant. involve, block, obstruct, fetter

exuberant (adj)
syn. cheerful, vivacious, animated, ebullient, high-spirited, lively, full of life, energetic, enthusiastic, excited, elated, vigorous

ant. apathetic, lifeless, repressed, lethargic

exult (v)

syn. delight, rejoice, celebrate, boast, triumph, relish, jubilate

ant. lament, bemoan, mourn, dismay, depress

exultant (adj)

syn. delighted, joyful, rejoicing, elated, triumphant, jubilant, revelling, gleeful

ant. miserable, mournful, depressed, unhappy

exultation (n)

syn. delight, glee, joy, jubilation, boasting, elation, triumph, joyfulness, celebration, rejoicing

ant. depression, mourning, unhappiness

extrovert (adj)

syn. sociable, lively, unreserved, friendly, outgoing, ebullient

ant. introvert

eye-catching (adj)

syn. impressive, showy, stunning, attractive, beautiful

ant. unattractive, plain

Ff

fabulous (adj)
syn. exceptional, fantastic, incredible, superb, wonderful
ant. moderate, small

facetious (adj)
syn. comical, joking, flippant, frivolous, funny, witty, humorous
ant. serious, sober, sombre

facilitate (v)
syn. promote, make, easier, enable, speed up, assist, advance
ant. impede, hinder

fact (n)
syn. truth, reality, aspect, detail, point, actuality
ant. fiction, lie

factitious (adj)
syn. counterfeit, fabricated, false, fake, insincere, unreal, artificial
ant. genuine, natural, authentic

factual (adj)
syn. genuine, truthful, exact, authentic, objective, real
ant. fictitious, false

fade (v)
syn. discolour, dim, grow faint, decline
ant. brighten

fagged (adj)
syn. exhausted, weary, beat, worn out, jaded, fatigued
ant. refreshed

failing (n)
syn. defect, fault, imperfection, deficiency, weakness, blemish, decay, decline
ant. strength, advantage

failure (n)
syn. defeat, fiasco, disaster, debacle, underachiever, oversight, breakdown, bankruptcy, collapse
ant. success, accomplishment

faint-hearted (adj)
syn. timid, faint-heart, hen-hearted, spiritless, lily-livered, weak

ant. courageous, brave

fair (adj)

syn. honest, unprejudiced, impartial, bright, sunny, light, pale, white, reasonable, tolerable, decent

ant. biased, inclement, harsh, dark, poor

faith (n)

syn. trust, conviction, belief, reliance, doctrine, religion, ideology, loyalty, fidelity, dogma

ant. mistrust, treachery, unfaithfulness

faithful (adj)

syn. trusty, loyal, realistic, staunch, trustworthy, true

ant. unfaithful, disloyal, treacherous

fake (adj)

syn. bogus, counterfeit, pirated, false, sham, fraudulent, forged, phoney, replica, artificial, dummy, invented, feigned

ant. genuine, bona fide, original, authentic

fallacious (adj)

syn. deceptive, erroneous, fictitious, false, incorrect, illusory, illogical, untrue, misleading

ant. correct, true, veritable, sound, valid

fallacy (n)

syn. deceit, delusion, deception, illusion, error, flaw, misconception, mistake, untruth

ant. truth, understanding, comprehension, verity

false (adj)

syn. incorrect, wrong, untrue, fictitious, fabricated, faithless, disloyal, fake, synthetic, dummy

ant. correct, faithful, genuine, reliable, true

fame (n)

syn. esteem, celebrity, stardom, popularity, renown, glory, name

ant. obscurity, oblivion

familiar (adj)

syn. routine, well known, acquainted, well informed, knowledgeable, bold, forward

ant. unfamiliar, formal, reserved, ignorant

famous (adj)

syn. popular, well known, noted, renowned, celebrated, great

ant. unknown

fanatic (n)
syn. radical, extremist, bigot, militant, maniac
ant. moderate

fanaticism (n)
syn. bigotry, immoderacy, devotion, immoderation, obsessiveness, infatuation, overenthusiasm, madness
ant. moderation, sobriety, composure, judiciousness

fancy (n)
syn. craze, caprice, whim, fascination, passion, imagination, fantasy, dreaming, irrationality
ant. fact, reality, perception

fantastic (adj)
syn. irrational, fanciful, extraordinary, unthinkable, unlikely, crazy, surreal, strange, wonderful, superb, fabulous, brilliant
ant. realistic, ordinary, plain, common, poor

fantasy (n)
syn. vision, imagination, daydreaming, wish, dream, delusion, illusion, fancy, conceiving.
ant. realism, reality, actuality

farce (n)
syn. pretence, mockery, comedy, joke, parody, satire
ant. tragedy

farcical (adj)
syn. absurd, comic, funny, silly, ridiculous, laughable
ant. sensible, tragic

far-fetched (adj)
syn. doubtful, crazy, fantastic, implausible, incredible, unconvincing, unrealistic, unlikely
ant. plausible, believable, conceivable, reasonable

far-sighted (adj)
syn. judicious, canny, wise, prudent, acute, shrewd
ant. unwise, imprudent

fascinating (adj)
syn. attractive, interesting, enchanting, charming
ant. boring

fascination (n)
syn. passion, interest, obsession, attraction, captivation, enchantment
ant, boredom, repulsion

fascism (n)
syn. dictatorship, absolutism, autocracy, totalitarianism, authoritarianism, despotism, monarchism, oppression
ant. democracy, liberalism, egalitarianism, tolerance

fastidious (adj)
syn. critical, particular, choosy, meticulous, precise, difficult, demanding
ant. undemanding, uncritical, cursory

fat (adj)
syn. stout, pot-bellied, obese, chubby, fatty, thick
ant. thin, slim, lean

fatal (adj)
syn. deadly, untreatable, disastrous, dire, harmful, fateful
ant. harmless, beneficial

fatigue (n)
syn. tiredness, lethargy, exhaustion, weariness, failure
ant. energy, vigour, freshness, liveliness

fault (n)
syn. defect, blemish, weakness, error, flaw, blunder
ant. strength, merit, advantage

faulty (adj)
syn. defective, malfunctioning, unsound, flawed, wrong, erroneous
ant. working, faultless, sound, excellent

favour (n)
syn. kindness, approval, benevolence, backing, good deed, regard
ant. disfavour, disapproval, disservice

favourable (adj)
syn. kind, approving, good, positive, advantageous, auspicious, encouraging, convenient, promising
ant. unfavourable, critical, disapproving, censorious

favourite (adj)
syn. best-loved, favoured, chosen, dearest, pet, preferred, beloved
ant. unfavourite, hated, despised, rejected

fawning (adj)
syn. bootlicking, slavish, cringing, sycophantic, servile, abject, flattering, toadying
ant. cold, proud, insolent, domineering

fear (n)
syn. phobia, horror, antipathy, terror, panic, alarm, apprehension,

hang-up, anxiety, awe
ant. fearlessness, courage, fortitude, gallantry, valour
fearless (adj)
syn. bold, brave, heroic, confident, daring, gallant, unapprehensive, valorous
ant. fearful, afraid, timid, cowardly
fearsome (adj)
syn. awesome, alarming, frightening, inspiring, horrific, terrible, dismaying
ant. delightful
feasible (adj)
syn. realistic, workable, possible, practicable, reasonable
ant. impracticable, impossible
feckless (adj)
syn. hopeless, aimless, irresponsible, useless, incompetent, worthless, unpurposed, unreliable
ant. efficient, sensible, meticulous, attentive, trustworthy
fecundity (n)
syn. productivity, productiveness, prodigality, profusion, lavishness
ant. infecundity, infertility, barrenness
federation (n)
syn. coalition, alliance, syndicate, league, combination, amalgamation, association, confederation, union, consortium
ant. estrangement, hostility, divorce, enmity
feeble (adj)
syn. delicate, weak, poor, fearful, dim, faint, frail, ineffective, thin
ant. strong, robust, worthy
feeble-minded (adj)
(offensive, old use)
syn. weak-minded, dull, irresolute, idiotic, half-witted, stupid
ant. strong-minded, bright, intelligent
feigned (adj)
syn. fake, counterfeit, assumed, artificial, insincere, sham, pseudo, spurious, fabricated
ant. genuine, sincere, heartfelt
felicitous (adj)
syn. suitable, apt, fitting, delightful, happy, well chosen, appropriate, well-timed
ant. inappropriate

feminine (adj)
syn. ladylike, womanish, delicate, tender, unmanly, womanly
ant. masculine

feminity (n)
syn. gentleness, womanhood, unmanliness, softness
ant. masculinity

ferment (n)
syn. commotion, frenzy, unrest, disruption, uproar, furore, turbulence, heat, turmoil, chaos, anarchy
ant. calm, peace, tranquillity

ferocious (adj)
syn. dangerous, wild, violent, bloody, savage, fierce, pitiless, harsh
ant. gentle, mild

fertile (adj)
syn. rich, productive, creative, prolific, profuse
ant. barren, arid

fertility (n)
syn. productiveness, fruitfulness, abundance, potency, richness, virility
ant. infertility, barrenness, aridity, sterility

fervent (adj)
syn. heartfelt, passionate, enthusiastic, keen, committed
ant. apathetic

fervor (n)
syn. passion, emotion, excitement, enthusiasm, spirit, zeal
ant. apathy

festive (adj)
syn. happy, cheerful, jolly, jovial, celebratory, merry, gay, joyful
ant. gloomy, sober, sombre, mournful

fetching (adj)
syn. charming, attractive, alluring, enchanting, captivating, pretty, fascinating, beguiling
ant. repellent, repulsive

feud (n)
syn. quarrel, row, fight, clash, dispute, discord, vendetta, antagonism, enmity
ant. peace, agreement

feverish (adj)
syn. excited, fevered, anxious, burning, hot, frantic, obsessive, impatient,

frenzied, nervous, fanatical
ant. calm, cool, composed
fiasco (n)
syn. disaster, failure, force, flop, washout, cock-up
ant. success
fib (n)
(informal)
syn. fiction, story, falsehood, concoction, white lie, untruth, tale, lie, invention
ant. truth, reality
fickle (adj)
syn. changeable, unsteady, capricious, giddy, unreliable, inconstant
ant. constant
fiction (n)
syn. story, creative writing, novels, literature, fabrication, untruth, fantasy, nonsense, falsehood
ant. fact, truth
fictional (adj)
syn. mythical, unreal, fabulous, legendary, invented, imaginary
ant. real, true, authentic, genuine
fictitious (adj)
syn. bogus, assumed, false, invented, phoney
ant. true, genuine
fidelity (n)
syn. loyalty, devotion, faithfulness, accuracy, correctness, authenticity
ant. infidelity, disloyalty, treachery
fidget (n)
syn. discomposure, anxiety, nervousness, willies, uneasiness, restlessness, agitation, jitters
ant. calmness, coolness
fiendish (adj)
syn. devilish, atrocious, cruel, diabolic, malign, malicious, inhuman, vicious, savage, impious, baleful, nefarious
ant. kind, compassionate, benign, gentle, sympathetic
fierce (adj)
syn. aggressive, ferocious, strong, intense, passionate, powerful
ant. gentle, mild

fiery (adj)
syn. excitable, impatient, impulsive, passionate, hot-headed, burning, violent, irritable, inflamed, ardent, feverish, fervent
ant. cold, impassive, spiritless, icy, apathetic, dull

figment (n)
syn. deception, illusion, fancy, fiction, delusion, concoction, fabrication, creation
ant. reality, fact, truth

figurative (adj)
syn. symbolic, non-literal, representative
ant. literal

filial (adj)
syn. devoted, fond, loyal, loving, respectful
ant. unfilial, disloyal

filthy (adj)
syn. dirty, foul, vulgar, obscene, bad, cranky
ant. clean, pleasant

finale (n)
syn. conclusion, end, climax, finish, close
ant. beginning, opening

finicky (adj)
syn. meticulous, particular, scrupulous, critical, choosy, difficult, tricky
ant. easy, easy-going

finite (adj)
syn. limited, fixed, restricted, calculable, bounded
ant. infinite, boundless, unlimited

firm (adj)
syn. hard, stiff, strong, decided, close, loving, definite
ant. soft, unstable

fishy (adj)
(informal)
syn. funny, doubtful, odd, suspicious, unlikely
ant. honest, legitimate

fitful (adj)
syn. disturbed, fluctuating, broken, haphazard, occasional, sporadic, variable, unstable
ant. regular, constant, steady, systematic

flabbergasted (adj)
(*informal*)
syn. astonished, amazed, confounded, nonplussed, stunned, speechless, stupefied
ant. indifferent, expected

flabbiness (n)
(*informal*)
syn. fat, flesh, bloatedness, heaviness, plumpness, laxness, overweight, fleshiness
ant. leanness, firmness, strength

flag (v)
syn. decline, diminish, fade, decrease, tire, weaken, droop
ant. revive

flagging (adj)
syn. declining, diminishing, fading, decreasing, subsiding, tiring, weakening, waning, sinking, deteriorating
ant. reviving, returning

flagrant (adj)
syn. atrocious, blatant, brazen, conspicuous, flaunting, heinous, infamous, notorious, shameless, scandalous, bold
ant. covert, secret, hidden, unimportant

flair (n)
syn. talent, gift, aptitude, skill, ability, style, class
ant. ineptitude

flak (n)
(*informal*)
syn. criticism, censure, condemnation, disparagement, opposition, disapproval, fault-finding, denunciation
ant. praise, commendation, compliment

flamboyant (adj)
syn. lively, vibrant, colourful, showy, dazzling, flashy
ant. plain, restrained

flattery (n)
syn. compliments, praise, honeyed words, fawning, sweet talk, buttering up, soft-soap
ant. criticism, abuse

flaw (n)
syn. fault, defect, imperfection, bug, glitch

ant. strength
flee (v)
syn. take off, run away, take to your heels, abscond, escape, beat it, scarper
ant. stand, stay
fleece (v)
syn. overcharge, defraud, rob, cheat, con, squeeze, swindle, plunder
ant. give, provide
fleeting (adj)
syn. short-lived, quick, brief, cursory, transitory
ant. lasting
fleshly (adj)
syn. physical, bodily, lustful, earthly, carnal, material, erotic, worldly
ant. spiritual, divine, religious
fleshy (adj)
syn. beefy, plump, chubby, hefty, flabby, obese, stout
ant. thin, lean, emaciated
flexibility (n)
syn. stretchiness, give, adjustability, freedom, tolerance
ant. rigidity
flippant (adj)
syn. frivolous, disrespectful, cheeky, superficial, impudent, brash, impertinent, silly
ant. serious, earnest
float (v)
syn. buoyant, hang, sail, stay on the surface, launch, introduce
ant. sink
flop (n)
syn. fiasco, failure, catastrophe, disaster, debacle, washout
ant. success
florid (adj)
syn. bombastic, flamboyant, showy, embellished, over-elaborate, fussy, high-coloured, ornate
ant. pale, plain, unadorned
flourish (v)
syn. grow, prosper, bloom, make progress, expand, shake, display
ant. wither, decline
flout (v)
syn. break, disobey, defy, breach, ignore, disregard

ant. observe, respect
fluctuating (adj)
syn. fickle, capricious, unstable, unsteady, irresolute, oscillatory, variable, rising and falling
ant. stable, constant, invariable, fixed
fluency (n)
syn. eloquence, articulateness, command, smoothness, slickness
ant. incoherence, inarticulacy
fluent (adj)
syn. communicative, natural, eloquent, articulate, silver-tongued, smooth, easy
ant. stilted, inarticulate, tongue-tied
flummoxed (adj)
(informal)
syn. confused, puzzled, confounded, bewildered, baffled, perplexed, at sea, nonplussed
ant. clear, lucid, enlightened
flurry (n)
syn. commotion, agitation, excitement, bustle, furore, ferment, flaw, fuss, tumult, hurry, turbulence
ant. calm, tranquillity
foe (n)
(old-fashioned, formal)
syn. enemy, adversary, opponent, rival
ant. friend
foggy (adj)
syn. murky, misty, dim, vague
ant. clear
foible (n)
syn. fault, oddity, eccentricity, idiosyncrasy, quirk, strangeness, defect, peculiarity, failing, imperfection
ant. normality, prudence, sanity, rationality
following (n)
syn. supporters, fans, admirers, backers, devotees, public
ant. opposition
following (adj)
syn. successive, next, ensuing, coming
ant. preceding

folly (n)
syn. stupidity, foolishness, lunacy, madness, nonsense, silliness, imprudence
ant. sense, prudence, wisdom

fond (adj)
syn. affectionate, caring, credulous, loving, devoted, warm, foolish, optimistic
ant. cold, indifferent, uncaring, hostile

fondness (n)
syn. affection, love, liking, fancy, attachment, penchant, partiality, susceptibility
ant. aversion, hate, disgust

fool (n)
syn. halfwit, idiot, ass, donkey, clod, dork, ignoramus
ant. genius, scholar

foolhardy (adj)
syn. incautious, hot-headed, ill-advised, ill-considered, adventurous, reckless, irresponsible, unheeding, daredevil, bold
ant. cautious, careful, prudent, calculating, wary

foolish (adj)
syn. idiotic, mindless, stupid, unwise, silly, imprudent
ant. sensible, wise

foolproof (adj)
syn. reliable, infallible, trustworthy, sure, guaranteed, tried and tested, perfect, flawless
ant. unreliable, untrustworthy, doubtful

forbearance (n)
syn. tolerance, endurance, avoidance, abstinence, patience, clemency, restraint, lenience
ant. intolerance, harshness, inflexibility, rigidity, vindictiveness

forbearing (adj)
syn. tolerant, restrained, patient, lenient, forgiving, merciful, clement, self-controlled
ant. intolerant, merciless, inflexible, harsh, grim

forbid (v)
syn. veto, prohibit, bar, proscribe, rule out
ant. permit, allow

forced (adj)
syn. mandatory, enforced, unnatural, synthetic, compulsory, unspontaneous, false

ant. voluntary, spontaneous, natural
foreigner (n)
syn. stranger, settler, alien, outsider, immigrant
ant. native, national
foremost (adj)
syn. first, leading, main, prime, supreme, highest, central, eminent, uppermost, earliest, number one
ant. last, final, secondary, minor
foresight (n)
syn. vision, planning, anticipation, care, forehandedness, forethought, prudence
ant. hindsight, improvidence
forethought (n)
syn. foresight, anticipation, providence, precaution, prudence, sense
ant. improvidence, rashness
foretold (adj)
syn. predicted, forecast, prophesied
ant. unforeseen
foreword (n)
syn. introduction, preface, prologue, preamble
ant. epilogue, postscript
forged (adj)
syn. false, fake, copied, pirate, bogus, dud, sham
ant. genuine
forgery (n)
syn. fraudulence, fraud, counterfeit, coining, imitation, fake, phoney
ant. original
forgive (v)
syn. excuse, pardon, overlook, tolerate, absolve, let off
ant. punish, blame, resent
forlorn (adj)
syn. dejected, sorrowful, unhappy, depressed, hopeless, vain, miserable
ant. happy, hopeful
formality (n)
syn. convection, politeness, etiquette, ritual, protocol, custom, decorum, red tape, aloofness
ant. informality

formerly (adv)
syn. before, previously, once, earlier, in the past
ant. currently, presently

formidable (adj)
syn. dangerous, dreadful, alarming, dismaying, appalling, fearful, awesome, mighty, onerous, terrific, shocking, challenging, accomplished, superb
ant. easy, genial, comforting

forsake (v)
syn. abandon, discard, desert, disown, renounce, quit, reject, give up, abdicate, jettison, vacate
ant. resume, return to

forte (n)
syn. specialty, strong suit, strength, talent, thing, strong point
ant. foible, inadequacy

forthright (adj)
syn. honest, frank, open, outspoken, candid, blunt
ant. tactful, evasive

fortitude (n)
syn. endurance, backbone, bravery, courage, guts, resolution, strength, perseverance
ant. cowardice, weakness

fortuitous (adj)
syn. coincidental, accidental, chance, fortunate, lucky, unexpected, incidental, unplanned, unintentional, unforeseen
ant. intentional, schemed, deliberate

fortunate (adj)
syn. blessed, lucky, auspicious, fortuitous, timely, helpful, favourable
ant. unfortunate, unlucky, disastrous

foster (v)
syn. help, promote, encourage, bring up, raise, support
ant. neglect, discourage

foul (adj)
syn. offensive, disgusting, polluted, dirty, vulgar, blue, unclean, stinking
ant. pleasant, pure, worthy

foxy (adj)
syn. artful, sharp, tricky, wily, cunning, crafty
ant. artless, open

fractious (adj)
syn. quarrelsome, bad-tempered, peevish, irritable, petulant, crabbed, awkward, unruly, fretful, refractory, cranky
ant. placid, complaisant, peaceable
fragile (adj)
syn. delicate, breakable, shaky, weak, unwell
ant. sturdy, robust
fragility (n)
syn. delicacy, weakness, frailty, feebleness
ant. durability, strength, robustness
fragrance (n)
syn. aroma, odour, scent, perfume, smell, balm, incense
ant. stench, stink
frail (adj)
syn. feeble, fragile, delicate, tender, breakable, brittle, weak, puny, vulnerable, unsound
ant. strong, firm, robust, tough
frankly (adv)
syn. candidly, bluntly, honestly, directly
ant. evasively, insincerely
frantic (adj)
syn. desperate, mad, panicky, hectic
ant. calm
fraternize (v)
syn. associate, consort, mingle, affiliate, cooperate, socialize, unite, mix
ant. ignore, shun
fraudulent (adj)
syn. cheating, dishonest, crooked, double-dealing, deceitful, false
ant. honest, genuine
fraught (adj)
syn. anxious, distressed, tense, agitated, worrisome, troublesome, distracted
ant. calm, untroublesome
fray (n)
syn. brawl, combat, fight, affray, battle, quarrel, rumpus, ruckus, melee
ant. calm, order
freedom (n)
syn. release, liberty, independence, exemption, license, liberty, privilege

ant. captivity, obligation, restriction, confinement

frenetic (adj)

syn. excited, distraught, frantic, insane, mad, frenzied, unbalanced, hyperactive, obsessive, fanatical

ant. placid, calm

frenzy (n)

syn. passion, hysteria, panic, fever, mania, fury, madness, agitation

ant. calm, composure, placidness

frequently (adv)

syn. regularly, often, again and again, continually

ant. infrequently, seldom

fresh (adj)

syn. novel, modern, new, energetic, strong

ant. stale, old

fretful (adj)

syn. irritable, complaining, peevish, short-tempered, petulant, uneasy, fractious, critical

ant. calm, patient, forbearing, submissive

friendly (adj)

syn. sociable, amiable, cordial, warm, amicable, genial, outgoing, close

ant. unfriendly, cold, hostile, unsociable

friendship (n)

syn. relationship, bond, comradeship, unity, intimacy, rapport, love, amity, amicability, harmony

ant. animosity, antagonism, hostility, enmity, antipathy

fright (n)

syn. fear, apprehension, panic, scare, terror, alarm, eyesore, shock, spectacle, horror

ant. assurance, confidence, composure

frightening (adj)

syn. fearful, appalling, alarming, fearsome, shocking, intimidating, scary, terrifying

ant. reassuring

frigid (adj)

syn. passive, passionless, stiff, unfeeling, unresponsive, unloving, cold, formal, icy, lifeless, cold-hearted, aloof, chill

ant. responsive, warm, ardent, amorous, loving

frivolity (n)
syn. fun, folly, silliness, superficiality, shallowness, childishness, flippancy, nonsense, light-heartedness
ant. seriousness

frivolous (adj)
syn. joking, flippant, jokey, foolish, silly, unimportant, flip
ant. serious

frown (n)
syn. grimace, dirty look, scowl, glare
ant. smile

frowzy (adj)
syn. dirty, ungroomed, untidy, dishevelled, unwashed, unkempt, neglectful
ant. well-groomed, trim, smart

frugal (adj)
syn. prudent, provident, economical, thrifty, careful, meagre, inexpensive
ant. lavish, extravagant, wasteful

fruitful (adj)
syn. helpful, rewarding, productive, profitable
ant. futile, barren, fruitless

fruition (n)
syn. accomplishment, fulfilment, perfection, completion, achievement, attainment
ant. failure

frustration (n)
syn. disappointment, irritation, vexation, failure
ant. promoting, fulfilment

fuddled (adj)
syn. confused, inebriated, stupefied, intoxicated, drunk, bemused, muddled, hazy
ant. sober, clear

fulminate (v)
syn. criticize, denounce, protest, thunder, fume, rage, curse
ant. praise, extol

fuming (adj)
syn. angry, raging, enraged, incensed, boiling, spitting, roused
ant. calm

fun (n)
syn. enjoyment, entertainment, cheerfulness, ridicule, mockery

ant. boredom, misery

functional (adj)

syn. useful, serviceable, practical, in use, running, operative

ant. useless, inoperative

fundamental (adj)

syn. core, basic, root, principal, chief, essential, vital

ant. secondary, incidental

funeral (adj)

syn. depressing, mournful, woeful, deathlike, lamenting, dismal, sad, sombre, dark

ant. happy, lively, festive, vivacious

funny (adj)

syn. droll, laughable, comic, farcical, absurd, odd, humorous, ridiculous, witty, entertaining, amusing, suspicious

ant. unfunny, serious, sad, unamusing, melancholy, dolorous

furious (adj)

syn. outraged, very angry, mad, violent, wrathful, irate, stormy, savage

ant. calm, pleased

furore (n)

syn. upset, stir, commotion, fuss, uproar, hoo-ha, outcry, mania, craze

ant. apathy, calm

furthest (adj)

syn. farthest, outer, most distant, remotest

ant. nearest

furtive (adj)

syn. secret, hidden, sneaky, conspiratorial, shifty, surreptitious

ant. open

fury (n)

syn. anger, rage, outrage, violence, ire, ferocity

ant. calm, peace

fuss (n)

syn. confusion, commotion, bustle, agitation, fidget, fluster, furore, worry, unrest, trouble

ant. calm, composure, peace

futile (adj)

syn. useless, hopeless, forlorn, fruitless, pointless, vain, unimportant

ant. useful, fruitful, profitable

futility (n)
syn. idleness, pointlessness, aimlessness, unimportance, ineffectiveness, vanity
ant. profitability, fruitfulness
fuzzy (adj)
syn. blurred, frizzy, unclear, vague, misty, obscure
ant. smooth, sharp, clear

Gg

gaiety (n)
(old-fashioned)
syn. celebration, colourfulness, fun, festivity, show, joy, jubilation, elation
ant. mourning, sadness, dreariness, drabness

gaily (adv)
syn. cheerfully, happily, merrily, joyfully
ant. sadly, dully

gain (n)
syn. profit, income, benefit, increment, rise
ant. loss

gallant (adj)
syn. daring, fearless, brave, courageous, heroic, courteous, respectful
ant. cowardly, discourteous

galore (adv)
syn. in abundance, in profusion, tons of, lots of, aplenty
ant. scarce

galvanize (v)
syn. inspire, excite, arouse, animate, electrify, quicken, provoke, startle, shock, activate
ant. retard, damp, restrain

gargantuan (adj)
syn. huge, big, large, gigantic, massive, mountainous, vast, titanic, immense
ant. small, Lilliputian, minute

garish (adj)
syn. showy, vulgar, gaudy, loud, tasteless, flamboyant
ant. subdued, plain, modest

garner (v)
syn. assemble, amass, gather, stockpile, deposit, store, accumulate
ant. dissipate, spread, waste

garnish (v)
syn. beautify, embellish, trim, decorate, enhance, adorn, enrich
ant. strip, disfigure, spoil

garrulous (adj)
syn. chatty, babbling, talkative, chattering, effusive, prattling, wordy
ant. taciturn, concise, terse
gathering (n)
syn. accumulation, aggregate, procurement, acquisition, heap
ant. scattering
gauche (adj)
syn. graceless, clumsy, awkward, unsophisticated, inept, ill-mannered, uncultured, unpolished
ant. graceful, elegant, sophisticated
gay^1 (adj)
syn. cheerful, festive, fun-loving, jovial, playful, lively, jolly, sunny, convivial, animated
ant. gloomy, sad
gay^2 (adj)
syn. homosexual, queer, lesbian
ant. heterosexual
generosity (n)
syn. unselfishness, charity, liberality, altruism, benevolence
ant. selfishness, meanness
generous (adj)
syn. unselfish, liberal, plentiful, rich, lavish, ample
ant. selfish, mean, meagre
genesis (n)
syn. beginning, dawn, inception, commencement, birth, start, foundation, generation, outset
ant. end, conclusion, cessation, finish
genial (adj)
syn. cordial, friendly, sympathetic, warm, easy-going, sociable, chummy
ant. cold, unfriendly
genius^1 (n)
syn. expert, brain, maestro, master, intellect, ace
ant. incompetent, bungler
genius^2 (n)
syn. competence, ability, intellect, brilliance, aptitude, flair, propensity, talent
ant. incompetence, inability

genocide (n)
syn. annihilation, extermination, holocaust, pogrom, slaughter, massacre, mass murder
ant. creation, generation, genesis

genteel (adj)
syn. polite, refined, courteous, dignified, respectable, gracious, well-bred, mannerly, elegant
ant. boorish, uncouth, crude, rough, unpolished

gentle (adj)
syn. pathetic, humane, kind, understanding, soft, slow, light
ant. rough, strong, loud

genuine (adj)
syn. real, true, authentic, honest, natural, pure
ant. bogus, insincere, artificial

germane (adj)
syn. appropriate, akin, apt, fitting, related, applicable, relevant, allied, suitable
ant. irrelevant, incompatible, inappropriate, unassociated

ghastly (adj)
syn. terrible, horrible, shocking, dreadful, fearful, awful
ant. pleasant, delightful

ghostly (adj)
syn. spooky, supernatural, phantom, eerie, uncanny, illusory, unnatural
ant. natural

giant (adj)
syn. large, vast, immense, titanic, elephantine, huge, enormous
ant. small, little, Lilliputian, trivial

giddy (adj)
syn. unsteady, faint, dizzy, silly, unbalanced
ant. sensible, sober

gifted (adj)
syn. able, talented, skilled, expert, clever, intelligent, ace, genius
ant. inept, dull

gigantic (adj)
syn. immense, huge, vast, titanic, mega, enormous
ant. small, tiny

gild (v)
syn. adorn, beautify, embellish, ornament, garnish, enhance, brighten, trim

ant. disfigure, spoil
gingerly (adv)
syn. cautiously, carefully, gently, reluctantly, suspiciously, timidly
ant. carelessly, roughly, boldly
glad (adj)
syn. cheerful, delightful, happy, jovial, over the moon, animated, pleased
ant. sad, blue, joyless, downcast
glamorous (adj)
syn. stylish, beautiful, chic, elegant, fashionable, exciting, charming, enchanting, attractive, alluring
ant. dull, dowdy, plain, boring
glamour (n)
syn. attraction, charm, allure, beauty, enchantment, appeal, fascination, magnetism
ant. repulsion, ugliness
glaring (adj)
syn. strong, dazzling, harsh, obvious, striking, unmistakable, blatant
ant. hidden, minor, dull
gleaming (adj)
syn. bright, glowing, shining, lustrous, brilliant, polished
ant. dull
glee (n)
syn. joy, cheerfulness, mirth, delight, gladness, pleasure, gaiety, elation, enjoyment
ant. gloom, blues, sadness, depression, melancholy
global (adj)
syn. international, world, worldwide, universal, general, comprehensive, overall
ant. limited, parochial
gloomy (adj)
syn. dim, sunless, dark, glum, depressed, dejected, pessimistic, unfavourable
ant. cheerful, bright
glory (n)
syn. prestige, fame, honour, recognition, nobility, greatness
ant. shame, blame
glossy (adj)
syn. brilliant, glassy, shiny, polished, gleaming
ant. dull

glum (adj)
syn. dejected, gloomy, sulky, doleful, morose, crestfallen, moody, pessimistic, depressed, taciturn
ant. cheerful, joyful, glad, happy

godless (adj)
syn. impious, irreligious, pagan, profane, ungodly
ant. godly, pious

good-for-nothing (n)
(informal)
syn. worthlessness, lazybones, idler, black sheep, loafer, drone
ant. winner, success, achiever

goodness (n)
syn. excellence, good, virtue, honesty, righteousness, decency, worth, merit
ant. wickedness, badness

goodwill (n)
syn. charity, decency, goodness, kindness, benevolence, compassion
ant. ill will, hostility

gorgeous (adj)
syn. beautiful, good-looking, pretty, attractive, cute, comely, superb, wonderful, elegant, dazzling
ant. drab, ugly, dull

gracious (adj)
syn. polite, well mannered, courteous, kind, hospitable, tactful, diplomatic, amiable, amenable, congenial
ant. ungracious, blunt, sullen, boorish, uncivilized

grandeur (n)
syn. glory, greatness, splendour, ceremony, pomp, bombast
ant. simplicity, humbleness

grandiloquent (adj)
syn. bombastic, high-sounding, pompous, rhetorical, pretentious, flowery, showy, exaggerated, grand
ant. simple, plain, ungarnished, homely, restrained

grandiose (adj)
syn. bombastic, grand, lofty, flamboyant, impressive, showy, extravagant, pompous
ant. ordinary, unpretentious, simple

grapple (v)
syn. clash, wrestle, scuffle, combat, confront, struggle, deal, tackle, face
ant. avoid, evade

grasping (adj)
syn. greedy, rapacious, materialistic, mean, miserly, parsimonious, tight-fisted, saving, acquisitive
ant. generous, liberal, lavish, open-handed, spendthrift

grateful (adj)
syn. obliged, thankful, beholden, appreciative
ant. ungrateful

gratification (n)
syn. delight, enjoyment, joy, thrill, contentment, elation
ant. frustration

grating (adj)
syn. disagreeable, annoying, displeasing, irritating, discordant, cacophonous, unpleasant, unharmonious, harsh
ant. pleasing, harmonious

gratitude (n)
syn. acknowledgement, thanks, appreciation, thankfulness, gratefulness
ant. ingratitude

grave (adj)
syn. terrible, important, serious, profound, sober, solemn
ant. trivial, light-hearted

gravity (n)
syn. seriousness, significance, magnitude, importance, urgency, acuteness, solemnity, grimness, sobriety
ant. triviality, gaiety, levity

great (adj)
syn. exceptional, considerable, substantial, large, huge, celebrated, eminent, prominent, impressive, magnificent, expert, eager, enjoyable, terrific
ant. small, little, minor, modest, unimportant, insignificant

greed (n)
syn. materialism, avarice, money-grubbing, hunger, gluttony, piggishness, desire, longing
ant. unselfishness, generosity, indifference, temperance

greedy (adj)
syn. voracious, gluttonous, piggish, materialistic, hungry, selfish
ant. unselfish, abstemious, moderate

greeting (n)
syn. welcome, hello, salutation, regards, compliments
ant. farewell

gregarious (adj)
syn. friendly, convivial, sociable, outgoing, affable, extrovert, cordial, warm, genial
ant. unsociable, unfriendly, solitary

grief (n)
syn. distress, pain, sorrow, sadness, heartbreak, agony
ant. joy, happiness

grief-stricken (adj)
syn. sorrowful, unhappy, broken-hearted, heartbroken, grieving, distracted, desolate, devastated, sad
ant. overjoyed, joyful, delighted, thrilled

grievance (n)
syn. complaint, ill feeling, objection, resentment, trouble, distress, unhappiness, grumble
ant. contentment, happiness, comfort

grieve (v)
syn. sorrow, cry, mourn, upset, sadden, pain, hurt
ant. rejoice

grim (adj)
syn. unsmiling, stern, horrible, dreadful, shocking, depressing, miserable, gloomy
ant. pleasant, amiable, congenial

grimy (adj)
syn. contaminated, foul, dirty, murky, smudgy, soiled
ant. clean, pure

gripping (adj)
syn. enthralling, fascinating, exciting, action-packed, exciting
ant. boring

grisly (adj)
syn. frightful, horrible, grim, appalling, terrifying, macabre, shocking, awful, abominable
ant. delightful, enjoyable, pleasant

groan (n)
syn. complaint, moan, grievance, protest
ant. cheer

groom (v)
syn. clean, brush, comb, arrange, prepare, train, teach, coach, smarten
ant. spoil, damage

grotesque (adj)
syn. deformed, distorted, unnatural, strange, abnormal, shocking, outrageous, ridiculous, unbelievable, incredible, ludicrous, absurd, silly
ant. logical, rational, sensible

grouchy (adj)
(informal)
syn. bad-tempered, complaining, discontented, dissatisfied, irritable, peevish, sulky, grumbling, ill-tempered
ant. contented, pleased, comfortable

grovelling (adj)
syn. bootlicking, flattering, sycophantic, fawning, backscratching
ant. outspoken, straightforward

grow (v)
syn. expand, enlarge, spread, sprout, cultivate
ant. decline, shrink, decrease, halt

growth (n)
syn. increase, expansion, rise, development, progress, tumour, swelling, advancement
ant. decrease, stagnation, stoppage, failure

grubby (adj)
syn. filthy, dirty, soiled, unwashed, manky
ant. clean, hygienic

grudge (n)
syn. ill will, bitterness, grievance, animosity, antagonism, antipathy, a chip on your shoulder
ant. regard, favour

gruelling (adj)
syn. exhausting, tiring, demanding, strenuous, difficult, back-breaking, harsh, punishing, laborious, tough, hard, arduous
ant. easy, simple, relaxing

gruesome (adj)
syn. ghastly, horrifying, grisly, horrible, horrific, grim, awful, terrible, fearful, loathsome, shocking
ant. pleasant, charming, congenial

grumble (n)
syn. complaint, grievance, grouse, protest, moan, objection
ant. contentment, happiness, comfort

grumpy (adj)
(informal)
syn. discontented, irritable, bad-tempered, grumbling, peevish, sulky, ratty, cranky
ant. good-humoured, contented

guile (n)
syn. artfulness, cleverness, cunning, deception, deceit, treachery, wiliness, trickery, duplicity
ant. guilelessness, honesty, frankness, uprightness

guest (n)
syn. visitor, company, client, lodger
ant. host

guilt (n)
syn. culpability, remorse, regret, blameworthiness, self-reproach, stigma, shame
ant. innocence, impenitence

guilty (adj)
syn. culpable, blameworthy, remorseful, ashamed, sorry, repentant, regretful
ant. innocent

gullible (adj)
syn. unsuspecting, ingenuous, credulous, innocent, naïve
ant. suspicious, astute

gumption (n)
syn. common sense, astuteness, ability, acumen, sagacity, shrewdness, cleverness
ant. foolishness, folly

guru (n)
(informal)
syn. sage, spiritual, teacher, spiritual leader, expert, leading light
ant. disciple

gushing (adj)
syn. overenthusiastic, effusive, emotional, unrestrained, extravagant, lavish
ant. restrained, sincere

gusto (n)
syn. delight, enjoyment, liking, pleasure, zeal, enthusiasm, fervour
ant. apathy, displeasure
gutless (adj)
syn. chicken-hearted, cowardly, feeble, lily-livered, spineless, timid
ant. courageous
gutsy (adj)
syn. bold, courageous, spirited, gallant, brave, resolute, indomitable
ant. timid, quiet

Hh

habitual (adj)
syn. accustomed, endless, constant, never-ending, fixed, eternal, regular, chronic
ant. occasional, intermittent

hackneyed (adj)
syn. overworked, stale, overused, banal, tired, worn-out
ant. new, original

haggard (adj)
syn. wrinkled, tired, drawn, hollow-eyed, exhausted
ant. hale, fresh

halcyon (adj)
syn. calm, gentle, happy, placid, quiet, undisturbed, peaceful, prosperous
ant. stormy, raging, troubled

hale (adj)
syn. healthy, strong, sound, able-bodied, youthful, blooming
ant. ill, unhealthy, feeble, weak

half-baked (adj)
(informal)
syn. foolish, brainless, ill-judged, silly, senseless, stupid
ant. sensible, wise, prudent

half-hearted (adj)
syn. tepid, apathetic, unenthusiastic, cool, indifferent, careless
ant. enthusiastic, excited, zealous

half-wit (n)
(informal)
syn. fool, dunce, imbecile, nitwit, idiot, ass
ant. brain, genius

half-witted (adj)
syn. crazy, dull, foolish, silly, idiotic, stupid
ant. clever, sensible

hallucination (n)
syn. fantasy, delusion, mirage, illusion, vision, dream, phantom
ant. realism, reality, actuality

handful (n)
syn. small amount, few, some
ant. lot

handicap (n)
(old-fashioned)
syn. defect, block, disability, disadvantage
ant. benefit, assistance, advantage

handsome (adj)
syn. attractive, graceful, good-looking, hunky, ample, substantial, considerable
ant. unhandsome, ugly, stingy

handy (adj)
(informal)
syn. accessible, convenient, helpful, easy to use, within reach, skilled
ant. inconvenient, clumsy

hangdog (adj)
syn. miserable, shamefaced, browbeaten, guilty, defeated
ant. bold, brave

hankering (n)
syn. urge, yearning, desire, wish, longing
ant. aversion, dislike

hanky-panky (n)
(old-fashioned, informal)
syn. dishonesty, cheating, funny business, nonsense, trickery
ant. openness, honesty

haphazard (adj)
syn. aimless, random, chance, disorderly, unsystematic
ant. planned, methodical, deliberate

hapless (adj)
syn. miserable, ill-fated, unfortunate, unlucky
ant. lucky

happiness (n)
syn. joy, cheerfulness, gaiety, pleasure, delight, elation, good spirits, merriment, contentment
ant. unhappiness, sadness, despair, misery

happy (adj)
syn. joyful, cheerful, contented, jolly, pleased, sunny, delighted, elated, lucky

ant. unhappy, sad, cheerless, disappointed, horrified

harassment (n)
syn. annoyance, trouble, persecution, victimization, hassle, vexation
ant. assistance

hard-core (adj)
syn. die-hard, extreme, blatant, dedicated, rigid
ant. moderate

hard-headed (adj)
syn. cool, pragmatic, realistic, astute, shrewd, sensible, unsentimental, tough
ant. unrealistic, senseless

hard-hearted (adj)
syn. heartless, cruel, inhuman, callous, merciless, unkind, uncompassionate, cold, intolerant
ant. kind, merciful, compassionate

hard-hitting (adj)
syn. tough, strongly-worded, critical, unsparing, forceful, vigorous, condemnatory
ant. mild, gentle, amiable

hardiness (n)
syn. courage, fortitude, boldness, valour, resolution, toughness, resilience, intrepidity
ant. timidity, cowardice

hard-line (adj)
syn. extreme, tough, inflexible, uncompromising, militant, definite
ant. moderate, liberal, pragmatic

hardness (n)
syn. difficulty, laboriousness, toughness, inhumanity, rigidity
ant. ease, softness, mildness

hardship (n)
syn. poverty, suffering, difficulty, distress, need
ant. ease, prosperity

hardy (adj)
syn. bold, fit, robust, sturdy, strong, tough, sound
ant. weak, delicate, unhealthy

hare-brained (adj)
syn. foolish, mindless, careless, unstable
ant. sensible

harmful (adj)
syn. dangerous, hurtful, damaging, destructive
ant. beneficial, harmless
harmony (n)
syn. accord, melodiousness, agreement, cooperation, peace, unity, rapport
ant. disagreement, discord, dissonance
harried (adj)
syn. bothered, anxious, worried, troubled, harassed, pressurized, agitated, distressed
ant. untroubled, calm, composed, relaxed
harrowing (adj)
syn. alarming, terrifying, distressing, tormenting, chilling, agonizing
ant. calming, heartening
harsh (adj)
syn. abrasive, abusive, cruel, severe, cold, rude
ant. mild, gentle, kind
hassle (n)
(informal)
syn. argument, trouble, inconvenience, fuss, altercation, irritation, nuisance
ant. agreement, peace
haste (n)
syn. speed, quickness, hurriedness, alacrity, urgency
ant. delay, slowness
hasten (v)
syn. hurry, speed, rush, accelerate, quicken
ant. delay, dawdle
hasty (adj)
syn. reckless, brisk, speedy, hurried, rash
ant. considered, careful, placid
hate (n)
syn. loathing, disgust, hatred, abhorrence, abomination
ant. love, liking, adoration
hatred (n)
syn. hate, animosity, aversion, enmity, dislike, antipathy
ant. love, liking, adoration
haughty (adj)
syn. proud, arrogant, lofty, scornful, immodest, conceited

ant. humble, modest, friendly

havoc (n)
syn. pandemonium, mayhem, chaos, bedlam, disorder, destruction, devastation
ant. calm, order, reconstruction

haywire (adj)
syn. confused, chaotic, disordered, erratic, disorganized, crazy
ant. orderly, ordered, correct

hazard (n)
syn. peril, danger, mishap, risk
ant. safety

hazy (adj)
syn. cloudy, misty, foggy, dull, uncertain, unclear
ant. definite, clear

headstrong (adj)
syn. rash, obstinate, reckless, stubborn, wilful, headless, pig-headed
ant. obedient, docile, tractable

heal (v)
syn. treat, cure, mend, repair, resolve, settle, patch up
ant. break, destroy

health (n)
syn. fitness, condition, well-being, vigour, haleness, strength
ant. illness, disease

healthy (adj)
syn. fine, well, blooming, nourishing, sound, wholesome, in the pink
ant. unhealthy, ill, diseased

heartache (n)
syn. distress, agony, suffering, anguish, pain, hurt, heartbreak, sorrow, grief
ant. happiness, joy, delight, ecstasy, bliss, euphoria

heartbreaking (adj)
syn. upsetting, painful, bitter, distressing, harrowing
ant. joyful, comforting, heart-warming

heartbroken (adj)
syn. disappointed, miserable, desolate, broken-hearted
ant. elated, delighted, rapturous

hearten (v)
syn. cheer, animate, encourage, inspire, gladden, assure, incite

ant. dishearten, damp

heartfelt (adj)

syn. sincere, from the heart, honest, wholehearted, warm, hearty, cordial

ant. insincere, dishonest, false

heartily (adv)

syn. wholeheartedly, enthusiastically, warmly, completely, thoroughly, sincerely, cordially

ant. half-heartedly, insincerely, dishonestly

heartless (adj)

syn. unkind, unsympathetic, cold, unfeeling, cruel, inhuman, hard-hearted, merciless, callous

ant. compassionate, kind, sympathetic, considerate

heart-rending (adj)

syn. heartbreaking, deplorable, harrowing, pathetic, tragic, sad, distressing, affecting, poignant

ant. heartwarming, comforting, joyful, pleasing

heartwarming (adj)

syn. cheering, pleasing, heartening, satisfying, encouraging

ant. heartbreaking, depressing

hearty (adj)

syn. jovial, lively, exuberant, vivacious, spirited, heartfelt, wholehearted, sincere, healthy, strong, ample, substantial

ant. cold, emotionless, feeble, meagre

heated (adj)

syn. passionate, angry, vehement, furious, excited, violent

ant. dispassionate, calm, composed

heathen (n)

syn. pagan, unbeliever, infidel, barbarian

ant. believer

heavy-hearted (adj)

syn. depressed, disheartened, downhearted, crushed, sad, morose, forlorn, mournful, sorrowful

ant. light-hearted, happy, joyful, delighted

hectic (adj)

syn. chaotic, frantic, busy, active, frenzied, excited

ant. calm, leisurely

hector (v)
syn. threaten, bully, harass, browbeat, worry, torment, boast, provoke, intimidate
ant. cajole, persuade, sweet-talk, entice, coax
hedonism (n)
syn. voluptuousness, pleasure-seeking, sensualism, luxuriousness
ant. asceticism
heed (n)
syn. attention, consideration, care, regard, respect, notice
ant. disregard, inattention, indifference
heed (v)
syn. consider, note, listen, regard, attend, obey
ant. disregard, ignore
hefty (adj)
syn. strong, burly, big, beefy, hard, powerful, substantial, heavy, considerable
ant. light, slight, small
hegemony (n)
syn. supremacy, domination, dominion, leadership, rule, command, control
ant. subjection
height (n)
syn. acme, peak, summit, pinnacle, tallness, elevation
ant. depth, nadir
heighten (adj)
syn. increase, boost, intensify, augment, magnify, strengthen, enhance
ant. decrease, diminish, reduce
heinous (adj)
syn. horrific, awful, wicked, terrible
ant. admirable
hell-bent (adj)
syn. determined, inflexible, fixed, tenacious, resolved, unhesitating, bent, dogged
ant. undetermined, irresolute, half-hearted, weak
help (v)
syn. assist, aid, back, support, encourage, cooperate, serve, promote, alleviate, remedy, relieve
ant. hinder, aggravate

help (n)
syn. assistance, aid, encouragement, cooperation, relief, remedy, cure, alleviation
ant. hindrance, aggravation

helpless (adj)
syn. powerless, incompetent, incapable, defenceless, dependent, impotent
ant. strong, independent, competent, enterprising

henceforth (adv)
syn. hence, hereafter, from now on
ant. hitherto

henpecked (adj)
syn. dominated, browbeaten, meek, bullied, timid
ant. dominant

herald (v)
syn. announce, harbinger, publicize, advertise, promulgate
ant. suppress

herculean (adj)
syn. laborious, toilsome, arduous, formidable, difficult, mighty, strong, powerful
ant. easy, puny, weak

hereditary (adj)
syn. inherited, passed, down, family, genetic, innate, inborn
ant. acquired

heresy (n)
syn. free-thinking, error, impiety, heterodoxy, unorthodoxy
ant. orthodoxy, tradition

heretic (n)
syn. free-thinker, nonconformist, dissenter, infidel, separatist, apostate, unbeliever
ant. conformist, believer

heroic (adj)
syn. bold, brave, intrepid, courageous, daring, fearless, gutsy
ant. cowardly, timid, pusillanimous

hesitant (adj)
syn. hesitating, half-hearted, sceptical, doubtful, irresolute, undecided, uncertain, timid, shy
ant. resolute, certain, staunch, confident, decisive

hesitate (v)
syn. doubt, be uncertain, pause, fumble, think twice
ant. proceed, continue
hesitation (n)
syn. doubt, uncertainty, irresolution, pause, indecision
ant. decision, assurance, alacrity
heterodox (adj)
syn. unorthodox, heretical, iconoclastic, nonconformist, dissident, unbelieving, apostate, disagreeing
ant. orthodox, conventional, traditional, conformist
heterodoxy (n)
syn. unorthodoxy, iconoclasm, heresy, dissent, schism
ant. orthodoxy, tradition
heroism (n)
syn. valour, bravery, fearlessness, courage, guts, boldness, fortitude
ant. cowardice, timidity, pusillanimity
heterogeneous (adj)
syn. mixed, varied, miscellaneous, different, dissimilar
ant. homogeneous
hiatus (n)
syn. gap, lacuna, break, discontinuance, lapse, interval, chasm
ant. continuance, continuation, constancy
hidden (adj)
syn. unseen, invisible, concealed, secret, masked, cryptic
ant. obvious, visible, open
hide (v)
syn. conceal, stash, hole up, veil, obscure, keep, secret, hush up, disguise
ant. reveal, show, display
hidebound (adj)
syn. conventional, unprogressive, narrow-minded, narrow, rigid, ultra-conservative
ant. unconventional, liberal
hideous (adj)
syn. ugly, repellent, repulsive, revolting, awful, horrific, frightful, horrifying, gruesome, ghastly, shocking
ant. beautiful, pleasant

high-born (adj)
(old-fashioned)
syn. noble, of noble birth, aristocratic, well-born, lordly, blue-blooded, patrician, high-class
ant. low-born, lower-class, working-class. common

highbrow (adj)
syn. brainy, intellectual, bookish, sophisticated, serious, cultivated
ant. lowbrow, unlettered

high-minded (adj)
syn. honourable, lofty, moral, principled, noble, ethical
ant. immoral, unscrupulous

hilarious (adj)
syn. amusing, comical, very funny, jolly, humorous, merry, cheerful
ant. serious, grave

historical (adj)
syn. actual, factual, authentic, real, documented, archival, old, past
ant. unhistorical, legendary

histrionic (adj)
syn. dramatic, false, unnatural, artificial, theatrical, insincere, bogus
ant. normal, genuine

hitch (v)
syn. tie, fasten, unite, join, hoist, connect, pull
ant. unfasten, unhitch, loose

hitherto (adv)
syn. so far, up to now, till now, beforehand, previously
ant. henceforth

hoard (v)
syn. collect, gather, accumulate, amass, save, store, stockpile
ant. squander, spend

hoax (n)
syn. prank, deception, cheat, joke, practical joke, fraud, con, trick
ant. openness, artlessness

hold (v)
syn. grasp, hug, grip, detain, confine, take, fit, consider, think, conduct
ant. drop, release

holiness (n)
syn. devoutness, godliness, piety, sacredness, divinity, religiousness, spirituality

ant. profanity, impiety, wickedness
hindrance (n)
syn. delay, inconvenience, stumbling block, obstruction, impediment, obstacle
ant. help, aid, assistance
hollow (adj)
syn. void, empty, depressed, meaningless, insincere, false, untrue
ant. convex, solid, sincere
holocaust (n)
syn. destruction, annihilation, extermination, extinction, mass murder, genocide, pogrom, slaughter, massacre
ant. creation, generation, genesis
holy (adj)
syn. religious, blessed, saintly, devout, sacred, pure, virtuous, divine, spiritual
ant. profane, impious, sinful
homage (n)
syn. admiration, honour, respect, esteem, tribute, worship, veneration
ant. contempt, disrespect
homely (adj)
syn. homelike, comfortable, cosy, domestic, modest, natural, plain, simple
ant. grand, unfamiliar, formal
homespun (adj)
syn. artless, rude, unpolished, inelegant, unrefined, homely, rustic, coarse, home-made, plain
ant. sophisticated, advanced, cultured, refined
homogeneous (adj)
syn. alike, comparable, consistent, uniform, similar, akin
ant. heterogeneous, different
homosexual (n)
syn. gay, lesbian, homophile, queer, invert, nancy
ant. heterosexual, straight
hone (v)
syn. sharpen, polish, grind, file, whet
ant. blunt
honest (adj)
syn. principled, candid, upright, ethical, trustworthy, virtuous, open
ant. dishonest, covert

honesty (n)
syn. candour, bluntness, uprightness, integrity, virtue, sincerity, truthfulness, morality
ant. dishonesty, insincerity

honorary (adj)
syn. complimentary, nominal, in name only, titular, unofficial, unsalaried, formal
ant. salaried, gainful

honour (n)
syn. accolade, admiration, integrity, glory, reputation, dignity, virtue, respect
ant. dishonour, shame, disgrace

honourable (adj)
syn. honest, respectable, good, upright, principled, great, distinguished, eminent
ant. dishonourable, dishonest, unworthy

honours (n)
syn. awards, rewards, titles, dignities, laurels, trophies, prizes
ant. aspersions, abuse, defamation, indignities

hope (n)
syn. desire, ambition, aspiration, optimism
ant. despair, pessimism

hopeless (adj)
syn. dejected, desperate, forlorn, incompetent, useless
ant. hopeful, competent, optimistic

horrible (adj)
syn. awful, shocking, horrifying, dreadful, ghastly, disagreeable, obnoxious, nasty, unpleasant, repulsive
ant. wonderful, pleasant, agreeable

horrid (adj)
syn. horrible, disagreeable, unpleasant, unkind, alarming, horrific, frightening, awful, repulsive
ant. pleasant, wonderful, lovely, agreeable

horrific (adj)
syn. awful, frightening, scaring, appalling, shocking, horrifying, alarming
ant. pleasant, wonderful, reassuring

horror (n)
syn. terror, fright, panic, fear, alarm, dismay, distress

ant. delight, satisfaction, reassurance

hospitable (adj)

syn. welcoming, amicable, amenable, friendly, cordial, warm, gracious, sociable, receptive

ant. inhospitable, hostile, unfriendly

hospitality (n)

syn. generosity, welcome, friendliness, sociability, warmth, geniality, kindness

ant. inhospitality, hostility, unfriendliness

hostile (adj)

syn. inhospitable, unfriendly, antagonistic, belligerent, unfavourable, grim, opposed, against, unsympathetic, anti

ant. friendly, favourable, sympathetic, generous

hostilities (n)

syn. fighting, war, conflict, warfare

ant. peace

hostility (n)

syn. animosity, antagonism, hatred, opposition, antipathy

ant. sympathy, friendliness

hot-blooded (adj)

syn. excitable, ardent, bold, high-spirited, passionate, wild, rash, lustful, eager

ant. cool, dispassionate

hot-headed (adj)

syn. impetuous, quick-tempered, reckless, rash, daredevil, headstrong, impulsive, unruly

ant. calm, cool, composed

hub (n)

syn. centre, heart, core, focal point, kernel

ant. periphery, boundary

hubbub (n)

syn. noise, uproar, commotion, disorder, rumpus, clamour, confusion, din, pandemonium

ant. calm, quite, order, peace

huddle (v)

syn. crowd, gather, throng, collect, congregate, curl up, crouch

ant. disperse

huge (adj)
syn. immense, enormous, mega, vast, big, large
ant. tiny, dainty

hullabaloo (n)
syn. pandemonium, noise, commotion, hubbub, uproar, rumpus, din, bedlam, clamour, ruckus, chaos
ant. calm, quiet, order, peace

human (adj)
syn. weak, physical, kind, humane, compassionate
ant. inhuman

humane (adj)
syn. compassionate, sympathetic, kind, tolerant, merciful
ant. inhumane, cruel, ruthless

humanity (n)
syn. compassion, fellow feeling, sympathy, humaneness, humankind, mankind, the human race
ant. inhumanity, bestiality

humble (adj)
syn. modest, submissive, meek, respectful, simple, lowly, polite, docile
ant. haughty, arrogant, proud, conceited

humdrum (adj)
syn. dull, mundane, boring, monotonous, routine, prosaic, everyday, uninteresting, run-of-the-mill
ant. interesting, unusual, exceptional

humid (adj)
syn. sultry, moist, muggy, wet, vaporous, steamy
ant. dry, fresh

humidity (n)
syn. moisture, mugginess, wetness, humidness, steaminess
ant. dryness, freshness

humiliation (n)
syn. shame, dishonour, embarrassment, disgrace, abashment
ant. dignity, triumph

humility (n)
syn. modesty, meekness, humbleness, submissiveness, lowliness, obedience
ant. hauteur, pride, egoism, conceit, vanity, arrogance

humorous (adj)
syn. funny, amusing, hilarious, witty, comic, comical, satirical, entertaining

ant. humourless, serious
humour (n)
syn. satire, comedy, hilarity, wit
ant. seriousness
hunger (n)
syn. starvation, undernourishment, appetite, desire, lust
ant. satisfaction, contentment
hungry (adj)
syn. starving, undernourished, desirous, eager, avid
ant. satisfied, contented, full
hurdle (n)
syn. obstacle, barrier, hindrance, stumbling block, difficulty
ant. advantage, help, assistance
hurry (n)
syn. rush, speed, haste, hustle and bustle, urgency, quickness
ant. leisure
hurt (v)
syn. ache, harm, injure, damage, pain, upset, distress, annoy
ant. soothe, relieve, appease
hurtful (adj)
syn. unkind, distressing, upsetting, spiteful, malicious, harmful, damaging,
nasty
ant. helpful, kind, soothing, harmless
husband (v)
syn. save, store, conserve, economize
ant. waste
hush-hush (adj)
(informal)
syn. confidential, secret, restricted, top-secret
ant. open, public
hybrid (adj)
syn. composite, mixed, compound, bastard, heterogeneous
ant. pure, pure-bred
hygiene (n)
syn. cleanliness, purity, sanitation, salubriousness
ant. filth, insanitariness
hygienic (adj)
syn. healthy, clean, sanitary, germ-free, pure

ant. unhygienic, insanitary
hyperbole (n)
syn. excess, exaggeration, overplay, overstatement
ant. understatement, meiosis
hypercritical (adj)
syn. over-critical, captious, finicky, fault-finding, fussy, censorious, carping
ant. uncritical, tolerant
hypochondria (n)
syn. depression, hypochondriasis, melancholy, valetudinarianism, sadness, gloom
ant. cheerfulness, elation, ecstasy, prosperity
hypocrisy (n)
syn. deception, deceit, insincerity, pretence, lip-service, falseness
ant. sincerity, humility
hypocrite (n)
syn. pretender, deceiver, fraud, charlatan, imposter, swindler
ant. saint, gentleman, worthy
hypocritical (adj)
syn. insincere, deceitful, hollow, false, fraudulent, self-righteous, two-faced
ant. sincere, humble, genuine
hypothesis (n)
syn. assumption, premise, proposition, theory, presumption
ant. practice, confirmation, proof
hypothetical (adj)
syn. theoretical, supposed, academic, imaginary, assumed, proposed, postulated
ant. real, actual
hysteria (n)
syn. madness, panic, frenzy, mania, distress, feverishness
ant. calm, quiet, composure

icon (n)
syn. figure, image, symbol, icon, idol, representation, celebrity
ant. nobody
iconoclasm (n)
syn. questioning, dissidence, heresy, criticism, scepticism, radicalism, unbelief, disbelief
ant. trustfulness, credulity, belief
iconoclast (n)
syn. dissident, critic, opponent, unbeliever, radical, sceptic, rebel
ant. believer, devotee
idea (n)
syn. thought, concept, plan, proposition, theory, notion, viewpoint, doctrine
ant. fact
ideal (adj)
syn. model, perfect, exemplary, classic, supreme, fanciful, unreal, theoretical, illusory, abstract
ant. imperfect, real, actual
idealism (n)
syn. impracticality, romanticism, utopianism
ant. realism, pragmatism
idealist (n)
syn. visionary, dreamer, romanticist, utopian
ant. realist, pragmatist
idealistic (adj)
syn. impractical, romantic, unrealistic, visionary, optimistic, utopian
ant. realistic, pragmatic
identical (adj)
syn. same, matching, corresponding, congruous, alike, like
ant. different
identifiable (adj)
syn. recognizable, noticeable, distinguishable, perceptible, known
ant. unidentifiable, unfamiliar, unknown

ideology (n)
syn. belief, creed, dogma, theory, doctrine, faith, tenets, conviction
ant. disbelief, unfaithfulness
idiocy (n)
syn. foolishness, stupidity, absurdity, lunacy, imbecility, dementia, silliness, folly
ant. sense, sanity, wisdom
idiom (n)
syn. colloquialism, phrase, jargon, usage, set phrase, style, vernacular, language, locution, expression
ant. standard, formality
idiomatic (adj)
syn. colloquial, vernacular, conversational, native, natural, informal
ant. unidiomatic, formal
idiosyncrasy (n)
syn. eccentricity, quirk, peculiarity, mannerism, oddness, characteristic
ant. normality, prudence, sanity
idiot (n)
(informal)
syn. halfwit, dummy, fool, nitwit, moron, charlie
ant. genius, scholar
idiotic (adj)
syn. stupid, foolish, senseless, moronic, absurd, crazy, half-witted, imbecilic
ant. wise, sane, sensible, prudent
idle (adj)
syn. indolent, lazy, slothful, jobless, vain, inactive, foolish, useless
ant. busy, industrious, active
idler (n)
syn. dodger, good-for-nothing, loafer, waster, lazybones, sloth
ant. worker, achiever
idolatry (n)
syn. glorification, adoration, exaltation, hero-worship, idolizing, adulation
ant. vilification, criticism, abuse
idolize (v)
syn. glorify, iconize, worship, admire, exalt, venerate, love, hero-worship
ant. vilify, despise, defame

ignite (v)
syn. burn, fire, inflame, light
ant. extinguish, quench

ignoble (adj)
syn. dishonourable, disgraceful, abject, degraded, infamous, heinous, unworthy, shameless, vile
ant. noble, honourable

ignominious (adj)
syn. degrading, disgraceful, dishonourable, shameful, unworthy
ant. honourable, triumphant

ignominy (n)
syn. dishonour, disgrace, contempt, shame, stigma, disrepute, humiliation, degradation, scandal
ant. credit, honour, reputation, glory

ignoramus (n)
(old-fashioned, humorous)
syn. dunce, duffer, simpleton, blockhead, fool, ass, donkey
ant. scholar, genius, intellectual

ignorance (n)
syn. unawareness, illiteracy, naivety, innocence, inexperience
ant. knowledge, wisdom

ignorant (adj)
syn. uneducated, illiterate, inexperienced, unaware, unfamiliar, uninformed, unknowing
ant. educated, learned, knowledgeable, aware

ignore (v)
syn. disregard, overlook, snub, neglect, pass over, disobey, brush aside
ant. acknowledge, note, obey

ill (adj)
syn. sick, ailing, unwell, unhealthy, diseased, bad, wrong, unlucky, unkind, malicious, harsh, harmful, acrimonious
ant. well, good, kind, beneficial

ill-advised (adj)
syn. ill-considered, foolish, imprudent, unwise, incautious, coarse, rash, indiscreet, thoughtless
ant. sensible, wise, prudent

ill-considered (adj)
syn. ill-judged, imprudent, unwise, rash, hasty, foolish

ant. sensible, wise, prudent
illegal (adj)
syn. unlawful, corrupt, illicit, criminal, proscribed, prohibited, banned
ant. legal, lawful.
illegible (adj)
syn. unreadable, obscure, unintelligible, indistinct, unclear
ant. legible, readable
illegitimate (adj)
syn. fatherless, bastard, unlawful, illicit, illegal, dishonest, corrupt, unauthorized
ant. legitimate, legal, unlawful
ill-fated (adj)
syn. doomed, forlorn, hapless, unfortunate
ant. lucky
ill-humour (n)
syn. acrimony, disagreeableness, sulkiness, petulance
ant. amiability
illiberal (adj)
syn. intolerant, prejudiced, bigoted, narrow-minded, parsimonious, ungenerous
ant. liberal, broad-minded
illicit (adj)
syn. forbidden, illegal, unlicensed, unlawful, proscribed
ant. legal, licit, lawful
illiterate (adj)
syn. unlettered, ignorant, uneducated
ant. literate
ill-mannered (adj)
syn. bad-mannered, churlish, impolite, rude, discourteous, coarse, insolent, ill-bred
ant. well-mannered, polite, well-bred
illness (n)
syn. sickness, disease, malady, disorder, poor health, affliction
ant. fitness, health
illogical (adj)
syn. erroneous, absurd, irrational, unreasonable
ant. logical

illuminating (adj)
syn. helpful, informative, instructive, revealing, enlightening
ant. unhelpful, confusing

illusion (n)
syn. misconception, error, delusion, fallacy, fantasy, mirage
ant. reality

illusory (adj)
syn. false, imaginary, unreal, imagined, fallacious, misleading, delusive
ant. genuine, real

illustrate (v)
syn. explain, demonstrate, clarify, decorate, support
ant. obscure

ill-will (n)
syn. enmity, grudge, animosity, hostility, hatred, bad blood
ant. goodwill, friendship

imaginary (adj)
syn. unreal, fanciful, illusory, fictitious, mythical, visionary, hypothetical
ant. real, true, actual

imagination (n)
syn. vision, creativity, fancy, mind's eye, insight, fantasy, illusion
ant. reality

imbecile (adj)
syn. feeble-minded, stupid, idiotic, witless, moronic, ludicrous
ant. intelligent, clever, sensible

imbecility (n)
syn. feeble-mindedness, stupidity, foolishness, incompetence, idiocy, inanity
ant. intelligence, cleverness, sense

imitation (n)
syn. copy, impersonation, counterfeit, likeness, replica, mimicry
ant. original

immaculate (adj)
syn. perfect, clean, faultless, impeccable, innocent, sinless
ant. damaged, dirty

immaturity (n)
syn. childishness, imperfection, inexperience, youth
ant. maturity

immediate (adj)
syn. prompt, instant, speedy, quick, urgent, current, close, nearest, latest
ant. delayed, distant, future

immediately (adv)
syn. instantly, right away, directly, precisely, at once
ant. later, never

immemorial (adj)
syn. ancient, age-old, archaic, traditional, olden, fixed, ancestral
ant. modern, recent

immense (adj)
syn. vast, huge, giant, large
ant. tiny

immigrant (n)
syn. migrant, newcomer, non-native, foreigner
ant. native

imminent (adj)
syn. approaching, near, forthcoming, expected, coming
ant. distant, far-off

immodesty (n)
syn. audacity, coarseness, impudence, impurity, indecorum, shamelessness, obscenity
ant. modesty, humility, self-consciousness

immoral (adj)
syn. unethical, sinful, bad, corrupt, licentious, wrong, indecent
ant. moral, ethical, virtuous

immorality (n)
syn. corruption, vice, licentiousness, sin, indecency, unscrupulousness
ant. morality, virtue

immortal (adj)
syn. deathless, imperishable, undying, eternal, everlasting, perennial, perpetual
ant. mortal, ephemeral, perishable

immunity (n)
syn. protection, resistance, freedom, exemption
ant. liability, susceptibility

impair (v)
syn. reduce, harm, weaken, decrease
ant. enhance, improve

impart (v)
syn. communicate, disclose, make known, tell, pass on, give, confer, contribute
ant. suppress, withhold
impartial (adj)
syn. unbiased, neutral, disinterested, objective, fair, unprejudiced
ant. biased, prejudiced, partisan
impasse (n)
syn. dead end, deadlock, halt, standoff, standstill, stalemate
ant. progress
impassioned (adj)
syn. enthusiastic, animated, excited, furious, heated, passionate, inspired, warm, violent, zealous
ant. cool, apathetic, mild
impassive (adj)
syn. impassible, unemotional, cool, reserved, composed, apathetic, dispassionate, unconcerned, unfeeling
ant. warm, responsive, moved, susceptible
impeach (v)
syn. accuse, charge, indict, blame, censure, denounce, question, challenge, discredit
ant. vindicate, excuse, absolve
impeccable (adj)
syn. perfect, faultless, flawless, exemplary, blameless
ant. imperfect, flawed
impede (v)
syn. prevent, obstruct, interfere with, delay, hamper, disrupt, hinder, stop
ant. facilitate, aid, assist
impediment (n)
syn. bar, obstruction, hindrance, obstacle, restriction, block, defect, stammer
ant. aid, assistance
impel (v)
syn. compel, persuade, force, incite, influence, induce, instigate, inspire, motivate, urge
ant. dissuade, deter, restrain, discourage
impending (adj)
syn. approaching, imminent, coming, forthcoming, near, threatening, menacing

ant. remote
impenitent (adj)
syn. unrepentant, unabashed, defiant, unashamed, unremorseful, incorrigible, hardened
ant. penitent, repentant, sorry
imperative (adj)
syn. crucial, urgent, vital, necessary, authoritative, lordly, commanding
ant. unimportant, humble
imperceptible (adj)
syn. unnoticeable, invisible, indiscernible, inaudible, tiny, microscopic, faint, shadowy, slight
ant. perceptible, noticeable
imperial (adj)
syn. royal, regal, noble, exalted, majestic, great, grand, magnificent, supreme, august
ant. lowly, humble, modest, obscure
imperil (v)
syn. endanger, risk, expose, hazard, threaten, jeopardize
ant. protect, save
imperious (adj)
syn. bossy, arrogant, despotic, authoritarian, domineering, autocratic, commanding, dictatorial
ant. humble, gentle, considerate
impersonal (adj)
syn. unfriendly, detached, formal, aloof, businesslike, dispassionate, stiff, official
ant. personal, friendly
impertinent (adj)
syn. impolite, ill-mannered, rude, insolent, disrespectful
ant. polite, respectful
imperturbable (adj)
syn. calm, composed, placid, self-possessed, impassive, cool, unmoved, complacent, unexcitable
ant. agitated, jittery, nervous, anxious
impetuous (adj)
syn. rash, reckless, impulsive, ill-considered, hasty, passionate, thoughtless, heedless, furious, violent
ant. cautious, circumspect, considered

impetus (n)
syn. force, energy, push, momentum, inspiration, motivation, driving force
ant. discouragement, prevention

impiety (n)
syn. blasphemy, profanity, unholiness, wickedness, godlessness, irreligion, ungodliness, irreverence, sin, sacrilege, vice
ant. piety, devotion, piousness, holiness

implacable (adj)
syn. unbending, cruel, merciless, ruthless, unforgiving, inflexible, unrelenting, adamant
ant. merciful, kind, humane

implant (v)
syn. inculcate, infuse, insert, instil, plant, sow, plant
ant. eradicate

implement (v)
syn. execute, enact, perform, apply, carry out, discharge, perfect, accomplish
ant. abolish, cancel

implausible (adj)
syn. doubtful, unlikely, unconvincing
ant. convincing

implicate (v)
syn. associate, connect, involve, enmesh, incriminate
ant. absolve, exonerate

implicit (adj)
syn. implied, understood, suggested, hinted at, incorporated, inherent, complete, absolute, unconditional, firm, wholehearted
ant. explicit, open, reserved, definite

implicitly (adv)
syn. unconditionally, absolutely, utterly, unhesitatingly
ant. explicitly, openly, definitely

implied (adj)
syn. assumed, implicit, indirect, understood, unexpressed, hinted, tacit
ant. stated, declared

implore (v)
syn. plead, beg, ask, solicit, pray, beseech, petition
ant. demand, suggest

imply (v)
syn. suggest, denote, indicate, intimate, connote, hint, mean, involve
ant. state, declare

impolite (adj)
syn. bad-mannered, coarse, rude, ill-mannered, uncivil, insolent, discourteous, disrespectful, impertinent
ant. polite, courteous, genteel, elegant

impolitic (adj)
syn. foolish, imprudent, ill-advised, injudicious, unwise, undiplomatic, maladroit, rash, indiscreet
ant. politic, wise, prudent, diplomatic, discreet

importance (n)
syn. significance, note, gravity, seriousness, eminence, power, status, worth
ant. unimportance, insignificance

impose (v)
syn. press, force, foist, enforce, levy, charge, introduce, establish
ant. abolish, lift

imposing (adj)
syn. spectacular, impressive, commanding, striking, majestic, grand, awesome, effective
ant. modest, unimposing, insignificant

imposter (n)
syn. cheat, deceiver, fake, impersonator, fraud, hoaxer, swindler, hypocrite, phoney
ant. saint, gentleman, worthy

imposture (n)
syn. fraud, imposition, deception, artifice, hoax, cheat, swindle
ant. honesty

impotent (adj)
syn. helpless, incapable, powerless, unmanned
ant. strong, potent

impotence (n)
syn. helplessness, incapacity, disability, inability, inefficiency, weakness
ant. strength

impoverished (adj)
syn. poor, penniless, poverty-stricken, ruined, needy, destitute, bankrupt, exhausted, sterile, spent, depleted
ant. rich, wealthy

impractical (adj)
syn. unrealistic, idealistic, unfeasible, absurd, crazy, inappropriate, unsuitable
ant. realistic, practical

imprecation (n)
syn. curse, abuse, denunciation, vilification, profanity, malediction, slander, blasphemy
ant. blessing, grace, praise

impress (v)
syn. affect, influence, excite, move
ant. disappoint

impressive (adj)
syn. effective, imposing, touching, affecting, striking
ant. unimpressive

imprison (v)
syn. confine, lock up, jail, detain, cage
ant. free, release

imprisonment (n)
syn. confinement, detention, custody, duress, porridge
ant. freedom

improbable (adj)
syn. unlikely, uncertain, doubtful, unconvincing, implausible
ant. probable, likely

impromptu (adj)
syn. extempore, unprepared, unrehearsed, spontaneous, unplanned, unstudied, extemporary
ant. prepared, rehearsed, planned

impropriety (n)
syn. blunder, bad taste, indecency, immodest, indecorousness, indecorum, mistake, vulgarity, unsuitability
ant. propriety, decency, decorum, modesty

improve (v)
syn. boost, refine, make better, upgrade, progress, get better, recover, revive, enhance, rectify
ant. worsen, deteriorate, decline, diminish

improvement (n)
syn. development, upgrade, advance, betterment, enhancement, augmentation, amelioration, progress

ant. decline, deterioration, retrogression

improvident (adj)
syn. lavish, spendthrift, thriftless, extravagant, imprudent, careless, prodigal, reckless, heedless, rash, incautious
ant. provident, thrifty, economical, prudent, saving

impudence (n)
syn. rudeness, insolence, impertinence, audacity, disrespect, shamelessness, boldness, presumption
ant. politeness

impulse (n)
syn. impetus, stimulus, motive, force, incitement, urge, instinct, feeling, passion, rashness, recklessness
ant. discouragement, prevention, cautiousness

impunity (n)
syn. freedom, liberty, exemption, dispensation, permission, licence
ant. liability, accountability, responsibility

impure (adj)
syn. polluted, mixed, dirty, unclean, foul, unchaste, corrupt, lewd, coarse, indecent, immoral
ant. pure, chaste, decent

imputation (n)
syn. accusation, attribution, aspersion, blame, charge, slander, reproach, slur, censure
ant. commendation, praise, accolade

inactivity (n)
syn. inaction, idleness, inertia, apathy, indolence, dormancy, lethargy
ant. action, activeness

inadvertence (n)
syn. inattention, thoughtlessness, oversight, error, negligence, blunder, heedlessness
ant. attention, heed, alertness

inadvertently (adv)
syn. unintentionally, accidentally, by mistake
ant. intentionally

inadvisable (adj)
syn. ill-advised, ill-judged, foolish, imprudent, injudicious, unwise, indiscreet
ant. advisable, judicious, sound

inane (adj)
syn. foolish, stupid, idiotic, senseless, silly, unintelligent, worthless
ant. sensible, wise

inapposite (adj)
syn. inappropriate, unfit, unsuitable, impertinent, inapplicable, irrelevant, inapt
ant. apposite, appropriate, relevant

inapt (adj)
syn. inappropriate, inapposite, unsuitable, unfit
ant. appropriate, suitable

inaptitude (n)
syn. incompetence, inaptness, clumsiness, unsuitableness
ant. competence, aptitude

inattention (n)
syn. absent-mindedness, absence of mind, forgetfulness, inattentiveness, preoccupation, disregard, carelessness
ant. attentiveness, care

inaudible (adj)
syn. unclear, low, muted, indistinct, faint, murmured
ant. audible

inauspicious (adj)
syn. discouraging, ominous, unfavourable, untoward, unlucky, unfortunate
ant. auspicious, promising, favourable

inborn (adj)
syn. hereditary, inherent, innate, natural, instinctive
ant. learned, acquired

incapable (adj)
syn. inept, incompetent, unfit, ineffective, unqualified, weak, powerless
ant. capable, competent

incarcerate (v)
syn. jail, cage, imprison, lock up, confine
ant. free, release

incarceration (n)
syn. jail, imprisonment, confinement, detention, captivity, bondage
ant. freedom, release

incautious (adj)
syn. careless, heedless, imprudent, negligent, impulsive, unwise, rash, indiscreet

ant. cautious, alert, prudent

incense (v)

syn. anger, provoke, enrage, antagonize, irritate, inflame, rouse

ant. pacify, placate, calm

incentive (n)

syn. encouragement, inducement, bait, motivation, impulse, enticement, reward

ant. disincentive, deterrent

inception (n)

syn. commencement, dawn, beginning, initiation, birth, rise

ant. end, abolition

incessant (adj)

syn. continuous, uninterrupted, ceaseless, constant, everlasting, endless, unending, perpetual, never-ending, non-stop

ant. intermittent, irregular, sporadic, occasional

inchoate (adj)

syn. beginning, incipient, elementary, undeveloped, commencing, embryonic

ant. finished, complete, developed

incipient (adj)

syn. inchoate, beginning, developing, commencing, embryonic, starting

ant. finished, complete, developed

incisive (adj)

syn. sharp, acute, cutting, acid, biting, caustic, satirical, sarcastic

ant. unincisive, mild

incite (v)

syn. inflame, excite, provoke, instigate, encourage, rouse, inflame

ant. deter, discourage, restrain

incivility (n)

syn. bad manners, impoliteness, coarseness, disrespect, rudeness, discourtesy, boorishness, churlishness

ant. civility, politeness, courtesy

inclement (adj)

syn. cruel, merciless, harsh, unfeeling, rough, stormy, bad, foul, severe

ant. clement, kind, mild

inclination (n)

syn. desire, leaning, fondness, liking, tendency, taste

ant. disinclination, aversion

inclined (adj)
syn. likely, prone, willing, liable, sloping
ant. unlikely, flat
include (v)
syn. add, incorporate, comprise, put in, allow for
ant. exclude, omit, leave out
inclusion (n)
syn. addition, involvement, incorporation, insertion
ant. exclusion
incognito (adj)
syn. disguised, veiled, masked, in disguise, unrecognized, undercover
ant. undisguised, open
incoherent (adj)
syn. unconnected, disjoined, disordered, confused, illogical, inconsistent, unintelligible, unorganized
ant. coherent, connected, planned, orderly, organized
incommensurate (adj)
syn. disproportionate, unequal, insufficient, extreme, excessive
ant. commensurate, appropriate
incommunicable (adj)
syn. inexpressible, unspeakable, indescribable, ineffable
ant. expressible, communicable
incomparable (adj)
syn. matchless, brilliant, superb, supreme, unmatched, unique
ant. ordinary, poor, run-of-the-mill
incompatible (adj)
syn. contradictory, opposed, mismatched, opposite, unsuitable, antipathetic, antagonistic
ant. compatible, consistent, harmonious
incompetence (n)
syn. incompetency, inability, inefficiency, ineptness, incapability, bungling, unfitness
ant. competency, ability, efficiency, aptitude
incompetent (adj)
syn. inept, inexpert, unprofessional, unskilled, bungling, clumsy, useless
ant. competent, expert, skilled, adept
incomprehensible (adj)
syn. unclear, unintelligible, difficult, abstruse, obscure, incoherent,

inconceivable, enigmatic, unthinkable
ant. comprehensible, understandable, intelligible, clear, plain
incongruity (n)
syn. conflict, inconsistency, disparity, discrepancy, unsuitability, inharmoniousness
ant. consistency, harmoniousness
inconsiderable (adj)
syn. small, minor, slight, insignificant, negligible, unimportant, petty, trivial
ant. considerable, important
inconsistent (adj)
syn. conflicting, incompatible, contradictory, at odds, incongruous, changeable, inconstant, fickle, unstable
ant. consistent, constant, stable
inconsolable (adj)
syn. heartbroken, broken-hearted, desolated, hopeless, forlorn
ant. consolable, cheerful, happy
inconstant (adj)
syn. changeable, variable, uncertain, unstable, unsteady, erratic, inconsistent, fickle, unreliable
ant. constant, steady, reliable
incontinent (adj)
syn. uncontrolled, uncontrollable, unrestrained, ungovernable, unchecked, lustful, licentious, promiscuous, unchaste
ant. controlled, chaste
incontrovertible (adj)
syn. certain, established, indisputable, unquestionable, positive, sure
ant. controvertible, uncertain, dubious
inconvenience (n)
syn. trouble, nuisance, bother, disturbance, difficulty, awkwardness, untimeliness, inopportuneness, unsuitableness
ant. help, convenience
inconvenient (adj)
syn. awkward, badly timed, troublesome, annoying, difficult, unsuitable
ant, convenient, suitable
incorporate (v)
syn. amalgamate, absorb, blend, include, combine
ant. separate, split off

incorporeal (adj)
syn. immaterial, spiritual, disembodied, insubstantial
ant. material
incorrigible (adj)
syn. incurable, unreformable, unteachable, hopeless, hardened, irredeemable, lost
ant. reformable, curable
incorruptible (adj)
syn. incorrupt, honest, trustworthy, upright, everlasting, imperishable, immortal, deathless
ant. corrupt, dishonest, perishable
increase (v)
syn. grow, expand, lengthen, augment, rise, raise, enhance, enlarge
ant. decrease, reduce
increase (n)
syn. growth, expansion, augmentation, increment, addition, boost, enlargement
ant. decrease, reduction
incredible (adj)
syn. amazing, unbelievable, unimaginable, wonderful, fantastic
ant. credible, believable
incredulity (n)
syn. disbelief, unbelief, doubt, scepticism, mistrust
ant. credulity, belief
incredulous (adj)
syn. disbelieving, unbelieving, doubtful, sceptical, mistrustful
ant. credulous, trustful
increment (n)
syn. expansion, addition, increase, growth, supplement
ant. decrease, reduction
incriminate (v)
syn. accuse, indict, blame, charge, inculpate, implicate, involve, impeach, stigmatize
ant. exonerate, vindicate, exculpate, excuse, pardon
inculcate (v)
syn. instil, infuse, implant, indoctrinate, impress, drill
ant. purge, remove, eliminate

inculpate (v)
syn. accuse, incriminate, blame, implicate, censure, charge, impeach, drag into, indict
ant. exculpate, exonerate, acquit, excuse

incumbent (adj)
syn. compulsory, mandatory, obligatory, necessary, binding
ant. optional

incur (v)
syn. bring on yourself, earn, meet with, provoke, run up, suffer, expose oneself to
ant. avoid, prevent

incurable (adj)
syn. irremediable, inoperable, hopeless, hardened, incorrigible
ant. curable

incursion (n)
syn. attack, invasion, raid, infiltration, foray
ant. retreat, withdrawal

indebted (adj)
syn. grateful, thankful, in debt, beholden, obliged, obligated
ant. ungrateful, thankless, selfish

indecency (n)
syn. immodesty, indecorum, impropriety, licentiousness, lewdness, obscenity, coarseness, pornography
ant. decency, modesty, decorum, propriety

indecent (adj)
syn. coarse, lewd, vulgar, obscene, dirty, blue, improper, unseemly, indecorous, immodest, licentious
ant. decent, decorous, modest

indecipherable (adj)
syn. illegible, undecipherable, unintelligible, unreadable, unclear
ant. legible, readable

indecision (n)
syn. irresolution, uncertainty, indecisiveness, hesitation, doubt
ant. resolution, decisiveness

indecorous (adj)
syn. improper, ill-bred, vulgar, rude, immodest, indecent, churlish, unmannerly, undignified, boorish
ant. decorous, proper, decent, mannerly, dignified

indefatigable (adj)
syn. diligent, unfailing, tireless, undying, unresting, indomitable, persevering, assiduous, persistent
ant. indolent, lazy, slothful, flagging

indelible (adj)
syn. permanent, ineradicable, fixed, enduring, lasting
ant. impermanent, erasable

independence (n)
syn. freedom, liberty, autonomy, self-reliance, self-rule, self-sufficiency, individualism
ant. dependence

independent (adj)
syn. free, autonomous, unaided, sovereign, self-supporting, self-governing, absolute, impartial, neutral, unconnected, separate, privatized
ant. dependent, biased, related

indescribable (adj)
syn. incommunicable, inexpressible, beyond words, ineffable, unutterable
ant. describable, commonplace

indestructible (adj)
syn. unbreakable, imperishable, lasting, everlasting, enduring, durable, permanent
ant. breakable, perishable, mortal

indeterminate (adj)
syn. inexact, indefinite, imprecise, undetermined, undecided, unfixed, confused, vague
ant. determinate, exact, definite

indict (v)
syn. accuse, charge, impeach, prosecute, incriminate, inculpate
ant. exonerate, excuse, acquit, vindicate

indictment (n)
syn. accusation, allegation, charge, prosecution, impeachment, incrimination
ant. exoneration, excuse, acquittal, vindication

indifference (n)
syn. detachment, lack of interest, lack of concern, boredom, disinterest, apathy, callousness, inattention, dispassion
ant. concern, interest, bias

indifferent (adj)
syn. detached, uncaring, casual, unenthusiastic, uninterested, forgettable, mediocre, ordinary, impartial, unprejudiced, neutral
ant. concerned, brilliant, enthusiastic, biased, interested
indigenous (adj)
syn. local, original, native, inborn, inherent
ant. foreign, acquired
indigent (adj)
syn. poor, impoverished, needy, penniless, penurious, poverty-stricken
ant. rich, affluent
indignant (adj)
syn. annoyed, angry, furious, irate, mad, miffed, resentful, provoked
ant. pleased, calm, gratified
indignation (n)
syn. fury, anger, wrath, resentment, fury, annoyance, pique, vexation
ant. pleasure, composure, gratification
indignity (n)
syn. disrespect, dishonour, insult, humiliation, aspersion, outrage, abuse, incivility
ant. respect, honour
indiscernible (adj)
syn. invisible, hidden, indistinguishable, subtle, unapparent, indistinct, inconsiderable
ant. discernible, visible, clear, distinguishable
indiscreet (adj)
syn. incautious, rash, hasty, reckless, unwise, undiplomatic, tactless, unthinking, inconsiderate
ant. discreet, cautious, tactful, diplomatic, judicious
indiscretion (n)
syn. folly, foolishness, imprudence, rashness, recklessness, tactlessness, mistake
ant. discretion, caution, diplomacy, prudence
indispensable (adj)
syn. necessary, essential, needed, requisite, fundamental, crucial
ant. unnecessary, nonessential
indisposed[1] (adj)
syn. unwell, sick, ill, ailing, poorly
ant. well

indisposed² (adj)
syn. disinclined, reluctant, unwilling, loath, hesitant, averse
ant. inclined, eager
indisputable (adj)
syn. undeniable, unquestionable, irrefutable, absolute, certain, sure
ant. disputable, dubious, uncertain
indissoluble (adj)
syn. imperishable, permanent, indestructible, enduring, incorruptible, binding, fixed, unbreakable
ant. perishable, impermanent, breakable
indistinct (adj)
syn. dim, blurred, weak, indefinite, vague, unclear, confused, indistinguishable
ant. distinct, clear, definite
indistinguishable (adj)
syn. same, similar, identical, like, alike, twin, indistinct, invisible, indefinite, obscure
ant. distinguishable, different, conspicuous, clear, noticeable
individualism (n)
syn. egoism, free-thinking, anarchism, self-direction
ant. conventionality
indocile (adj)
syn. unruly, uncontrollable, unmanageable, ungovernable, headstrong, obstinate, stubborn, perverse, refractory
ant. docile, submissive, obedient, amenable, manageable
indoctrinate (v)
syn. inculcate, infuse, imbue, instil, teach, brainwash, instruct
ant. purge, remove, eliminate
indolence (n)
syn. laziness, lethargy, sloth, idleness, inertia, inactivity, languor
ant. activeness, diligence, enthusiasm
indolent (adj)
syn. lazy, lethargic, slothful, idle, apathetic, inactive, slow
ant. active, diligent, enthusiastic
indomitable (adj)
syn. bold, resolute, steadfast, intrepid, unbeatable, invincible, unwavering, staunch
ant. feeble, timid, compliant

inducement (n)
syn. incentive, motive, bait, impulse, persuasion, attraction, reward, lure, reason, encouragement
ant. disincentive, deterrent, discouragement, obstacle

induct (v)
syn. instal, initiate, introduce, inaugurate, invest
ant. oust

indulgence (n)
syn. satisfaction, excess, self-gratification, extravagance, pampering, luxury, tolerance, sympathy
ant. moderation, intolerance

indulgent (adj)
syn. easy-going, generous, tolerant, forgiving, kind, soft-hearted, understanding, compliant
ant. strict, moderate

industrious (adj)
syn. diligent, active, busy, hard-working, laborious, preserving, sedulous, assiduous, energetic
ant. lazy, indolent

inebriated (adj)
syn. drunk, befuddled, intoxicated, legless, tipsy, well-oiled
ant. sober

ineffable (adj)
syn. unspeakable, indescribable, inexpressible, beyond words
ant. commonplace, describable

ineffectual (adj)
syn. ineffective, futile, useless, fruitless, feeble, unproductive, incompetent, vain, powerless, impotent
ant. effectual, effective, efficient, productive, functional

inefficient (adj)
syn. inept, incompetent, ineffectual, wasteful, waste, inexpert
ant. efficient, competent, expert

inelegant (adj)
syn. unrefined, coarse, rude, crude, graceless, uncouth, clumsy, unsophisticated
ant. elegant, refined, polite, genteel

ineligible (adj)
syn. disqualified, unqualified, unacceptable, unsuitable, unfit

ant. eligible, qualified, fit

inept (adj)
syn. incompetent, inefficient, unskilful, absurd, inapt, unfit, clumsy
ant. competent, apt, adroit

inequality (n)
syn. disparity, disproportion, imbalance, unfairness, bias, prejudice, difference
ant. equality, impartiality, balance, objectivity

inert (adj)
syn. inactive, lazy, indolent, lethargic, dull, slow, motionless, apathetic
ant. active, alive, animated

inertia (n)
syn. inactivity, laziness, dullness, lethargy, stupor, indolence, sloth, apathy
ant. liveliness, activity

inevitable (adj)
syn. unavoidable, assured, certain, decreed, fated, destined, sure
ant. avoidable, uncertain

inexcusable (adj)
syn. unforgivable, unpardonable, unjustifiable, unacceptable, intolerable
ant. excusable, venial

inexorable (adj)
syn. adamant, harsh, cruel, merciless, remorseless, inflexible, unbending, implacable, uncompromising, relentless, irrevocable
ant. lenient, indulgent, flexible, yielding

inexpedient (adj)
syn. injudicious, imprudent, unwise, ill-advised, impolitic, indiscreet, misguided, foolish, senseless, unfavourable, disadvantageous
ant. expedient, judicious, prudent, wise

inexpensive (adj)
syn. cheap, low-priced, low-cost, affordable, economy, budget, cut-price
ant. expensive, dear, high-priced

inexperienced (adj)
syn. amateur, inexpert, green, fresh, untrained, unskilled
ant. experienced, expert

inexpert (adj)
syn. amateurish, clumsy, inept, unskilled, untrained
ant. expert, skilled

inexplicable (adj)
syn. unexplainable, baffling, incomprehensible, strange, enigmatic, unintelligible
ant. explicable, explainable, understandable
infallible (adj)
syn. sure, certain, reliable, perfect, unfailing, faultless, accurate
ant. fallible, imperfect, reliable
infamous (adj)
syn. scandalous, notorious, disgraceful
ant. glorious, reputable
infamy (n)
syn. dishonour, notoriety, disrepute, scandal, stigma, baseness, crime, disgrace, shame
ant. honour, glory, fame
infancy (n)
syn. early days, beginning, emergence, outset, birth, dawn, inception
ant. end, finish, close, conclusion, finale
infant (n)
syn. baby, young, newborn, child
ant. adult
infatuated (adj)
syn. fascinated, obsessed, mad, beguiled, captivated, bewitched, crazy, mesmerized, smitten
ant. disenchanted, indifferent, dispassionate, detached
infatuation (n)
syn. fascination, obsession, passion, captivation, madness, beguilement, fixation, crush
ant. disenchantment, indifference, detachment, boredom
infection (n)
syn. contamination, contagion, pollution, virus, influence, corruption
ant. asepsis
infelicitous (adj)
syn. ill-timed, unlucky, unfortunate, unfavourable, miserable, unhappy, unsuitable, inapt, unfit
ant. felicitous, timely, lucky, happy, appropriate
inference (n)
syn. assumption, guess, conclusion, presumption, surmise
ant. knowledge

inferior (adj)
syn. subordinate, lowly, unimportant, substandard, mediocre, poor, second-rate
ant. superior, excellent

infernal (adj)
syn. hellish, devilish, satanic, damnable, abominable, malicious
ant. heavenly, celestial

infertile (adj)
syn. barren, sterile, unproductive, unfruitful, dried-up
ant. fertile, productive

infertility (n)
syn. barrenness, sterility, unproductiveness, childlessness
ant. fertility, productiveness

infidel (n)
syn. iconoclast, atheist, disbeliever, pagan, sceptic, heretic, free-thinker, heathen
ant. believer

infinite (adj)
syn. unlimited, never-ending, boundless
ant. limited, finite

infirmity (n)
syn. feebleness, weakness, ill health, defect, disability, disorder, ailment, sickness
ant. strength, health

inflame (v)
syn. excite, incite, provoke, anger, animate, aggravate, intensify, increase
ant. pacify, cool, mitigate

inflammatory (adj)
syn. provocative, explosive, instigative, inflaming, riotous
ant. pacific, calming

inflate (v)
syn. amplify, blow out, increase, raise, hike up, expand
ant. lower, deflate

inflexible (adj)
syn. unbending, stiff, rigid, stubborn, adamant, resolute, unchangeable
ant. flexible, adjustable, amenable

influential (adj)
syn. powerful, controlling, significant, important, cogent

ant. insignificant, unimportant
informal (adj)
syn. casual, unofficial, vernacular, colloquial, familiar, idiomatic, slangy, unconventional
ant. formal, official, standard
informed (adj)
syn. educated, knowledgeable, learned, up to date, enlightened, familiar, well-read
ant. ignorant, unaware
infrequent (adj)
syn. rare, occasional, uncommon, unusual, sporadic, intermittent
ant. frequent, regular, constant, continuous
infuriate (v)
syn. anger, madden, provoke, enrage, vex, irritate, incense
ant. pacify, please, mollify
infuse (v)
syn. inculcate, implant, instil, imbue, introduce, inspire
ant. purge, remove, eliminate
ingenious (adj)
syn. innovative, creative, inventive, pioneering, clever, genius, shrewd, talented
ant. unimaginative, clumsy, stupid
ingenuity (n)
syn. innovativeness, creativity, inventiveness, cleverness, ingeniousness, shrewdness, genius, talent
ant. stupidity, clumsiness, dullness
ingenuous (adj)
syn. innocent, candid, open, simple, frank, childlike, trustful, honest
ant. sly, cunning, artful, crafty, dishonest
inglorious (adj)
syn. dishonourable, ignoble, base, humiliating, disreputable, infamous, humble, unknown
ant. glorious, famous
ingrain (v)
syn. instil, implant, infuse, imbue, impregnate, fix
ant. eradicate, purge
inhabitant (n)
syn. native, resident, denizen, citizen, tenant

ant. visitor
inhale (v)
syn. breathe in, whiff, sniff in, gasp, inspire
ant. exhale
inharmonious (adj)
syn. cacophonous, discordant, harsh, unmelodious, strident, clashing
ant. harmonious, melodious, friendly
inherent (adj)
syn. inborn, ingrained, natural, built-in, characteristic, intrinsic, hereditary
ant. extraneous, external, incidental
inherit (v)
syn. acquire, take over, be willed, receive, get succeed to
ant. bequeath, give, leave
inhibit (v)
syn. hinder, impede, interfere with, curb, stop, suppress, hold back, discourage, forbid, ban
ant. encourage, allow
inhibition (n)
syn. suppression, hindrance, prohibition, impediment, interference, obstruction, obstacle
ant. freedom, assistance
inimical (adj)
syn. unfavourable, antagonistic, hostile, opposed, unfriendly, contrary, harmful
ant. favourable, friendly
inimitable (adj)
syn. unique, matchless, incomparable, peerless, exceptionable, sublime, supreme, distinctive
ant. commonplace, common, ordinary
iniquity (n)
syn. sin, wickedness, offence, crime, evil, vice, wrong
ant. virtue, righteousness
initial (adj)
syn. first, beginning, introductory, opening, start
ant. final, last, closing
initiate (v)
syn. begin, commence, launch, set up, introduce, install, inculcate, coach
ant. end, expel

injudicious (adj)
syn. ill-judged, imprudent, foolish, incautious, hasty, indiscreet, unwise, stupid
ant. judicious, prudent, wise, sensible

injure (v)
syn. hurt, harm, wound, break, damage, spoil, blemish, tarnish
ant. benefit, help, aid, strengthen

injury (n)
syn. hurt, harm, wound, cut, damage, offence, injustice, insult, abuse
ant. reparation, compensation, restoration

inland (adj)
syn. internal, domestic, home, interior
ant. foreign

innate (adj)
syn. inborn, natural, inherited, inherent, instinctive, intrinsic, inbred, ingrained
ant. acquired, accidental, nurtured

innocent (adj)
syn. guiltless, blameless, honest, inculpable, not guilty, sinless, artless, trusting, impeccable, immaculate, harmless
ant. guilty, impure, injurious, mischievous

innocuous (adj)
syn. innocent, harmless, safe, inoffensive, bland
ant. harmful, troublesome

innovative (adj)
syn. enterprising, new, inventive, original, pioneering, ingenious, novel, ground breaking
ant. unimaginative, conservative

innumerable (adj)
syn. countless, incalculable, myriad, many, numerous
ant. few

inoffensive (adj)
syn. innocent, innocuous, unobjectionable, harmless, mild, gentle
ant. offensive, malicious

inordinate (adj)
syn. disproportionate, immoderate, exorbitant, excessive, extravagant, unreasonable, extreme
ant. moderate, restrained, reasonable

inquietude (n)
syn. anxiety, restlessness, unrest, uneasiness, apprehension, worry, disquiet, discomposure
ant. ease, quiet, composure

inquisitive (adj)
syn. curious, inquiring, eager, investigative, questioning, probing, snoopy
ant. uninquisitive, incurious, uninterested

insalubrious (adj)
syn. insanitary, dirty, unclean, unhealthy, unwholesome, unhygienic
ant. salubrious, healthy, hygienic

insane (adj)
(informal)
syn. psychotic, mad, crazy, stupid, foolish, daft, irrational
ant. sane, sensible, rational

insanity (n)
syn. madness, craziness, mental disorder, foolishness, folly, idiocy, stupidity
ant. sanity, sense, wisdom

insatiable (adj)
syn. greedy, unsatisfied, inordinate, immoderate, unappeaseable, voracious, gluttonous
ant. moderate, satisfied

inscribe (v)
syn. imprint, engrave, write, enlist, enter, register
ant. erase, delete

inscrutable (adj)
syn. incomprehensible, inexplicable, hidden, enigmatic, mysterious, unintelligible, baffling, unfathomable
ant. comprehensible, obvious, clear, expressive

insecure (adj)
syn. unsure, afraid, uncertain, perilous, unsafe, vulnerable, unstable, unsteady, weak
ant. confident, safe, stable

insensitive (adj)
syn. uncaring, unfeeling, callous, indifferent, hard, unsympathetic, unaffected
ant. caring, sensitive

insert (v)
syn. enter, put in, introduce, infuse, imbue, fix
ant. extract, detach

insidious (adj)
syn. cunning, treacherous, crafty, wily, deceptive, deceitful, subtle, stealthy, Machiavellian
ant. straightforward, candid, frank, honest

insight (n)
syn. intuition, understanding, perception, wisdom
ant. reasoning

insightful (adj)
syn. perceptive, observant, acute, astute, knowledgeable, intelligent
ant. superficial, shallow

insignificant (adj)
syn. unimportant, negligible, insubstantial, petty, paltry, irrelevant
ant. significant, important

insincere (adj)
syn. false, hollow, pretended, fake, hypocritical, phoney, dishonest, untruthful
ant. sincere, honest, truthful

insipid (adj)
syn. tasteless, bland, colourless, boring, dull, tedious, uninteresting, spiritless, lifeless, prosaic, characterless
ant. appetizing, tasty, high-spirited, exciting

insist (v)
syn. emphasize, stress, demand, assert, claim, maintain
ant. waive, deny

insobriety (n)
syn. intoxication, drunkenness, inebriety, excitement, frivolity, crapulence, intemperance
ant. sobriety, soberness, calmness, seriousness

insolence (n)
syn. arrogance, disrespect, offensiveness, abuse, rudeness, boldness, impudence, impertinence
ant. deference, respect, politeness

insolent (adj)
syn. arrogant, disrespectful, offensive, abusive, rude, bold, impudent, impertinent

ant. deferential, respectful, polite, courteous
insolvent (adj)
syn. bankrupt, beggared, ruined, defaulting, penniless
ant. rich, affluent
insomnia (n)
syn. sleeplessness, tension, stress, wakefulness, restlessness, insomnolence, inability to sleep
ant. sleep, slumber, rest, relaxation
inspiration (n)
syn. motivation, stimulus, encouragement, influence, enlightenment, creativity, imagination, brainstorm, bright idea
ant. deterrent, discouragement, hindrance, unimaginativeness
inspiring (adj)
syn. encouraging, heartening, exciting, moving, stimulating, uplifting
ant. uninspiring, discouraging, dull
inspirit (v)
syn. cheer, animate, inspire, excite, hearten, arouse, stimulate, gladden
ant. dispirit, depress, sadden
install (v)
syn. fix, put in, setup, place, introduce, induct, invest, reinstate
ant. oust, displace, depose
instantaneous (adj)
syn. quick, instant, immediate, on-the-spot, prompt, direct, unhesitating
ant. slow, late
instantly (adv)
syn. quickly, immediately, at once, without delay, right away, on the spot, directly
ant. slowly, eventually, later
instigate (v)
syn. provoke, incite, influence, encourage, rouse, initiate, impel, spur, goad, inflame
ant. suppress, curb, restrain
instil (v)
syn. infuse, infix, imbue, implant, introduce, inculcate, inject
ant. eradicate, purge, remove
instinct (n)
syn. intuition, feeling, inclination, sixth sense, ability, talent, skill, aptitude
ant. reason, ratiocination

instinctive (adj)
syn. natural, automatic, intuitive, innate, impulsive, inborn, unthinking, spontaneous, gut
ant. deliberate, voluntary, conscious, rational

institute (v)
syn. establish, initiate, begin, set up, found, launch, start, pioneer, install
ant. abolish, end, terminate

instructor (n)
syn. trainer, tutor, coach, teacher, counsellor, master, advisor, guide, guru
ant. pupil, student, trainee

insubordinate (adj)
syn. disobedient, defiant, refractory, rebellious, seditious, unruly, undisciplined
ant. docile, obedient, submissive

insufficient (adj)
syn. inadequate, wanting, deficient, short, lacking
ant. sufficient, excessive

insular (adj)
syn. narrow-minded, parochial, illiberal, detached, aloof, limited, provincial, prejudiced
ant. broad-minded, liberal, cosmopolitan

insult (n)
syn. abuse, jibe, slight, barb, aspersions, libel, slander, indignity, outrage, affront, contempt, insolence
ant. compliment, respect, honour, deference, homage

insurance (n)
syn. assurance, security, protection, indemnity, guarantee, providence, safeguard
ant. jeopardy, insecurity, peril

insurrection (n)
syn. revolution, uprising, revolt, mutiny, riot, insubordination, insurgency, coup
ant. subjugation, loyalty, obedience

intact (adj)
syn. perfect, undamaged, unbroken, unharmed, untouched, virgin, unviolated
ant. damaged, broken, harmed

intangible (adj)
syn. indefinable, vague, indefinite, insubstantial, imperceptible, unreal, invisible, dim
ant. tangible, definable, real, evident

integral (adj)
syn. whole, complete, total, essential, fundamental, intrinsic
ant. partial, non-essential

integrate (v)
syn. combine, mix, merge, join, unite, incorporate, amalgamate
ant. segregate, separate

integrity (n)
syn. fairness, sincerity, honesty, truthfulness, unity, soundness
ant. dishonesty, unreliability

intellect (n)
syn. reason, mind, sense, brain, brain power, understanding, intelligence
ant. stupidity, folly, foolishness

intellectual (n)
syn. academic, learned, highbrow, egghead, thinker, mastermind, scholar, genius
ant. dunce, lowbrow, fool, halfwit

intelligence (n)
syn. intellect, brain, comprehension, aptitude, acumen, sharpness, cleverness, sense, mind, knowledge, information
ant. stupidity, folly, foolishness

intelligent (adj)
syn. clever, bright, brainy, astute, smart, sharp, perceptive, insightful, genius, rational, wise, sensible
ant. unintelligent, stupid, foolish, unwise, senseless

intelligible (adj)
syn. understandable, comprehensible, clear, unambiguous, coherent, explicit
ant. unintelligible, vague, unclear

intemperate (adj)
syn. immoderate, extreme, excessive, uncontrolled, extravagant, self-indulgent, alcoholic, intoxicated, drunken
ant. temperate, moderate, controlled

intense (adj)
syn. extreme, acute, severe, strong, harsh, great, passionate, zealous,

impassioned, eager
ant. mild, calm, apathetic, unfeeling
intensify (n)
syn. extremity, severity, strength, greatness, power, passion, emotion, fervour, vehemence, fire, eagerness
ant. mildness, calmness, apathy, unfeelingness
intensive (adj)
syn. thorough, in-depth, exhaustive, detailed, meticulous, rigorous, comprehensive, deep
ant. superficial, shallow, cursory
intentional (adj)
syn. deliberate, intended, calculated, planned, conscious, wilful, purposeful
ant. unintentional, accidental, casual
intercept (v)
syn. stop, interrupt, block, obstruct, check, catch, curb
ant. allow, assist, release
interchangeable (adj)
syn. exchangeable, commutable, identical, similar
ant. different
interdict (n)
syn. prohibition, embargo, ban, veto, injunction, bar, proscription
ant. permission, sanction
interest (n)
syn. attentiveness, delight, curiosity, importance, relevance, hobby, pastime, recreation, passion, involvement
ant. disinterest, boredom, apathy, indifference
interested (adj)
syn. attentive, engaged, curious, fascinated, absorbed, involved, biased, partial, prejudiced
ant. uninterested, disinterested, indifferent, detached
interesting (adj)
syn. engrossing, absorbing, fascinating, enthralling, entertaining, gripping, amusing
ant. boring, dull, tedious, monotonous
interference (n)
syn. intervention, intrusion, meddling, disturbance, disruption, conflict
ant. assistance, forbearance

interim (adj)
syn. provisional, temporary, makeshift, acting, stand-in, stop-gap
ant. permanent, everlasting
interior (adj)
syn. internal, inner, inside, domestic, home, local, spiritual, personal, psychological
ant. exterior, external, extrinsic
interlink (v)
syn. interconnect, interlock, knit, link together, link, lock together
ant. separate
interlude (n)
syn. break, halt, hiatus, pause, interval, intermission, stop, rest, respite
ant. continuance, continuation, constancy
interminable (adj)
syn. unending, never-ending, endless, incessant, everlasting, boundless, eternal, limitless, boring, protracted, perpetual
ant. brief, limited, periodic, finished
intermingle (v)
syn. intermix, mix, combine, mingle, merge, amalgamate
ant. separate
intermission (n)
syn. interval, interlude, break, stop, respite, interruption, pause, lull
ant. continuance, continuation, constancy
intermittent (adj)
syn. discontinuous, irregular, periodic, sporadic, occasional, recurrent, broken
ant. continuous, constant, perpetual
internal (adj)
syn. inside, inner, inward, interior, domestic, national
ant. external, foreign
international (adj)
syn. global, universal, intercontinental, world, cosmopolitan, multinational, worldwide
ant. national, local
interpolate (v)
syn. add, introduce, insert, interject, enter
ant. delete, cancel

interpret (v)
syn. explain, clarify, expound, elucidate, define, decode, unravel, decipher
ant. mystify, misrepresent

interpretation (n)
syn. explanation, clarification, elucidation, analysis, version, exposition
ant. mystification, misrepresentation

interruption (n)
syn. disturbance, break, stoppage, disruption, discontinuance, hindrance, intrusion
ant. continuance, continuation

intimacy (n)
syn. rapport, attachment, closeness, warmth, friendliness
ant. formality

intimate[1] (adj)
syn. close, dear, bosom, firm, friendly, warm, informal, relaxed, cosy, secret, personal, thorough, detailed, in-depth
ant. distant, unfriendly, formal, cold, superficial

intimate[2] (v)
syn. disclose, announce, communicate, make known, reveal, suggest, imply, indicate
ant. conceal

intimate (n)
syn. associate, comrade, friend, crony, confident, bosom
ant. stranger, outsider

intimately (adv)
syn. closely, affectionately, familiarly, personally, confidentially, thoroughly
ant. coldly, distantly

intimidate (v)
syn. threaten, frighten, scare, browbeat, hound, bully, discourage, terrorize, coerce
ant. encourage, persuade, induce

intimidation (n)
syn. terror, terrorization, fear, threats, bullying, arm-twisting, browbeating, pressure
ant. encouragement, persuasion, inducement

intolerance (n)
syn. discrimination, bigotry, illiberality, xenophobia, jingoism, impatience, narrow-mindedness

ant. tolerance, forbearance, broad-mindedness

intoxicated (adj)

syn. drunk, excited, drunken, inebriated, legless, drunken

ant. sober

intoxication (n)

syn. drunkenness, inebriation, insobriety, inebriety, crapulence

ant. sobriety, soberness

intractable (adj)

syn. headstrong, stubborn, unmanageable, obstinate, indocile, difficult, unruly, insubordinate, perverse, bull-headed, uncooperative

ant. tractable, amenable, submissive, willing, docile

intransigent (adj)

syn. stubborn, intractable, uncompromising, obstinate, rigid, tough, unyielding, unbending, hardline

ant. amenable, submissive, willing, docile

intrepid (adj)

syn. unafraid, brave, fearless, courageous, heroic, bold, lion-hearted, stalwart, spirited, indomitable

ant. cowardly, timid, fearful, craven

intricate (adj)

syn. tangled, complex, elaborate, complicated

ant. simple, easy, uncomplicated

intrigue (v)

syn. attract, fascinate, charm, arouse, tantalize, interest

ant. bore

intrigue (n)

syn. plotting, conspiracy, collusion, scheming, double-dealing, conniving

ant. loyalty, faith

intriguing (adj)

syn. interesting, fascinating, beguiling, tantalizing, absorbing

ant. boring, uninteresting, dull

intrinsic (adj)

syn. basic, inherent, fundamental, essential, innate, inborn, genuine, real, natural

ant. extrinsic, external, added

introduction (n)

syn. initiation, institution, launch, presentation, meeting, preface, foreword, prelude, prologue, intro

ant. ending, conclusion, epilogue
introspection (n)
syn. self-analysis, heart-searching, soul-searching, self-examination, self-observation, self-questioning
ant. extrospection
introverted (adj)
syn. withdrawn, self-centred, introspective, contained
ant. extroverted
intrude (v)
syn. encroach, violate, interfere, meddle, trespass
ant. stand, back, withdraw
intuition (n)
syn. insight, instinct, sixth sense, knowledge, hunch, understanding, perception
ant. reason, reasoning
inundate (v)
syn. flood, submerge, engulf, deluge, overflow
ant. drain
invade (v)
syn. capture, annex, occupy, overrun, attack, violate, encroach
ant. liberate, leave
invalidate (v)
syn. nullify, cancel, quash, annul, repeal, weaken, overthrow, refute
ant. validate, certify, ratify
invaluable (adj)
syn. all-important, vital, valuable, indispensable, crucial
ant. worthless, dispensable
invariable (adj)
syn. unchangeable, changeless, unalterable, constant, consistent, unvarying
ant. variable, changeable
invasion (n)
syn. attack, aggression, annexation, incursion, foray, raid, offensive, trespass, intrusion, encroachment
ant. withdrawal, retreat, departure, recall
invective (n)
syn. abuse, censure, reproach, denunciation, sarcasm, castigation, revilement, scolding, vilification, obloquy
ant. praise, eulogy, glorification, accolade

inveigh (v)
syn. abuse, condemn, blame, denounce, protest, censure, reproach
ant. praise, eulogize, compliment

investigate (v)
syn. look into, probe, study, analyse, enquire into, examine, check out
ant. ignore, disregard, neglect

invigorate (v)
syn. energize, revitalize, rouse, revive, stimulate, exhilarate, pep up, animate
ant. enervate, tire, dishearten, weary

invincible (adj)
syn. unbeatable, invulnerable, inseparable, unyielding, unconquerable
ant. vulnerable, beatable

invisible (adj)
syn. unseen, out of sight, inconspicuous, concealed, hidden
ant. visible, conspicuous

inviting (adj)
syn. tempting, alluring, enticing, mouth-watering, appetizing, attractive, intriguing
ant. uninviting, repellent, repulsive

invocation (n)
syn. appeal, prayer, entreaty, petition
ant. order

invulnerable (adj)
syn. safe, secure, insusceptible, invincible
ant. vulnerable

inward (adj)
syn. inside, interior, inner, secret, internal, spiritual, incoming
ant. outward, external, outgoing

irascible (adj)
syn. bad-tempered, irritable, peevish, crabby, petulant, short-tempered, touchy, hasty, ill-natured
ant. placid, affable, friendly, sociable

irate (adj)
syn. angry, annoyed, enraged, furious, ireful, fuming, exasperated, incensed
ant. calm, placid, relaxed

ire (n)
(literary, formal)
syn. fury, anger, passion, rage, exasperation
ant. calmness, composure
iridescent (adj)
syn. glittering, shimmering, prismatic, rainbow-coloured, multicoloured
ant. dull, dim
irk (v)
(literary, formal)
syn. annoy, disgust, rile, irritate, provoke, vex
ant. please, delight
irksome (adj)
syn. troublesome, annoying, irritating, bothersome, vexations, boring, tedious
ant. pleasant, delightful
irony (n)
syn. sarcasm, derision, satire, mockery, ridicule, paradox, incongruity
ant. admiration, respect
irradiate (v)
syn. illuminate, brighten, enlighten
ant. darken
irrational (adj)
syn. unreasonable, illogical, absurd, stupid, foolish, senseless, ridiculous, unwise
ant. rational, logical, sensible, wise
irreconcilable (adj)
syn. conflicting, clashing, incompatible, opposed, uncompromising, inflexible, implacable
ant. reconcilable, compatible, appeaseable
irrecoverable (adj)
syn. unrecoverable, lost, irretrievable
ant. recoverable
irrefutable (adj)
syn. indisputable, certain, sure, invincible, unquestionable, undeniable, beyond question
ant. refutable, questionable
irregular (adj)
syn. inconstant, disorderly, variable, unsystematic, rough, crooked,

unequal, uneven, abnormal, odd, eccentric
ant. regular, level, smooth, normal
irrelevant (adj)
syn. unrelated, unconnected, inapt, impertinent, extraneous
ant. relevant, applicable, pertinent
irreligious (adj)
syn. atheistic, impious, godless, ungodly, profane, unbelieving, iconoclastic
ant. religious, pious
irreparable (adj)
syn. irrecoverable, beyond, repair, irremediable, incurable, irreclaimable
ant. reparable, remediable
irrepressible (adj)
syn. vivacious, lively, ebullient, high-spirited, full of life, animated, buoyant, uncontrollable
ant. repressible, depressed, despondent, dejected
irresistible (adj)
syn. compelling, overwhelming, fascinating, alluring, captivating, enchanting, uncontrollable, tempting
ant. resistible, avoidable, repulsive, disgusting
irresolute (adj)
syn. unresolved, undecided, uncertain, hesitant, inconstant, half-hearted, undetermined, weak
ant. resolute, resolved, determined, decided
irresponsible (adj)
syn. careless, light-hearted, unreliable, untrustworthy, rash, thoughtless
ant. responsible, dedicated, committed, trustworthy
irreverence (n)
syn. blasphemy, disrespect, impiety, profanity, mockery, derision, godlessness, impudence
ant. reverence, respect, honour, awe
irrevocable (adj)
syn. unchangeable, permanent, binding, final, irreversible, immutable, fixed
ant. revocable, alterable, reversible
irritable (adj)
syn. short-tempered, bad-tempered, grumpy, irascible, peevish, hasty, petulant, crabbed, ill-humoured, excitable
ant. cheerful, affable, good-humoured, complacent

irritate (v)
syn. anger, annoy, vex, hack off, hurt, inflame
ant. delight, please, soothe
irritation (n)
syn. anger, annoyance, vexation, displeasure, exasperation
ant. delight, pleasure, joy
irruption (n)
syn. invasion, foray, incursion, raid
ant. retreat
isolate (v)
syn. segregate, separate, detach, seclude, cut off, alienate, divorce, insulate, disconnect
ant. unite, integrate, incorporate, assimilate
isolation (n)
syn. friendlessness, loneliness, detachment, isolation, solitude, inaccessibility
ant. contact, company

Jj

jaded (adj)
syn. bored, dulled, exhausted, fatigued
ant. fresh, refreshed

jagged (adj)
syn. rough, spiky, barbed, broken, saw-edged, ragged, irregular
ant. smooth

jail (v)
syn. imprison, lock up, detain, confine, bang up
ant. release, acquit

jangle (n)
syn. clash, cacophony, jar, discord, din, rattle, dissonance
ant. euphony, harmony

jar (v)
syn. jerk, shake, disturb, agitate, jangle, clash, quarrel, disagree
ant. agree, consent

jar (n)
syn. jerk, shock, clash, agitation, jangle, discord, disagreement, cacophony
ant. euphony, harmony

jargon (n)
syn. idiom, slang, terminology, vocabulary, argot, usage, language, lingo, nonsense, balderdash
ant. formality

jaundiced (adj)
syn. cynical, biased, hostile, jealous, bitter, partial
ant. naive, fresh, optimistic

jealous (adj)
syn. envious, grudging, green, suspicious, protective, green-eyed, rival
ant. content, trusting

jealousy (n)
syn. envy, grudge, distrust, resentment, bitterness, suspicion, spite, heart-burning, the green-eyed monster
ant. contentment, happiness, trust

jeer (v)
syn. taunt, abuse, ridicule, tease, heckle, barrack, scorn, boo
ant. cheer, acclaim, applaud

jeopardize (v)
syn. risk, threaten, imperil, endanger, compromise
ant. protect, safeguard

jeopardy (n)
syn. danger, plight, peril, risk, insecurity
ant. safety, security

jest (n)
syn. joke, fun, quip, prank, play, hoax, banter
ant. seriousness, soberness

jettison (v)
syn. abandon, dump, ditch, discard, throw out
ant. retain

jibe (n)
syn. jeer, taunt, insult, ridicule, barb, quip, dig
ant. applause, cheer

jilt (v)
syn. abandon, leave, discard, throw over, forsake, reject, ditch, dump
ant. adopt, embrace, retain

jingoism (n)
syn. chauvinism, nationalism, flag-waving, xenophobia, insularity, parochialism, patriotism
ant. liberalism, moderation, tolerance, broadmindedness

jinx (n)
syn. curse, black magic, voodoo, the evil eye, spell, hex
ant. blessing, benediction

jitters (n)
syn. anxiety, nervousness, fidgets, the creeps, shivers, shakes, willies
ant. calmness, composure

jittery (adj)
(informal)
syn. anxious, nervous, fidgety, agitated, shaky, uneasy, shivery
ant. calm, composed

jocose (adj)
syn. jovial, merry, jesting, jocular, joking, humorous, funny, comical, sportive, witty

ant. melancholy, sorrowful, depressed, blue

jocular (adj)

syn. joking, comical, witty, funny, jocose, humorous, jesting, merry
ant. serious, sober

jolly (adj)

syn. cheery, gay, jovial, cheerful, happy, joyful, spirited, jocose, convivial
ant. sombre, miserable, sad

jovial (adj)

syn. cheerful, good-humoured, genial, sunny, cordial
ant. morose, miserable, sad

joviality (n)

syn. cheerfulness, gladness, happiness, glee, mirth
ant. sadness, merriment

joy (n)

syn. happiness, jubilation, delight, triumph, rejoicing, euphoria, ecstasy, pleasure
ant. misery, sorrow, mourning

jubilant (adj)

syn. joyful, overjoyed, thrilled, elated, ecstatic, rejoicing, over the moon
ant. despondent, depressed, mournful

jubilation (n)

syn. ecstasy, celebration, euphoria, elation, joy, exultation, festivity
ant. depression, mourning, lamentation

judicious (adj)

syn. wise, acute, sensible, prudent, reasonable, shrewd, careful, intelligent, sober
ant. injudicious, ill-advised

jumble (v)

syn. disorder, mix up, tangle, tumble, disarrange, muddle, confuse
ant. order, arrange

jumpy (adj)

(informal)

syn. tense, nervous, anxious, jittery, restless
ant. calm, composed

junior (adj)

syn. younger, minor, low-ranking, subordinate, inferior, lower
ant. senior, older

just (adj)
syn. impartial, unbiased, fair, disinterested, decent, honourable, upright, principled, rightful, deserved, appropriate
ant. unjust, unfair, inappropriate

justice (n)
syn. justness, fairness, impartiality, honesty, legality, propriety, morality, judge, magistrate, jurist
ant. injustice, defendant

justifiable (adj)
syn. justified, warranted, valid, just, defensible, acceptable, lawful, reasonable, vindicable, right
ant. unjustifiable, culpable, unwarranted

justification (n)
syn. vindication, rationale, defence, grounds, reason, exoneration, excuse, apology
ant. condemnation, accusation, blame

justify (v)
syn. vindicate, acquit, exculpate, substantiate, uphold, defend, explain, excuse
ant. condemn, accuse, blame

juvenile (n)
(law)
syn. adolescent, youngster, teenager, minor, child, kid
ant. adult

juxtaposition (n)
syn. nearness, closeness, adjacency, vicinity, proximity
ant. separation, dissociation

Kk

keen (adj)
syn. anxious, brilliant, eager, enthusiastic, acute, powerful, zealous, ambitious, diligent, sharp, incisive, shrewd, clever
ant. apathetic, reluctant, unenthusiastic, dull, stupid

keep (v)
syn. preserve, protect, maintain, obey, respect, fulfil, look after, support, withhold, carry on, continue, save, deposit, amass
ant. discard, break, neglect, cease, use

kid (n)
(informal)
syn. child, baby, youth, younger, girl, boy
ant. adult

kidnap (v)
syn. abduct, hijack, hold to ransom, capture
ant. free

kind (adj)
syn. kind-hearted, caring, kindly, warm, loving
ant. unkind

kind-hearted (adj)
syn. amicable, warm-hearted, compassionate, good-natured, humane, sympathetic, generous, gracious, humanitarian
ant. ill-natured, unkind, cruel, malicious, churlish

kindle (v)
syn. ignite, light, torch, stimulate, inspire, activate
ant. extinguish

kindly (adj)
syn. kind, benevolent, generous, kind-hearted, good-natured, compassionate, gentle, loving, considerate, warm
ant. ill-natured, unkind, cruel, malicious, churlish

kindness (n)
syn. affection, gentleness, kindliness, altruism, benevolence, sympathy, compassion, generosity, car
ant. unkindness, cruelty, inhumanity

king (n)
syn. ruler, monarch, majesty, supremo, chief
ant. subject
kingly (adv)
syn. royal, majestic, princely, regal, noble, grand, imperial, august
ant. lowly, humble, simple
knack (n)
(informal)
syn. talent, ability, gift, instinct, aptitude, capability, tendency, habit
ant. inability, incapability, ineptitude
knavery (n)
syn. dishonesty, fraud, deception, rascality, deceit, trickery, duplicity
ant. honesty, truthfulness, morality
knavish (adj)
syn. dishonest, fraudulent, deceitful, unscrupulous, tricky, unprincipled, roguish
ant. honest, virtuous, principled
knit (v)
syn. join, unite, fuse, merge, link, blend, unify
ant. separate
knock (v)
syn. hit, strike, beat, bump, slap, criticize, find fault, slam
ant. praise
knockout (n)
syn. bestseller, hit, smash, sensation, success, winner, stunner
ant. flop, loser
knot (v)
syn. bind, tie, knit, ravel, entangle
ant. untie
knotty (adj)
syn. complex, difficult, complicated, puzzling, rough, nodular
ant. simple, smooth
knowing (adj)
syn. sharp, clever, shrewd, sagacious, cunning, aware, perceptive, significant, meaningful, intentional, conscious
ant. artless, ignorant, unconscious
knowledge (n)
syn. comprehension, mastery, understanding, learning, scholarship, awareness

ant. ignorance
kudos (n)
syn. honour, prestige, glory, esteem, admiration, respect, status, fame, applause, praise
ant. disgrace, dishonour, shame, reproach

laborious (adj)
syn. onerous, difficult, tough, laboured, diligent, sedulous, thorough
ant. easy, effortless, indolent

labour (n)
syn. work, donkey-work, exertion, pains, sweat, effort, industry, toil
ant. idleness, ease, relaxation, leisure

labour (v)
syn. work, struggle, toil, strive, slog away
ant. rest, idle

labyrinth (n)
syn. complication, complexity, confusion, entanglement, intricacy, perplexity, maze
ant. simplicity, straight forwardness

labyrinthine (adj)
syn. twisting, meandering, complicated, confusing, intricate, puzzling, perplexing
ant. simple, straightforward

lacerate (v)
syn. cut, mutilate, tear, gash, hurt
ant. mend

lachrymose (adj)
syn. tearful, sad, dolorous, mournful, crying, weeping, woeful
ant. cheerful, happy, laughing

lack (n)
syn. dearth, absence, deficiency, shortage, void, need
ant. abundance, profusion

lack (v)
syn. require, need, want, be without, miss
ant. have

lacklustre (adj)
syn. uninspiring, uninspired, unimaginative, humdrum, dull, insipid, lifeless, prosaic, sombre
ant. inspired, brilliant, polished

laconic (adj)
syn. short, brief, terse, crisp, taciturn, concise, compact
ant. wordy, verbose, garrulous
lad (n)
(old-fashioned, informal)
syn. youngster, boy, juvenile, dude, chap, guy
ant. adult
laden (adj)
syn. loaded, overloaded, burdened, full
ant. empty
ladylike (adj)
(old-fashioned)
syn. elegant, genteel, polite, refined, mannerly, decorous
ant. unseemly, indecorous
lag (v)
syn. fall behind, hang back, delay, trail
ant. hurry, lead
laid-back (adj)
syn. relaxed, free and easy, unconcerned, calm, cool, leisurely, chilled
ant. uptight, tense
lambaste (v)
(also lambast)
syn. beat, flay, rebuke, scold, reprimand, thrash
ant. praise
lame (adj)
syn. crippled, limping, disabled, feeble, weak, implausible, poor
ant. strong
lament (v)
syn. grieve, mourn, keen, deplore, sorrow, rue
ant. celebrate, rejoice, welcome
languid (adj)
syn. feeble, week, languishing, tired, lethargic, sluggish, unenthusiastic, apathetic, uninterested
ant. strong, spirited, lively, vivacious
languish (v)
syn. grieve, decline, deteriorate, waste away, suffer
ant. flourish, thrive

languor (n)
syn. feebleness, weakness, tiredness, weariness, fatigue, lethargy, apathy, torpor, sleepiness, stillness, calm
ant. energy, enthusiasm, alacrity, gusto

lank (adj)
syn. dull, lifeless, slim, thin, bony, skinny, lanky, drooping, flaccid
ant. burly, dumpy

lapse (n)
syn. decline, fall, omission, failing, interval, pause, break
ant. improvement, continuation

large (adj)
syn. big, substantial, huge, great, immense, heavy, burly, mega, jumbo
ant. small, tiny, little

largely (adv)
syn. principally, mainly, greatly, by and large, mostly
ant. partly

lascivious (adj)
syn. lustful, lecherous, lewd, salacious, unchaste, randy, sensual, blue, obscene, pornographic, dirty
ant. chaste, decent, virtuous

lassitude (n)
syn. lethargy, apathy, languor, weariness, sluggishness, tiredness, dullness, fatigue
ant. vigour, energy

last (adj)
syn. concluding, final, ultimate, extreme, latest
ant. first

lasting (adj)
syn. long-lived, enduring, eternal, everlasting, durable, permanent, constant, persisting, strong
ant. transient, ephemeral, passing, short lived

latent (adj)
syn. hidden, undeveloped, potential, concealed, invisible, unexpressed, unrealized, unseen, secret
ant. conspicuous, live, active

later (adj)
syn. following, subsequent, next, upcoming, succeeding
ant. earlier, preceding

latitude (n)
syn. freedom, liberty, licence, independence
ant. restriction
latter (adj)
syn. last-mentioned, last, later, second, final
ant. earlier, former
laud (v)
syn. applaud, extol, hail, praise, acclaim, glorify, honour, magnify
ant. blame, curse, decry, damn, condemn
laudable (adj)
syn. praiseworthy, admirable, commendable, exemplary, worthy
ant. shameful, blameworthy
laughter (n)
syn. laughing, tittering, giggling, amusement, mirth, glee, merriment
ant. crying, gloom
lawless (adj)
syn. unruly, anarchic, riotous, rebellious, chaotic, mutinous
ant. law-abiding, lawful
lawlessness (n)
syn. disorder, anarchy, insurgency, chaos
ant. order
laxity (n)
syn. laxness, negligence, freedom, licence, permissiveness, slackness
ant. strictness
laziness (n)
syn. indolence, idleness, sluggishness, sloth
ant. industriousness
lavish (adj)
syn. luxurious, expensive, grand, liberal, wasteful, sumptuous, abundant, copious
ant. frugal, meagre, economical, scant
lazy (adj)
syn. drowsy, lethargic, sleepy, indolent, slow, slothful, inactive
ant. industrious, active, diligent
lead (v)
syn. guide, escort, accompany, cause, prompt, control, be ahead, outrun, live
ant. follow

leader (n)
syn. head, chief, captain, chair, manager, principal, premier, master, monarch, boss
ant. follower, supporter
leading (adj)
syn. main, top, prime, chief, greatest, foremost, central, star
ant. minor, subordinate
lean (adj)
syn. slim, thin, slender, bony, skinny, lank, meagre, barren, poor, scanty
ant. fat, fleshy, rich, abundant
leaning (n)
syn. tendency, inclination, preference, prosperity, penchant, predisposition
ant. avoidance, dislike
leap (v)
syn. jump, hop, skip, rise, surge, increase
ant. drop, fall
learned (adj)
syn. scholarly, academic, knowledgeable, erudite, intellectual, cultured, bookish, genius, brainy
ant. ignorant, uneducated, illiterate
learner (n)
syn. novice, trainee, student, pupil, neophyte, rookie
ant. expert, veteran
learning (n)
syn. study, education, scholarship, schooling, erudition, tuition, wisdom, understanding
ant. ignorance
least (adj)
syn. slightest, smallest, poorest, lowest
ant. most
leave (v)
syn. depart, quit, go, disappear, set out
ant. arrive
lecherous (adj)
syn. lustful, unchaste, lewd, salacious, concupiscent, licentious, lascivious, randy
ant. chaste, decent, virtuous

lechery (n)
syn. lustfulness, lewdness, salaciousness, licentiousness, carnality, lust, profligacy, womanizing, randiness
ant. chastity, decency, virtue
left-wing (adj)
syn. communist, socialist, labour, leftist, lefty, red
ant. right-wing, conservative
legal (adj)
syn. lawful, valid, licensed, legitimate, allowable, permissible, judicial
ant. illegal
legalize (v)
syn. authorize, legitimize, license, allow, permit
ant. veto
legend (n)
syn. myth, epic, saga, fable, folk tale, mythology, celebrity, icon, star, inscription
ant. history, obscurity
legendary (adj)
syn. mythical, fabled, fabulous, fanciful, fictitious, famous, celebrated
ant. historical, obscure, unknown
legible (adj)
syn. intelligible, clear, neat, readable
ant. illegible
legitimate (adj)
syn. legal, permitted, licensed, lawful, valid, proper, authorized
ant. illegitimate, invalid, illegal
leisure (n)
syn. relaxation, rest, time off, break, holiday, ease
ant. work.
leisurely (adj)
syn. relaxed, unhurried, sedate, slow, restful, comfortable
ant. hurried, hasty
lengthy (adj)
syn. long, prolonged, extended, verbose, wordy, long-winded, protracted
ant. short
leniency (n)
syn. mercy, compassion, mildness, softness, tolerance, clemency
ant. severity

lend (v)
syn. loan, advance, provide, add, contribute, give, lease
ant. borrow
lenient (adj)
syn. merciful, compassionate, easy-going, humane, forgiving, tolerant
ant. strict, severe
lenitive (adj)
syn. soothing, balmy, emollient, mitigative, alleviating
ant. irritant
lessen (v)
syn. reduce, minimize, decrease, allay, alleviate, diminish, subside, decline, ease off, recede
ant. increase
lesser (adj)
syn. minor, lower, less important, subsidiary, second-class, inferior, lowly, subordinate
ant. greater, superior
let (v)
syn. allow, permit, sanction, license, enable, grant, rent
ant. prevent, prohibit
let-down (n)
(informal)
syn. disappointment, comedown, anticlimax, fiasco, washout
ant. success, boost
lethal (adj)
syn. deadly, dangerous, fatal, life-threatening, toxic
ant. safe, harmless
lethargic (adj)
syn. lazy, inactive, lifeless, sluggish, apathetic, drowsy, sleepy
ant. energetic, lively
lethargy (n)
syn. laziness, dullness, apathy, inertia, drowsiness, sleepiness, sluggishness
ant. liveliness, vitality
lettered (adj)
syn. well-read, educated, literate, learned, erudite, scholarly, cultured
ant. ignorant
let-up (n)
syn. breather, pause, lull, break, interval, respite, remission

ant. continuation
levity (n)
syn. silliness, light-heartedness, frivolity, triviality, flippancy, giddiness
ant. seriousness, gravity, sobriety
lewd (adj)
syn. blue, indecent, dirty, loose, lustful, obscene, vulgar, bawdy
ant. decorous, polite, chaste
liabilities (n)
syn. debts, duties, responsibilities, obligations
ant. assets
liable (adj)
syn. accountable, responsible, answerable, exposed, subject, open, likely, apt, probable
ant. unaccountable, unlikely
libel (n)
syn. slander, slur, vilification, character assassination, misrepresentation, obloquy, defamation (of character), mud-slinging
ant. praise, eulogy
liberal (adj)
syn. broad-minded, tolerant, easy-going, modern, flexible, generous, unselfish
ant. narrow-minded, strict, reactionary
liberalism (n)
syn. free-thinking, progressivism, humanitarianism, radicalism, latitudinarianism
ant. conservatism, narrow-mindedness
liberality (n)
syn. broad-mindedness, open-mindedness, tolerance, latitude, permissiveness, kindness, profusion, generosity
ant. illiberality, narrow-mindedness, meanness
liberate (v)
syn. free, release, emancipate, discharge, let out, rescue
ant. imprison, confine, enslave
liberation (n)
syn. liberty, freedom, release, emancipation, unfettering
ant. imprisonment, enslavement
liberty (n)
syn. freedom, autonomy, sovereignty, independence, privilege

ant. slavery, servitude
libidinous (adj)
syn. lustful, unchaste, lecherous, sensual, salacious, lascivious, carnal, lewd, loose, randy
ant. chaste, modest, temperate
licence (n)
syn. permission, certificate, right, freedom, franchise
ant. prohibition, restriction
licentiousness (n)
syn. lust, lewdness, promiscuity, abandon, debauchery, salacity
ant. modesty
lifelike (adj)
syn. graphic, exact, pictorial, true, realistic, vivid, true-to-life, expressive
ant. unnatural, inexact
lighten^1 (v)
syn. brighten, light up, illumine
ant. darken
lighten^2 (v)
syn. reduce, decrease, cheer, encourage, inspire, restore
ant. increase, depress
light-headed (adj)
syn. fickle, foolish, bird-brained, silly, superficial, thoughtless
ant. sober
light-hearted (adj)
syn. cheerful, carefree, amusing, elated, gay, jovial
ant. miserable, sad, serious
likeable (adj)
syn. agreeable, pleasant, genial, friendly, good-natured, congenial, amiable
ant. unpleasant, disagreeable
likelihood (n)
syn. possibility, chance, probability, hope, threat, prospect
ant. unlikeliness
likely (adj)
syn. possible, probable, anticipated, plausible, acceptable, believable, appropriate
ant. unlikely, implausible, inappropriate
like-minded (adj)
syn. agreeing, unanimous, in accord, in agreement, of the same mind

ant. disagreeing
liken (v)
syn. compare, associate, equate, relate
ant. contrast
likeness (n)
syn. similitude, resemblance, similarity, depiction, sketch, representation, picture
ant. unlikeness, dissimilarity
likewise (adv)
syn. also, moreover, too, besides, furthermore, similarly
ant. otherwise, contrariwise
liking (n)
syn. affection, fondness, taste, love, affinity, fancy
ant. dislike, aversion
lily-white (adj)
syn. incorrupt, innocent, virgin, chaste, pure, milk-white
ant. corrupt
limelight (n)
syn. attention, publicity, celebrity, fame, stardom, prominence
ant. obscurity
limitation (n)
syn. control, curb, restriction, defect, weak point, imperfection, weakness
ant. extension, strength
limitless (adj)
syn. boundless, endless, infinite, immense, unlimited
ant. limited
limpid (adj)
syn. clear, comprehensible, lucid, intelligible, transparent, quiet, calm, peaceful
ant. incomprehensible, opaque, agitated
linger (v)
syn. remain, hang around, persist, last, continue, carry on
ant. leave, rush
lion-hearted (adj)
syn. brave, fearless, bold, valorous, courageous, valiant, daring, intrepid
ant. cowardly, fearful, spineless
lionize (v)
syn. eulogize, acclaim, glorify, exalt, honour, praise, hero-worship

ant. vilify, defame

listen (v)

syn. hear, pay attention, give ear, concentrate, heed, take notice

ant. ignore

listless (adj)

syn. lethargic, sluggish, lifeless, apathetic, uninterested, passive, inactive

ant. energetic

listlessness (n)

syn. lethargy, sluggishness, lifelessness, apathy, spiritlessness, sloth, indolence

ant. liveliness

literacy (n)

syn. education, learning, scholarship, knowledge, erudition, culture

ant. illiteracy

literary (adj)

syn. scholarly, bookish, erudite, academic, cultured, artistic

ant. illiterate

literate (adj)

syn. learned, educated, widely read, scholarly, cultured

ant. illiterate, ignorant

litigious (adj)

syn. argumentative, combative, quarrelsome, contentious, belligerent, disputatious

ant. genial, friendly

litter (n)

syn. waste, junk, rubbish, refuse, garbage, trash, untidiness, disorder, mess

ant. tidiness

little (adj)

syn. small, tiny, compact, short, young, brief, minor, trivial, paltry, short-lived, negligible

ant. big, important, large, elder, major

live^1 (v)

syn. be alive, exist, reside, stay, pass, experience, undergo, survive

ant. die, perish

live^2 (adj)

syn. conscious, vital, living, active, explosive, current, relevant, important

ant. dead, apathetic

lively (adj)
syn. spirited, alert, vivacious, energetic, eager, animated, busy, gay, bustling, refreshing
ant. dull, quiet, apathetic

liverish (adj)
syn. disagreeable, peevish, ill-humoured, crabbed, snappy, grumpy
ant. calm, easy-going

livid (adj)
syn. angry, enraged, fuming, boiling, furious, outraged, exasperated, mad, discoloured
ant. calm

loaf (v)
syn. idle, loiter, waste time, stand about
ant. toil

loafer (n)
syn. time-waster, drone, idler, lazybones, good-for-nothing, sluggard
ant. worker, achiever

loan (n)
syn. credit, advance, mortgage, accommodation
ant. borrowing

loath (adj)
syn. unwilling, opposed, reluctant, disinclined
ant. willing, eager

loathe (v)
syn. hate, despise, abhor, abominate, execrate, dislike
ant. love, adore

loathing (n)
syn. hate, hatred, dislike, abhorrence, antipathy, revulsion
ant. love, liking

loathsome (adj)
syn. hateful, abhorrent, disgusting, repulsive, abominable, horrible, obnoxious, horrid
ant. delightful, likeable

lofty (adj)
syn. high, tall, noble, elevated, arrogant, haughty, proud, lordly
ant. lowly, humble, modest

logical (adj)
syn. sound, analytical, judicious, reasoned, rational, natural, sensible, coherent

ant. illogical, irrational
loiter (v)
syn. idle, loaf, linger, hang around, stand around
ant. hurry
lone (adj)
syn. unaccompanied, isolated, solitary, single, separated
ant. accompanied
loneliness (n)
syn. isolation, abandonment, friendlessness, solitariness, separation, solitude, aloneness
ant. society
long (adj)
syn. lengthy, extended, protracted, prolonged, endless
ant. short, brief
longing (n)
syn. aspiration, thirst, desire, yearning, hope, craving, wish, hankering, itch
ant. apathy
long-lasting (adj)
syn. continuing, long-lived, long-standing, permanent, unfading, enduring, prolonged
ant. short-lived, transient, ephemeral
long-lived (adj)
syn. long-lasting, enduring, durable, long-standing
ant. short-lived
long-standing (adj)
syn. long-lived, long-lasting, enduring, well established, traditional, fixed
ant. new, recent, short-lived
long-winded (adj)
syn. wordy, lengthy, long, verbose, repetitive, meandering, prolix
ant. concise, terse, brief
loom (v)
syn. emerge, appear, threaten, be imminent, brew
ant. recede
loose (adj)
syn. untied, not secure, unsteady, free, shapeless, oversized, imprecise, rough, vague, random, unchaste, immoral, licentious
ant. secure, tight, precise, chaste

loose (v)
syn. free, release, unfasten, untie, loosen, relax
ant. confine, bind, tighten
loosen (v)
syn. unbind, free, release, loose, relax
ant. tighten
loquacious (adj)
syn. talkative, chatty, garrulous, babbling, voluble
ant. taciturn, quiet
lord (n)
syn. noblemen, baron, earl, monarch, master, king, chief
ant. commoner
lordly (adj)
syn. majestic, grand, princely, arrogant, lofty, proud
ant. lowly, humble
lose (v)
syn. misplace, evade, drop, throw off, waste, miss, be defeated
ant. gain, find, win
loss (n)
syn. reduction, death, fatality, deficit, damage, losing, waste, destruction
ant. benefit, gain, profit, recovery
loud (adj)
syn. noisy, roaring, blaring, sonorous, clamorous, vociferous, showy, vulgar
ant. quiet, low, soft
loudly (adv)
syn. noisily, shrilly, clamorously, vehemently, vociferously
ant. quietly, softly
lounge (v)
syn. idle, relax, repose, rest, kill time, loaf, loiter
ant. work
lousy (adj)
(informal)
syn. bad, hateful, dirty, miserable, poor, trashy, mean
ant. superb, excellent
lovable (adj)
syn. sweet, lovely, dear, adorable, likable, endearing
ant. hateful, loathsome, detestable

love (v)
syn. like, be fond of, adore, worship, be infatuated with, cherish, crazy about, fancy
ant. hate, loathe, detest

love (n)
syn. liking, fondness, adoration, passion, attachment, infatuation, lust, compassion, regard, dearest, beloved, honey, sweetheart
ant. hatred, hate, loathing, detestation

lovely (adj)
syn. pretty, beautiful, handsome, charming, exquisite, delightful, enchanting, pleasing, fabulous, terrific
ant. horrible, ugly

loving (adj)
syn. fond, close, affectionate, devoted, warm, passionate
ant. cold, cruel

low (adj)
syn. small, short, shallow, insufficient, meagre, vulgar, mean, nasty, unworthy, moderate, cheap, soft, quiet, depressed, sad
ant. high, honourable, expensive, loud, happy

lower (adj)
syn. low-level, junior, inferior, subordinate, secondary, bottom
ant. upper

lower (v)
syn. drop, let down, quieten, soften, hush, decrease, lessen, reduce
ant. raise, increase

low-key (adj)
syn. restrained, quiet, modest, low-profile, low-pitched, discreet, inconspicuous, understand, unobtrusive
ant. ostentatious, showy, obtrusive

lowly (adj)
syn. simple, modest, humble, ordinary, common, low, low-ranking, obscure, meek, docile
ant. lofty, exalted, aristocratic

loyal (adj)
syn. faithful, trusty, true, trustworthy, reliable, staunch, patriotic, devoted
ant. disloyal, perfidious, treacherous

loyalty (n)
syn. allegiance, faithfulness, patriotism, fidelity, devotion

ant. disloyalty, treachery, infidelity
lucid (adj)
syn. clear, intelligible, coherent, rational, sane, sober, bright, beaming
ant. unintelligible, confused, unclear
lucrative (adj)
syn. profitable, well paid, rewarding, moneymaking, gainful
ant. unprofitable
ludicrous (adj)
syn. ridiculous, stupid, mad, absurd, comic, laughable
ant. sensible
lugubrious (adj)
syn. sad, sorrowful, sombre, dismal, mournful, doleful, depressing, melancholy, miserable
ant. cheerful, merry, jovial
lukewarm (adj)
syn. half-hearted, tepid, uninterested, unenthusiastic
ant. warm, cold, enthusiastic
lull (n)
syn. calm, calmness, peace, respite
ant. agitation
lumbering (adj)
syn. awkward, lumpish, clumsy, blundering, unwieldy, heavy, overgrown, massive, lubberly
ant. dainty, agile, nimble
luminary (n)
syn. celebrity, VIP, dignitary, notable, star, superstar, leader, bigwig, big shot
ant. nobody
luminous (adj)
syn. brilliant, shining, bright, dazzling, glowing, lucid, intelligible, clear, comprehensible
ant. dark, unintelligible
lumpy (adj)
syn. clotted, bumpy, cloggy, curdled, grainy
ant. smooth, even
lunacy (n)
syn. insanity, madness, mania, craziness, folly, foolishness, stupidity, dementia

ant. sanity, sense, wisdom
lunatic (n)
syn. madman, madwoman, maniac, nutter, screwball, psychopath, idiot,
loony
ant. genius
lunatic (adj)
syn. insane, mad, senseless, stupid, absurd, foolish, crazy
ant. sane, sensible
lure (v)
syn. attract, coax, tempt, draw, entice, allure, seduce
ant. repel, deter
lurid (adj)
syn. bright, glaring, loud, gaudy, sensational, graphic, colourful, shocking,
gruesome, dazzling, exaggerated
ant. run-of-the-mill, ordinary, common
luscious (adj)
syn. appetizing, delicious, mouth-watering, aromatic, tasty, attractive,
delightful, pleasurable, flavoursome, rich
ant. revolting, austere
lust (n)
syn. passion, desire, longing, sex drive, lasciviousness, lecherousness,
carnality, randiness, greed, eagerness, appetite, hunger
ant. frigidity, apathy, indifference
lustful (adj)
syn. passionate, lewd, lecherous, sensual, lascivious, salacious, carnal,
sexually excited, hot, randy
ant. chaste, virtuous, modest
lustre (n)
syn. brightness, dazzle, glitter, shine, sparkle, sheen, brilliance, splendour,
fame, honour, glory, distinction
ant. dullness
lustrous (adj)
syn. bright, dazzling, glittering, shiny, sparkling
ant. dull, lustreless.
lusty (adj)
syn. strong, sturdy, robust, hale, healthy, energetic, rugged, stalwart
ant. weak

luxuriant (adj)
syn. dense, plentiful, lush, fertile, rich, productive, abundant, ample, fancy, flamboyant, elaborate
ant. sparse, infertile, meagre, few, simple

luxuriate (v)
syn. enjoy, bask, revel, delight, prosper, boom, flourish, thrive
ant. wither, shrink, decay

luxurious (adj)
syn. grand, rich, opulent, magnificent, palatial, sumptuous, posh, plush, swanky, sensual, voluptuous
ant. plain, basic, austere, ascetic

luxury (n)
syn. affluence, opulence, grandeur, splendour, comfort, delight, magnificence, enjoyment, voluptuousness, self-indulgence
ant. austerity, necessity, simplicity

lying (n)
syn. dishonesty, deceit, untruthfulness, fibbing, fabrication
ant. honesty, truthfulness

lying (adj)
syn. dishonest, deceitful, untruthful, false, two-faced
ant. truthful, honest

lyrical (adj)
syn. emotional, expressive, deeply felt, ecstatic, passionate, enthusiastic, rapturous
ant. unenthusiastic, apathetic

Mm

macabre (adj)
syn. horrible, grim, gruesome, ghastly, ghostly, frightful, frightening, morbid, death like, eerie, dreadful
ant. pleasant, wonderful, attractive

Machiavellian (adj)
syn. cunning, crafty, wily, artful, deceitful, astute, opportunist, shrewd, scheming, unscrupulous, sly, intriguing, foxy
ant. honest, artless, naïve, innocent, candid

macho (adj)
syn. manly, virile, male, masculine, red-blooded, strong, robust, bold, forceful, potent
ant. unmanly, womanly, effeminate

mad (adj)
syn. insane, fanatical, lunatic, crazy, unbalanced, angry, passionate, hysterical
ant. sane, sensible, rational, lucid

madcap (adj)
(informal)
syn. hot-headed, crazy, heedless, bird-brained, imprudent, foolhardy, rash, thoughtless, ill-advised, wild, silly, impulsive
ant. sensible, cautious, calm, cool

madden (v)
syn. annoy, irritate, provoke, craze, vex, anger, exasperate, inflame, enrage, infuriate, incense, tick off
ant. pacify, please, calm

madness (n)
syn. lunacy, insanity, dementia, mayhem, frenzy, craziness, stupidity, foolishness, folly, anger, exasperation, wrath
ant. sanity, sense, composure

maelstrom (n)
syn. pandemonium, chaos, turmoil, disorder, bedlam, confusion, whirlpool, uproar
ant. order, peace, calm

magisterial (adj)
syn. commanding, authoritative, dictatorial, imperative, despotic, arrogant, haughty, lofty, assertive, lordly
ant. humble, modest, meek, polite

magnanimity (n)
syn. kindness, generosity, unselfishness, selflessness, tolerance, benevolence, forbearance, charity
ant. meanness, parsimony, selfishness

magnanimous (adj)
syn. charitable, altruistic, generous, big-hearted, unselfish, noble, kind, philanthropic
ant. mean, parsimonious, selfish

magnate (n)
syn. chief, notable, VIP, tycoon, mogul, baron, personage, big shot, leader.
ant. nobody

magnificence (n)
syn. impressiveness, glory, grandeur, luxury, nobility, pomp, splendour, brilliance, sublimity
ant. modesty, simplicity, plainness

magnificent (adj)
syn. impressive, glorious, splendid, superb, grand, spectacular, excellent, luxurious, sublime
ant. ordinary, modest, uninspiring, humble

magnify (v)
syn. extend, increase, intensify, enlarge, boost, expand, blow up, exaggerate
ant. minimize, reduce

magniloquent (adj)
syn. pompous, bombastic, lofty, high-flown, elevated, sonorous, high-sounding
ant. simple, straightforward

magnitude (n)
syn. immensity, enormity, size, vastness, importance, significance, consequence, mass
ant. smallness, insignificance

maiden (n)
syn. girl, miss, virgin, damsel, lass
ant. lad, boy

maim (v)
syn. disable, disfigure, injure, cripple, wound
ant. heal, repair
main (adj)
syn. important, essential, chief, first, crucial, supreme, absolute
ant. minor, unimportant
mainstream (adj)
syn. conventional, accepted, established, orthodox, standard, normal, received
ant. heterodox, peripheral, inessential
maintenance (n)
syn. preservation, continuation, care, repair, support
ant. neglect
majestic (adj)
syn. grand, dignified, royal, stately, impressive, noble, magnificent, imperial, kingly
ant. lowly, modest, unimpressive
majesty (n)
syn. dignity, nobility, glory, grandeur, magnificence, loftiness, haughtiness
ant. unimportance, unimpressiveness, humility
major (adj)
syn. main, important, greatest, leading, vital, crucial, big, considerable, paramount, serious
ant. minor, trivial
majority (n)
syn. mass, most, greater part, preponderance, adulthood, maturity, seniority
ant. minority, childhood
make (v)
syn. manufacture, build, create, construct, force, cause, appoint, get, prepare
ant. destroy
make-believe (n)
syn. daydreaming, fantasy, fabrication, pretence, unreality, imagination, masquerade
ant. reality, realism, actuality
maker (n)
syn. creator, builder, manufacturer, producer, constructor, architect, author

ant. dismantler
makeshift (adj)
syn. provisional, temporary, rough-and-ready, substitute, improvised
ant. permanent, finished
maladministration (n)
syn. misrule, mismanagement, misgovernment, corruption, incompetence
ant. order
maladroit (adj)
syn. inept, incompetent, unskilful, inexpert, inapt, bungling, clumsy, awkward
ant. competent, skilled, dexterous
malady (n)
syn. sickness, illness, disease, ailment, complaint, disorder, breakdown, affliction
ant. fitness, health
malaise (n)
syn. anxiety, depression, anguish, discomfort, illness, uneasiness, doldrums, melancholy
ant. happiness, well-being
malcontent (adj)
syn. discontented, dissatisfied, disgruntled, displeased, uneasy
ant. contented, happy
malediction (n)
syn. curse, damnation, condemnation, anathema, slander, denunciation
ant. blessing, praise
malefactor (n)
syn. criminal, sinner, lawbreaker, offender, culprit, felon, miscreant
ant. saint
malevolent (adj)
syn. ill-natured, bitter, malicious, vindictive, resentful, vengeful, malign, malignant, vicious, venomous, hostile
ant. benevolent, kind, kind-hearted, charitable
malice (n)
syn. ill will, enmity, spite, vindictiveness, animosity, malevolence, vengefulness, hostility, bitterness, venom, grudge
ant. love, benevolence, kindness
malicious (adj)
syn. bitter, vindictive, malevolent, malignant, hurtful, hateful, cruel,

resentful, spiteful, mischievous, vicious
ant. benevolent, kind, thoughtful
malign (v)
syn. abuse, defame, injure, slander, derogate, vilify
ant. praise, admire
malignant (adj)
syn. malign, malevolent, venomous, harmful, bitter, destructive, hostile, spiteful, deadly
ant. benign, kind, harmless
malodorous (adj)
syn. foul-smelling, evil-smelling, niffy, stinking, smelly, offensive
ant. sweet-smelling
mammon (n)
syn. wealth, riches, money, affluence, opulence
ant. poverty
mammoth (adj)
syn. huge, gigantic, massive, colossal, titanic, immense, leviathan, vast
ant. tiny, small
manacle (v)
syn. bind, chain, handcuff, fetter, curb, restrain
ant. free
manageable (adj)
syn. achievable, feasible, practicable, compliant, accommodating, easy
ant. unmanageable
manful (adj)
syn. brave, determined, courageous, bold, intrepid, manly, stalwart, resolute, heroic, gallant, unflinching
ant. timid, half-hearted
mangle (v)
syn. disfigure, spoil, tear, mutilate, destroy, cut, cripple, mar
ant. mend, repair, restore
mangy (adj)
syn. dirty, mean, ratty, shabby, scruffy, tatty
ant. neat, clean
manhood (n)
syn. maturity, adulthood, manliness, masculinity, resolution, stamina, courage, bravery, fortitude
ant. boyhood, womanhood, timidness

mandatory (adj)
syn. compulsory, obligatory, requisite, essential
ant. optional

mania (n)
syn. obsession, desire, rage, fixation, enthusiasm, fascination, craze, madness, lunacy, frenzy
ant. phobia, coolness, self-possession, sanity

maniac (n)
syn. madman, madwoman, fanatic, psychopath, lunatic, loony, screwball
ant. genius

manifest (v)
syn. exhibit, present, show, display, reveal, evince
ant. hide

manifestation (n)
syn. show, display, exposure, exhibition, sign, indication, demonstration, revelation
ant. concealment, hiding, cover-up

manifold (adj)
syn. various, abundant, multiple, many, varied, numerous
ant. few, simple

manliness (n)
syn. courage, boldness, fearlessness, manhood, masculinity, virility, vigour, resolution, heroism
ant. unmanliness, timidity

manly (adj)
syn. masculine, muscular, well built, tough, rugged, powerful, virile, macho, resolute, hunky
ant. unmanly, womanly, timid, effeminate

man-made (adj)
syn. artificial, fake, synthetic, manufactured, spurious, counterfeit
ant. natural, real, genuine

mannered (adj)
syn. artificial, pseudo, posed, pretentious, affected, put-on
ant. natural

mannerism (n)
syn. idiosyncrasy, quirk, peculiarity, habit, oddity, characteristic, trait
ant. normality, rationality, prudence

mannerly (adj)
syn. well-mannered, polite, respectful, courteous, genteel, well-bred, well-behaved, refined, civil
ant. unmannerly, rude

manners (n)
syn. behaviour, decorum, politeness, demeanour, etiquette
ant. impoliteness, indecorousness

mansion (n)
syn. villa, house, palace, castle, big house
ant. hovel

manumission (n)
syn. liberation, enfranchisement, deliverance, emancipation, release
ant. servitude, slavery

manumit (v)
syn. liberate, set free, release, free, emancipate, deliver
ant. enslave, bind, subjugate

many (adj)
syn. myriad, innumerable, numerous, several, countless, manifold
ant. few

mar (v)
syn. damage, disfigure, spoil, ruin, deface, tarnish
ant. enhance

marginal (adj)
syn. small, slight, negligible, insignificant
ant. considerable

marine (adj)
syn. oceanic, naval, maritime, pelagic, sea, seafaring
ant. land

marital (adj)
syn. married, nuptial, conjugal, matrimonial, wedded
ant. celibate

maroon (v)
syn. abandon, forsake, desert, cut off, isolate, leave
ant. keep

martial (adj)
syn. warlike, military, bellicose, brave, belligerent, courageous
ant. pacific, gentle

marvel (n)
syn. wonder, phenomenon, miracle, prodigy, spectacle, genius, sensation
ant. disinterest, ordinariness
marvellous (adj)
syn. wonderful, excellent, magnificent, superb, sublime, amazing, smashing
ant. dreadful, awful, ordinary
masculine (adj)
syn. male, manly, virile, strong, macho, robust, vigorous, unfeminine
ant. feminine, effeminate
massacre (n)
syn. genocide, mass murder, slaughter, holocaust, carnage, annihilation, butchery, ethnic cleansing
ant. creation, generation, genesis
massive (adj)
syn. huge, big, large, immense, heavy, gigantic, bulky
ant. tiny, slight
masterly (adj)
syn. expert, skilled, adept, adroit, accomplished, excellent, ace
ant. inept, unskilled
mastery (n)
syn. ability, understanding, proficiency, command, expertise, authority, comprehension
ant. clumsiness, unfamiliarity
matchless (adj)
syn. unique, peerless, incomparable, unequalled, unmatched, perfect, ideal
ant. ordinary
material (adj)
syn. physical, worldly, corporeal, earthly, bodily, tangible, important, vital, serious, significant, essential
ant. spiritual, immaterial
mature (adj)
syn. adult, fully grown, fully developed, ripened, ripe, mellow, sensible
ant. immature
maturity (n)
syn. adulthood, manhood, fullness, ripeness, majority, wisdom
ant. immaturity
maverick (n)
syn. individualist, eccentric, dissident, rebel, nonconformist, dissenter

ant. conformist
mawkish (adj)
syn. emotional, maudlin, sentimental, feeble, insipid, mushy, tasteless
ant. matter-of-fact, pleasant
mayhem (n)
syn. pandemonium, havoc, uproar, anarchy, chaos, turmoil, bedlam
ant. order, peace, calm
maze (n)
syn. confusion, bewilderment, labyrinth, tangle, intricacy, web, complexity, perplexity
ant. order, clarity, simplicity, straightforwardness
meagre (adj)
syn. scant, inadequate, limited, negligible, stingy, poor, little
ant. ample, abundant, substantial
mean (adj)
syn. miserly, parsimonious, unkind, unfair, loathsome, nasty, malicious, horrible, rotten
ant. kind, generous
meandering (adj)
syn. serpentine, roundabout, tortuous, wandering, twisting
ant. straight
measureless (adj)
syn. immeasurable, limitless, infinite, incalculable, endless, immense, boundless
ant. measurable, finite
meddle (v)
syn. interfere, intervene, intrude, mess about, fiddle, butt in, muck about
ant. disregard, ignore, overlook
mediate (v)
syn. make peace, intervene, arbitrate, liaise, referee, negotiate, reconcile
ant. estrange, divide
mediation (n)
syn. reconciliation, diplomacy, arbitration, intervention
ant. separation, estrangement
mediocre (adj)
syn. average, inferior, uninspired, undistinguished, run-of-the-mill, ordinary, mean, second-rate, prosaic, unremarkable, so-so
ant. excellent, exceptional

mediocrity (n)
syn. inferiority, ordinariness, poorness, insignificance, indifference, unimportance, amateurishness
ant. excellence, superiority

meek (adj)
syn. quiet, obedient, submissive, timid, docile, modest, gentle, shy, peaceful, spiritless
ant. arrogant, assertive, rebellious

meekness (n)
syn. compliance, gentleness, humility, humbleness, softness, modesty, submissiveness, timidity, lowliness, docility
ant. arrogance, assertiveness, conceit

megalomania (n)
syn. self-admiration, self-love, self-glorification, self-esteem, self-regard, self-contentment, egoism, egomania
ant. altruism, generosity, self-abandonment, self-forgetfulness

megalomaniac (n)
syn. narcissist, egocentric, egoist, egomaniac, boaster, bighead
ant. altruist, humanitarian, philanthropist

melancholy (adj)
syn. sorrowful, unhappy, gloomy, sad, despondent, dejected, depressed, downhearted, low-spirited, doleful
ant. happy, elated, cheerful, gay, joyful

melancholy (n)
syn. sorrow, sadness, unhappiness, dejection, misery, despondency, gloom, gloominess, blues
ant. happiness, elation

mellifluous (adj)
syn. melodious, mellow, sweet, euphonious, smooth, soft, harmonious, sweet-sounding
ant. harsh, discordant

mellow (adj)
syn. melodious, mellifluous, smooth, sweet-sounding, good-natured, amiable, genial, easy-going, pleasant
ant. harsh, rough

melodious (adj)
syn. harmonious, lyrical, tuneful, melodic, musical, euphonious
ant. discordant, harsh

melody (n)
syn. song, tune, theme, strain, melodiousness, euphony, harmony
ant. discord, harshness

memorable (adj)
syn. unforgettable, significant, remarkable, historic, famous, striking, celebrated, noteworthy
ant. forgettable, insignificant

memorize (v)
syn. learn by heart, remember, learn
ant. forget

memory (n)
syn. recall, recollection, reminiscence, remembrance, retrospection, honour, commemoration, respect
ant. forgetfulness, oblivion

menace (n)
syn. threat, oppression, intimidation, risk, danger, peril, nuisance, troublemaker, pest
ant. reassurance, safety

menacing (adj)
syn. threatening, hostile, frightening, ominous, sinister, intimidating
ant. friendly

mend (v)
syn. repair, patch, stitch, renovate, restore, patch up
ant. break, damage

mendacity (n)
syn. untruthfulness, dishonesty, deceit, deception, falsity, fraudulence, falsehood
ant. honesty, truthfulness

menial (n)
syn. servant, attendant, slave, domestic
ant. master

mental (adj)
syn. psychological, intellectual, rational, abstract, insane, mentally ill, mad, loony, crazy
ant. physical, sane, balanced

mephitic (adj)
syn. stinking, foul, malodorous, rank, noxious, noisome, unwholesome, poisonous, miasmatic

ant. pleasant, salubrious

mercenary (adj)

syn. greedy, grasping, covetous, sordid, selfish, money-grubbing, hired, bought, venal, paid

ant. liberal, voluntary

merciful (adj)

syn. compassionate, forbearing, forgiving, kind, soft-hearted, generous, sympathetic, humane, mild, magnanimous, liberal

ant. merciless, cruel

mercurial (adj)

syn. active, spirited, vivacious, lively, energetic, fickle, inconstant, changeable, unstable

ant. saturnine, gloomy

mercy (n)

syn. pity, leniency, compassion, kindness, forgiveness, sympathy, magnanimity, generosity

ant. cruelty, ruthlessness

meretricious (adj)

syn. showy, garish, flashy, cheap, false, bogus, counterfeit, spurious, insincere

ant. genuine

merge (v)

syn. join, combine, blend, converge, mingle, fuse

ant. separate

merger (n)

syn. combination, amalgamation, union, coalition, corporation, fusion

ant. separation

meridian (n)

syn. peak, height, acme, zenith, culmination, apex, pinnacle, summit, climax, highest point

ant. nadir, bottom, lowest point, zero

merit (n)

syn. worth, excellence, value, calibre, distinction, benefit, good point, advantage

ant. fault, disadvantage

meritorious (adj)

syn. deserving, exemplary, good, excellent, worthy, commendable, admirable

ant. despicable, unworthy
merriment (n)
syn. joy, jollity, fun, hilarity, mirth, merrymaking, pleasure, festivity, levity, laughter
ant. gloom, sadness, seriousness
merry (adj)
syn. smiling, sunny, cheerful, joyful
ant. miserable
mesmerize (v)
syn. hypnotize, enthral, fascinate, spellbound, captivate, stupefy
ant. bore
mess (n)
syn. untidiness, clutter, disorder, muddle, disarray, chaos, shambles, difficult, plight, trouble, dilemma, fix
ant. tidiness, order
messy (adj)
syn. confused, dirty, untidy, complex, bitter
ant. neat, tidy, ordered
metamorphosis (n)
syn. change, transformation, modification, conversion, mutation, alteration, change-over
ant. immutability, constancy, permanence
metaphysical (adj)
syn. immaterial, spiritual, abstract, theoretical, philosophical, intellectual, speculative
ant. material
methodical (adj)
syn. systematic, orderly, organized, structured, meticulous, neat, precise, planned
ant. disorganized
meticulous (adj)
syn. careful, diligent, precise, thorough, fussy, perfectionist, studious
ant. careless, slapdash
mettle (n)
syn. courage, boldness, bravery, resolution, energy, vigour, animation, fire, spirit, temperament, character
ant. cowardice, timidity, fear

miasmatic (adj)
syn. foul, stinking, miasmal, mephitic, malodorous, noisome, unwholesome, noxious, poisonous
ant. pleasant, salubrious

middling (adj)
syn. average, mediocre, medium, tolerable, moderate, run-of-the-mill, passable, ordinary, OK, so-so
ant. excellent, exceptional

miffed (adj)
syn. annoyed, displeased, hurt, aggrieved, offended, upset
ant. pleased, delighted

might (n)
syn. power, strength, force, capability, energy, potency, vigour
ant. weakness

mighty (adj)
syn. powerful, strong, forceful, stalwart, robust, lusty, vigorous, huge, massive, colossal, immense
ant. weak, frail, feeble, tiny

migrate (v)
syn. move, immigrate, emigrate, relocate, journey, travel, wander
ant. remain

mild (adj)
syn. soft, sympathetic, meek, compassionate, genial, gentle, lenient, pacific, moderate, docile, tasteless, insipid
ant. harsh, violent, strong, severe, fierce

mildness (n)
syn. softness, sympathy, meekness, compassion, geniality, gentleness, leniency, docility, kindness, mellowness, warmth, forbearance
ant. harshness, violence, ferocity

militant (adj)
syn. extremist, radical, hard-line, fanatical, belligerent, aggressive, bellicose, combative, contending
ant. pacific, gentle, peace-loving, mild

military (adj)
syn. armed, soldierly, warlike, martial
ant. civil

militate (v)
syn. oppose, conflict with, war, go against, counter, contend

ant. agree

mindless (adj)

syn. senseless, heedless, thoughtless, careless, stupid, foolish, unthinking, negligent, routine, boring

ant. mindful, thoughtful, intelligent

mingle (v)

syn. mix, intermix, fuse, merge, blend, amalgamate, unite, join, socialize, get together, hobnob

ant. separate, divide, split

miniature (adj)

syn. small, little, baby, tiny, mini, pygmy

ant. giant, large

minimal (adj)

syn. minimum, very small, very little, nominal, negligible, slightest

ant. maximum

minion (n)

syn. follower, favourite, pet, bootlicker, yes man, parasite, toady, flatterer, henchman, sycophant

ant. master, boss

minuscule (adj)

syn. little, miniature, tiny, microscopic, Lilliputian, diminutive

ant. huge, gigantic

miraculous (adj)

syn. amazing, astonishing, incredible, divine, remarkable, unbelievable, phenomenal, wonderful

ant. ordinary, normal, natural

mirth (n)

syn. cheerfulness, frolic, amusement, pleasure, fun, merriment, joy, glee, levity, festivity

ant. melancholy, gloom, sorrow

mirthful (adj)

syn. cheerful, happy, gay, jovial, jolly, joyful, blithe, light-hearted, vivacious, lively, festive

ant. gloomy, sorrowful, sad

misanthropy (n)

syn. selfishness, inhumanity, malevolence, cynicism, egoism

ant. philanthropy

miscarriage (n)
syn. failure, mishap, abortion, defeat, misfortune, mischance, breakdown, error
ant. success, victory

miscellany (n)
syn. variety, mixture, diversity, assortment, jumble, anthology
ant. similarity, likeness

mischief (n)
syn. naughtiness, misbehaviour, rascality, misconduct, damage, nuisance
ant. good, benefit

mischievous (adj)
syn. troublesome, naughty, annoying, playful, harmful, injurious, bad, damaging, evil
ant. good, well behaved, beneficial

misconception (n)
syn. delusion, misunderstanding, fallacy, misapprehension, error, misconstruction
ant. reality

misconduct (n)
syn. misbehaviour, misdemeanour, wrongdoing, delinquency, transgression, impropriety, malpractice
ant. propriety, morality, decorum

miscreant (n)
syn. rouge, scoundrel, rascal, criminal, knave, sinner, wrongdoer
ant. worthy, saint

miser (n)
syn. niggard, penny-pincher, tightwad, hoarder
ant. spendthrift

miserable (adj)
syn. sorrowful, sad, unhappy, depressed, dejected, gloomy, cheerless, poor, poverty-stricken
ant. cheerful, lovely, rich

miserly (adj)
syn. parsimonious, niggardly, mean, ungenerous, tight-fisted, stingy, penurious
ant. generous, charitable, lavish

misery (n)
syn. unhappiness, suffering, sorrow, sadness, depression, distress, torment,

gloom, the blues, despondency, melancholy, poverty, want
ant. joy, contentment, pleasure, affluence
misfortune (n)
syn. adversity, difficulty, problem, trouble, bad luck, mischance, tragedy, tribulation, calamity, setback
ant. success, luck
misgiving (n)
syn. doubt, uncertainty, hesitation, distrust, mistrust, suspicion, apprehension, anxiety, fear
ant. assurance, confidence
mishap (n)
syn. accident, misfortune, bad luck, disaster, ill luck, misadventure
ant. success, luck
mislay (v)
syn. lose, miss, be unable to find, misplace
ant. find
mislead (v)
syn. misguide, deceive, fool, misinform, misdirect, trick
ant. enlighten
mismatched (adj)
syn. unmatching, unsuited, clashing, antipathetic, incongruous, incompatible, ill-assorted, incompatible, irreconcilable
ant. matching, compatible, harmonious, agreeable
misprize (v)
syn. underestimate, undervalue, depreciate, misunderstand, belittle, despise, mistake
ant. appreciate, value, understand
misshapen (adj)
syn. deformed, distorted, twisted, malformed, crooked, unshapely, grotesque, crippled
ant. shapely, comely, neat
mistaken (adj)
syn. incorrect, wrong, false, inexact, imprecise, misinformed, untrue, inaccurate, unsound
ant. correct, justified
mistimed (adj)
syn. ill-timed, untimely, inopportune, badly timed, unfortunate
ant. opportune, timely

mistreatment (n)
syn. abuse, ill-treatment, bullying, cruelty, ill-use, molestation, misuse, unkindness, harm, brutalization
ant. pampering, cosseting

mistrust (n)
syn. distrust, scepticism, misgiving, doubt, wariness, suspicion, apprehension, hesitancy
ant. trust, confidence

misty (adj)
syn. foggy, vague, hazy, cloudy, blurred
ant. clear, bright

misunderstanding (n)
syn. misconception, misinterpretation, misapprehension, mistake, misjudgement, disagreement, clash, argument, difference, discord
ant. understanding, agreement

mitigate (v)
syn. reduce, moderate, lessen, alleviate, relieve, calm, lighten, subdue, pacify, mollify
ant. aggravate, increase, exacerbate

mitigation (n)
syn. reduction, moderation, lessening, alleviation, relief, decrease, appeasement, mollification
ant. aggravation, increase, exacerbation

moan (v)
syn. groan, complain, sorrow, bemoan, grumble, grieve, mourn, deplore, sigh, weep
ant. rejoice, joy, delight

mobile (adj)
syn. movable, travelling, moving, animated, changeable
ant. immobile

mock (v)
syn. ridicule, make fun of, tease, sneer, delude, mimic, counterfeit, imitate, satirize
ant. praise, respect, flatter

mockery (n)
syn. ridicule, derision, jeering, gibe, contempt, taunt, parody, sham, burlesque, satire, travesty, sarcasm
ant. respect, admiration

mocking (adj)
syn. cynical, disrespectful, insulting, sneering, sarcastic, satirical
ant. laudatory, glorifying
moderate (adj)
syn. calm, modest, tolerable, reasonable, affordable, pragmatic, liberal
ant. immoderate, extreme
moderate(v)
syn. decrease, lessen, subside, recede, diminish, control, check, curb, appease
ant. increase, aggravate
modest (adj)
syn. humble, chaste, reserved, reticent, meek, moderate, tolerable, quiet, simple, decent, limited
ant. immodest, conceited, indecent, grand, excessive
modesty (n)
syn. humility, decency, humbleness, propriety, bashfulness, reserve, meekness, shyness, reticence, discreetness
ant. immodesty, conceit, vanity
modulate (v)
syn. modify, change, inflect, tune, adjust, harmonize, balance
ant. increase, raise
moiety (n)
(law/literary)
syn. half, fragment, share, piece, part, a half share
ant. whole
mogul (n)
syn. baron, magnate, notable, supremo, big shot, personage
ant. nobody
moist (adj)
syn. humid, damp, wet, soft, juicy
ant. dry
moisture (n)
syn. humidity, dampness, wetness, water, liquid
ant. dryness
molest (v)
syn. disturb, harass, annoy, pester, irritate, vex, abuse, mistreat, accost, maltreat, ill-use, attack
ant. soothe, calm, pamper, cosset

mollycoddle (v)
syn. overprotect, spoon-feed, pamper, ruin, spoil, pet, cosset, coddle, baby
ant. discipline, ill-treat, neglect
monarch (n)
syn. ruler, king, sovereign, emperor, crowned head
ant. subject, citizen
monastic (adj)
syn. ascetic, reclusive, eremitic, celibate, austere, hermitical, withdrawn
ant. materialistic, worldly, secular
moneyed (adj)
(also *monied*)
syn. rich, affluent, wealthy, well-off, prosperous, well-to-do
ant. poor
monologue (n)
syn. lecture, sermon, harangue, speech, oration, soliloquy
ant. dialogue, discussion
monopoly (n)
syn. control, domination, ascendancy, exclusive right, corner
ant. competition
mollify (v)
syn. appease, calm, soothe, quiet, pacify, ease, lessen, reduce, moderate, soften
ant. provoke, anger, aggravate
momentary (adj)
syn. short, short-lived, brief, passing, transient, ephemeral
ant. lengthy
momentous (adj)
syn. important, historic, crucial, significant, serious, major, decisive, critical
ant. insignificant, trivial
monotonous (adj)
syn. uninteresting, dull, humdrum, uniform, unchanging, boring, tedious, deadly
ant. interesting, lively
monotony (n)
syn. boredom, dullness, prosaicness, sameness, colourlessness, uniformity
ant. colour, liveliness

monstrous (adj)
syn. horrible, awful, shocking, heinous, diabolical, infamous, unnatural, deformed, huge, massive, gigantic
ant. wonderful, normal, tiny

monumental (adj)
syn. historic, immense, enormous, memorable, significant, majestic, striking, classic, important
ant. trivial, unimportant

moody (adj)
syn. angry, sulky, emotional, peevish, morose, temperamental, irritable
ant. cheerful, equable

moor (v)
syn. tie up, fasten, anchor, secure
ant. untie

moot (adj)
syn. controversial, disputable, unresolved, arguable, debatable, at issue, questionable, open
ant. indisputable, unquestionable, positive

moral (adj)
syn. ethical, blameless, good, proper, honest, principled, virtuous, noble, upright
ant. immoral, unethical, corrupt

morale (n)
syn. confidence, spirit, will, heart, self-esteem, self-confidence, motivation
ant. enervation

morality (n)
syn. ethics, virtue, uprightness, good behaviour, morals, integrity, righteousness, propriety, decency, honesty
ant. immorality, vice, impropriety, dishonesty

morass (n)
syn. chaos, confusion, swamp, marsh, muddle, clutter, bog, mess
ant. order, peace

moratorium (n)
syn. ban, halt, embargo, delay, stay, suspension, postponement, standstill, respite
ant. go-ahead, green light

morbid (adj)
syn. unhealthy, sick, macabre, unwholesome, ghoulish, gruesome,

pessimistic, sombre, morose, unsound, diseased, grisly
ant. wholesome, healthy, sound, well

mordant (adj)
syn. sarcastic, bitter, acid, acerbic, biting, sharp, cutting, mordacious, incisive, trenchant, harsh
ant. soothing, gentle, sparing

moribund (adj)
syn. collapsing, doomed, dying, failing, crumbling, declining, stagnating, weak, waning
ant. flourishing, alive, lively

moron (n)
syn. idiot, fool, halfwit, donkey, ass, ignoramus, imbecile, blockhead
ant. genius, mastermind, maestro

morose (adj)
syn. cheerless, depressed, gloomy, humourless, melancholy, mournful, sulky, sullen, moody, pessimistic, ill-tempered, unsociable
ant. cheerful, communicative, genial, friendly, sunny

mortal (adj)
syn. perishable, human, corporeal, ephemeral, temporal, deadly, bitter
ant. immortal, eternal

mortality (n)
syn. temporality, fatality, ephemerality, death, perishability
ant. immortality

mortification (n)
syn. embarrassment, shame, humiliation, discomposure, confusion, abashment, vexation, displeasure, dissatisfaction
ant. delight, joy, ease, contentment

moth-eaten (adj)
(informal)
syn. shabby, ragged, worn-out, decayed, dilapidated, moribund, outworn, tattered, outdated, ancient
ant. fresh, new, smart

motivate (v)
syn. inspire, activate, incite, provoke, induce, instigate, stimulate, encourage
ant. deter, prevent, discourage

motivation (n)
syn. inspiration, incitement, provocation, inducement, instigation,

stimulus, encouragement, motive
ant. deterrent, prevention, discouragement
motive (n)
syn. reason, motivation, cause, rationalize, basis, inducement, intention, impulse, inspiration, drive, purpose
ant. deterrent, discouragement
motely (adj)
syn. mixed, diverse, miscellaneous, heterogeneous, varied, multicoloured, variegated
ant. uniform, homogeneous
mouldy (adj)
syn. bad, stale, decaying, musty, rotten, blighted
ant. fresh, wholesome
mourn (v)
syn. deplore, regret, sorrow, lament, weep, wail, grieve
ant. rejoice, joy, bless
mournful (adj)
syn. sorrowful, sad, unhappy, grievous, distressing, depressing, gloomy, sombre, heartbroken, doleful, melancholy, dejected
ant. joyful, cheerful, happy, sunny
mourning (n)
syn. sorrow, lamentation, grief, woe, sadness, bereavement, wailing
ant. rejoicing, joy, delight
movable (adj)
syn. transferable, mobile, changeable, transportable
ant. fixed
much (adj)
syn. ample, plentiful, great, a lot of, considerable
ant. little
mucky (adj)
(informal)
syn. dirty, grubby, muddy, filthy, soiled, messy
ant. clean
muddle (n)
syn. disorder, mess, chaos, confusion, jumble, disarray
ant. order
muddy (adj)
syn. dirty, boggy, mucky, swampy, cloudy, unclear, dingy, murky

ant. clean, clear

muffle (v)
syn. cover, wrap, conceal, disguise, mask, mute, deaden, suppress, silence
ant. expose, amplify

muggy (adj)
syn. humid, airless, sticky, sultry, sweltering, oppressive
ant. fresh, dry

mulish (adj)
syn. stubborn, headstrong, inflexible, obstinate, refractory, perverse, wilful
ant. amenable, agreeable, flexible

multiply (v)
syn. increase, extend, expand, augment, spread, intensify, propagate, boost, proliferate
ant. decrease, lessen

multitude (n)
syn. swarm, crowd, mass, throng, congregation, myriad, assembly, army
ant. handful, scattering

mum (adj)
(informal)
syn. silent, mute, quiet, uncommunicative, taciturn, speechless
ant. talkative, chatty

mumble (v)
syn. murmur, mutter, fumble
ant. exclaim, shout

mundane (adj)
syn. everyday, routine, dull, boring, unexciting, prosaic, uninteresting, humdrum
ant. extraordinary, cosmic

munificent (adj)
syn. generous, liberal, bountiful, beneficent, charitable, magnanimous, princely, philanthropic, lavish, benevolent, big-hearted
ant. mean, ungenerous, miserly, parsimonious

murky (adj)
syn. dull, dark, sunless, foggy, gloomy, dirty, obscure, dismal
ant. bright, clear

muscular (adj)
syn. burly, brawny, strong, stalwart, robust, lusty, athletic, energetic, beefy
ant. puny, weak, feeble

muse (v)
syn. think, think over, ponder, consider, meditate, contemplate, brood, ruminate
ant. ignore

mushroom (v)
syn. grow, increase, boom, expand, flourish, spring up, thrive, prosper
ant. decline, reduce

musical (adj)
syn. melodious, mellifluous, euphonious, lyrical, tuneful, dulcet, harmonious
ant. unmusical, discordant

muster (v)
syn. assemble, gather, round up, meet, convene, congregate, rally
ant. disperse

musty (adj)
syn. stale, dank, old, ancient, mouldy, ill-smelling, decayed, moth-eaten
ant. fresh, new

mutable (adj)
syn. changeable, fickle, flexible, inconsistent, uncertain, unstable
ant. constant, permanent

mute (adj)
syn. silent, mum, speechless, voiceless, taciturn, unspoken, uncommunicative, unexpressed, quiet, dumb
ant. loud, spoken, voluble, articulate

mutilate (v)
syn. disfigure, slash, maim, hack up, cripple, damage, desecrate, vandalize
ant. mend, restore, renovate

mutinous (adj)
syn. rebellious, turbulent, insurgent, ungovernable, revolutionary, unruly, refractory, riotous
ant. obedient, compliant, dutiful

mutiny (n)
syn. rebellion, revolt, uprising, disobedience, sedition, insurrection, riot, revolution
ant. obedience, compliance, docility

mutter (v)
syn. murmur, mumble, grumble, complain
ant. exclaim, shout

myopic (adj)
syn. short-sighted, near-sighted
ant. long-sighted
myriad (adj)
(literary)
syn. many, countless, incalculable, boundless, innumerable, untold
ant. limited, few
mysterious (adj)
syn. peculiar, puzzling, odd, funny, perplexing, cryptic, baffling, secret, secretive, hidden, reticent, enigmatic, unexplainable
ant. unmysterious, plain, frank, comprehensible, straightforward
mystify (v)
syn. puzzle, bewilder, perplex, confuse, baffle, confound
ant. enlighten, educate
myth (n)
syn. legend, fable, saga, story, tradition, allegory, tale, fiction, untruth, falsehood, fabrication, illusion, fantasy, cock and bull story
ant. truth, fact, reality
mythical (adj)
syn. mythological, fabled, traditional, storied, legendary, fabulous, unreal, invented, false, imaginary, fanciful, fictitious
ant. truthful, historical, factual, real

Nn

nab (v)
(informal)
syn. grab, catch, seize, arrest
ant. release

nadir (n)
syn. low point, bottom, rock bottom, all-time low, lowest point, zero
ant. zenith, peak, apex

nag (v)
syn. harass, annoy, chivvy, hound, criticize, moan, henpeck, hassle, trouble, scold, irritate
ant. assist, praise

naive (adj)
syn. candid, frank, artless, ingenuous, innocent, unworldly, credulous, immature, trusting, unsophisticated
ant. worldly, artful, sophisticated

naivety (n)
syn. inexperience, frankness, openness, simplicity, credulity, candour
ant. sophistication, experience

naked (adj)
syn. undressed, nude, unclothed, stripped, open, unadorned, plain, manifest, undisguised
ant. clothed, dressed, concealed

narcissism (n)
syn. self-love, self-admiration, self-glorification, self-contentment, complacency, ego, conceit, egocentricity, egoism, self-regard, egomania
ant. altruism, generosity, self-abandonment, self-forgetfulness, unselfishness

narcissist (n)
syn. megalomaniac, egomaniac, egoist, boaster, bighead
ant. altruist, humanitarian, philanthropist

narrator (n)
syn. storyteller, author, chronicler, presenter, commentator
ant. listener, audience

narrow (adj)
syn. tight, restricted, close, cramped, slender, thin, attenuated
ant. broad, wide
narrow (v)
syn. limit, reduce, shrink, decrease
ant. widen
narrow-minded (adj)
syn. small-minded, prejudiced, insular, intolerant, biased, illiberal, bigoted, parochial, conservative
ant. broad-minded, tolerant
nascent (adj)
syn. beginning, developing, embryonic, young, budding, incipient
ant. mature, dying
nasty (adj)
syn. unpleasant, abusive, offensive, revolting, objectionable, loathsome, disagreeable, malicious, wicked, spiteful, mean, ill-tempered, malevolent
ant. pleasant, nice, decent, benevolent
native (n)
syn. resident, citizen, inhabitant, national, dweller
ant. foreigner, outsider
natural (adj)
syn. normal, usual, reasonable, common, pure, genuine, authentic, real, naive, ingenuous, candid, artless, frank, inborn, inherent, innate, indigenous
ant. abnormal, artificial, artful, acquired
naughty (adj)
syn. unruly, annoying, bad, disobedient, indecent, rude, coarse
ant. polite, good, well behaved
nauseous (adj)
syn. sickening, nauseating, loathsome, disgusting, distasteful, revolting, repulsive, offensive
ant. pleasant, delightful
nearby (adj)
syn. accessible, handy, near, not far away
ant. distant
neat (adj)
syn. tidy, clean, smart, trim, skilful, clever, expert, apt, elegant
ant. untidy, messy, clumsy

nebulous (adj)
syn. vague, obscure, cloudy, indistinct, hazy, shapeless, imprecise
ant. clear, transparent
necessary (adj)
syn. needed, obligatory, required, requisite, essential, compulsory, indispensable, inescapable, inevitable
ant. unnecessary, inessential, unimportant
need (adj)
syn. demand, requirement, want, necessity, distress, poverty
ant. sufficiency
needless (adj)
syn. unnecessary, pointless, causeless, redundant, superfluous, useless, uncalled-for
ant. necessary, needful
needy (adj)
syn. underprivileged, penniless, impoverished, in need, poor, poverty-stricken, skint
ant. wealthy, well off, affluent
nefarious (adj)
syn. criminal, heinous, infamous, sinful, horrible, evil, base, wicked, vile, scandalous
ant. admirable, exemplary
negation (n)
syn. opposite, contrary, reverse, contradiction, refusal, void, nothing, denial, veto
ant. affirmation
negative (adj)
syn. opposing, contradictory, contrary, denying, pessimistic, antagonistic, cynical, gloomy, apathetic, harmful, unfavourable
ant. positive, optimistic, favourable
negligent (adj)
syn. neglectful, careless, forgetful, heedless, remiss, unmindful, indifferent, lax, inattentive, uncaring, thoughtless, irresponsible
ant. careful, heedful, dutiful, attentive, scrupulous
neglect (v)
syn. disregard, leave alone, ignore, forget, fail, overlook, abandon, omit
ant. remember, cherish, nurture

negligence (n)
syn. carelessness, disregard, laxity, neglect, oversight, slackness, heedlessness, thoughtlessness, inattention
ant. care, regard, attentiveness, attention

negligible (adj)
syn. insignificant, trivial, unimportant, minor, slight, small
ant. important, significant

neighbouring (adj)
syn. adjacent, adjoining, connecting, nearby, bordering, next, next-door, proximate, close
ant. remote, distant, faraway

neighbourly (adj)
syn. friendly, cordial, sociable, amiable, amicable, generous, kind, civil, helpful, hospitable, attentive, obliging
ant. unneighbourly, unsociable, unfriendly, aloof

neophyte (n)
syn. convert, novice, learner, beginner, proselyte, pupil, student, trainee
ant. master

nerve (n)
syn. confidence, bravery, valour, will power, determination, guts, audacity, presumption, arrogance, cheek, boldness, insolence
ant. cowardice, timidity, weakness

nervous (adj)
syn. worried, apprehensive, anxious, stressed, tense
ant. relaxed, calm, cool, confident

nervousness (n)
syn. anxiety, tension, agitation, worry, heebie-jeebies, disquiet, excitability, perturbation
ant. calmness, coolness, composure

nether (adj)
syn. lower, bottom, inferior, under
ant. upper

nettle (v)
syn. irritate, vex, provoke, annoy, pique, enrage, harass, exasperate, ruffle, irk, incense
ant. soothe, calm, pacify, relieve

neurotic (adj)
syn. nervous, paranoid, hysterical, tense, obsessive, oversensitive,

abnormal, anxious
ant. calm, normal, stable
neutral (adj)
syn. impartial, disinterested, unprejudiced, unbiased, harmless, safe, innocuous, pale, dull, insipid
ant. biased, provocative, partisan
neutralize (v)
syn. counterbalance, negate, counteract, undo, nullify, invalidate, annul
ant. intensify
never (adv)
syn. at no time, not at all
ant. always
newfangled (adj)
syn. modern, contemporary, new, trendy, fashionable, recent, novel
ant. old-fashioned
newness (n)
syn. freshness, uniqueness, innovation, strangeness, novelty, unfamiliarity
ant. oldness, ordinariness
niggardly (adj)
syn. parsimonious, miserly, mean, tight, close-fisted, frugal, tight-fisted, meagre, insufficient
ant. generous, ample
nightfall (n)
syn. dusk, evening, sunset, twilight, sundown
ant. dawn, daybreak
nightmare (n)
syn. ordeal, misery, suffering, torture, trial, agony, hell, tribulation, hardship, trouble, purgatory, the pits
ant. ecstasy, joy, euphoria
nightmarish (adj)
syn. alarming, frightening, agonising, creepy, horrible, disturbing, harrowing, terrifying, scaring, ominous, shocking
ant. soothing, calming, peaceful, reassuring
nihilist (n)
syn. disbeliever, sceptic, cynic, agonistic, revolutionary, atheist, agitator
ant. believer
nimble (adj)
syn. active, agile, lively, active, ready, prompt, quick, swift, clever, intelligent

ant. clumsy, awkward

nice (adj)

syn. pleasant, lovely, amiable, friendly, civil, kind, mild, fine

ant. unpleasant, nasty

nimbly (adv)

syn. actively, quickly, briskly, acutely, smartly, sharply, alertly

ant. clumsily, awkwardly

nitwit (n)

(informal)

syn. fool, half-wit, ass, idiot, simpleton, dummy, numbskull, dimwit

ant. genius, brain

nobility (n)

syn. aristocracy, nobles, lords, gentry, upper class, eminence, greatness, loftiness, nobleness, exaltation, virtue, magnificence

ant. commonalty, lowliness

noble (adj)

syn. aristocratic, high-born, worthy, honourable, magnificent, grand, majestic

ant. lowborn, humble, lowly

noble (n)

syn. aristocrat, lord, patrician, baron, aristo

ant. commoner

noise (n)

syn. sound, clamour, outcry, cry, row, din, commotion, pandemonium, uproar, hullabaloo

ant. silence, quiet

noisome (adj)

syn. foul, offensive, unwholesome, poisonous, noxious, malodorous, unhealthy, hurtful, injurious, mischievous

ant. wholesome, healthy, beneficial

non compos mentis (adj)

(also non compos)

syn. crazy, mentally ill, mad, unbalanced, insane, deranged, of unsound mind

ant. compos mentis, sane, stable

noisy (adj)

syn. clamorous, chattering, loud, blaring, rioting, turbulent, cacophonous, strident ant. quiet, peaceful

nominal (adj)

syn. formal, supposed, theoretical, inconsiderable, small, token

ant. actual, real, considerable

nonchalance (n)

syn. composure, calm, cool, indifference, unconcern

ant. worriedness, anxiousness

nonchalant (adj)

syn. careless, unconcerned, apathetic, dispassionate, casual, calm, cool, composed, indifferent

ant. concerned, anxious

nondescript (adj)

syn. indefinite, dull, ordinary, unremarkable, commonplace, unexceptional, bland

ant. distinctive, remarkable

nonentity (n)

syn. nobody, nothing, cipher, zero

ant. somebody

nonpareil (adj)

syn. unique, matchless, supreme, peerless, incomparable, unparalleled, unmatched, unequalled

ant. ordinary, common

nonplus (v)

syn. puzzle, stump, bewilder, confound, astonish, perplex, taken aback, mystify, confuse, baffle

ant. enlighten, educate

nonsense (n)

syn. folly, absurdity, foolishness, balderdash, rubbish, trash, silliness, stupidity, senselessness, humbug, bullshit

ant. sense, understanding, wisdom, intellect

nonsensical (adj)

syn. senseless, foolish, silly, ludicrous, meaningless, crazy, absurd, incomprehensible, irrational

ant. sensible, logical, rational

normal (adj)

syn. accustomed, common, natural, routine, usual, regular, ordinary, sane, rational

ant. abnormal, insane, peculiar, odd

normality (n)
syn. commonness, ordinariness, regularity, balance, rationality, routine
ant. abnormality, peculiarity
normally (adv)
syn. as a rule, naturally, conventionally, usually
ant. abnormally
nostalgic (adj)
syn. sentimental, regretful, emotional, wistful, homesick, maudlin
ant. realistic
nosy (adj)
(informal)
syn. curious, inquisitive, interfering, prying, meddlesome, snooping
ant. incurious, uninterested
notability (n)
syn. celebrity, dignitary, esteem, notable, fame, eminence, luminary, VIP
ant. nonentity, nobody
notable (adj)
syn. noted, remarkable, memorable, noteworthy, celebrated, important, prominent
ant. unremarkable, unknown
notable (n)
syn. celebrity, dignitary, VIP, personage, worthy, somebody, big shot
ant. nonentity, nobody
noted (adj)
syn. notable, famous, eminent, celebrated, great, well-known, renowned, distinguished
ant. unknown, undistinguished
noteworthy (adj)
syn. significant, notable, remarkable, unique, unusual, exceptional, important, memorable
ant. unexceptional, usual, ordinary
nothing (n)
syn. nil, nought, nothingness, cipher, zero, nonexistence
ant. something
notice (v)
syn. observe, see, detect, note, perceive, heed, clock
ant. overlook, miss

noticeable (adj)
syn. conspicuous, clear, obvious, distinct, perceptible, apparent, manifest
ant. inconspicuous, obscure

notify (v)
syn. inform, advise, tell, alert, apprise, disclose, announce, warn
ant. suppress

notoriety (n)
syn. infamy, disrepute, disgrace, scandal, obloquy, shame, opprobrium
ant. renown, honour, illustriousness, fame, glory

notorious (adj)
syn. infamous, disreputable, dishonourable, scandalous, disgraceful, ignominious
ant. famous, honoured, illustrious

nourish (v)
syn. feed, nurse, nurture, care for, encourage, support, maintain
ant. starve

nourishing (adj)
syn. nutritious, healthy, beneficial, nutritive, health-giving, wholesome
ant. unhealthy

novel (adj)
syn. fresh, new, different, uncommon, unfamiliar, unconventional, unusual, original, innovative
ant. stale, traditional, familiar, ordinary

novice (n)
syn. trainee, student, tyro, learner, beginner, amateur, neophyte, probationer, rookie
ant. master, expert, veteran, professional

now (adv)
syn. at the moment, nowadays, today, right away, at once, immediately
ant. then, later

noxious (adj)
syn. deadly, dangerous, harmful, detrimental, poisonous, unfriendly, baleful, unpleasant, unhealthy, unwholesome, destructive
ant. innocuous, beneficial, wholesome

nude (adj)
syn. naked, undressed, unclothed, uncovered, exposed, bare
ant. clothed, dressed

nugatory (adj)
syn. worthless, useless, insignificant, trifling, vain, futile, bootless
ant. valuable, useful

nuisance (n)
syn. annoyance, bother, pest, inconvenience, vexation, trouble, headache, pain
ant. pleasure, delight

null (adj)
syn. invalid, void, useless, worthless, nugatory, ineffectual
ant. valid

nullify (v)
syn. revoke, abolish, cancel, void, annul, invalidate, quash, abrogate, repeal, veto
ant. validate, ratify, certify, approve

numb (adj)
syn. benumbed, immobile, dead, deadened, paralysed, unfeeling, insensible, insensitive, anesthetized, unconscious
ant. sensitive, alert, conscious

numerous (adj)
syn. many, countless, copious, a lot of
ant. few

numskull (n)
(also numbskull)
syn. dimwit, fool, blockhead, dummy, simpleton, dunce, a stupid person
ant. genius, brain, scholar

nurse (v)
syn. care for, look after, treat, nurture, feed, encourage, keep, promote foster
ant. neglect, banish

nurture (v)
syn. train, rear, bring up, develop, raise, educate, foster, feed
ant. neglect

nutritious (adj)
syn. nourishing, healthy, health-giving, nutritive, beneficial, wholesome, good, substantial, invigorating
ant. unhealthy, unwholesome, bad

Oo

obdurate (adj)
syn. adamant, harsh, callous, unfeeling, inflexible, obstinate, headstrong, pig-headed, hard-hearted, stubborn
ant. amenable, submissive, tender

obedient (adj)
syn. compliant, good, docile, submissive, respectful, law-abiding, tractable
ant. disobedient, rebellious

obeisance (n)
syn. respect, homage, reverence, curtsy, worship, deference, salutation, salaam
ant. disrespect, insolence, disregard

obese (adj)
syn. fat, heavy, overweight, bulky, fleshy, corpulent, tubby
ant. skinny, thin

obey (adj)
syn. abide by, act upon, comply, heed, discharge, respect, carry out
ant. disobey, ignore, defy

obfuscate (v)
syn. obscure, cloud, darken, perplex, confuse, muddle
ant. clear, clarify

objection (n)
syn. challenge, demur, opposition, disapproval, grievance, dissent
ant. agreement, assent

objective (adj)
syn. unprejudiced, neutral, impartial, disinterested, fair, non-partisan, unbiased, real, factual, actual
ant. subjective, biased, emotional

objurgate (v)
syn. scold, rebuke, reprimand, chide, reprove, upbraid
ant. praise, commend

oblation (n)
syn. offering, donation, sacrifice, contribution, present, gift
ant. gain

obligation (n)
syn. commitment, bond, accountability, charge, responsibility, duty, contract
ant. choice, discretion
obligatory (adj)
syn. compulsory, bounden, necessary, enforced, requisite, binding
ant. optional
obliged (adj)
syn. thankful, grateful, indebted, appreciative, beholden, compelled
ant. ungrateful, thankless
obliging (adj)
syn. agreeable, amiable, amenable, kind, civil, courteous, friendly, cooperative, willing, accommodating
ant. unobliging, unhelpful, unkind
obliterate (v)
syn. annihilate, eradicate, erase, destroy, wipeout, delete, cancel, hide, blot out
ant. restore, preserve
obliteration (n)
syn. annihilation, eradication, elimination, erasure, extirpation, blotting out, effacement
ant. restoration, preservation
oblivion (n)
syn. darkness, coma, disregard, limbo, forgetfulness, neglect, unconsciousness, obscurity
ant. awareness, consciousness
oblivious (adj)
syn. unaware, ignorant, unconscious, insensible, unmindful, deaf, forgetful, absent-minded
ant. aware, conscious
obloquy (n)
syn. criticism, censure, denunciation, slander, defamation, aspersion, vilification, blame, reproach, ignominy, disgrace, dishonour, shame
ant. praise, commendation, accolade, approval
obnoxious (adj)
syn. disagreeable, foul, objectionable, hateful, abhorrent, loathsome, intolerable, disgusting, odious, unpleasant, nasty
ant. pleasant, delightful, agreeable

obscene (adj)
syn. pornographic, dirty, foul, immoral, salacious, lewd, indecent, vulgar, coarse, immodest, scandalous, blue
ant. clean, decorous, decent

obscure (adj)
syn. ambiguous, vague, uncertain, intricate, unclear, unknown, unsung, unheard-of, incomprehensible, dim, cloudy
ant. clear, famous

obscurity (n)
syn. ambiguity, darkness, haziness, vagueness, lowliness, inconspicuousness, incomprehensibility, insignificance, namelessness
ant. clarity, fame, limelight

obsequious (adj)
syn. flattering, sycophantic, fawning, servile, submissive, slavish
ant. independent, assertive

observant (adj)
syn. alert, attentive, mindful, watchful, sharp-eyed, vigilant, perceptive
ant. unobservant, inattentive

obsessed (adj)
syn. immersed, bedevilled, haunted, possessed, infatuated, smitten, hung up
ant. detached, unconcerned, indifferent

obsession (n)
syn. mania, fixation, passion, preoccupation, infatuation, compulsion, phobia, neurosis, crush
ant. indifference, disenchantment

obsolescent (adj)
syn. declining, dying out, moribund, waning, disappearing, fading, on the way out
ant. flourishing, alive, lively

obsolete (adj)
syn. out of date, ancient, old-fashioned, archaic, dead, discarded, dated, antiquated, old
ant. modern, current, new

obstacle (n)
syn. hurdle, bar, barrier, difficulty, obstruction, block, problem, snag, impediment, hindrance
ant. assistance, help, aid, advantage

obstinacy (n)
syn. stubbornness, firmness, inflexibility, perseverance, perversity,
pig-headedness, tenacity, obduracy, persistence
ant. flexibility, cooperativeness, submissiveness
obstinate (adj)
syn. stubborn, bull-headed, pig-headed, headstrong, firm, unbending,
rusty, adamant, inflexible, tenacious, wilful
ant. amenable, compliant, flexible, submissive
obstreperous (adj)
syn. noisy, turbulent, boisterous, disorderly, clamorous, loud, uproarious,
rowdy, unmanageable, uncontrolled, undisciplined
ant. quiet, calm, serene, disciplined
obstruct (v)
syn. block, choke, clog, barricade, bar, impede, stop, curb, prevent,
interfere, interrupt, delay
ant. assist, help, facilitate, clear
obstruction (n)
syn. barricade, obstacle, barrier, hindrance, stumbling block, stop,
stoppage, restriction, hold-up, blockage, impediment
ant. assistance, help, facilitation, clearance
obtrusive (adj)
syn. noticeable, conspicuous, obvious, protruding, prominent, interfering,
intrusive, pushy
ant. unobtrusive, retiring
obtuse (adj)
syn. dull, inattentive, slow, boneheaded, stupid, unintelligent,
uncomprehending, imperceptive, thick-skinned, retarded
ant. sharp, keen, bright, intelligent
obvious (adj)
syn. clear, apparent, evident, conspicuous, perceptible, noticeable, visible,
unmistakable, unconcealed
ant. unclear, hidden, obscure, imperceptible
occasional (adj)
syn. infrequent, casual, incidental, intermittent, irregular, sporadic, periodic
ant. frequent, regular, constant
occasionally (adv)
syn. sometimes, seldom, periodically, rarely, now and then, at times,
sporadically

ant. frequently, often
odd (adj)
syn. abnormal, bizarre, strange, puzzling, occasional, various, sundry, unmatched, mismatched, leftover
ant. normal, ordinary, regular
odious (adj)
syn. abhorrent, annoying, disgusting, hateful, foul, heinous, horrible
ant. pleasant
odium (n)
syn. dislike, hatred, hate, abhorrence, antipathy, obloquy, disfavour, dishonour, censure, shame
ant. liking, love, honour
odorous (adj)
syn. sweet-smelling, perfumed, fragrant, scented, aromatic, balmy, pungent
ant. inodorous, odourless, scentless
offend (v)
syn. upset, hurt, insult, humiliate, miff, irritate, violate, displease, annoy, disgust
ant. please, delight, enchant
offender (n)
syn. miscreant, criminal, wrongdoer, culprit, sinner, lawbreaker
ant. saint, worthy
offensive (adj)
syn. rude, disrespectful, insulting, unpleasant, dreadful, horrible, hostile, bellicose, aggressive, warlike
ant. complimentary, pleasant, defensive
offensive (n)
syn. attack, invasion, incursion, campaign, onslaught, raid, blitz
ant. defence, retreat
offer (v)
syn. present, extend, give, hold out, furnish, bid, put forward
ant. withdraw, refuse
offhand (adj)
syn. careless, indifferent, casual, uninterested, dismissive, nonchalant, cursory
ant. planned, calculated

officious (adj)
syn. self-important, self-assertive, intrusive, meddling, interfering, obtrusive, dictatorial, impertinent, pushy, bossy
ant. humble, meek, compliant, self-effacing

offspring (n)
syn. child, children, descendant, seed, progeny, posterity, heirs, successors
ant. parent(s)

often (adv)
syn. frequently, regularly, repeatedly, again and again, commonly, generally
ant. seldom, occasionally

old-fashioned (adj)
syn. out of fashion, outdated, out of date, unfashionable, antiquated, archaic, obsolete, old hat
ant. modern, up-to-date, contemporary

ominous (adj)
syn. threatening, baleful, fateful, dark, sinister, unpromising, menacing, inauspicious
ant. promising, auspicious

omission (n)
syn. exclusion, avoidance, leaving out, deletion, negligence, exception, neglect, oversight, forgetfulness
ant. inclusion, addition

omit (v)
syn. exclude, leave out, skip, miss, miss out, cut, overlook, forget, fail, neglect
ant. include, add, remember

omnipotent (adj)
syn. almighty, all-powerful, sovereign, supreme
ant. impotent, feeble

omniscient (adj)
syn. all-knowing, all-seeing, all-wise
ant. ignorant

once (adv)
syn. previously, long ago, formerly, at one time, once upon a time
ant. now

oncoming (adj)
syn. forthcoming, upcoming, advancing, approaching, impending, imminent
ant. previous

onerous (adj)
syn. burdensome, responsible, heavy, hard, oppressive, difficult, arduous, laborious, toilsome
ant. easy, light, effortless

one-sided (adj)
syn. biased, partial, partisan, unfair, prejudiced, unbalanced, unequal
ant. impartial, equal

onset (n)
syn. start, arrival, commencement, beginning, outbreak, inception, kick-off
ant. end, finish

onslaught (n)
syn. attack, offensive, assault, blitz, charge, bombardment, onset, barrage, advance
ant. defence, retreat

onus (n)
syn. burden, responsibility, obligation, load, encumbrance, duty
ant. irresponsibility

oodles (n)
(old-fashioned, informal)
syn. loads, lots, abundance, heaps, tons, large amount
ant. scarcity

opaque (adj)
syn. cloudy, hazy, non-transparent, blurred, misty, dull, obscure, unintelligible, incomprehensible, unclear
ant. transparent, clear

open (adj)
syn. unlocked, unclosed, unfolded, exposed, unenclosed, unfilled, free, vulnerable, frank, candid, out-spoken, plain, clear, undisguised
ant. shut, closed

open-handed (adj)
syn. generous, bountiful, liberal, lavish, free
ant. tight-fisted, mean

openly (adv)
syn. blatantly, publicly, overtly, honestly, frankly, candidly, sincerely
ant. secretly

open-minded (adj)
syn. broad-minded, neutral, unbiased, objective, liberal, impartial,

unprejudiced, tolerant, fair
ant. narrow-minded, prejudiced, bigoted
opiate (n)
syn. tranquillizer, narcotic, soporific, sedative
ant. stimulant
opinion (n)
syn. belief, view, viewpoint, idea, conviction, standpoint, point of view, fancy, theory
ant. knowledge
opinionated (adj)
syn. arrogant, overconfident, dogmatic, opinionative, pig-headed, bigoted, dictatorial, biased, prejudiced, overbearing
ant. meek, open-minded, liberal, unbiased
opponent (n)
syn. rival, enemy, competitor, challenger, antagonist, adversary, critic, dissenter, objector
ant. ally, supporter, proponent, advocate
opportune (adj)
syn. timely, well-timed, convenient, apt, fit, fitting, favourable, suitable, auspicious, lucky
ant. inopportune, untimely, unfavourable
oppose (v)
syn. resist, disagree with, challenge, be against, confront, counter, thwart, defy
ant. support, favour
opposing (adj)
syn. antagonistic, clashing, conflicting, contrary, antipathetic, opposed, irreconcilable, rival
ant. similar, allied, related
opposition (n)
syn. antagonism, dissent, resistance, hostility, adversary, opponent(s), rival(s), opposing side
ant. agreement, support, co-operation
oppressed (adj)
syn. downtrodden, persecuted, underprivileged, troubled, henpecked, subjugated, exploited, victimized, underfoot
ant. free, liberated

oppression (n)
syn. persecution, tyranny, misery, subjugation, subjection, abuse, hardship, cruelty, injustice, repression, injustice, despotism, ill-treatment
ant. freedom, liberty

oppressive (adj)
syn. brutal, harsh, despotic, merciless, cruel, repressive, ruthless, unjust, hot, humid, sultry
ant. lenient, gentle, mild, fresh

opprobrious (adj)
syn. dishonourable, shameful, ignominious, disgraceful, reprehensible, infamous, defamatory, slanderous, contemptuous, offensive, derogatory
ant. honourable, virtuous, laudatory, complimentary

opprobrium (n)
syn. dishonour, shame, ignominy, disgrace, infamy, degradation, stigma, censure, scurrility, reproach, disfavour, debasement
ant. esteem, respect, admiration, honour

optimistic (adj)
syn. positive, hopeful, encouraging, buoyant
ant. pessimistic, depressing

optimum (adj)
syn. best, perfect, A1, ideal, top, highest, optimal
ant. worst

optional (adj)
syn. elective, voluntary, unforced, open, discretionary
ant. compulsory

opulence (n)
syn. prosperity, luxuriance, luxury, affluence, abundance, profusion, fortune, plenty, riches, wealth
ant. poverty, penury

opulent (adj)
syn. affluent, luxurious, grand, prolific, rich, splendid, well-off, wealthy, plush
ant. spartan, poor, penurious

ordeal (n)
syn. trial, suffering, hell, tribulation, torture, agony, trauma, affliction, hardship, nightmare
ant. ecstasy, joy, euphoria

orderly (adj)
syn. tidy, neat, well-ordered, trim, methodical, well-organized, systematic, logical, coherent, disciplined, well-behaved, peaceful
ant. untidy, disorderly, unruly

ordinary (adj)
syn. usual, common, everyday, normal, routine, average, prosaic, conventional, run-of-the-mill, humdrum
ant. unusual, extraordinary, uncommon, special

organic (adj)
syn. living, natural, biological, animate, structural, basic, integral, inherent, fundamental, organized, methodical, ordered, systematic
ant. inorganic, extraneous, external, unsystematic

origin (n)
syn. beginning, birth, start, genesis, inception, descent, ancestry, pedigree, family, source, base, cause, root, derivation
ant. end, termination, result, outcome

original (adj)
syn. indigenous, first, early, earliest, native, actual, authentic, genuine, creative, new, novel, innovative, distinctive, different, unique, edgy
ant. unoriginal, latest, hackneyed, clichéd

original (n)
syn. source, prototype, archetype, master, standard, model
ant. copy, replica

originate (v)
syn. start, begin, arise, emerge, create, develop, invent, conceive, pioneer, think up
ant. abolish, terminate, end

ornate (adj)
syn. decorated, adorned, fancy, elaborate, fussy, showy, beautiful, elegant, flashy
ant. plain, austere

orthodox (adj)
syn. conventional, accepted, customary, true, traditional, conservative, observant, strict, devout
ant. unorthodox, unconventional

ostensible (adj)
syn. pretended, superficial, seeming, outward, professed, manifest, alleged, apparent, pseudo, bogus

ant. real, actual, true
ostentation (n)
syn. boasting, display, parade, pretentiousness, flamboyance, show, window-dressing, flaunting, pomp, flourish, showiness, pageantry, swank
ant. unpretentiousness, reserve, propriety, modesty, simplicity
ostentatious (adj)
syn. showy, vulgar, brash, pretentious, mannered, flamboyant, pompous, conspicuous, boastful, aggressive
ant. quiet, restrained, subdued
ostracize (v)
syn. shun, avoid, exclude, banish, bar, boycott, exile, freeze out, blacklist, blank
ant. accept, welcome, reinstate
oust (v)
syn. expel, depose, eject, drive out, dismiss, turnout
ant. reinstate, install, settle
outcast (n)
syn. outsider, castaway, expatriate, pariah, refugee, vagabond, untouchable, exile
ant. favourite, idol, celebrity, luminary
outcome (n)
syn. result, consequence, upshot, aftermath, issue, effect, end
ant. cause
outcry (n)
syn. noise, uproar, protest, hue and cry, clamour, commotion, howl, vociferation, yell, shout, hullaballoo
ant. quiet, calm, silence, tranquillity
outer (adj)
syn. outside, external, distant, faraway
ant. inner, central
outgoing (adj)
syn. extrovert, chatty, cordial, convivial, gregarious, communicative, friendly, sociable, warm, open, unreserved, retiring
ant. introverted, introspective, unsociable, withdraw, incoming
outlandish (adj)
syn. unconventional, bizarre, unfamiliar, odd, strange, alien, eccentric, grotesque, unheard-of, queer, extraordinary
ant. conventional, familiar, ordinary

outlaw (v)
syn. ban, banish, bar, proscribe, make illegal, disallow, prohibit, embargo, debar
ant. allow, legalize, permit

outlay (n)
syn. expenditure, outgoings, disbursement, spending, expense, cost
ant. income, revenue, earnings

outline (n)
syn. shape, silhouette, contours, profile, lines, form, summary, gist, synopsis, precis, sketch, rough idea, abstract, epitome
ant. amplification, expansion, enlargement, augmentation

outrage (n)
syn. anger, hurt, fury, indignation, rage, shock, wrath, annoyance, ire, scandal, insult, disgrace, abuse
ant. calm, happiness

outrageous (adj)
syn. shocking, appalling, dreadful, intolerable, horrible, violent, disgraceful, ridiculous, exaggerated, excessive
ant. acceptable, reasonable, irreproachable

outright (adj)
syn. absolute, complete, utter, perfect, sheer, undeniable, definite, total, thorough, unconditional, direct
ant. indefinite, ambiguous, provisional

outset (n)
syn. beginning, opening, starting point, commencement, inauguration, inception, start, kick off
ant. end, conclusion, finish

outskirts (n)
syn. borders, fringes, edges, vicinity, suburbs, periphery, environs
ant. centre, city-centre

outspoken (adj)
syn. candid, direct, frank, explicit, unreserved, blunt, forthright, free, straightforward, open
ant. reserved, reticent, tactful, diplomatic

outspread (adj)
syn. spread out, extended, unfolded, outstretched, open, unfurled
ant. closed

outstanding (adj)
syn. excellent, superb, marvellous, impressive, exceptional, striking, notable, conspicuous, ace, remarkable, fine, wonderful, terrific, great, unpaid, due
ant. insignificant, ordinary, unexceptional, paid
outward (adj)
syn. external, superficial, ostensible, surface, seeming, outside, visible
ant. inward, inner
outwardly (adv)
syn. externally, superficially, ostensibly, seemingly, evidently, apparently
ant. inwardly, internally
outworn (adj)
syn. outdated, out of date, stale, abandoned, overused, worn-out, exhausted, rejected, clichéd, obsolete
ant. new, fresh
ovation (n)
syn. praise, applause, cheering, laudation, acclamation, acclaim, plaudits, commendation, accolade, eulogy
ant. denunciation, condemnation, censure, criticism
overawe (v)
syn. frighten, intimidate, scare, browbeat, abash, domineer, terrify, alarm, perturb
ant. reassure, cheer, encourage
overbearing (adj)
syn. domineering, dominating, arrogant, despotic, tyrannical, high-handed, autocratic, haughty, imperious, bossy
ant. humble, modest, unassertive, liberal
overcast (adj)
syn. cloudy, sunless, black, hazy, murky, dull, sombre, gloomy
ant. clear, bright, sunny
overcome (v)
syn. conquer, subdue, defeat, vanquish, crush, beat, surmount, overpower
ant. submit, surrender
overdo (v)
syn. exaggerate, overact, overstate, overindulge, overplay, go to extremes, overcook
ant. neglect, underuse

overdue (adj)
syn. late, delayed, behind time, tardy, owed, due, unpaid, outstanding, unsettled
ant. early, punctual

overemphasize (v)
syn. overstress, exaggerate, overdramatize, labour
ant. underemphasize, understate

overestimate (v)
syn. overvalue, overrate, exaggerate, over praise
ant. underestimate

overflow (v)
syn. overspill, surge, run over, swamp, deluge, flood
ant. subside

overheated (adj)
syn. excited, overexcited, agitated, impassioned, passionate, flaming, roused
ant. calm, dispassionate

overindulgence (n)
syn. excess, debauch, immoderation, surfeit, intemperance, overeating
ant. abstention, abstemiousness

overjoyed (adj)
syn. delighted, elated, thrilled, ecstatic, jubilant, euphoric, delirious, over the moon, on cloud nine
ant. upset, sad, disappointed

overload (v)
syn. overburden, overcharge, burden, encumber, oppress
ant. relieve

overlook (v)
syn. ignore, leave out, omit, miss, disregard, forget, pass over, excuse, forgive, condone
ant. note, notice, punish

overpowering (adj)
syn. overwhelming, forceful, strong, uncontrollable, irresistible, powerful, weighty, intolerable, oppressive
ant. weak, controllable

overriding (adj)
syn. dominant, compelling, essential, major, paramount, prime, ultimate, supreme, most important, cardinal, number one, central

ant. unimportant, insignificant

overrule (v)

syn. cancel, revoke, repeal, recall, annul, countermand, quash, disallow, overthrow, override, reverse, overturn, veto, reject

ant. approve, allow, confirm, enact

overrun (v)

syn. invade, attack, occupy, ravage, permeate, storm, overwhelm, run riot, infest, exceed

ant. evacuate, desert

overt (adj)

syn. open, apparent, evident, unconcealed, visible, clear

ant. covert, secret

overthrow (v)

syn. unseat, oust, dethrone, depose, bring down, defeat, overturn, abolish, demolish, raze, vanquish, conquer

ant. restore, reinstate, install

overthrow (n)

syn. unseating, ousting, dethronement, deposition, defeat, abolition, demolition, displacement, removal, end

ant. restoration, reinstatement

overture (n)

syn. proposal, approach, advance, invitation, proposition, offer, opening, introduction, prologue

ant. rejection, finale

overweight (adj)

syn. fat, obese, heavy, fleshy, stout, hefty, pot-bellied, tubby, podgy

ant. underweight, skinny, thin

overwhelming (adj)

syn. immense, breathtaking, invincible, stunning, massive, irresistible

ant. negligible, insignificant

overwrought (adj)

syn. tense, agitated, frantic, excited, overexcited, overheated, emotional, overworked, elaborate, ornate, fancy, overdone

ant. calm, cool, plain

owing (adj)

syn. due, owed, in arrears, payable, unpaid, unsettled, outstanding

ant. paid

Pp

pacific (adj)
(literary)
syn. peaceable, nonviolent, conciliatory, mild, peace-making, peace-loving, placatory, gentle, quiet, peaceful, serene, still, calm
ant. belligerent, aggressive, turbulent, agitated

pacify (v)
syn. appease, placate, assuage, calm, silence, tame, lull, soothe, subdue, allay, mitigate
ant. aggravate, enrage, anger

packed (adj)
syn. crowded, filled, full, jammed, swarming, crammed, overloaded, jam-packed
ant. deserted, empty

pact (n)
syn. agreement, bond, concord, compact, entente, alliance, deal, treaty, league
ant. disagreement, breach, quarrel

pagan (n)
syn. atheist, heathen, idolater, infidel, unbeliever
ant. believer

pageant (n)
syn. parade, show, tableau, procession, extravaganza, spectacle, display
ant. modesty, humbleness

pageantry (n)
syn. magnificence, grandeur, show, pomp, spectacle, splendour, display, glamour, ceremony, ostentation, showiness
ant. modesty, reserve, propriety, simplicity

pain (n)
syn. suffering, ache, hurt, agony, pang, trouble, misery, grief, anguish, sorrow
ant. relief, joy

pained (adj)
syn. hurt, aggrieved, injured, miffed, upset

ant. gratified, pleased
painful (adj)
syn. aching, agonizing, hurting, sore, unpleasant, unhappy, distressing, harrowing, difficult, hard, troublesome, arduous
ant. painless, pleasant, easy
painstaking (adj)
syn. careful, assiduous, rigorous, meticulous, attentive, thorough, scrupulous, sedulous, diligent
ant. slapdash, careless, negligent
pal (n)
(informal)
syn. friend, comrade, companion, buddy, partner, crony
ant. enemy
palatable (adj)
syn. tasty, delicious, luscious, toothsome, mouth-watering, pleasant, satisfactory, acceptable, agreeable
ant. unpalatable, unpleasant, unacceptable, disagreeable
palatial (adj)
syn. splendid, luxurious, lavish, fancy, sumptuous, grand, majestic, splendid, regal, magnificent, posh, swanky, plush
ant. modest, mean, cramped, poky
pale (adj)
syn. colourless, white, wan, anaemic, sickly, faded, washed out, light, feeble, weak, dim
ant. ruddy, bright, dark
palliate (v)
syn. relieve, allay, alleviate, assuage, soften, soothe, abate, lessen, minimize, diminish, excuse, cover up, conceal
ant. aggravate, provoke, expose
palliative (adj)
syn. calming, soothing, alleviative, mollifying, mitigative, lenitive
ant. irritant, annoying
pallid (adj)
syn. pale, white, whitish, insipid, colourless, wan, ashen, lifeless, tired, spiritless
ant. ruddy, high-complexioned, vigorous
pallor (n)
syn. paleness, whiteness, pallidity, pallidness, wanness

ant. ruddiness

pally (adj)
syn. friendly, intimate, close, affectionate, thick, familiar, chummy
ant. unfriendly

palmy (adj)
syn. flourishing, glorious, prosperous, fortunate, halcyon, happy
ant. unfortunate, ill-fated

palpable (adj)
syn. touchable, tangible, substantial, real, visible, observable, transparent, clear, open, overt, conspicuous, apparent, unmistakable
ant. impalpable, imperceptible, unnoticeable, invisible, elusive

paltry (adj)
syn. meagre, small, negligible, trivial, little, insignificant, insufficient, petty, miserable, pitiful, poxy
ant. considerable, significant, substantial

pamper (v)
syn. indulge, ruin, spoil, humour, coddle, cosset, baby, fondle, mollycoddle, gratify
ant. discipline, neglect, ill-treat

panacea (n)
syn. elixir, remedy, cure-all, medicine, nostrum, antidote, solution
ant. poison, toxin

panache (n)
syn. flair, style, flamboyance, self-assurance, confidence, spirit, liveliness, vivacity, energy, vitality, pizzazz
ant. diffidence, shyness, modesty, restraint

pandemonium (n)
syn. uproar, chaos, din, maelstrom, confusion, disorder, ruckus, bedlam, clamour, commotion, noise
ant. calm, peace, order, serenity

panegyric (n)
syn. praise, eulogy, accolade, commendation, tribute, encomium
ant. tirade, denunciation

pang (n)
syn. pain, ache, prick, spasm, twinge, discomfort, anguish, agony, trouble
ant. relief, joy

panic (n)
syn. fear, alarm, terror, hysteria, anxiety, apprehension, dismay,

consternation, confusion, cold sweat, flap
ant. calm, composure, confidence, assurance
panoramic (adj)
syn. extensive, comprehensive, wide, widespread, scenic, far-reaching
ant. limited
parable (n)
syn. fable, story, tale, allegory, lesson, legend, myth
ant. truth, fact
parade (n)
syn. march, procession, display, pageant, ostentation, exhibition, show, spectacle
ant. modesty, humbleness
parallel (adj)
syn. similar, corresponding, aligned, like, equidistant, analogous, equal, equivalent, matching, akin
ant. divergent, separate
parallel (n)
syn. match, counterpart, twin, equivalent, likeness, analogy, similarity, comparison, resemblance, correspondence
ant. converse, opposite, difference,
paradise (n)
syn. heaven, utopia, bliss, delight, happiness, joy
ant. hell, purgatory
paradoxical (adj)
syn. absurd, illogical, ambiguous, baffling, contradictory, puzzling, improbable, conflicting
ant. logical, sensible, rational
paramount (adj)
syn. chief, foremost, prime, most, important, supreme, central, topmost, principal, leading, number-one
ant. minor, lowest, inferior, last
paranoia (n)
(informal, medical)
syn. mistrust, suspicion, anxiety, insecurity, obsession, fear, apprehension
ant. calm, composure, trust
paranoid (adj)
(also paranoiac)
syn. mistrustful, suspicious, anxious, insecure, obsessive, fearful, apprehensive

ant. calm, normal, trustful

paraphrase (n)

syn. explanation, interpretation, restatement, rewording, translation, recapitulation

ant. mystification, misrepresentation

parched (adj)

syn. dried up/out, baked, withered, arid, burned, scorched, dry, dehydrated, thirsty, gasping

ant. flooded, fertile

pardon (v)

syn. condone, forgive, excuse, absolve, exonerate, reprieve, acquit, release, let off

ant. punish, blame, condemn

pardon (n)

syn. condonation, forgiveness, excuse, absolution, exoneration, reprieve, acquittal, amnesty, release

ant. punishment, blame, conviction, condemnation

pardonable (adj)

syn. condonable, forgivable, excusable, permissible, justifiable, remissible, allowable, dispensable, venial, understandable

ant. unpardonable, unforgivable, inexcusable, reprehensible

pariah (n)

syn. outcast, untouchable, castaway, outsider, exile, outlaw, leper

ant. favourite, idol, celebrity

parity (n)

syn. equality, equivalence, uniformity, sameness, par, analogy, identity, agreement, similarity, parallelism

ant. disparity, difference, contrast, dissimilarity

parlance (n)

syn. idiom, jargon, tongue, vernacular, language, talk, speech, lingo

ant. formality

parochial (adj)

syn. narrow-minded, confined, narrow, insular, provincial, conservative, small-minded, illiberal

ant. broad-minded, unprejudiced, liberal

parody (n)

syn. satire, burlesque, imitation, mockery, mimicry, spoof, send up, travesty, distortion, perversion, misrepresentation

ant. respect, admiration
parry (v)
syn. deflect, ward off, block, avert, fend off, evade, avoid, dodge, sidestep
ant. direct, encourage
parsimonious (adj)
syn. frugal, miserable, miserly, ungenerous, money-grubbing, saving, mean, penurious, tight-fisted
ant. generous, open-handed, liberal
parsimony (n)
syn. meanness, stinginess, frugality, tight-fistedness, niggardliness
ant. generosity, liberality
parson (n)
syn. cleric, clergyman, churchman, preacher, priest, pastor, rector
ant. layman
partial ^{1} (adj)
syn. imperfect, limited, incomplete, unfinished, fragmentary
ant. complete, total
partial ^{2} (adj)
syn. biased, discriminatory, prejudiced, partisan, one-sided, unjust, unfair
ant. impartial, disinterested, unbiased, fair
partiality (n)
syn. bias, prejudice, discrimination, affinity, penchant, fondness, love, favouritism
ant. justice, dislike
partially (adv)
syn. partly, fractionally, somewhat, incompletely
ant. wholly, entirely
parting (n)
syn. farewell, valediction, goodbye, going, separation, division, break, disunion, split
ant. meeting, convergence, union
parting (adj)
syn. farewell, departing, valedictory, closing, concluding, last, final, deathbed
ant. arriving, opening, first
partisan (n)
syn. follower, adherent, guerilla, underground fighter, enthusiast, devotee, stalwart, supporter, champion

ant. opponent, adversary, antagonist
partisan (adj)
syn. biased, partial, prejudiced, discriminatory, one-sided, factional, partial
ant. nonpartisan, neutral, unbiased
partly (adv)
syn. partially, a little, slightly, in part, somewhat, incompletely, up to a point
ant. wholly, completely
partner (n)
syn. associate, collaborator, colleague, co-worker, teammate, comrade, accomplice, sidekick, mate, spouse
ant. rival, competitor, antagonist
passable (adj)
syn. satisfactory, all right, not excellent, acceptable, ordinary, unexceptional, OK, so-so, open, clear, navigable, unobstructed
ant. excellent, exceptional, sterling, impassable, blocked
passion (n)
syn. emotion, vigour, zeal, enthusiasm, intensity, love, lust, fascination, mania, obsession, fanaticism, addiction
ant. apathy, coolness, calm
passionate (adj)
syn. emotional, intense, fervent, excited, impassioned, heartfelt, crazy, very keen, erotic, lustful, sensual, hot-blooded
ant. apathetic, cool, calm, frigid
passive (adj)
syn. inactive, non-active, lifeless, uninvolved, docile, submissive, compliant
ant. active, resistant
pastime (n)
syn. entertainment, activity, hobby, amusement, sport, recreation
ant. vocation, business, work
past master (n)
syn. expert, ace, wizard, adept, connoisseur, specialist
ant. incompetent, novice
pastoral (adj)
syn. rural, agricultural, country, rustic, priestly, clerical
ant. urban

pasty (adj)
syn. anaemic, pale, pasty-faced, sickly, unhealthy, wan, gluey, sticky, waxy
ant. healthy, rubicund, ruddy

patent (adj)
syn. explicit, apparent, clear, indisputable, open, overt
ant. hidden, opaque

patent (n)
syn. copyright, right, licence, privilege, invention, grant
ant. disadvantage

pathetic (adj)
syn. sad moving, pitiful, poignant, heart-rending, poor, deplorable, sorry, weak, feeble, lamentable
ant. cheerful, admirable

patience (n)
syn. tolerance, forbearance, restraint, understanding, endurance, perseverance, tenacity
ant. impatience, intolerance

patient (adj)
syn. forbearing, tolerant, calm, stoical, enduring, persevering, tenacious, submissive
ant. impatient, intolerant

patrician (adj)
syn. aristocratic, gentle, noble, high-born, lordly, blue-blooded
ant. humble, common, plebeian

patrician (n)
syn. aristocrat, noble, nobleman, earl, peer, gentleman, lord
ant. plebeian, commoner

patriotic (adj)
syn. nationalistic, loyalist, chauvinistic, jingoistic, loyal
ant. traitorous

patronage (n)
syn. aid, aegis, backing, assistance, help, encouragement, sponsorship, support, subscription, commerce
ant. opposition, hindrance

paucity (n)
syn. shortage, fewness, poverty, meagreness, dearth, scarcity, want, lack, insufficiency
ant. abundance, plenty, prosperity, affluence

pause (v)
syn. stop, halt, break, discontinue, delay, cease, wait, rest
ant. proceed, continue, resume
pause (n)
syn. stop, halt, break, intermission, interval, delay, cessation, rest
ant. continuance, continuation, resumption
peace (n)
syn. quiet, stillness, serenity, truce, treaty, concord, amity
ant. disturbance, noise, war
peaceable (adj)
syn. peaceful, pacific, peace-loving, amicable, nonviolent, gentle, friendly, mild, placatory
ant. warlike, belligerent, offensive
peak (n)
syn. apex, climax, point, zenith, top, pinnacle, acme, summit
ant. nadir, base, bottom
peccant (adj)
syn. sinful, corrupt, bad, wicked, criminal, wrong, faulty, guilty, culpable, morbid
ant. righteous, virtuous, upright, honest
peculiar (adj)
syn. strange, odd, eccentric, curious, abnormal, unusual, distinctive, typical, specific, unique
ant. ordinary, normal, general
peculiarity (n)
syn. characteristic, mannerism, idiosyncrasy, curiosity, oddity, quirk
ant. ordinariness, normality
pedagogue (n)
(old use/formal)
syn. teacher, tutor, educator, instructor
ant. pupil
pedantic (adj)
syn. fussy, finicky, dogmatic, fastidious, erudite, particular, formal, precise
ant. casual, informal, imprecise
pedestrian (adj)
syn. boring, humdrum, dull, tedious, ordinary, mundane, uninteresting, mediocre, prosaic
ant. exciting, bright, imaginative

pedigree (n)
syn. ancestry, descent, lineage, parentage, bloodline, genealogy, family tree, origin, race
ant. posterity, descendants, progeny

pedlar (n)
syn. vendor, hawker, seller, dealer, pusher
ant. buyer

peerless (adj)
syn. unique, matchless, unmatched, unparalleled, unequalled, unsurpassed, incomparable, remarkable, excellent, special
ant. ordinary, common, normal, mediocre

peevish (adj)
syn. ill-tempered, short-tempered, acrimonious, childish, ill-natured, grumpy, irritable, sour, petulant, sulky, sullen
ant. genial, friendly, amicable, good-tempered, good-natured

pejorative (adj)
syn. derogatory, uncomplimentary, unpleasant, damning, condemnatory, bad, debasing, detractive, negative, insulting, defamatory
ant. complimentary, laudatory, flattering, appreciative

pellucid (adj)
syn. transparent, clear, crystalline, translucent, coherent, lucid, intelligible, comprehensible, plain
ant. opaque, impenetrable, unintelligible, unclear

penalize (v)
syn. punish, correct, discipline, disadvantage, handicap
ant. reward

penalty (n)
syn. fine, punishment, forfeit
ant. reward

penchant (n)
syn. liking, preference, love, taste, passion, inclination, fondness, propensity, bias
ant. aversion, dislike

pendent (adj)
syn. hanging, dangling, pendulous, jutting out, suspended, swinging
ant. erect, firm, stiff

pending (adj)
syn. undecided, unresolved, unsettled, outstanding, impending, imminent,

coming, forthcoming, near, approaching
ant. decided, settled, finished, closed

penetrable (adj)
syn. accessible, permeable, porous, fathomable, vulnerable, passable, open, understandable, comprehensible
ant. impenetrable, sealed, incomprehensible, enigmatic

penetrating (adj)
syn. cutting, sharp, harsh, cold, chill, bitter, piercing, shrill, keen, intent, insightful, perceptive, intelligent
ant. mild, gentle, soft, dull

penitence (n)
syn. regret, contrition, remorse, repentance, sorrow, self-reproach, rue, shame
ant. impenitence, adamancy, stubbornness

penitent (adj)
syn. regretful, contrite, remorseful, repentant, sorry, sorrowful, apologetic, conscience-stricken
ant. impenitent, unrepentant, remorseless

penniless (adj)
syn. poor, penurious, needy, impoverished, poverty-stricken, impecunious, indigent, bankrupt, skint
ant. rich, wealthy, affluent, well off, prosperous, loaded

penny-pinching (adj)
syn. parsimonious, frugal, miserly, mean, ungenerous, niggardly, tight-fisted
ant. generous, liberal, open-handed

pensive (adj)
syn. thoughtful, absorbed, absent-minded, contemplative, dreamy, musing, brooding, sad, mournful, serious, sober
ant. realistic, carefree, outgoing

pent-up (adj)
syn. suppressed, repressed, restrained, confined, held back
ant. released

penury (n)
syn. poverty, beggary, need, destitution, shortage, paucity, scarcity
ant. prosperity, luxury, abundance

peppery (adj)
syn. hot, pungent, spicy, incisive, trenchant, biting, irritable,

bad-tempered, hot-tempered, quick-tempered, fiery
ant. mild, moderate, gentle, affable, sociable
perceptible (adj)
syn. perceivable, appreciable, noticeable, apparent, visible, distinct, obvious, clear, distinguishable
ant. imperceptible, unnoticeable, invisible
perception (n)
syn. understanding, knowledge, comprehension, intuition, feeling, insight, conception, idea, sense
ant. ignorance, unawareness
perceptive (adj)
syn. insightful, acute, clever, observant, shrewd, sharp, responsive, alert
ant. slow, unobservant, obtuse
percipient (adj)
syn. alert, aware, knowing, astute, intelligent, penetrating, judicious, sharp
ant. unaware, obtuse, slow, dull
perdition (n)
syn. damnation, ruin, destruction, downfall, doom, hell
ant. salvation, redemption
perennial (adj)
syn. long-lived, long-lasting, continual, continuing, perpetual, immortal, eternal, endless, undying, constant
ant. ephemeral, short-lived, transitory
perfect (adj)
syn. absolute, flawless, ideal, exact, complete
ant. imperfect, flawed
perfidious (adj)
syn. disloyal, dishonest, corrupt, faithless, unfaithful, untrustworthy, traitorous, treacherous, two-faced
ant. loyal, honest, faithful
perfidy (n)
syn. disloyalty, dishonesty, faithlessness, treachery, infidelity, betrayal, deceit, treason, double-dealing
ant. loyalty, honesty, faithfulness
perfume (n)
syn. scent, fragrance, cologne, smell, aroma, bouquet, odour
ant. stench

perfunctory (adj)

syn. superficial, cursory, hasty, careless, thoughtless, headless, indifferent, negligent, cool, uninterested, impersonal

ant. thorough, cordial, friendly, warm

perhaps (adv)

syn. maybe, possibly, conceivably, perchance

ant. definitely

peril (n)

syn. danger, insecurity, jeopardy, threat, hazard, menace, uncertainty

ant. safety, security

perimeter (n)

syn. circumference, border, boundary, periphery, frontier

ant. centre, middle

peripatetic (adj)

syn. roaming, nomadic, wandering, migratory, itinerant, travelling

ant. fixed.

peripheral (adj)

syn. incidental, secondary, marginal, subsidiary, unimportant, glossy, irrelevant

ant. central, crucial

periphery (n)

syn. boundary, edge, circumference, border, margin, outside

ant. centre

perish (v)

syn. die, be killed, be lost, fall, vanish, decay, decompose, rot, spoil

ant. survive, flourish, grow, ripen

perishable (adj)

syn. destructible, fragile, impermanent, temporary, short-lived, decomposable

ant. imperishable, enduring

perjury (n)

(law)

syn. false swearing, false oath, mendacity, falsification, false witness, false statement

ant. honesty, truthfulness

perky (adj)

(informal)

syn. cheerful, lively, animated, vivacious, spirited, jaunty, sparkling, sunny, gay

nat. cheerless, lethargic, dull, gloomy
permeable (adj)
syn. penetrable, porous, passable, pervious
ant. impermeable, impenetrable
permissible (adj)
syn. allowable, permitted, admissible, right, acceptable, legitimate, authorized, lawful, OK
ant. impermissible, prohibited, banned, disallowed
permission (n)
syn. authorization, approval, sanction, clearance, consent, licence, freedom, permit, allowance, go-ahead
ant. prohibition, ban
permissive (adj)
syn. liberal, easy-going, forbearing, lenient, open-minded, complaisant
ant. strict, harsh
permit (v)
syn. allow, sanction, license, let, warrant, authorize
ant. forbid, prohibit
pernicious (adj)
syn. harmful, deadly, destructive, damaging, detrimental, hurtful, ruinous, noisome
ant. beneficial, harmless, innocuous
perpetual (adj)
syn. continuous, constant, unending, everlasting, deathless, endless, never-ending, interminable, non-stop, eternal
ant. temporary, intermittent, ephemeral, transient
perpetuate (v)
syn. continue, keep alive, keep up, keep going, sustain, conserve, preserve, maintain, eternalize
ant. end, erase, annihilate, obliterate
perplex (v)
syn. puzzle, bewilder, nonplus, baffle, confuse, complicate, mix up, jumble, entangle
ant. enlighten, simplify
perplexity (n)
syn. puzzlement, bewilderment, bafflement, confusion, incomprehension, complication, complexity, entanglement, enigma, muddle, dilemma
ant. enlightenment, simplification, solution

perplexing (adj)
syn. amazing, baffling, puzzling, confusing, mysterious, strange, difficult, complex
ant. simple, easy
persecute (v)
syn. oppress, victimize, abuse, torture, ill-treat, harass, pester, intimidate, hound, hassle
ant. pamper, humour, gratify, accommodate
perseverance (n)
syn. diligence, persistence, dedication, zeal, resolution, determination, endurance, sedulity, steadfastness, tenacity
ant. irresolution, carelessness, inattention, apathy
persevere (v)
syn. continue, keep going, persist, go on, carry on, hold fast, maintain, pursue, hang on, endure
ant. stop, give up, discontinue, waver
persist (v)
syn. carry on, persevere, continue, keep going, endure, remain, stay
ant. give up, stop, desist
persistence (n)
syn. perseverance, determination, tenacity, stickability, endurance, diligence, resolution, steadfastness, staying power, pertinacity
ant. irresolution, indecision, carelessness
persistent (adj)
syn. resolute, insistent, tenacious, determined, stubborn, unshakable, continuous, constant, never-ending, frequent, chronic
ant. irresolute, wavering, intermittent
personable (adj)
syn. agreeable, affable, amiable, good-looking, attractive, pleasing, charming, outgoing
ant. disagreeable, unfriendly, unattractive
perspicacious (adj)
syn. perceptive, shrewd, acute, sharp, intelligent, wise, clever, sagacious, keen, far-sighted, observant
ant. dull, obtuse, slow, stupid, unobservant
perspicacity (n)
syn. perception, shrewdness, acuteness, sharpness, acumen, cleverness, sagacity, keenness, insight

ant. dullness, obtuseness, stupidity

perspicuity (n)
syn. clarity, lucidity, comprehensibility, intelligibility, plainness, clearness, transparency, precision
ant. obscurity, vagueness, imprecision

perspicuous (adj)
syn. clear, lucid, comprehensible, intelligible, plain, transparent, distinct, precise
ant. obscure, vague, imprecise

persuade (v)
syn. convince, win over, induce, influence, coax, advise, sweet-talk, urge, cause, move, counsel
ant. dissuade, discourage, deter

persuasive (adj)
syn. convincing, telling, impressive, compelling, sound, logical, strong
ant. unconvincing

pertinacious (adj)
syn. resolute, stubborn, tenacious, unshakable, firm, persistent, steadfast, headstrong, pig-headed, inflexible, determined
ant. irresolute, half-hearted, loose, weak

pertinent (adj)
syn. relevant, appropriate, suitable, applicable, proper, fitting, apposite, apt, to the point, analogous
ant. irrelevant, inappropriate, unsuitable

perturb (v)
syn. alarm, disturb, trouble, worry, upset, vex, confuse, discompose, bother, ruffle, rattle
ant. compose, calm, soothe, reassure

peruse (v)
syn. browse, examine, study, scan, scrutinize, read, inspect, investigate
ant. ignore

perverse (adj)
syn. abnormal, unreasonable, awkward, stubborn, troublesome, irrational, illogical, peevish, ill-tempered, petulant
ant. docile, normal, reasonable, affable, genial

perverted (adj)
syn. abnormal, corrupt, distorted, immoral, misguided, twisted, unnatural, unhealthy, vicious, wicked

ant. normal, natural, virtuous
pervious (adj)
syn. porous, permeable, passable, accessible, penetrable, receptive
ant. impervious, impassable, impenetrable
pessimism (n)
syn. cynicism, despondency, despair, depression, melancholy, hopelessness, dejection, negativity
ant. optimism, cheerfulness
pessimist (n)
syn. cynic, sceptic, fatalist, doom merchant
ant. optimist
pessimistic (adj)
syn. cynical, despondent, despairing, depressed, melancholic, hopeless, dejected, negative
ant. optimistic, cheerful
pest (n)
syn. annoyance, nuisance, problem, menace, worry, pestilence, pain in the neck
ant. blessing
pester (v)
syn. harass, annoy, badger, disturb, irritate, hound, plague, hassle, bug
ant. soothe, calm, pacify
pestilence (n)
(old use/literary)
syn. epidemic, disease, curse, bane, plague, scourge, blight
ant. blessing, boon
pettish (adj)
syn. peevish, petulant, irritable, fretful, touchy, waspish
ant. genial, friendly
petty (adj)
syn. insignificant, trivial, unimportant, paltry, narrow-minded, small-minded, cheap, niggardly
ant. important, generous, magnanimous, noble
petulant (adj)
syn. bad-tempered, sulky, sullen, peevish, pettish, irritable, ratty, cranky
ant. genial, friendly, good-humoured
phantom (n)
syn. ghost, spirit, apparition, phantasm, illusion, vision, hallucination, spook

ant. reality
phenomenal (adj)
syn. extraordinary, remarkable, wonderful, marvellous, fantastic, prodigious, uncommon, exceptional
ant. ordinary, common, unexceptional
philanthropic (adj)
syn. generous, charitable, altruistic, liberal, public-spirited, kind, unselfish
ant. misanthropic, selfish, mean
philanthropist (n)
syn. altruist, benefactor, giver, patron, donor, humanitarian
ant. misanthropist
philanthropy (n)
syn. altruism, benevolence, charity, generosity, humanitarianism, liberality, brotherly love
ant. misanthropy
phlegmatic (adj)
syn. apathetic, uninterested, lethargic, sluggish, unemotional, unfeeling, dull, impassive, philosophical, placid
ant. passionate, emotional, demonstrative
phobia (n)
syn. fear, aversion, terror, revulsion, dislike, anxiety, obsession, loathing, hang-up
ant. liking, love, mania
phoney (adj)
(informal)
syn. false, bogus, assumed, forged, fraudulent, counterfeit, fake, insincere, cod
ant. authentic, real, true
physical (adj)
syn. bodily, carnal, non-spiritual, blue-collar, manual, material, actual, palpable
ant. mental, spiritual
pictorial (adj)
syn. illustrative, illustrated, graphic, expressive, vivid, striking
ant. unclear
picturesque (adj)
syn. pretty, attractive, scenic, beautiful, charming, lovely, delightful, pleasing

ant. ugly, unattractive, unlovely
piercing (adj)
syn. high-pitched, shrill, loud, strident, probing, penetrating, searching, shrewd, sharp
ant. dull, soft
piety (n)
syn. devotion, faith, piousness, godliness, holiness, reverence, grace, sanctity, saintliness
ant. impiety, unholiness, irreverence, sin, profanity
piffle (n)
(old-fashioned, informal)
syn. rubbish, nonsense, balderdash, trash, rot, humbug, absurdity, folly, stupidity, bosh
ant. sense, wisdom, sanity
pig-headed (adj)
syn. stubborn, inflexible, bull-headed, obstinate, perverse, self-willed, intractable, stupid
ant. flexible, tractable, manageable
pilfer (v)
syn. steal, rob, thieve, purloin, lift, knock off, nick
ant. return
pillage (n)
syn. plunder, looting, loot, devastation, marauding, robbery, spoils, sack
ant. help, protection
pinnacle (n)
syn. high point, apex, height, zenith, top, acme, peak, summit
ant. nadir, base
pious (adj)
syn. god-fearing, saintly, religious, godly, holy, devout, righteous, reverent
ant. impious, irreligious
piquant (adj)
syn. tasty, spicy, hot, sharp, strong, interesting, exciting, fascinating, juicy
ant. bland, dull, banal
pique (v)
syn. hurt, offend, wound, annoy, upset, vex, irritate, irk, provoke, excite
ant. please, cheer, entertain
pique (n)
syn. annoyance, irritation, displeasure, resentment, indignation, offence

ant. pleasure, delight

pirate (n)

syn. robber, rover, plunderer, corsair

ant. saint

pithy (adj)

syn. concise, short, brief, terse, compact, meaningful, forceful, cogent

ant. verbose, wordy

pitiable (adj)

syn. pitiful, piteous, sorry, pathetic, miserable, deplorable, poor, distressing

ant. enviable, fortunate, lucky

pitiless (adj)

syn. merciless, ruthless, unmerciful, unsympathetic, unfeeling, cruel, callous, cold, unkind, harsh

ant. merciful, compassionate

pity (n)

syn. compassion, sympathy, condolence, mercy, misfortune, shame

ant. cruelty, indifference, scorn

placable (adj)

syn. appeaseable, forgiving, reconcilable, magnanimous, mild, merciful

ant. implacable, intractable, inflexible, cruel

placate (v)

syn. pacify, appease, soothe, calm, satisfy, mollify, reconcile

ant. anger, provoke, incense

placid (adj)

syn. calm, composed, gentle, unexcitable, self-possessed, easy-going, peaceful, quiet, undisturbed

ant. excitable, agitated, jumpy

plague (v)

syn. trouble, afflict, curse, harass, torment, pester, bother, irk, annoy, bug

ant. soothe, calm, pacify

plain (adj)

syn. clear, lucid, unmistakable, comprehensible, simple, ordinary, austere, ugly, unattractive, candid, frank, sincere, honest, level, flat, plane

ant. unclear, obscure, fancy, attractive, devious, deceitful, uneven

plaintiff (n)

(law)

syn. accuser, complainant, petitioner, suitor, prosecutor, claimant

ant. defendant, respondent, accused

plaintive (adj)
syn. mournful, sorrowful, woeful, pitiful, pathetic, sad, forlorn, unhappy
ant. joyous, gleeful, happy

plaudits (n)
syn. praise, applause, commendation, ovation, acclamation, eulogy
ant. denunciation, condemnation

plausible (adj)
syn. reasonable, likely, possible, probable, convincing, believable, credible, conceivable, imaginable
ant. implausible, improbable, unlikely

playful (adj)
syn. high-spirited, lively, full of fun, frisky, humorous, frivolous, teasing, light-hearted
ant. serious, stern, pensive

plea (n)
syn. appeal, petition, request, prayer, pretext, vindication, excuse, exoneration
ant. accusation, imputation, blame

pleasant (adj)
syn. nice, delightful, pleasurable, enjoyable, great, lovely, genial, amiable, friendly, polite
ant. unpleasant, nasty, repugnant, harsh

please (v)
syn. delight, entertain, make happy, satisfy, amuse, think fit, like, desire, wish, want
ant. displease, annoy, anger

pleased (adj)
syn. glad, happy, gratified, contented, content, satisfied, delighted, thankful, on cloud nine
ant. displeased, unhappy, upset, annoyed

pleasing (adj)
syn. good, acceptable, pleasant, great, pleasurable, amiable, nice, friendly, charming, lovely, likeable
ant. unpleasant, obnoxious, hateful

pleasure (n)
syn. happiness, joy, delight, comfort, amusement, contentment, satisfaction, recreation, fun
ant. displeasure, pain, sorrow

plebeian (adj)
syn. common, unrefined, working-class, coarse, mean, low, low-born, lower-class
ant. noble, aristocratic, patrician

plebeian (n)
syn. common man, commoner, peasant, worker, proletarian, pleb
ant. noble, aristocrat, patrician

plenary (adj)
syn. complete, full, whole, general, absolute, unrestricted, unqualified, unlimited, unconditional
ant. restricted, conditional

plenitude (n)
syn. abundance, plenty, fullness, profusion, completeness, copiousness, bounty
ant. scarcity, scantiness, dearth

plenty (n)
syn. abundance, opulence, prosperity, luxury, wealth, plenitude, excess, plethora, copiousness, profusion
ant. scarcity, lack, want, scantiness

plethora (n)
syn. excess, surplus, abundance, profusion, surfeit
ant. dearth, scarcity

plight (n)
syn. difficulty, difficult situation, predicament, trouble, dilemma, quandary, fix
ant. ease, comfort

plucky (adj)
(informal)
syn. brave, courageous, daring, fearless, bold, mettlesome, valorous, spirited, unflinching, intrepid
ant. cowardly, timid, feeble, spineless

plump (adj)
syn. fat, fleshy, stout, chubby, tubby, ample, full, podgy
ant. thin, slim, skinny

plunder (v)
syn. pillage, rob, strip, loot, ransack, steal, pilfer, thieve
ant. preserve, help, protect

plush (adj)
(informal)
syn. rich, affluent, sumptuous, expensive, luxury, luxurious, lavish, opulent, posh, swank
ant. austere, abstemious, simple

podgy (adj)
syn. fat, chubby, fleshy, plump, tubby, corpulent
ant. skinny, thin

poetic (adj)
syn. artistic, lyric, lyrical, expressive, imaginative, figurative, rhythmical
ant. prosaic, unimaginative

poignant (adj)
syn. sad, touching, pitiful, heartbreaking, heart-rendering, moving, pathetic, painful, biting, sharp, acute, caustic
ant. cheerful, pleasant, soothing, dull

pointless (adj)
syn. senseless, useless, worthless, aimless, hopeless, fruitless, unproductive, futile, vain
ant. valuable, worthwhile, meaningful

poise (n)
syn. composure, calmness, self-possession, equanimity, coolness, self-control, presence of mind, grace, stability, control, balance
ant. agitation, disturbance, discomposure, instability

poisonous (adj)
syn. venomous, deadly, noxious, toxic, lethal, fatal, polluting, spiteful, malicious, malign, malevolent, bitter
ant. harmless, innoxious, safe

poky (adj)
syn. little, small, cramped, boxy, tiny, confined
ant. spacious

polemic (adj)
(also polemical)
syn. controversial, contentious, disputatious, argumentative, quarrelsome, belligerent
ant. complaisant, agreeable

polemic (n)
(also polemics)
syn. controversy, dispute, debate, argument, contention

ant. complaisance, agreement
polished (adj)
syn. shiny, lustrous, gleaming, expert, adept, skilful, adroit, superb, accomplished, genteel, sophisticated, refined, elegant
ant. dull, inexpert, incompetent, coarse
polite (adj)
syn. courteous, well-mannered, genteel, well-bred, civilized, urbane, cultured
ant. impolite, rude
politic (adj)
syn. astute, prudent, wise, judicious, sensible, shrewd, advantageous
ant. impolitic, unwise
pollute (v)
syn. contaminate, infect, adulterate, corrupt, taint, poison, spoil
ant. purify, clean
pollution (n)
syn. contamination, dirt, impurity, infection, uncleanness, corruption, violation
ant. purification, purity
poltroon (n)
(old use)
syn. coward, dastard, faint-heart, craven, yellow-belly, chicken
ant. hero.
pomp (n)
syn. ceremony, show, splendour, magnificence, parade, grandeur, glory, majesty
ant. simplicity, austerity
pompous (adj)
syn. pretentious, arrogant, inflated, self-important, proud, bombastic, haughty, conceited, grandiose
ant. humble, modest, economical, simple
ponder (v)
syn. contemplate, think, think about, muse on, consider, examine
ant. ignore
pooh-pooh (v)
(informal)
syn. dismiss, brush aside, disregard, minimize, scorn, ridicule, reject
ant. consider, regard, exaggerate

popular (adj)
syn. celebrated, famous, well-liked, admired, familiar, general, common, universal
ant. unpopular, exclusive

populous (adj)
syn. crowded, populated, overpopulated, swarming
ant. deserted

pornographic (adj)
syn. porn, obscene, offensive, coarse, salacious, lewd, filthy, indecent, dirty, blue
ant. inoffensive, innocent

pornography (n)
(also porn, informal)
syn. obscenity, indecency, bawdiness, erotica, dirt, smut, filth
ant. decency, decorum

porous (adj)
syn. permeable, penetrable, absorbent, pervious
ant. impermeable, impenetrable

portable (adj)
syn. handy, compact, light, transportable, manageable, convenient, movable, lightweight
ant. fixed, ponderous

portentous (adj)
(literary)
syn. significant, pivotal, crucial, threatening, ominous, inauspicious, pompous, miraculous, phenomenal, extraordinary, remarkable
ant. insignificant, unimportant, ordinary, common, unimpressive

portly (adj)
syn. fat, burly, stout, heavy, plump, well-built, corpulent
ant. slim, thin, slight

posh (adj)
(informal)
syn. fashionable, stylish, smart, fancy, luxurious, high-class, classy, swank, aristocratic, upper-class
ant. cheap, inferior, vulgar

positive (adj)
syn. favourable, helpful, affirmative, supportive, constructive, cheerful, hopeful, optimistic, encouraging, good, certain, sure, convinced

ant. negative, pessimistic, uncertain, indefinite
possible (adj)
syn. conceivable, imaginable, likely, probable, feasible, hopeful, achievable
ant. impossible, unlikely
possibly (adv)
syn. perhaps, maybe, conceivably, hopefully
ant. certainly
posterity (n)
syn. descendants, heirs, children, progeny, successors, offspring
ant. ancestry
postpone (v)
syn. adjourn, delay, put off, hold over, suspend, reschedule, put back
ant. prepone, advance, forward
potency (n)
syn. strength, power, influence, force, cogency, energy, muscle, vigour
ant. impotence, weakness, powerlessness
potent (adj)
syn. strong, powerful, influential, forceful, cogent, compelling
ant. impotent, weak, powerless
pout (v)
syn. frown, glower, scowl, sulk, grimace, brood
ant. smile, grin
poverty (n)
syn. penury, pennilessness, impoverishment, hardship, indigence, neediness, destitution, shortage, scarcity, dearth
ant. wealth, affluence, abundance, plenty
poverty-stricken (adj)
syn. poor, impoverished, penurious, penniless, needy, bankrupt, indigent, distressed
ant. rich, affluent
powerful (adj)
syn. strong, burly, solid, well-built, potent, forceful, mighty, intense, fierce, influential, dominant, cogent, effective
ant. powerless, weak, impotent, gentle, ineffective
practicable (adj)
syn. possible, realistic, workable, achievable, feasible
ant. impracticable

pragmatic (adj)
syn. practical, realistic, opinionated, factual, sensible, unidealistic, hard-headed, hard-nosed
ant. impractical, unrealistic, idealistic

pragmatism (n)
syn. practicalism, realism, practicality, humanism, opportunism
ant. idealism, romanticism

pragmatist (n)
syn. practicalist, realist, humanist, utilitarian, opportunist
ant. idealist, romantic

praise (v)
syn. applaud, congratulate, acclaim, admire, cheer, commend, eulogize, compliment
ant. censure, criticize, condemn

praise (n)
syn. applause, congratulation, acclaim, admiration, commendation, eulogy, accolade, acclamation
ant. censure, criticism, condemnation

praiseworthy (adj)
syn. commendable, excellent, honourable, sterling, admirable, exemplary, worthy, laudable
ant. reprehensible, dishonourable

preamble (n)
syn. introduction, preface, foreword, prelude, prologue
ant. epilogue

precarious (adj)
syn. insecure, dangerous, uncertain, unsafe, unsteady, unpredictable, risky, dodgy
ant. safe, certain, secure

precede (v)
syn. prefix, come first, herald, go ahead of, forerun, lead
ant. follow

precedence (n)
syn. priority, antecedence, lead, precession, superiority, supremacy, seniority, pre-eminence
ant. subordination

preceding (adj)
syn. earlier, above, past, foregoing, former, prior, previous, anterior

ant. subsequent, following, succeeding, later

precious (adj)
syn. valuable, expensive, costly, dear, valued, special, affected, artificial, pretentious
ant. worthless, cheap, natural, artless

precipitate (adj)
syn. hasty, incautious, hurried, rash, impetuous, reckless, imprudent, injudicious, ill-advised
ant. cautious, unhurried, prudent, judicious

precise (adj)
syn. specific, explicit, exact, correct, accurate, meticulous, scrupulous, rigid, strict, particular, distinct
ant. imprecise, inaccurate, vague

precision (n)
syn. accuracy, exactness, scrupulousness, strictness, correctness, rigour, meticulousness
ant. imprecision, vagueness

preclude (v)
syn. stop, restrain, rule out, debar, prohibit, hinder, prevent
ant. encourage, persuade

precocious (adj)
syn. forward, advanced, clever, quick, bright, smart
ant. backward

precursor (n)
syn. forerunner, harbinger, messenger, antecedent, ancestor
ant. follower

precursory (adj)
syn. introductory, preliminary, antecedent, prior, previous
ant. final, following

predecessor (n)
syn. ancestor, forerunner, forefather, antecedent
ant. descendant, successor

predicament (n)
syn. plight, crisis, mess, muddle, difficulty, dilemma, fix
ant. ease, comfort

predictable (adj)
syn. anticipated, foreseeable, unsurprising, reliable, likely, inevitable
ant. unpredictable, unlikely

predilection (n)
syn. liking, affection, preference, inclination, bias, fondness, predisposition, fancy, partiality, affinity, love, taste
ant. aversion, antipathy, disinclination

predominant (adj)
syn. forceful, dominant, paramount, prime, superior, supreme, strong, principal, controlling
ant. weak, ineffective, minor

pre-eminent (adj)
syn. outstanding, supreme, paramount, matchless, peerless, incomparable, predominant, superior, main, distinguished
ant. inferior, unknown, undistinguished

preface (n)
syn. introduction, foreword, preamble, prologue, prelude
ant. epilogue, postscript

prefatory (adj)
syn. introductory, preliminary, opening, antecedent, preparatory
ant. closing, final

preferable (adj)
syn. better, best, chosen, desirable, favoured
ant. undesirable

preferment (n)
syn. promotion, advancement, rise, elevation
ant. demotion

pregnable (adj)
syn. defenceless, exposed, unprotected, open to attack, assailable, vulnerable
ant. fortified

prejudice (n)
syn. preconception, discrimination, bias, bigotry, injustice, racism, unfairness, intolerance
ant. fairness, impartiality, tolerance

prejudiced (adj)
syn. biased, discriminatory, bigoted, partisan, unjust, unfair, jaundiced, narrow-minded, intolerant
ant. impartial, fair, tolerant

prejudicial (adj)
syn. damaging, harmful, injurious, detrimental, mischievous,

disadvantageous, inimical, hostile
ant. beneficial, advantageous
preliminary (adj)
syn. introductory, opening, preparatory, exploratory, initial, prior, prefatory
ant. final, closing
prelude (n)
syn. beginning, preliminary, opening, introduction, foreword, preamble, preface, prologue
ant. epilogue, finale
premier (adj)
syn. leading, prime, top, primary, highest, outstanding, foremost, top-ranking
ant. lowest, minor, secondary
premise (v)
syn. assume, postulate, assert, hypothesize, take as true, state
ant. conclude
premonition (n)
syn. anxiety, apprehension, intuition, worry, fear, uneasiness, foreboding, misgiving, omen
ant. reassurance, composure, calmness
preoccupied (adj)
syn. pensive, lost in thought, wrapped up, distracted, absent-minded, deep in thought, engrossed, oblivious, inattentive
ant. unpreoccupied, attentive, alert, mindful
preponderant (adj)
syn. dominant, leading, paramount, greater, predominant, prevalent, chief, major, supreme
ant. minor, lowest, insignificant
prepossessing (adj)
syn. charming, good-looking, attractive, pleasing, captivating, appealing, enchanting, alluring, delightful, inviting, likable
ant. unprepossessing, unattractive, repulsive, obnoxious
preposterous (adj)
syn. ludicrous, ridiculous, absurd, laughable, foolish, illogical, irrational, senseless, excessive, incredible, unbelievable, unreasonable
ant. reasonable, rational, logical

prescient (adj)
syn. perceptive, divining, far-sighted, prophetic, foresighted, shrewd, aware
ant. imperceptive, slow, unintelligent
prescribe (v)
syn. advise, suggest, recommend, advocate, direct, dictate, order, stipulate
ant. prohibit, forbid, stop
presentable (adj)
syn. acceptable, decent, tidy, suitable, respectable, proper
ant. unpresentable, untidy
preservation (n)
syn. protection, conservation, care, upholding, perpetuation, maintenance, continuation
ant. destruction, ruination, eradication
preserve (v)
syn. protect, conserve, guard, save, maintain, perpetuate, safeguard, uphold, continue
ant. destroy, ruin, eradicate, abandon, attack
pressing (adj)
syn. crucial, critical, demanding, urgent, serious, important, high-priority
ant. unimportant, trivial
prestige (n)
syn. status, stature, standing, repute, prominence, esteem, honour, importance
ant. unimportance, humbleness
presumption[1] (n)
syn. hypothesis, guess, assumption, inference, belief, supposition, opinion, conjecture
ant. knowledge, proof
presumption[2] (n)
syn. boldness, impertinence, temerity, audacity, arrogance, insolence, impudence, nerve
ant. humility, modesty, politeness
prestigious (adj)
syn. high-status, distinguished, celebrated, reputable, respected, influential, eminent
ant. obscure, humble, modest

presumptive (adj)
syn. likely, believed, assumed, expected, believable, inferred, hypothetical, supposed
ant. unlikely, known

presumptuous (adj)
syn. bold, impertinent, audacious, disrespectful, impudent, forward, pushy, overconfident, arrogant
ant. modest, humble, decorous

pretence (n)
syn. trickery, acting, deception, falsehood, make-believe, show, guise, facade, semblance, pretext
ant. honesty, openness, truth

pretension (n)
syn. show, showiness, self-importance, vanity, ostentation, conceit, hypocrisy, assumption, pretext
ant. modesty, humility, simplicity

pretentious (adj)
syn. showy, mannered, ostentatious, flamboyant, bombastic, pompous, arrogant, conceited
ant. unpretentious, modest, humble

pretty (adj)
syn. cute, nice-looking, good-looking, attractive, charming, nice, lovely, neat, pleasing, fair, comely
ant. ugly, unattractive, plain

prevalent (adj)
syn. common, widespread, usual, popular, current, everyday, frequent
ant. rare, uncommon

prevarication (n)
syn. evasion, deception, pretence, deceit, fibbing, lie, falsehood, untruth
ant. openness, honesty, truth

prevent (v)
syn. stop, prohibit, inhibit, forbid, thwart, nip in the bud, obstruct, foil, impede, hinder, check, avoid, block
ant. allow, aid, help, foster

previous (adj)
syn. preceding, prior, past, antecedent, former, one-time, earlier, erstwhile
ant. next, later

prey (n)
syn. kill, booty, plunder, target, victim, mug
ant. predator
priceless (adj)
syn. expensive, invaluable, costly, dear, irreplaceable, precious, beyond price, treasured
ant. worthless, cheap, run-of-the-mill
pride (n)
syn. self-esteem, honour, dignity, delight, sense of achievement, satisfaction, arrogance, vanity, conceit, self-importance
ant. shame, modesty, humility, self-consciousness
priggish (adj)
syn. self-righteous, self-satisfied, narrow-minded, puritanical, smug, prim, prudish, goody-goody
ant. informal, broad-minded, easy-going
prim (adj)
syn. formal, priggish, puritanical, stiff, fussy, precise, fastidious, prudish, particular, demure
ant. informal, broad-minded, easy-going
primacy (n)
syn. superiority, command, seniority, supremacy, dominance, leadership
ant. inferiority
prime (adj)
syn. primary, main, central, first, foremost, major, best, top-quality, finest, top, A1
ant. secondary, minor, inferior
prime (n)
syn. peak, zenith, heyday, bloom, pinnacle
ant. decline, decrease
primeval (adj)
syn. ancient, early, prehistoric, primitive, primordial, first, original
ant. modern, developed, later
primitive (adj)
syn. earliest, ancient, primeval, first, rude, crude, barbaric, uncivilized, rough, savage
ant. modern, civilized, sophisticated
prince (n)
syn. ruler, monarch, lord, sovereign

ant. subject

princely (adj)

syn. regal, royal, majestic, noble, dignified, generous, gracious, magnanimous, liberal, rich, lavish

ant. lowly, humble, mean, parsimonious

principal (adj)

syn. main, leading, foremost, first, top, pre-eminent, chief, number-one

ant. minor, dependent

principal (n)

syn. head, head teacher, headmaster, dean, chancellor, vice chancellor, president, director

ant. subordinate, dependant

principle (n)

syn. rule, standard, law, precept, doctrine, code, belief, tenet, ethics, morals, goodness, virtue, honesty, integrity

ant. practice, wickedness, unscrupulousness

prior (adj)

syn. earlier, preceding, previous, former

ant. later, subsequent

privacy (n)

syn. isolation, secrecy, concealment, solitude, seclusion

ant. publicity, publicness

privation (n)

syn. penury, poverty, hardship, distress, beggary, indigence, need, want

ant. affluence, wealth, prosperity

privilege (n)

syn. advantage, benefit, liberty, favour, right, honour

ant. disadvantage

privy (adj)

syn. aware, informed, cognizant, confidential, private, secret, personal

ant. public, known, exposed

probably (adv)

syn. likely, most likely, possibly, perhaps, doubtless, maybe

ant. improbably, definitely

probity (n)

syn. honesty, uprightness, honour, integrity, principle, morality, virtue, goodness, truthfulness

ant. improbity, dishonesty, fraudulence

problem (n)
syn. difficulty, complication, quandary, worry, dilemma, nuisance, pain, puzzle, riddle
ant. solution, answer

proceed (v)
syn. begin, move, carry on, continue, advance, go, go ahead
ant. stop, retreat

proceeds (n)
syn. earnings, profit, returns, revenue, income, receipts
ant. expenses, losses

proclaim (n)
syn. announce, declare, advertise, trumpet, make known, state
ant. suppress, conceal

proclivity (n)
syn. inclination, disposition, bent, tendency, predilection, liking, penchant, bias, partiality, fondness
ant. disinclination, indisposition, aversion, dislike

procrastinate (v)
syn. adjourn, delay, defer, postpone, gain time, dilly-dally, prolong, put off
ant. proceed, expedite, advance

procure (v)
syn. obtain, gain, earn, get, acquire, pick up, secure, effect, buy, manage
ant. lose, waste, squander

prodigal (adj)
syn. wasteful, excessive, extravagant, spendthrift, reckless, lavish, improvident
ant. thrifty, economical, modest

prodigious (adj)
syn. remarkable, amazing, fabulous, wonderful, extraordinary, marvellous, astonishing, huge, vast, immense, tremendous
ant. unremarkable, ordinary, small

prodigy (n)
syn. genius, mastermind, wonder child, wunderkind, whizz, whizz-kid
ant. dunce, idiot

productive (adj)
syn. constructive, fruitful, creative, inventive, fertile, profitable, rich
ant. unproductive, fruitless, infertile

profane (adj)
syn. blasphemous, irreligious, pagan godless, impious, sinful, wicked, unholy, worldly, temporal, secular
ant. religious, reverent, sacred, pious

profanity (n)
syn. irreverence, blasphemy, ungodliness, sacrilege, impiety, cursing, irreligion
ant. reverence, worship, piety

profess (v)
syn. admit, acknowledge, confess, declare, maintain, confirm, claim, pretend
ant. deny, repudiate, ignore

professional (adj)
syn. qualified, competent, white-collar, expert, skilled, experienced
ant. non-professional, amateur

professional (n)
syn. expert, specialist, master, maestro, old hand, virtuoso, ace, pro
ant. non-professional, amateur, layman, dabbler

proffer (v)
syn. offer, extend, present, hold out, submit, volunteer
ant. withhold, retain

proficiency (n)
syn. competence, aptitude, ability, expertise, mastery, skill, talent
ant. incompetence, clumsiness

proficient (adj)
syn. competent, skilled, accomplished, trained, able, efficient, talented
ant. incompetent, clumsy

profit (n)
syn. gain, income, proceeds, return, revenue, benefit, advantage, mileage
ant. loss, disadvantage

profitable (adj)
syn. gainful, lucrative, moneymaking, money-spinning, successful, advantageous, fruitful, worthwhile
ant. unprofitable, disadvantageous

profligacy (n)
syn. immorality, licentiousness, corruption, promiscuity, debauchery, shamelessness, extravagance, lavishness, prodigality, unthrift
ant. morality, virtue, thrift, parsimony

profligate (adj)
syn. immoral, loose, debauched, corrupt, shameless, unprincipled, extravagant, wasteful, lavish, prodigal, spendthrift
ant. moral, virtuous, thrifty, parsimonious

profound (adj)
syn. extreme, deep, acute, heartfelt, sincere, extensive, wise, intelligent, insightful
ant. superficial, shallow, mild

profuse (adj)
syn. abundant, ample, excessive, lavish, liberal, prolific, plentiful, prodigal
ant. sparse, sparing, scanty

profusion (n)
(formal/literary)
syn. abundance, bounty, excess, plethora, plenty, surplus, wealth, extravagance, lavishness
ant. sparsity, sparingness, lack

progeny (n)
syn. offspring, descendants, posterity, children, family
ant. ancestry

progress (n)
syn. advancement, growth, development, improvement, breakthrough, amelioration
ant. retrogression, decline

progressive (adj)
syn. continuing, gradual, developing, advanced, liberal, modern, pioneering, reforming
ant. retrogressive, conservative, traditional

prohibit (v)
syn. ban, disallow, forbid, proscribe, prevent, preclude, stop, rule out, veto
ant. allow, permit

prohibition (n)
syn. ban, bar, prevention, injunction, proscription, embargo, veto
ant. allowance, permission

proletariat (n)
syn. masses, commonalty, commoners, lower classes, working class, common people
ant. aristocracy, nobility, elite

proliferate (v)
syn. increase, spread, expand, mushroom, burgeon, breed
ant. decrease, dwindle
prolific (adj)
syn. productive, creative, profuse, plentiful, abundant, rich
ant. unproductive, meagre, scarce
prologue (n)
syn. preamble, foreword, preface, introduction, prelude
ant. epilogue
prolix (adj)
syn. wordy, verbose, lengthy, long-winded, prosaic, boring
ant. terse, concise, short
prolong (v)
syn. delay, extend, lengthen, drag out, perpetuate, continue
ant. shorten, curtail
prominent (adj)
syn. eminent, notable, important, famous, conspicuous, obvious,
noticeable, evident, bulging, projective
ant. minor, unimportant, inconspicuous
promiscuity (n)
syn. lechery, licentiousness, immorality, amorality, looseness, laxity,
abandon
ant. chastity, virtue
promiscuous (adj)
syn. immoral, loose, unchaste, abandoned, licentious, unselective, careless,
mixed, disorderly
ant. chaste, virtuous, selective
promising (adj)
syn. hopeful, encouraging, rosy, optimistic, favourable, reassuring
ant. unpromising, hopeless
promote (v)
syn. upgrade, elevate, raise, advance, support, boost, encourage, advertise,
endorse, push
ant. demote, hinder, obstruct
promotion (n)
syn. advancement, elevation, exaltation, rise, encouragement, backing,
support, publicity
ant. demotion, hindrance, obstruction

prompt (v)
syn. motivate, induce, persuade, encourage, produce, remind, help out, provoke
ant. deter, dissuade

prompt (adj)
syn. punctual, fast, timely, quick, on time, early
ant. slow, late

promptly (adv)
syn. punctually, on time, immediately, without delay, rapidly, fast
ant. late, unpunctually

promulgate (v)
syn. announce, proclaim, declare, advertise, disseminate, broadcast
ant. suppress, conceal, hide

propaganda (n)
syn. publicity, advertising, promotion, brainwashing, indoctrination
ant. obstruction

propel (v)
syn. push, impel, drive, throw, move, launch, shoot
ant. stop

propensity (n)
syn. inclination, proclivity, tendency, leaning, disposition, penchant, bent, liking
ant. disinclination, aversion, dislike

propinquity (n)
syn. closeness, nearness, neighbourhood, proximity, kinship, relationship
ant. remoteness, distance

propitiate (v)
syn. placate, pacify, appease, satisfy, reconcile, satisfy, soothe
ant. offend, provoke, anger

propitious (adj)
syn. favourable, promising, auspicious, advantageous, lucky, friendly, kind, benevolent
ant. unfavourable, inauspicious, hostile

proponent (n)
syn. advocate, backer, partisan, supporter, friend, defender, patron
ant. opponent, adversary

proportional (adj)
syn. proportionate, balanced, equivalent, corresponding, commensurate

ant. disproportionate, unbalanced
propose (v)
syn. recommend, suggest, proffer, put forward, design, intend
ant. oppose, withdraw
propound (v)
syn. propose, suggest, postulate, put forward, submit
ant. oppose
propriety (n)
syn. decorum, etiquette, decency, good manners, refinement, correctness, modesty, politeness, courtesy
ant. impropriety, indecorum, indecency, discourtesy
prosaic (adj)
syn. unimaginative, uninspired, boring, dull, mundane, uninteresting, routine, humdrum
ant. imaginative, interesting
proscribe (v)
syn. ban, prohibit, bar, reject, boycott, exclude, doom, condemn, denounce
ant. allow, permit, admit, approve
proscription (n)
syn. ban, prohibition, bar, rejection, boycott, exclusion, denunciation, condemnation, banishment
ant. allowing, permission, admission
prosecute (v)
syn. charge, sue, execute, put on trial, indict, take to court, put in the dock, impeach
ant. defend, desist
proselyte (n)
syn. convert, neophyte, disciple, novice, beginner, learner
ant. master
prospect (n)
syn. chance, likelihood, probability, hope, outlook
ant. unlikelihood
prospective (adj)
syn. potential, likely, anticipated, imminent, would be, soon-to-be, future, intended
ant. agreed, current, present
prosper (v)
syn. progress, flourish, bloom, grow rich, succeed

ant. fail

prosperity (n)
syn. riches, success, wealth, affluence, well-being, plenty, luxury
ant. poverty, penury, hardship

prosperous (adj)
syn. successful, flourishing, thriving, booming, rich, affluent, well off, lucky, in the money
ant. unprosperous, unsuccessful, poor

protect (v)
syn. defend, guard, insulate, save, keep safe, cover, shelter, preserve
ant. attack, harm, expose

protest (n)
syn. dissent, fuss, objection, complaint, outcry, demonstration, demo
ant. acceptance, agreement

protocol (n)
syn. etiquette, decorum, formalities, convention, custom, the rules, manners
ant. boorishness

prototype (n)
syn. model, archetype, original, ideal, standard, example
ant. copy

protract (v)
syn. lengthen, drag out, prolong, extend, stretch, continue
ant. shorten, curtail

proud (adj)
syn. pleased, happy, satisfying, arrogant, haughty, conceited, big-headed
ant. ashamed, modest, humble

provident (adj)
syn. prudent, far-sighted, judicious, wise, cautious, careful, thrifty, economical, frugal
ant. improvident, imprudent, reckless, careless

providential (adj)
syn. timely, fortunate, lucky, heaven-sent
ant. untimely

provisional (adj)
syn. temporary, interim, conditional, tentative, provisory, qualified, acting
ant. permanent, absolute, definite

provocation (n)
syn. incitement, instigation, irritation, encouragement, cause, annoyance, aggravation
ant. appeasement, pacification

provoke (v)
syn. annoy, irk, anger, vex, infuriate, incite, inspire, encourage, instigate, motivate
ant. appease, pacify, deter, discourage

prowess (n)
syn. mastery, skill, ability, talent, expertise, proficiency, aptitude, command, genius, competence
ant. incompetence, inability, ineptitude, mediocrity

proximity (n)
syn. closeness, nearness, adjacency, vicinity, neighbourhood
ant. remoteness, distance

prudent (adj)
syn. judicious, wise, shrewd, well judged, canny, sensible, provident, cautious, careful, frugal, economical, thrifty
ant. imprudent, unwise, improvident, reckless, extravagant

prudish (adj)
syn. moralistic, puritanical, prim, priggish, narrow-minded, strict, goody-goody
ant. easy-going, broad-minded

prurient (adj)
syn. lecherous, lustful, salacious, erotic, dirty, obscene, pornographic, lewd
ant. virtuous, chaste, decent

pseudo (adj)
syn. bogus, false, fake, phoney, artificial, spurious
ant. genuine

psychic (adj)
syn. paranormal, supernatural, metaphysical, mystic, mental, psychological, telepathic
ant. natural, normal

publicity (n)
syn. promotion, advertisement, spotlight, attention, splash, hype
ant. obscurity, secrecy

puerile (adj)
syn. childish, silly, immature, foolish, trivial
ant. mature, adult
pugnacious (adj)
syn. aggressive, bellicose, combative, antagonistic, hostile, argumentative, quarrelsome
ant. peaceable, easy-going
punctilious (adj)
syn. strict, precise, particular, meticulous, fussy, scrupulous
ant. easy-going, lax
punctual (adj)
syn. prompt, precise, on time, punctilious, timely
ant. unpunctual, late
punish (v)
syn. discipline, scold, chastise, penalize, beat
ant. reward
puny (adj)
syn. feeble, weak, small, undersized, paltry, petty, insignificant
ant. strong, sturdy, important
pungent (adj)
syn. powerful, strong, sharp, biting, spicy, acrimonious, hot, acrid, trenchant
ant. mild, weak, tasteless
puritan (n)
syn. fanatic, moralist, disciplinarian, pietist
ant. hedonist
puritanism (n)
syn. fanaticism, bigotry, rigidity, self-discipline, austerity, asceticism, narrow-mindedness
ant. hedonism, broad-mindedness
purity (n)
syn. cleanliness, cleanness, freshness, goodness, righteousness, virtue, integrity, piety, honesty, morality
ant. impurity, immorality, corruption
purloin (v)
(formal/humorous)
syn. steal, rob, pilfer, thieve, take
ant. restore

purposeful (adj)
syn. resolute, committed, determined, steadfast, resolved, decided, fixed
ant. purposeless, aimless, indecisive
pursue (v)
syn. follow, hunt, hound, continue, strive for, practice, seek
ant. shun, abandon
pushy (adj)
(informal)
syn. assertive, forceful, overbearing, aggressive, domineering, enterprising, overconfident, ambitious, bossy
ant. submissive, meek, docile, gentle
pusillanimous (adj)
syn. cowardly, fearful, timid, feeble, spineless, lily-livered
ant. brave, courageous
putrid (adj)
syn. decayed, rotten, decomposed, rancid, bad, corrupt, offensive
ant. fresh, wholesome
puzzle (v)
syn. bewilder, baffle, nonplus, confuse, perplex, stump
ant. enlighten, inform
pygmy (n)
(also pigmy)
syn. midget, dwarf, manikin
ant. giant

Qq

quack (adj)
(informal)
syn. phoney, bogus, fake, sham, counterfeit, false
ant. genuine, authentic

quaint (adj)
syn. old-fashioned, picturesque, antiquated, unusual, peculiar, odd, unique, fanciful, extraordinary
ant. modern, contemporary, ordinary

qualm (n)
syn. anxiety, misgiving, apprehension, doubt, remorse, pang, sickness
ant. ease, confidence, assurance

quandary (n)
syn. dilemma, plight, predicament, uncertainty, trouble, perplexity, bewilderment, doubt
ant. ease, comfort

quarrel (n)
syn. fight, argument, clash, brawl, wrangle, altercation, feud, row, tiff
ant. agreement, understanding, harmony

quarrelsome (adj)
syn. argumentative, bellicose, antagonistic, quick-tempered, peevish, contentious, belligerent
ant. genial, peaceable, placid

quash (v)
syn. cancel, revoke, nullify, overthrow, annul, overrule, repeal, stop, squash, nip in the bud, curb
ant. confirm, reinstate, justify

queer (adj)
syn. abnormal, strange, odd, funny, unusual, peculiar, eerie, cranky, spooky
ant. normal, ordinary, common

quell (v)
syn. crush, suppress, quash, put down, crack down, subdue, pacify, calm, silence, soothe

ant. incite, aggravate, foment

querulous (adj)

syn. complaining, discontented, dissatisfied, petulant, peevish, irritable, critical, grumbling, quarrelsome

ant. contented, uncomplaining, placid

query (n)

syn. question, enquiry, doubt, issue

ant. answer

query (n)

syn. question, suspect, doubt, disbelieve, enquire

ant. accept

quick-tempered (adj)

syn. hot-tempered, quarrelsome, impatient, irritable, touchy, petulant, temperamental

ant. cool, self-possessed, dispassionate

quiescent (adj)

syn. inactive, motionless, calm, restful, peaceful, serene

ant. active

quiet (adj)

syn. silent, noiseless, hushed, calm, peaceful

ant. loud, busy

quiet (n)

syn. silence, quietness, hush, calm, serenity, peace

ant. disturbance, din, uproar

quirk (n)

syn. idiosyncrasy, oddity, characteristic, eccentricity, peculiarity, mannerism, chance

ant. normality, sanity, rationality

quirky (adj)

syn. idiosyncratic, unconventional, eccentric, strange, unusual, peculiar

ant. conventional, normal

quite (adv)

syn. totally, completely, wholly, entirely, altogether, reasonably, somewhat, rather

ant. partly, very

quixotic (adj)

syn. unrealistic, impractical, fanciful, idealistic, visionary, romantic, impetuous

ant. realistic, practical
quondam (adj)
syn. former, previous, past, earlier, one-time
ant. present

rabble (n)
syn. masses, mob, commonalty, crowd, peasantry, commoners
ant. elite, aristocracy

rabid (adj)
syn. mad, frantic, furious, fanatical, violent, zealous, extreme
ant. rational, restrained

rack (v)
syn. torture, harass, pain, torment, afflict, agonize, distress
ant. comfort, soothe, relieve

radiant (adj)
syn. bright, luminous, shining, glorious, dazzling, joyful, thrilled, elated, delighted
ant. dark, gloomy, miserable

radical (adj)
syn. fundamental, basic, natural, inherent, thorough, complete, fanatical, revolutionary, extreme
ant. superficial, conservative

radical (n)
syn. revolutionary, revolutionist, fanatic, rebel, militant
ant. moderate, conservative

rage (n)
syn. anger, fury, outrage, spleen, indignation, ire, passion, craze, madness, mania
ant. composure, calmness, self-possession

ragged (adj)
syn. tattered, torn, worn, shabby, tatty, rough, serrated, jagged
ant. neat, smart, smooth

raillery (n)
syn. joking, teasing, banter, pleasantry, mockery, satire, ridicule
ant. respect, admiration, seriousness

rake (v)
syn. gather, collect, level, comb, search, rummage, hunt
ant. lose, abandon, ignore, hide

rake (n)
(old-fashioned)
syn. debauchee, profligate, libertine, playboy, pleasure-seeker, womanizer, sensualist
ant. ascetic, hermit, puritan, saint

raise (v)
syn. uplift, elevate, increase, boost, collect, bring up, produce, nurture, rear, promote, upgrade
ant. lower, decrease, reduce, demote

rambling (adj)
syn. wordy, long-winded, disjoined, verbose, incoherent, labyrinthine, sprawling
ant. direct, concise, compact

rampage (n)
syn. rage, storm, fury, violence, uproar, frenzy, destruction, tempest
ant. calmness, order

rampant (adj)
syn. uncontrolled, unchecked, unrestrained, out of control, spreading, wild, violent
ant. controlled, restrained, curbed

ramshackle (adj)
syn. crumbling, tumbledown, broken-down, dilapidated, shaky, unsafe, decrepit
ant. solid, sturdy, stable

rancid (adj)
syn. foul, bad, sour, stale
ant. sweet

rancour (n)
syn. malice, bitterness, malevolence, spite, animosity, enmity, hatred, hostility, antipathy, grudge, resentment
ant. love, compassion, benevolence, goodwill

random (adj)
syn. non-specific, chance, unsystematic, arbitrary, hit-or-miss, unfocussed, unplanned
ant. systematic, deliberate

rankle (v)
syn. annoy, vex, irritate, irk, fester
ant. pacify, soothe

ransack (v)
syn. plunder, rob, pillage, ravage, strip, raid, loot, search, comb
ant. help, preserve, protect

rapacious (adj)
syn. greedy, grasping, voracious, avaricious, insatiable, predacious
ant. unselfish, abstemious

rapine (n)
(literary)
syn. pillage, plunder, looting, robbery, spoliation, raid
ant. help, protection

rapid (adj)
syn. quick, speedy, brisk, fast
ant. slow

rapport (n)
syn. affinity, harmony, bond, empathy, sympathy, understanding, close relationship
ant. antipathy, aversion, hostility

rapt (adj)
syn. preoccupied, absorbed, spellbound, fascinated, rapturous, lost
ant. bored

rapture (n)
syn. joy, bliss, delight, ecstasy, ravishment, happiness
ant. sadness, sorrow, grief

rare (adj)
syn. uncommon, unusual, infrequent, outstanding, unique
ant. common, usual

rarely (adv)
syn. infrequently, scarcely, seldom, once in a blue moon
ant. often

rascal (n)
(old-fashioned)
syn. rogue, scoundrel, wretch, blackguard, miscreant, devil
ant. gentleman, saint, worthy

rash (adj)
syn. hot-headed, careless, reckless, thoughtless, indiscreet, imprudent, incautious
ant. prudent, careful, cautious

ratify (v)
syn. approve, authorize, confirm, accept, recognize, certify, endorse
ant. reject, repudiate
rational (adj)
syn. sensible, realistic, sound, logical, cogent, intelligent, sagacious, reasoning, judicious
ant. irrational, illogical, crazy, injudicious
ratty (adj)
(informal)
syn. angry, irritable, short-tempered, annoyed, peeved, crabbed
ant. calm, cool, patient
raucous (adj)
syn. harsh, noisy, shrill, loud, wild, rough
ant. soft, quiet
ravage (v)
syn. destroy, plunder, spoil, pillage, loot, ruin, devastate
ant. preserve, protect
ravenous (adj)
syn. starving, greedy, hungry, voracious, rapacious, insatiable
ant. sated, contented
raving (adj)
syn. irrational, furious, hysterical, mad, insane, crazy, delirious
ant. calm, composed, self-possessed
ravishing (adj)
syn. enchanting, fascinating, captivating, bewitching, dazzling, charming, stunning, beautiful, lovely, delightful
ant. loathsome, repulsive, obnoxious, ugly
raw (adj)
syn. fresh, uncooked, crude, natural, untrained, new, sore, painful
ant. cooked, processed, refined, healed
reactionary (adj)
syn. right-wing, diehard, conservative, rightist, traditionalist
ant. progressive, radical
readable (adj)
syn. legible, intelligible, clear, comprehensible, understandable, pleasant, interesting, absorbing, entertaining
ant. unreadable, crabbed, illegible, tedious, boring

readily (adv)
syn. quickly, promptly, willingly, happily, easily
ant. reluctantly
real (adj)
syn. true, actual, factual, concrete, authentic, genuine, complete, absolute, right
ant. unreal, imaginary, false
realism (n)
syn. practicality, pragmatism, truthfulness, accuracy
ant. idealism, romanticism
realistic (adj)
syn. pragmatic, sensible, practical, reasonable, achievable, genuine, authentic, truthful
ant. unrealistic, irrational, fanciful
reality (n)
syn. realism, fact, accuracy, truth, actuality, authenticity
ant. fantasy, imagination
reap (v)
syn. cut, harvest, obtain, crop, derive
ant. sow
reasoned (adj)
syn. rational, sound, sensible, judicious, methodical, logical
ant. irrational, illogical
reassure (v)
syn. comfort, cheer, encourage, embolden, hearten, soothe, buoy up, bolster, console
ant. alarm, perturb, trouble, worry
rebate (n)
syn. refund, deduction, discount
ant. surcharge
rebel (n)
syn. mutineer, revolutionary, insurgent, dissident, dissenter
ant. loyalist, conformist
rebellion (n)
syn. mutiny, insurgence, revolt, revolution, disobedience, uprising, insurrection
ant. compliance, obedience, submission

rebuff (v)
syn. snub, dismiss, reject, decline, refuse, brush off, turn down
ant. accept
rebuke (v)
syn. scold, reproach, admonish, reprimand, blame, castigate, tick off
ant. commend, praise
rebut (v)
syn. refute, invalidate, disprove, overturn, contradict, negate, quash
ant. agree, confirm
rebuttal (n)
syn. refutation, invalidation, disproof, overthrow, contradiction, negation
ant. agreement, confirmation
recalcitrant (adj)
syn. wilful, defiant, stubborn, uncooperative, perverse, headstrong, intractable, rebellious, awkward, disobedient, bloody-minded
ant. amenable, docile, flexible, submissive
recall (v)
syn. recollect, remember, evoke, call back, withdraw, nullify
ant. forget
recant (v)
syn. withdraw, disown, disclaim, repudiate, retract, take back, abjure, deny
ant. maintain, acknowledge, assert
recapitulate (v)
(also *recap*)
syn. repeat, recount, restate, sum up, summarize, review
ant. expand
recede (v)
syn. retreat, subside, diminish, fade, decrease, decline
ant. advance, proceed, grow
recent (adj)
syn. new, modern, contemporary, fresh, up-to-date
ant. old, out-of-date
receptive (adj)
syn. responsive, flexible, accessible, open-minded, sympathetic, amenable, approachable
ant. unreceptive, unresponsive, closed-minded
recession (n)
syn. depression, slowdown, decline, downturn, slump

ant. boom, upturn

reciprocal (adj)
syn. mutual, shared, corresponding, give-and-take, interchangeable
ant. one-sided

reckless (adj)
syn. careless, heedless, rash, impetuous, inattentive, impulsive, irresponsible
ant. cautious, careful

recluse (n)
syn. hermit, monk, ascetic, anchorite, loner, solitary, eremite
ant. philanderer, rake, romeo

recommend (v)
syn. praise, propose, approve, promote, advocate, suggest, advise
ant. disapprove, veto, discourage

reconcile (v)
syn. pacify, reunite, settle, harmonize, resolve, accept
ant. estrange, alienate

reconciliation (n)
syn. agreement, harmony, reunion, appeasement, understanding, compromise, settlement
ant. estrangement, separation

recrimination (n)
syn. retaliation, countercharge, accusation, squabbling, quarrel, name-calling
ant. agreement, harmony

rectitude (n)
syn. virtue, morality, uprightness, righteousness, goodness, honour, correctness, precision
ant. vice, corruption, immorality, profligacy

rector (n)
syn. cleric, pastor, parson, clergyman
ant. layman

recuperate (v)
syn. improve, get better, mend, regain, recover, revive, pickup
ant. worsen, decline

recur (v)
syn. reappear, return, repeat, persist, come back
ant. depart

refined (adj)
syn. processed, purified, polished, cultivated, elegant, cultured, fine, impeccable
ant. crude, coarse, rude
reform (v)
syn. improve, amend, rectify, rebuild, correct, renovate
ant. deteriorate, worsen
refractory (adj)
syn. stubborn, obstinate, unmanageable, recalcitrant, perverse, intractable, disobedient, headstrong, contentious, unruly
ant. amenable, docile, compliant, obedient, submissive
refresh (v)
syn. freshen, reanimate, revitalize, cool, rejuvenate, stimulate
ant. weary, exhaust, tire
refreshing (adj)
syn. revitalizing, energizing, invigorating, exhilarating, fresh, imaginative, stimulating
ant. wearying, exhausting, tiring
refrigerate (v)
syn. cool, freeze, chill, chilly
ant. heat
refulgent (adj)
syn. shining, very bright, radiant, lustrous, glittering, gleaming, beaming
ant. dull
refute (v)
syn. rebut, disprove, confute, invalidate, prove wrong, deny, discredit, contradict
ant. confirm, validate, accept
regal (adj)
syn. royal, kingly, majestic, magnificent, imperial, grand, noble, august
ant. lowly, humble, simple, ordinary
regale (v)
syn. entertain, delight, amuse, feast, fascinate, captivate, refresh
ant. bore, weary, vex, bother
regardful (adj)
syn. attentive, thoughtful, mindful, heedful, considerate, vigilant, canny
ant. regardless, heedless, inattentive

regardless (adj)
syn. inattentive, thoughtless, mindless, heedless, inconsiderate, unmindful, indifferent, uncaring
ant. regardful, mindful, heedful, attentive

regimented (adj)
syn. disciplined, controlled, regulated, strict, stern, ordered, methodical
ant. free, loose, lax

regress (v)
syn. recede, relapse, decline, retreat, lapse, go back
ant. progress

regret (v)
syn. deplore, mourn, rue, bemoan, lament, repent
ant. rejoice, welcome

regret (n)
syn. disappointment, remorse, sorrow, grief, repentance, self-reproach, lamentation
ant. satisfaction, delight, rejoicing, celebration

regular (adj)
syn. constant, steady, fixed, unchanging, orderly, uniform, normal, customary, routine, commonplace, conventional
ant. irregular, erratic, unconventional

reinforce (v)
syn. boost, increase, brace, strengthen, top up, augment, support
ant. weaken, undermine

reinstate (v)
syn. reappoint, reinstall, recall, put back, restore, re-establish
ant. remove, expel

reject (v)
syn. decline, refuse, turn down, shun, discard, desert, rebuff
ant. accept, welcome

rejoice (v)
syn. delight, celebrate, joy, exult, make merry, be over the moon, be happy
ant. mourn, lament, grieve

rejoicing (n)
syn. delight, celebration, joy, exultation, gaiety, happiness, merrymaking, festivity, revelry
ant. mourning, grief, lamentation, sorrow

rejuvenate (v)
syn. revive, regenerate, revitalize, refresh, rekindle, restore, recharge, breathe new life into
ant. suppress, curb
relapse (v)
syn. regress, slip back, revert, lapse, fail, deteriorate
ant. improve
relax (v)
syn. de-stress, rest, relieve, weaken, loosen, ease, moderate, reduce
ant. tense, tighten
release (v)
syn. free, let go, liberate, acquit, drop, discharge, publish, disseminate, circulate, broadcast, put out
ant. imprison, hold, suppress
relegate (v)
syn. demote, put down, downgrade, lower
ant. promote, upgrade
relevant (ad)
syn. pertinent, appropriate, apposite, to the point, applicable, related, germane, apt
ant. irrelevant, impertinent, inapplicable, inapt
relieved (adj)
syn. glad, happy, grateful, thankful, reassured, pleased
ant. worried
reliable (ad)
syn. trustworthy, sound, loyal, faithful, truthful, genuine, honest, trusty
ant. unreliable, suspect, doubtful
religious (adj)
syn. devout, godly, pious, holy, spiritual, scrupulous, strict, meticulous
ant. irreligious, atheistic, profane, secular, lax
relinquish (v)
syn. abandon, leave, quit, renounce, drop, give up, abdicate
ant. retain, keep
relish (v)
syn. enjoy, adore, taste, take pleasure in, appreciate, savour, love
ant. dislike, loath
reluctance (n)
syn. unwillingness, disinclination, misgivings, vacillation, dislike, hesitation

ant. willingness, eagerness
reluctant (adj)
syn. unwilling, disinclined, hesitant, unenthusiastic, loath, averse
ant. willing, eager
remarkable (adj)
syn. wonderful, notable, outstanding, extraordinary, amazing, striking, exceptional
ant. ordinary, average
remember (v)
syn. recall, recollect, call to mind, retain, memorize, honour, commemorate
ant. forget
remiss (adj)
syn. careless, heedless, negligent, thoughtless, forgetful, derelict, sloppy, unmindful, indolent
ant. careful, diligent, scrupulous
remission (n)
syn. pardon, forgiveness, absolution, reprieve, exoneration, lessening, decrease, respite, relaxation
ant. punishment, increase
remonstrance (n)
syn. protest, objection, expostulation, complaint, grievance, reprimand
ant. acquiescence, acceptance, agreement
remonstrate (v)
syn. protest, dissent, object, argue, expostulate, challenge, complain
ant. acquiesce, accept, agree
remorse (n)
syn. repentance, sorrow, penitence, regret, guilt, anguish, shame, contrition
ant. gaiety, joy, satisfaction, happiness
remorseful (adj)
syn. repentant, sorrowful, sorry, regretful, self-reproachful, conscience stricken, penitent, apologetic, ashamed
ant. remorseless, impenitent, unrepentant, regretless
remunerative (adj)
syn. lucrative, profitable, rewarding, gainful
ant. unprofitable
renegade (n)
syn. traitor, mutineer, rebel, defector, outlaw, deserter, apostate, rat
ant. loyalist

renege (v)
syn. fail to honour, break your promise, default on
ant. honour
renounce (v)
syn. abandon, quit, give up, reject, deny, shun, disown, repudiate
ant. retain, keep, acknowledge
renovate (v)
syn. modernize, revamp, restore, upgrade, recondition, repair, revive, do up
ant. damage, ruin, mutilate
renown (n)
syn. fame, glory, repute, reputation, distinction, prominence, eminence, notability, celebrity
ant. notoriety, infamy, obloquy, shame
renowned (adj)
syn. celebrated, famed, prominent, noted, famous, esteemed, illustrious, eminent
ant. unknown, obscure, anonymous
repair (v)
syn. mend, renovate, restore, correct, fix, renew, patch up, put right, redress
ant. damage, harm, ruin, spoil
repartee (n)
syn. pleasantry, quip, banter, wit, witticism, raillery, jest, joke
ant. seriousness, argument
repeal (v)
syn. abolish, nullify, cancel, revoke, quash, annul, invalidate, abrogate
ant. enact, establish, ratify, authorize
repel (v)
syn. repulse, resist, rebuff, reject, revolt, disgust, put off
ant. welcome, attract
repellent (adj)
syn. repulsive, disgusting, obnoxious, hateful, horrible, revolting, loathsome, resistant
ant. attractive, pleasing, enticing, charming
repent (v)
syn. regret, lament, feel, remorse, deplore, rue, be penitent
ant. rejoice, celebrate, welcome

repentance (n)
syn. regret, grief, penitence, remorse, guilt, contrition, sorrow, self-reproach
ant. gaiety, joy, satisfaction, happiness

repentant (adj)
syn. regretful, remorseful, penitent, apologetic, shamefaced, ashamed, sorry
ant. unrepentant, impenitent, unashamed

replenish (v)
syn. fill up, refill, recharge, top up, recruit, restock
ant. empty, squander

replica (n)
syn. copy, duplicate, model, facsimile, dummy
ant. original

repose (n)
syn. peace, relaxation, ease, slumber, rest, inactivity, calmness, composure, poise
ant. activity, agitation, strain, stress

reprehend (v)
syn. criticize, blame, censure, reprimand, chide, admonish, scold, rebuke
ant. commend, laud, extol, praise

reprehensible (adj)
syn. dishonourable, culpable, deplorable, unforgivable, condemnable, remiss, shameful, blameworthy
ant. commendable, praiseworthy, creditable

repress (v)
syn. subdue, suppress, crush, oppress, control, curb, quell
ant. express, release

repression (n)
syn. suppression, crushing, subduing, oppression, despotism, tyranny, restraint, control
ant. encouragement, liberty

reprieve (n)
syn. pardon, remission, amnesty, stay of execution, respite
ant. punishment

reprimand (v)
syn. admonish, scold, rebuke, blame, chide, reproach, chastise, castigate, tell off

ant. commend, praise
reprisal (n)
syn. retaliation, revenge, requital, retribution, vengeance
ant. forgiveness, submission
reproach (n)
syn. criticism, censure, rebuke, blame, admonition, disapproval, dishonour, obloquy, stigma, disgrace, shame
ant. commendation, praise, approval, honour, fame
reproachful (adj)
syn. disapproving, critical, accusatory, abusive, scolding, censorious
ant. complimentary, approving
reprobate (adj)
syn. immoral, shameless, corrupt, profligate, base, wicked, depraved, evil
ant. moral, virtuous, upright, ethical
reprobate (n)
(formal/humorous)
syn. rogue, rascal, villain, sinner, scoundrel, miscreant, wrongdoer, rake
ant. paragon, hero, exemplar, saint
reproof (n)
syn. reprimand, reproach, blame, censure, reproval, rebuke, reprehension, criticism
ant. commendation, praise, compliment
reprove (v)
syn. scold, reproach, rebuke, admonish, reprehend, censure, blame, chide, reprimand, tell off
ant. commend, praise, applaud, compliment
repudiate (v)
syn. reject, disown, cast off, abandon, deny, dismiss, refute, brush aside, rebut
ant. embrace, acknowledge, admit, adopt
repugnant (adj)
syn. loathsome, repellent, nasty, foul, abhorrent, hateful, appalling, disgusting, obnoxious, hostile
ant. congenial, pleasant, tolerable, acceptable
repulse (v)
syn. repel, reject, rebuff, drive back, turn down, disregard
ant. welcome, captivate, attract

repulsive (adj)

syn. disgusting, foul, obnoxious, vile, horrible, nasty, loathsome, repellent

ant. attractive, delightful, pleasant, friendly

reputation (n)

syn. repute, renown, name, fame, honour, esteem, character, stature

ant. infamy, notoriety, shame

repute (n)

syn. reputation, name, fame, esteem, celebrity, renown, stature

ant. infamy, notoriety, shame

requisite (adj)

syn. mandatory, needed, vital, essential, required, indispensable, compulsory

ant. optional, inessential, non-essential

rescind (v)

syn. cancel, quash, revoke, recall, nullify, repeal, invalidate

ant. confirm, establish, enforce

rescission (n)

syn. cancellation, abrogation, repeal, revocation, nullification

ant. enforcement

resemblance (n)

syn. similarity, analogy, similitude, parallel, closeness, facsimile, likeness

ant. dissimilarity

resemble (v)

syn. mirror, look alike, correspond to, be similar

ant. differ, vary

resent (v)

syn. dislike, grumble at, grudge, feel bitter about

ant. welcome, accept

resentment (n)

syn. animosity, anger, bitterness, irritation, dissatisfaction, acrimony, hatred, displeasure

ant. contentment, satisfaction

reserved[1] (adj)

syn. aloof, unfriendly, quiet, unsociable, silent, cool, uncommunicative

ant. outgoing, friendly, frank, informal

reserved[2] (adj)

syn. booked, engaged, held, retained, taken

ant. unreserved, free

resigned (adj)
syn. patient, forbearing, long-suffering, stoical, uncomplaining, submissive
ant. resisting, rebellious

resilience (n)
syn. flexibility, strength, toughness, buoyancy, unshockability, adaptability
ant. rigidity, inflexibility

resistance (n)
syn. hostility, opposition, combat, fight, defiance, struggle, immunity
ant. acceptance, submission

resolute (adj)
syn. resolved, determined, firm, bold, purposeful, strong-willed, tenacious, preserving, staunch
ant. irresolute, half-hearted

resolution (n)
syn. determination, decision, commitment, intention, perseverance, proposal, motion, proposition, firmness, settlement
ant. irresolution, indecision

respectful (adj)
syn. polite, courteous, civil, mannerly, deferential, gracious, humble
ant. disrespectful, rude, insolent

resplendent (adj)
syn. bright, dazzling, splendid, shining, sparkling, glittering, brilliant
ant. dull, dim

restful (adj)
syn. relaxing, calm, soothing, peaceful, untroubled, undisturbed, leisurely, comfortable
ant. exciting, tumultuous, disturbed

restive (adj)
syn. uneasy, restless, fretful, impatient, nervous, refractory, stubborn, obstinate
ant. relaxed, calm, docile

restoration (n)
syn. renovation, reconstruction, repair, revival, reinstatement, return, recovery, replacement
ant. decline, damage, removal

restrained (adj)
syn. unemotional, sober, self-controlled, mild, discreet, quiet, soft, muted
ant. unrestrained, impetuous, impulsive, rash

restriction (n)
syn. limitation, control, constraint, curb, stipulation
ant. freedom
result (n)
syn. conclusion, outcome, consequence, product
ant. cause
resume (v)
syn. renew, continue, recommence, restart, proceed, go on, carry on
ant. stop, cease, suspend
resume (n)
syn. outline, synopsis, summary, abridgement, precis, abstract, overview, compendium, epitome
ant. amplification, expansion
resumption (n)
syn. continuation, restart, renewal, reopening, recommencement
ant. stop, suspension, cessation
resurgence (n)
syn. revival, comeback, renewal, renaissance, reawakening, re-emergence, resurrection, reappearance
ant. decrease, extinction, quashing
resurrection (n)
syn. revival, comeback, renaissance, rebirth, resurgence, return, reappearance, renewal
ant. extinction, quashing, burying
retain (v)
syn. keep, hold back, save, preserve, recollect, remember
ant. abandon, relinquish, forget
retaliation (n)
syn. reprisal, revenge, vengeance, counter-attack, retribution, retort
ant. forgiveness, submission
retard (v)
syn. brake, delay, detain, slow down, keep back, halt, impede
ant. advance, accelerate
reticent (adj)
syn. mute, reserved, silent, uncommunicative, mum, tight-lipped, unresponsive, taciturn
ant. garrulous, communicative, frank

retiring (adj)
syn. shy, reticent, reserved, modest, diffident, unassertive, bashful, meek, shamefaced
ant. forward, assertive, outgoing

retract (v)
syn. cancel, disown, deny, reverse, repeal, withdraw, revoke, pull back
ant. confirm, maintain

retreat (v)
syn. quit, leave, withdraw, retire, flee
ant. advance

retrench (v)
syn. reduce, lessen, decrease, cut, curtail, trim, clip, shorten, restrain
ant. increase, enhance

retribution (n)
syn. punishment, reprisal, revenge, retaliation, vengeance, nemesis, redress
ant. forgiveness, pardon

retrieve (v)
syn. recover, regain, get back, recapture
ant. lose

retrograde (adj)
syn. backward, regressive, retrogressive, waning, inverse, declining, downward
ant. progressive, forward

retrogress (v)
syn. regress, decline, retrograde, worsen, recede, fall
ant. progress

retrospect (n)
syn. contemplation, remembrance, recollection, review
ant. prospect

reveal (v)
syn. disclose, tell, make known, release, exhibit, show
ant. hide, conceal

revel (v)
syn. celebrate, rejoice, roister, make merry, luxuriate, live it up
ant. mourn, lament

revelation (n)
syn. disclosure, unmasking, broadcast, leak, exposition, exposure, announcement

ant. hiding, concealment, masking
revelry (n)
syn. festivity, merrymaking, revel, celebration, fun, partying
ant. mourning, sobriety
revenge (n)
syn. reprisal, retaliation, vengeance, retribution, requital
ant. pardon, forgiveness
revengeful (adj)
syn. vindictive, spiteful, vengeful, bitter, implacable, malicious, malevolent, merciless
ant. forgiving, kind, merciful
revenue (n)
syn. income, earnings, proceeds, profit, return, gain
ant. expenditure, spending
revere (v)
syn. respect, venerate, admire, esteem, adore
ant. despise, scorn, dislike
reverence (n)
syn. admiration, great respect, high esteem, honour, veneration, homage, high regard, awe, adoration
ant. scorn, contempt, mockery, insult
reverent (adj)
syn. reverential, respectful, humble, devout, solemn, deferential, pious
ant. irreverent, disrespectful
reverie (n)
syn. daydream, fantasy, preoccupation, dream, trance
ant. attention
revert (v)
syn. regress, return, default, go back, relapse
ant. progress
revile (v)
syn. malign, abuse, scorn, defame, reproach, vilify, slander, decry
ant. commend, extol, praise
revitalize (v)
syn. boost, reactivate, reenergize, rejuvenate, refresh, reinvigorate, revive, stimulate
ant. suppress, dampen, curb

revival (n)
syn. upturn, resurgence, improvement, restoration, rebirth, comeback
ant. downturn, suppression
revocation (n)
syn. abolition, quashing, nullification, repeal, rescinding, revoking, cancellation
ant. enforcement, imposition, implementation
revoke (v)
syn. abolish, repeal, cancel, nullify, retract, annul, dissolve, abrogate, overrule
ant. enforce, confirm, establish
revolt (n)
syn. revolution, insurgence, rebellion, riot, uprising, coup, mutiny
ant. loyalty, allegiance, faithfulness
revolting (adj)
syn. repulsive, disgusting, offensive, foul, nauseating, horrid, vomitous, loathsome, obnoxious
ant. pleasant, attractive, delightful
revolutionary (n)
syn. revolutionist, rebel, insurgent, mutineer, anarchist
ant. loyalist
revulsion (n)
syn. abhorrence, dislike, disgust, aversion, loathing, repulsion, nausea, repugnance
ant. delight, pleasure, attraction
rhetorical (adj)
syn. eloquent, oratorical, stylistic, silver-tongued, bombastic, pompous, ornate, extravagant, pretentious
ant. unrhetorical, simple, plain, unpretentious
ribald (adj)
syn. bawdy, licentious, obscene, vulgar, coarse, lewd, indecent, naughty, blue, foul-mouthed
ant. polite, pure, decorous, decent
ribaldry (n)
syn. bawdiness, licentiousness, obscenity, vulgarity, coarseness, indecency, naughtiness, baseness, filth
ant. politeness, decorum, propriety, decency

rich (adj)
syn. opulent, wealthy, affluent, prosperous, moneyed, well-off, flush, fertile, productive, precious, splendid, spicy, delicious, intense
ant. poor, miserly, unfertile, barren, plain
riches (n)
syn. wealth, cash, capital, money, richness
ant. poverty
rickety (adj)
syn. shaky, unsteady, unstable, infirm, weak, broken-down, ramshackle
ant. stable, sturdy, strong
riddle (n)
syn. puzzle, brain-teaser, enigma, problem, conundrum
ant. solution
ridicule (n)
syn. laughter, mockery, scorn, derision
ant. respect, praise
ridiculous (adj)
syn. absurd, funny, laughable, hilarious, ludicrous, foolish
ant. sensible, serious
rife (adj)
syn. common, general, widespread, endemic, prevalent, plentiful
ant. rare, uncommon, few
rift (n)
syn. breach, crack, split, disagreement, feud, quarrel, bust-up, row
ant. unity, agreement, reconciliation, understanding
righteous (adj)
syn. virtuous, ethical, good, honest, decent, upright, moral, principled
ant. unrighteous, wicked, corrupt, immoral
right-wing (adj)
syn. traditionalist, conservative, rightist, conventional
ant. left-wing
rigid (adj)
syn. firm, hard, stiff, strict, uncompromising
ant. flexible
rigorous (adj)
syn. meticulous, strict, careful, precise, draconian, rigid, inflexible, extreme, harsh
ant. mild, lenient, lax, slapdash, easy-going

rigour (n)
syn. severity, hardship, ordeal, austerity, harshness, strictness, suffering, rigidity, precision
ant. mildness, leniency, laxity, freedom

rile (v)
syn. anger, irritate, annoy, exasperate, irk, vex, provoke
ant. pacify, soothe, calm

rinse (v)
syn. wash, clean, dip, bathe
ant. dry

riot (n)
syn. anarchy, disorder, uproar, row, commotion, fray, rumpus
ant. calm, order

rip (v)
syn. tear, split, slash, pluck, yank
ant. mend, repair

ripe (adj)
syn. mature, fully developed, perfect, ready, favourable, opportune
ant. unripe, immature, inopportune

risk (n)
syn. danger, hazard, jeopardy, peril
ant. safety

risky (adj)
syn. dangerous, hazardous, perilous, precarious
ant. safe

rival (n)
syn. competitor, enemy, opponent, challenger, nemesis, adversary, contender
ant. ally, associate, colleague, friend

rivalry (n)
syn. competition, opposition, contention, conflict, antagonism
ant. cooperation, collaboration

riveting (adj)
syn. captivating, absorbing, fascinating, enthralling, mesmerising
ant. boring, uninteresting

roar (v)
syn. bellow, bawl, thunder, bay, shout, yell, holler, howl
ant. whisper, murmur

robber (n)
syn. burglar, pirate, swindler, thief, brigand, highwayman
ant. saint, gentleman
robust (adj)
syn. strong, powerful, hale, vigorous, healthy, tough, durable, hearty, sturdy
ant. weak, frail, delicate
rogue (n)
(old-fashioned)
syn. miscreant, rascal, criminal, crook, scamp, swindler, scoundrel
ant. gentleman, saint, worthy
rollicking (adj)
syn. jovial, carefree, frolicsome, boisterous, merry, hearty, sportive, spirited, lively
ant. serious, staid, restrained, sober
romantic (adj)
syn. passionate, amorous, loving, sentimental, charming, idealistic, fanciful, unrealistic, imaginary, impractical
ant. unromantic, realistic, unsentimental, sober
romantic (n)
syn. idealist, dreamer, visionary, utopian, sentimentalist
ant. realist
roomy (adj)
syn. spacious, big, wide, large, sizeable, extensive, ample, generous
ant. narrow, cramped
rosy (adj)
syn. pink, healthy, blooming, fresh, hopeful, bright, promising, favourable, optimistic
ant. pale, depressing, hopeless, sad, bleak
rot (v)
syn. decompose, decay, spoil, taint, corrupt
ant. preserve
rotten (adj)
syn. decomposing, bad, decaying, rancid, spoiled, off, dishonest, corrupt, immoral, crooked
ant. good, fresh, honest

rotter (n)
(old-fashioned)
syn. scoundrel, blackguard, fink, swine, bastard
ant. gentleman, saint

rouse (v)
syn. arouse, anger, disturb, incite, provoke, stir, stimulate
ant. soothe, calm

route (n)
syn. defeat, retreat, thrashing, beating, overthrow
ant. victory

rowdy (adj)
syn. disorderly, unruly, undisciplined, boisterous, noisy, out of control
ant. peaceful

rowdy (n)
syn. ruffian, hooligan, brawler, rouge, rascal, miscreant
ant. gentleman, saint, worthy

royal (adj)
syn. regal, noble, imperial, kingly, princely, magnificent, august, grand, majestic
ant. lowly, humble, simple, ordinary

ruckus (n)
(informal)
syn. commotion, disorder, uproar, turmoil, rumpus, agitation, fuss, pandemonium
ant. calm, peace, serenity

ruction (n)
syn. commotion, disturbance, quarrel, uproar, rumpus, brawl, fuss
ant. calm, peace

ruddy (adj)
syn. reddish, red, rubicund, blooming, rosy, pink, healthy
ant. pale, unhealthy

rude (adj)
syn. impolite, impudent, indecent, insolent, ill-mannered, vulgar, blue, filthy, unrefined
ant. polite, courteous, refined, civilized

rudimentary (adj)
syn. fundamental, basic, essential, crude, primitive, rough, undeveloped
ant. advanced, developed

rue (v)
(old-fashioned)
syn. regret, deplore, grieve, lament, repent, sorrow, mourn
ant. rejoice, revel, celebrate
ruffian (n)
(old-fashioned)
syn. rowdy, rouge, rascal, thug, scoundrel, hooligan, brute
ant. gentleman, saint, worthy
ruffle (v)
syn. disarrange, mess up, rumple, upset, disturb, irritate
ant. arrange, compose, calm
rugged (adj)
syn. rough, rocky, strong, robust, tough, solid, muscular, manly
ant. smooth, delicate, puny
ruin (n)
syn. destruction, decay, havoc, devastation, collapse, downfall, insolvency, bankruptcy
ant. restoration, reconstruction, development, prosperity
ruinous (adj)
syn. destructive, catastrophic, disastrous, harmful, excessive, extortionate
ant. beneficial, advantageous
ruminate (v)
syn. ponder, muse, brood, meditate, consider, think
ant. ignore
rumour (n)
syn. gossip, speculation, story, talk, hearsay, the buzz
ant. truth, fact
rumpus (n)
(informal)
syn. commotion, pandemonium, disturbance, fuss, furore, uproar, row, confusion, noise
ant. calm, peace, serenity
run-of-the-mill (adj)
syn. ordinary, unexceptional, unremarkable, average, mediocre, common
ant. exceptional, remarkable, excellent
ruse (n)
syn. trick, ploy, tactic, wile, scheme, stratagem, deception
ant. honesty

rupture (n)
syn. breach, break, feud, altercation, disagreement, rift, split, estrangement, quarrel, dissolution
ant. agreement, unity, reconciliation, understanding
rustic (adj)
syn. rural, agricultural, rough, unsophisticated, unpolished, simple, rude, uncultured
ant. urban, polished, sophisticated, cultured
rustic (n)
(humorous)
syn. countryman, peasant, yokel, bumpkin, hick
ant. townie, sophisticate
ruthless (adj)
syn. merciless, cruel, brutal, harsh, pitiless, callous, unfeeling, heartless, inexorable, implacable, savage
ant. merciful, compassionate, kind, forgiving, humane

Ss

sabotage (n)
syn. destruction, damage, disruption, vandalism, treachery
ant. construction, development

sack^1 (v)
syn. dismiss, layoff, discharge, axe, fire
ant. appoint

sack^2 (v)
syn. ravage, ransack, plunder, loot, pillage, destroy, spoil
ant. preserve, protect

sacred (adj)
syn. holy, sanctified, devotional, religious, divine, spiritual
ant. profane, secular

sacrilege (n)
syn. blasphemy, heresy, impiety, profanity, desecration, disrespect, mockery, violation, irreverence
ant. reverence, respect, piety

sad (adj)
syn. unhappy, dejected, sorrowful, depressed, miserable, heartbroken, downcast, lamentable, sorry, depressing, sombre
ant. happy, glad, joyful, cheerful, gay

sadism (n)
syn. cruelty, ruthlessness, brutality, inhumanity, spite, malevolence, callousness
ant. compassion, mercy

safeguard (v)
syn. protect, shield, keep safe, look after, save, preserve, guard
ant. jeopardize, imperil, endanger

sagacious (adj)
syn. wise, able, intelligent, astute, shrewd, sharp, judicious, clever, far-sighted
ant. obtuse, stupid, foolish, short-sighted

sagacity (n)
syn. wisdom, sense, acumen, insight, foresight, prudence, shrewdness,

sharpness, judiciousness
ant. obtuseness, stupidity, foolishness, folly
sage (n)
syn. scholar, expert, wise man/woman, genius, mystic, master, philosopher, guru
ant. ignoramus, fool, donkey, ass
saintly (adj)
syn. godly, devout, holy, virtuous, religious, spiritual, pious, good
ant. ungodly, godless, unholy
salacious (adj)
syn. lustful, erotic, lecherous, bawdy, lewd, indecent, licentious, obscene, blue
ant. pure, decent, clean, decorous
salient (adj)
syn. prominent, conspicuous, significant, noticeable, marked, outstanding, remarkable
ant. inconspicuous, insignificant, unnoticeable, ordinary
salubrious (adj)
syn. nice, healthy, pleasant, agreeable, classy, posh, wholesome
ant. insalubrious, unhealthy, unwholesome
salutary (adj)
syn. advantageous, beneficial, helpful, profitable, salubrious, valuable
ant. harmful, unhelpful
salvage (v)
syn. save, rescue, restore, recover, retrieve
ant. demolish, destroy
salvation (n)
(in religion)
syn. liberation, restoration, redemption, lifeline, rescue
ant. damnation, destruction, loss
sanctimonious (adj)
syn. self-righteous, self-satisfied, false, insincere, hypocritical, goody-goody, superior
ant. unsanctimonious, humble, modest
sanctity (n)
syn. holiness, purity, sacredness, grace, devotion, righteousness, godliness, piety
ant. unholiness, impurity, godlessness, profanity

sane (adj)
syn. sensible, rational, prudent, intelligent, realistic, sound, lucid, judicious
ant. insane, foolish, mad

sanguinary (adj)
syn. bloody, bloodthirsty, brutal, ruthless, cruel, murderous, savage
ant. unsanguinary, merciful, gentle, humane

sanguine (adj)
syn. optimistic, cheerful, hopeful, positive, confident, upbeat, buoyant, lively
ant. pessimistic, gloomy, melancholy, cynical

sanity (n)
syn. wisdom, sense, prudence, judiciousness, rationality, common sense, lucidity
ant. insanity, foolishness, folly, lunacy

sapient (adj)
(literary)
syn. wise, clever, sharp, sagacious, judicious, intelligent, astute, shrewd
ant. unwise, stupid, unintelligent, slow

sarcasm (n)
syn. mockery, cynicism, scorn, irony, ridicule, satire, contempt
ant. admiration, respect

sarcastic (adj)
syn. mocking, cynical, scornful, ironic, satirical, contemptuous, acrimonious
ant. admiring, respectful

satire (n)
syn. irony, parody, sarcasm, ridicule, wit, caricature, burlesque, spoof
ant. admiration, respect

satirical (adj)
syn. ironic, mocking, critical, disrespectful, bitter, cynical, sarcastic
ant. admiring, respectful

satisfaction (n)
syn. contentment, pride, fullness, happiness, content
ant. frustration, discontent

saturnine (adj)
(literary)
syn. gloomy, sombre, grave, dismal, morose, uncommunicative
ant. jovial, cheerful, gay

saucy (adj)
syn. rude, impertinent, impudent, insolent, disrespectful, cheeky
ant. respectful, polite
savage (adj)
syn. cruel, violent, harsh, sadistic, vicious, merciless, fierce, pitiless, uncivilized, rude
ant. humane, gentle, compassionate, mild, civilized
savant (n)
syn. scholar, sage, intellectual, expert, philosopher
ant. ignoramus, fool, donkey
save (adj)
syn. liberate, rescue, protect, preserve, shield
ant. abandon, discard, expose
scamp (n)
(old-fashioned)
syn. scallywag, ruffian, rogue, rascal, devil, wretch, villain
ant. saint, gentleman
scandal (n)
syn. crime, offence, dishonour, infamy, shame, outrage, gossip, slander
ant. honour, fame
scant (adj)
syn. meagre, little, insufficient, minimal, bare
ant. ample, abundant
scarcity (n)
syn. shortage, paucity, dearth, insufficiency, want, lack, poverty
ant. plenty, abundance, sufficiency
scathing (adj)
syn. withering, savage, scornful, caustic, critical, bitter, sarcastic, biting
ant. pleasant, mild, complimentary
scatter-brained (adj)
(informal)
syn. bird-brained, forgetful, inattentive, dizzy, silly, empty-headed, madcap
ant. sober, careful, sensible
scenic (adj)
syn. panoramic, spectacular, impressive, picturesque, striking, beautiful
ant. dull, unspectacular, ugly
sceptic (n)
syn. agnostic, cynic, unbeliever, atheist, doubting Thomas

ant. believer
sceptical (adj)
syn. doubtful, cynical, hesitating, distrustful, unconvinced
ant. convinced, trusting
scheming (adj)
syn. cunning, artful, wily, crafty, devious, tricky, unscrupulous, deceitful
ant. honest, ingenuous, artless, open
schism (n)
syn. breach, break, division, disagreement, separation
ant. unity
scholar (n)
syn. intellectual, academic, expert, learned person, authority, brain, genius, egghead
ant. ignoramus, dunce, fool, idiot, ass
scintillating (adj)
syn. exciting, lively, brilliant, vibrant, dazzling, glittering
ant. dull, boring
scold (v)
syn. rebuke, admonish, reprimand, chide, reproach
ant. praise, commend
scorching (adj)
syn. hot, sweltering, blazing, sizzling, flaming, fiery
ant. mild, freezing
scorn (n)
syn. contempt, ridicule, mockery, sarcasm, sneering, derision
ant. respect, admiration
scornful (adj)
syn. mocking, arrogant, contemptuous, derisive, sarcastic, scathing
ant. respectful, admiring
scoundrel (n)
(old-fashioned)
syn. rogue, miscreant, wretch, rascal, blackguard
ant. gentleman, worthy
scourge (n)
syn. misfortune, plague, affliction, curse, bane, menace, torture
ant. blessing, benediction
scowl (v)
syn. frown, glower, grimace, lower, glare

ant. smile

scrappy (adj)
syn. disjoined, bitty, incomplete, fragmentary, slapdash, superficial
ant. finished, complete

scrimmage (n)
syn. scuffle, brawl, melee, row, riot, rumpus, struggle, fight
ant. calmness, peace, order

scrooge (n)
(informal)
syn. miser, penny-pincher, money-grubber, niggard, cheapskate
ant. spendthrift, squanderer

scruffy (adj)
(informal)
syn. shabby, dirty, untidy, tattered, messy, ungroomed, disreputable.
ant. smart, tidy, well-dressed.

scrupulous (adj)
syn. meticulous, careful, attentive, assiduous, rigorous, thorough, principled, ethical
ant. careless, lax

scrutinize (v)
syn. examine, investigate, study, check
ant. ignore

scuffle (n)
syn. struggle, fight, rumpus, riot, melee, brawl
ant. peace, calmness, order

scurrility (n)
syn. abuse, vilification, obloquy, maligning, offensiveness, nastiness
ant. praise, politeness

scurrilous (adj)
syn. defamatory, insulting, abusive, offensive, obscene, slanderous, libellous, vulgar, bitchy
ant. appreciate, complimentary, polite

seamy (adj)
syn. unpleasant, nasty, sordid, low, repulsive, degraded, rough
ant. pleasant, respectable

secession (n)
syn. split, disaffiliation, withdrawal, schism, break, seceding
ant. unification, affiliation, amalgamation

secluded (adj)
syn. isolated, sheltered, remote, private, retired, solitary
ant. public, busy
sectarian (adj)
syn. separatist, factional, narrow-minded, bigoted, partisan, intolerant, dogmatic
ant. non-sectarian, broad-minded
secular (adj)
syn. non-religious, profane, worldly
ant. religious
sedentary (adj)
syn. seated, inactive, motionless, unmoving
ant. active
sedition (n)
syn. treason, disloyalty, agitation, insurrection, mutiny
ant. loyalty, calm
seduce (v)
syn. lure, allure, attract, entice, manipulate, beguile, mislead, tempt
ant. repel, put off, deter
seductive (adj)
syn. tempting, alluring, inviting, enticing, attractive, appealing
ant. repulsive, unattractive
sedulous (adj)
syn. diligent, scrupulous, active, assiduous, busy, persevering, laborious, industrious
ant. idle, half-hearted, passive, lethargic
segment (n)
syn. part, portion, section, division, piece
ant. whole, entire
segregate (v)
syn. isolate, separate, keep apart, divide, cut off
ant. integrate, unite
seize (v)
syn. snatch, grab, grip, capture, confiscate, hijack, snatch
ant. release
seldom (adv)
syn. infrequently, rarely, occasionally, once in a blue moon
ant. often, frequently

self-centred (adj)
syn. self-obsessed, vain, inconsiderate, selfish, thoughtless, egocentric, narcissistic
ant. altruistic, philanthropic, unselfish

self-conscious (adj)
syn. shy, uneasy, timid, embarrassed, nervous, uncomfortable, sheepish
ant. confident, unaffected

self-esteem (n)
syn. self-worth, self-respect, self-regard, self-assurance, self-confidence, pride, dignity
ant. humility, modesty, humbleness

selfish (adj)
syn. self-seeking, self-obsessed, egocentric, egotistic, greedy
ant. unselfish, altruistic

self-possessed (adj)
syn. self-assured, cool, composed, poised, unruffled, confident
ant. nervous, worried

self-righteous (adj)
syn. self-satisfied, pious, hypocritical, smug, sanctimonious, superior, goody-goody
ant. humble, modest, meek, submissive

send-off (n)
syn. farewell, adieu, goodbye, departure
ant. arrival

sensational (adj)
syn. thrilling, momentous, shocking, explicit, stunning, superb, fantastic, smashing
ant. unremarkable, dull, run-of-the-mill

sense (n)
syn. awareness, faculty, perception, feeling, comprehension, understanding, reason, wisdom, use, purpose, tact
ant. stupidity, folly, foolishness, absurdity

senseless (adj)
syn. absurd, idiotic, futile, pointless, stupid, illogical, useless
ant. sensible, wise

sensible (adj)
syn. reasonable, logical, realistic, sound, wise, practical, rational, realistic
ant. insensible, senseless, foolish, stupid

sensitive (adj)
syn. reactive, delicate, tender, easily, offended, touchy, irritable
ant. insensitive, unresponsive

sensual (adj)
syn. physical, bodily, erotic, sexual, lewd, lecherous, salacious, voluptuous, passionate, animal
ant. spiritual, puritan, ascetic

sensuality (n)
syn. eroticism, sexiness, lewdness, lecherousness, salaciousness, voluptuousness, lustfulness, debauchery, licentiousness, animalism
ant. spirituality, puritanism, asceticism

sentimental (adj)
syn. nostalgic, loving, emotional, romantic, mawkish, corny, touching
ant. unsentimental, realistic

sepulchral (adj)
(literary)
syn. mournful, funeral, sombre, gloomy, melancholy, grave, dismal, sad, heartbroken
ant. elated, cheerful, joyful

sensuous (adj)
syn. pleasurable, sensory, luxurious, sexy, voluptuous, lush, hedonistic
ant. ascetic, simple

serene (adj)
syn. placid, tranquil, calm, peaceful, composed, undisturbed, chilled
ant. agitated, troubled

serenity (n)
syn. calm, calmness, peace, placidity, composure, quietness
ant. disruption, disturbance, anxiety

servile (adj)
syn. bootlicking, submissive, fawning, humble, slavish, low, controlled, abject
ant. bold, aggressive, independent

servitude (n)
syn. slavery, bondage, serfdom, captivity, obedience, enslavement, subjection
ant. freedom, liberty, liberation

setback (n)
syn. blow, difficulty, issue, problem, upset, misfortune, disappointment, hiccup

ant. breakthrough, boost, advantage
shabby (adj)
syn. ramshackle, dilapidated, old, faded, tattered, unfair, unkind, mean, unworthy
ant. smart, honourable
shallow (adj)
syn. superficial, empty, trivial, surface, unanalytical, unscholarly, foolish, frivolous, ignorant
ant. profound, deep, analytical, thorough
sham (adj)
syn. false, fake, counterfeit, artificial, bogus, phoney
ant. genuine, real
shambles (n)
syn. mess, havoc, confusion, muddle, disorder, chaos
ant. order
shame (n)
syn. humiliation, remorse, guilt, disgrace, dishonour, obloquy, infamy
ant. pride, honour
shameless (adj)
syn. unashamed, unrepentant, brazen, flagrant, insolent, unabashed, blatant
ant. ashamed, shamefaced, sheepish
sharp (adj)
syn. keen, sharpened, intense, severe, bitter, caustic, intelligent, clever
ant. blunt, gentle, mild, stupid, dull
sheen (n)
syn. brightness, polish, lustre, shine, brilliance
ant. dullness
sheepish (adj)
syn. shamefaced, ashamed, embarrassed, abashed, self-conscious, comfortable, bashful
ant. shameless, unabashed, confident
shifty (adj)
syn. crafty, furtive, tricky, dishonest, artful, crooked
ant. honest, upright
shimmering (adj)
syn. glittering, glowing, luminous, shiny, shining, lustrous

ant. dull, dim
shocking (adj)
syn. awful, horrific, appalling, terrible, outrageous, disgusting, abominable, upsetting
ant. delightful, lovely, pleasant
shoddy (adj)
syn. second-rate, poor-quality, cheap, inferior, poor, tatty
ant. first-rate, excellent
shortage (n)
syn. dearth, insufficiency, scarcity, shortfall, poverty, deficit
ant. glut, abundance, plenty
shortcoming (n)
syn. imperfection, defect, weakness, fault, drawback
ant. strength
shorten (v)
syn. reduce, cut, abridge, abbreviate, contract, condense, curtail
ant. lengthen, extend, enlarge
short-sighted (adj)
syn. ill-considered, ill-advised, imprudent, careless, unthinking, injudicious, myopic
ant. long-sighted, far-sighted
short-tempered (adj)
syn. hot-tempered, impatient, fiery, irritable, touchy
ant. calm, placid
showy (adj)
syn. fancy, exotic, loud, ostentatious, vulgar, pretentious, flamboyant
ant. restrained, quiet, subdued
shrewd (adj)
syn. clever, intelligent, astute, perceptive, smart, sharp, canny, wise
ant. stupid, unwise, obtuse, slow
shrewdness (n)
syn. intelligence, astuteness, perceptiveness, smartness, sharpness, acumen, wisdom, sagacity
ant. stupidity, foolishness, obtuseness
shrewish (adj)
syn. complaining, ill-tempered, bad-tempered, fault-finding, petulant, peevish, discontented, quarrelsome
ant. genial, friendly, placid, composed

shy (adj)
syn. bashful, introverted, withdrawn, diffident, self-effacing, nervous, modest
ant. confident, bold
shyness (n)
syn. bashfulness, diffidence, self-consciousness, nervousness, modesty
ant. confidence, boldness
sickening (adj)
syn. nauseating, revolting, repulsive, disgusting, offensive, vomitous, distasteful, obscene
ant. delightful, pleasing, attractive
shun (v)
syn. avoid, ignore, evade, freeze out, spurn
ant. welcome, accept
significance (n)
syn. importance, gravity, magnitude, seriousness
ant. unimportance
silly (adj)
syn. stupid, inane, foolish, unwise, petty, trivial
ant. sensible
similar (adj)
syn. alike, same, like, corresponding, analogous, equivalent
ant. dissimilar, different
similarity (n)
syn. similitude, resemblance, equivalence, likeness, correspondence, uniformity, comparability
ant. dissimilarity, difference, unlikeness
similitude (n)
syn. similarity, resemblance, likeness, copy, replica, analogy
ant. dissimilitude, difference
simulated (adj)
syn. fake, artificial, bogus, inauthentic, phoney, spurious, sham
ant. genuine, real
simultaneous (adj)
syn. coinciding, parallel, coincident, synchronized
ant. separate
sin (n)
syn. misdeed, wrong, offence, crime, immorality, vice

ant. virtue, morality, righteousness

sincerity (n)

syn. integrity, honesty, candour, frankness, genuineness, openness, truthfulness

ant. insincerity, deceit, guile

single-minded (adj)

syn. committed, determined, resolute, dedicated, purposeful, tenacious, devoted

ant. half-hearted, apathetic, unenthusiastic

sinister (adj)

syn. menacing, alarming, ominous, disturbing, threatening, criminal, evil, shady, bad

ant. innocent, harmless

sinner (n)

syn. wrongdoer, offender, transgressor, criminal, trespasser, miscreant

ant. saint, gentleman, worthy

sizeable (adj)

syn. large, substantial, significant, considerable

ant. small

sketchy (adj)

syn. rough, unfinished, incomplete, cursory, scrappy, insufficient

ant. detailed, thorough

skilful (adj)

syn. skilled, talented, adept, expert, competent, able, gifted, accomplished, experienced, ace

ant. unskilful, clumsy, inept, incompetent

skill (n)

syn. expertise, talent, competence, prowess, accomplishment, mastery

ant. ineptitude, incompetence

skinny (adj)

syn. lean, thin, bony, skeletal, underweight, emaciated

ant. plump, fat

skirmish (n)

syn. fight, battle, tussle, combat, conflict, fray, clash, encounter

ant. peace, harmony, understanding

slander (n)

syn. defamation, libel, obloquy, aspersion, abuse, backbiting, calumny

ant. eulogy, accolade, commendation, praise

slander (v)
syn. defame, malign, smear, vilify, backbite, decry, scandalize
ant. eulogise, glorify, commend, praise

slapdash (adj)
syn. careless, hurried, rash, hasty, disorderly
ant. careful, orderly

slavery (n)
syn. bondage, servitude, captivity, enslavement
ant. freedom

slavish (adj)
syn. servile, submissive, fawning, menial, base
ant. independent

sleek (adj)
syn. shiny, lustrous, smooth, silky, graceful, elegant
ant. rough, scruffy

slender (adj)
syn. lean, slim, thin, slight, small, feeble, inadequate, insufficient
ant. plump, strong, ample

slighting (adj)
syn. insulting, slanderous, abusive, disrespectful, uncomplimentary, derogatory, offensive
ant. flattering, complimentary, appreciative

slim (adj)
syn. thin, lean, slight, slender, small, faint
ant. fat, chubby, strong

slipshod (adj)
syn. slapdash, careless, negligent, untidy, disorderly
ant. careful, tidy

sloth (n)
syn. laziness, inactivity, slothfulness, sluggishness, idleness, indolence, inertia, lethargy
ant. industry, diligence, labour, activity

slothful (adj)
syn. lazy, inactive, sluggish, idle, indolent, inert, lethargic
ant. industrious, diligent, laborious, active

slovenly (adj)
syn. scruffy, messy, untidy, ill-groomed, careless, negligent, slack
ant. tidy, careful

slow (adj)
syn. leisurely, unhurried, lazy, inactive, prolonged, lengthy, stupid, obtuse, unintelligent, dim, dull
ant. fast, quick, smart, intelligent

sluggish (adj)
syn. lethargic, lazy, lifeless, slow, inactive, torpid, sleepy, unresponsive, slothful
ant. vigorous, quick, brisk, dynamic, energetic

slump (n)
syn. fall, decrease, decline, downturn, recession, depression, collapse
ant. boom, rise

slur (n)
syn. insult, slander, imputation, allegation, aspersion, disgrace, smear
ant. respect, honour, eulogy

sly (adj)
syn. cunning, tricky, artful, foxy, mischievous, clever, roguish, wicked, covert, scheming
ant. artless, honest, straightforward, open

small-minded (adj)
syn. narrow-minded, intolerant, illiberal, petty, bigoted, ungenerous, insular, prejudiced, biased, chauvinistic
ant. broad-minded, tolerant, liberal, unprejudiced

smart (adj)
syn. fashionable, chic, well dressed, stylish, elegant, intelligent, clever, sharp, bright, witty, quick, energetic
ant. scruffy, untidy, stupid, slow

smile (v)
syn. beam, smirk, leer
ant. frown

smitten (adj)
(humorous)
syn. enchanted, obsessed, infatuated, in love, captivated, affected, afflicted
ant. disenchanted, unaffected

smug (adj)
syn. conceited, proud, complacent, self-satisfied, self-righteous, superior
ant. modest, humble, self-effacing

smutty (adj)
(informal)
syn. filthy, dirty, indecent, pornographic, vulgar, coarse, obscene, blue, bawdy
ant. decent, clean, polite, decorous

snazzy (adj)
(informal)
syn. smart, fashionable, jazzy, stylish, attractive
ant. shabby, unfashionable

sneer (n)
syn. smirk, jibe, dig, jeer, insult, mockery
ant. respect

snide (adj)
(informal)
syn. derogatory, hurtful, malicious, cynical, nasty, scornful, sarcastic, sneering
ant. flattering, complimentary, smooth-tongued

snobbery (n)
syn. arrogance, pride, loftiness, pretension, haughtiness
ant. humility, modesty

snub (n)
syn. rebuff, insult, humiliation, put-down, brush-off, slap in the face, affront
ant. flattery, praise

soar (v)
syn. escalate, climb, rise, increase, shoot up
ant. fall, plummet

sober (adj)
syn. abstinent, clear-headed, sensible, rational, quiet, serious, dignified, sombre, restrained
ant. drunk, excited, irrational

sobriety (n)
syn. abstinence, self-restraint, composure, calmness, solemnity, seriousness
ant. drunkenness, excitement

sociable (adj)
syn. genial, friendly, affable, amicable, amiable, cordial, outgoing, warm
ant. unsociable, unfriendly, hostile

sojourn (n)
(literary)
syn. rest, a temporary stay, holiday, visit
ant. travel
solace (n)
syn. comfort, relief, consolation, cheer, support
ant. distress, misfortune
solemn (adj)
syn. serious, sincere, sober, sombre, dignified, formal, magnificent, ceremonial
ant. frivolous, light-hearted, silly, informal
solemnity (n)
syn. seriousness, dignity, gravity, sacredness, sanctity, grandeur
ant. frivolity, nonsense, silliness
solidarity (n)
syn. unity, unanimity, agreement, accord, consensus, concord, cohesion
ant. dissent, disagreement, discord
solitary (adj)
syn. friendless, alone, lonely, withdrawn, unsociable, isolated, single
ant. sociable, gregarious
solitude (n)
syn. solitariness, privacy, loneliness, isolation
ant. companionship, society
sombre (adj)
syn. dark, dull, sober, solemn, serious, sad, cheerless, melancholy, joyless, mournful
ant. bright, cheerful, joyful, happy
somnolent (adj)
syn. sleepy, drowsy, slumberous, dozy
ant. alert
soothe (v)
syn. comfort, quiet, pacify, calm, ease, appease, lessen, reduce
ant. irritate, annoy, aggravate
soothing (adj)
syn. relaxing, calming, restful, peaceful, balmy
ant. annoying, irritating
sophisticated (adj)
syn. cultured, refined, urbane, worldly-wise, advanced, the latest

ant. unsophisticated, unrefined, crude
sorcery (n)
syn. witchcraft, magic, wizardry, black magic
ant. exorcism
sordid (adj)
syn. shameful, cheap, ignominious, dirty, filthy, disreputable
ant. respectable, worthy
sorrow (n)
syn. sadness, misery, regret, heartache, despair, grief, woe, affliction, misfortune, trouble
ant. joy, happiness, bliss, delight
sorrowful (adj)
syn. sad, miserable, heartbroken, depressed, mournful, tearful, melancholy, sorry, unhappy, dejected
ant. joyful, gleeful, happy, delighted, gay
sorry (adj)
syn. regretful, repentant, apologetic, ashamed, shamefaced, compassionate, sorrowful, sad, miserable, pathetic, pitiful
ant. impenitent, unrepentant, glad, splendid, fine
sound (adj)
syn. healthy, undamaged, fit, solid, strong, reliable, sensible, wise, untroubled
ant. unsound, unhealthy, unfit, unreliable
sovereign (n)
syn. king, emperor, ruler, monarch, lord, autocrat
ant. subject
sow (v)
syn. plant, strew, scatter, seed
ant. reap
spacious (adj)
syn. large, broad, roomy, capacious, wide
ant. cramped, small
sparing (adj)
syn. frugal, prudent, parsimonious, thrifty, economical, cautious, careful, saving
ant. lavish, extravagant, liberal, unsparing
sparse (adj)
syn. meagre, paltry, scanty, scant, scarce, limited

ant. abundant, plentiful
spartan (adj)
syn. austere, ascetic, strict, rigorous, harsh, plain, frugal
ant. luxurious, lavish
spectacular (adj)
syn. magnificent, dazzling, impressive, stunning, striking, eye-catching, sensational, grand
ant. unspectacular, unimpressive, ordinary, dull
spellbound (adj)
syn. fascinated, enchanted, enthralled, transfixed, rapt, mesmerized
ant. bored, uninterested
spendthrift (n)
syn. spender, waster, prodigal, squanderer
ant. miser, saver
spine-chilling (adj)
syn. frightening, horrifying, terrifying, hair-raising, spooky, scary
ant. reassuring, comforting
spineless (adj)
syn. pusillanimous, timid, weak, cowardly, lily-livered, faint-hearted
ant. bold, brave, daring
spirited (adj)
syn. enthusiastic, active, lively, passionate, bold, feisty
ant. lazy, apathetic, timid
spiritual (adj)
syn. non-material, mental, inner, psychological, holy, religious, divine, sacred
ant. physical, material, secular, profane
spite (n)
syn. malice, malevolence, spleen, hate, animosity, grudge, venom, pique, ill will
ant. benevolence, compassion, love, goodwill
spleen (n)
(literary)
syn. anger, malice, spite, peevishness, venom, acrimony, bitterness, pique, ill will
ant. benevolence, compassion, love, goodwill
splendid (adj)
syn. grand, superb, magnificent, rich, plush, wonderful, excellent,

smashing, fantastic
ant. simple, ordinary, modest, poor
splendour (n)
syn. grandeur, richness, magnificence, majesty, brilliance, glory
ant. simplicity, humility
splenetic (adj)
syn. malicious, spiteful, peevish, irritable, touchy, petulant
ant. genial, friendly
spontaneous (adj)
syn. unplanned, free, unprompted, impulsive, instinctive, natural, extempore
ant. planned, studied, forced
spooky (adj)
syn. frightening, scary, weird, spine-chilling, ghostly
ant. reassuring, comforting
sporadic (adj)
syn. infrequent, periodic, occasional, odd, erratic, random
ant. continuous, frequent, regular
sprightly (adj)
(also *spry*)
syn. lively, active, vivacious, animated, frolicsome, cheerful
ant. inactive, lifeless, lethargic
sprout (v)
syn. grow, shoot, develop, germinate
ant. wither, decay
spruce (adj)
syn. neat, smart, well groomed, well dressed, trim
ant. untidy, dishevelled
spry (adj)
(also *sprightly*)
syn. lively, active, vivacious, animated, frolicsome, cheerful
ant. inactive, lifeless, lethargic
spur (n)
syn. motivation, encouragement, stimulus, inducement, incentive, incitement
ant. curb, deterrent, disincentive
spurious (adj)
syn. fake, bogus, artificial, false, phoney

ant. genuine, real

spurn (v)

syn. reject, disregard, rebuff, snub, scorn, turn down, despise, disdain

ant. welcome, respect, accept, embrace

squabble (n)

syn. quarrel, argument, disagreement, altercation, row, wrangle, clash, tiff

ant. agreement, harmony, amity

squalid (adj)

syn. filthy, grimy, dirty, miserable, shabby, improper, sordid, dishonest, corrupt

ant. clean, pleasant, respectable

squander (v)

syn. waste, lavish, misspend, throw away, spend like water, run through

ant. save

squanderer (n)

syn. spendthrift, spender, waster, prodigal

ant. miser, saver

squeal (n)

syn. scream, cry, shriek, wail

ant. laugh

stagnant (adj)

syn. motionless, standing, still, dirty, slow-moving, inactive, sluggish, static

ant. flowing, continuous

staid (adj)

syn. conventional, formal, traditional, sedate, serious, sober

ant. unstaid, frivolous, silly

stale (adj)

syn. rancid, old, stuffy, overused, decayed, stereotyped

ant. fresh

stalemate (n)

syn. impasse, standstill, halt, deadlock, stand-off, stop

ant. progress, growth, development

stalwart (adj)

syn. staunch, faithful, devoted, loyal, dedicated, committed, reliable, resolute, daring

ant. disloyal, timid, weak

stamina (n)
syn. strength, energy, endurance, toughness, tenacity, determination
ant. weakness, feebleness
standstill (n)
syn. halt, impasse, lapse, pause, rest, stay, stoppage
ant. progress
staple (adj)
syn. main, major, first, chief, prime, basic
ant. minor
starchy (adj)
syn. formal, stiff, conventional, ceremonious
ant. informal, liberal
stare (v)
syn. gaze, look, gape
ant. ignore
startle (v)
syn. surprise, shock, frighten, alarm, scare, taken aback
ant. calm, composed
stately (adj)
syn. dignified, grand, majestic, royal, solemn, ceremonious, pompous, magnificent, splendid
ant. undignified, unimpressive, informal, lowly
static (adj)
syn. stable, unchanging, constant, unchanged, fixed, stationary, standstill
ant. variable, active, dynamic, moving
stationary (adj)
syn. static, unmoving, motionless, at rest
ant. moving, mobile
stature (n)
syn. importance, rank, height, reputation, prestige, status
ant. unimportance, humbleness
staunch (adj)
syn. loyal, faithful, stalwart, trustworthy, devoted, committed, reliable, firm, resolute, steadfast
ant. disloyal, unfaithful, unreliable, wavering, weak
steadfast (adj)
syn. steady, unwavering, fixed, firm, staunch, faithful, loyal, resolute
ant. wavering, unreliable, weak

stentorian (adj)
syn. thundering, loud, deafening, clamorous, loud-voiced
ant. soft
stereotyped (adj)
syn. conventional, stale, overused, standard, tired
ant. unconventional, different
sterile (adj)
syn. unproductive, unfruitful, infertile, barren, sterilized, antiseptic, clean
ant. fertile, fruitful, septic
sterility (n)
syn. infertility, impotence, barrenness, unfruitfulness, futility
ant. fertility, fruitfulness
sterling (adj)
syn. excellent, first-class, pure, worthy, great, standard, genuine, real
ant. inferior, poor, worthless, false
stern (adj)
syn. serious, unsmiling, grim, unfriendly, frowning, strict, severe, hard, harsh, tough
ant. genial, mild, lax, lenient
stick-in-the-mud (n)
(informal)
syn. traditionalist, conservative, fogey, reactionary
ant. modernist, radical
stiff-necked (adj)
syn. stubborn, uncompromising, arrogant, proud, haughty, opinionated
ant. humble, modest, flexible
stigma (n)
syn. shame, disgrace, taint, humiliation, dishonour, ignominy, blot, stain, blemish
ant. honour, fame, esteem, credit
stimulate (v)
syn. motivate, excite, encourage, trigger, inspire, arouse
ant. discourage, deter
stimulating (adj)
syn. thought-provoking, inspirational, inspiring, exciting, interesting, exhilarating, rousing, provoking
ant. boring, uninspiring, depressing

stimulus (n)
syn. encouragement, motivation, inducement, impetus, spur, inspiration
ant. deterrent, discouragement

stingy (adj)
syn. ungenerous, parsimonious, mean, miserly, niggardly, penurious, meagre, insufficient
ant. generous, charitable, ample

stir (n)
syn. commotion, fuss, agitation, disturbance, uproar, excitement, hoo-ha
ant. calm, tranquillity

stirring (adj)
syn. stimulating, exciting, animated, lively, thrilling, rousing, exhilarating, impassioned, intoxicating
ant. boring, uninspiring, calming, dull

stoical (adj)
(also *stoic*)
syn. long-suffering, cool, calm, patient, dispassionate, stoic, philosophical
ant. excitable, anxious

stoicism (n)
syn. long-suffering, calmness, patience, acceptance, forbearance, fortitude
ant. excitement, anxiety

stolid (adj)
syn. dull, apathetic, slow, obtuse, stoical, unemotional, indifferent, impassive
ant. vivacious, lively, exciting, interested

stony (adj)
syn. merciless, pitiless, cold, hard, cruel, inflexible, adamant, unforgiving
ant. genial, friendly, forgiving

stormy (adj)
syn. blowy, wild, blustery, thundery, angry, passionate, furious
ant. calm, peaceful

strait-laced (adj)
(also *straight-laced*)
syn. moralistic, stuffy, strict, narrow-minded, puritanical, prudish
ant. easy-going, broad-minded

strange (adj)
syn. peculiar, odd, uncommon, abnormal, queer, unusual, novel, new, unfamiliar

ant. ordinary, common, normal, familiar
stranger (n)
syn. newcomer, outsider, foreigner, alien, unknown
ant. acquaintance, native
strapping (adj)
(informal)
syn. sturdy, strong, burly, well-built, powerful, beefy
ant. puny, feeble, weak
strengthen (v)
syn. energize, encourage, fortify, make strong, back up, support, reinforce
ant. weaken, enfeeble, enervate
strenuous (adj)
syn. hard, tough, tiring, difficult, forceful, vigorous, resolute, spirited,
energetic
ant. easy, effortless, half-hearted, feeble
stress (n)
syn. strain, anxiety, pressure, worry, hassle, emphasis, accent
ant. relaxation
stressful (adj)
syn. difficult, tense, demanding, hard, frustrating
ant. relaxing
stricken (adj)
syn. afflicted, struck, smitten, hit
ant. unaffected
stricture (n)
syn. rebuke, blame, criticism, flak, censure
ant. commendation, praise
strident (adj)
syn. clamorous, loud, harsh, cacophonous, unmusical, shrill, discordant
ant. soft, sweet, quiet
strife (n)
(literary)
syn. conflict, quarrel, struggle, animosity, dispute, discord, argument,
disagreement
ant. peace, amity, accord, harmony
striking (adj)
syn. impressive, wonderful, stunning, marvellous, imposing, breathtaking,
noticeable, visible, remarkable

ant. unimpressive, commonplace, unremarkable

stringent (adj)
syn. strict, severe, tough, rigorous, rigid, tight, inflexible
ant. lax, loose, easy-going, flexible

strong-arm (adj)
syn. threatening, bullying, aggressive, intimidatory
ant. gentle, compassionate

stroppy (adj)
(informal)
syn. uncooperative, quarrelsome, bad-tempered, difficult, perverse, awkward, unhelpful
ant. cooperative, obliging, sweet-tempered

stubborn (adj)
syn. pig-headed, obstinate, headstrong, refractory, inflexible, intractable, perverse, recalcitrant, wilful, obdurate
ant. amenable, compliant, obliging, docile, submissive

stuck-up (adj)
(informal)
syn. conceited, arrogant, haughty, proud, swollen-headed, big-headed
ant. humble, modest, meek

studious (adj)
syn. academic, scholarly, intellectual, bookish, diligent, hard-working, erudite, brainy
ant. lazy, slothful, sluggish

stuffy (adj)
syn. stale, airless, sultry, uninteresting, conservative, prim, old-fashioned, dull
ant. fresh, airy, interesting, modern

stumbling-block (n)
syn. hindrance, bar, obstacle, hurdle, barrier, obstruction
ant. boost

stump (v)
(informal)
syn. baffle, puzzle, perplex, flummox, nonplus, confuse
ant. enlighten

stupefy (v)
syn. shock, amaze, baffle, bewilder, confuse
ant. enlighten

stunning (adj)
syn. beautiful, wonderful, spectacular, magnificent, superb, lovely, terrific, fantastic, awesome, sublime
ant. ordinary, poor, ugly, unimpressive

stupendous (adj)
syn. tremendous, staggering, amazing, extraordinary, marvellous, fabulous, wonderful, huge, vast, astonishing
ant. ordinary, unimpressive, common, normal, unexceptional

stupid (adj)
syn. foolish, brainless, unintelligent, unwise, feeble-minded, imprudent
ant. clever, intelligent, sensible

stupor (n)
syn. coma, insensibility, trance, lethargy, daze, unconsciousness
ant. alertness, agility

sturdy (adj)
syn. strong, strapping, muscular, robust, long-lasting, durable
ant. weak, feeble

stylish (adj)
syn. fashionable, smart, elegant, modish, chic, modern, trendy
ant. unstylish, unfashionable, dowdy

subdue (v)
syn. crush, control, defeat, quieten, reduce, suppress, conquer
ant. arouse, excite

subdued (adj)
syn. depressed, sad, sombre, dejected, gloomy, quiet, hushed, dim, soft, low
ant. unsubdued, aroused, cheerful, lively, loud

subjection (n)
syn. servitude, dependence, mastery, enslavement, subordination
ant. independence, liberty

subjugate (v)
syn. conquer, subdue, crush, quell, defeat, suppress, oppress
ant. liberate, free

sublime (adj)
syn. eminent, glorious, noble, exalted, lofty, elevated, lofty, elevated, magnificent, majestic
ant. lowly, ridiculous

submissive (adj)
syn. compliant, docile, obedient, tractable, yielding, passive, obliging, amenable, humble
ant. intractable, obstinate, rebellious, assertive

subnormal (adj)
syn. feeble-minded, low, retarded, inferior
ant. gifted

subsequent (adj)
syn. following, succeeding, next, later, coming
ant. previous

subside (v)
syn. calm, abate, fall, decline, quieten, decrease, recede, collapse
ant. intensity, rise, increase

subsidiary (adj)
syn. subordinate, assistant, secondary, helpful, auxiliary, aiding
ant. chief, primary, principal

substantial (adj)
syn. considerable, major, significant, sizeable, useful, strong, sturdy, durable
ant. insubstantial, insignificant, small

substantiate (v)
syn. prove, confirm, authenticate, corroborate, establish, validate
ant. refute, disprove

subterfuge (n)
syn. deception, artifice, ruse, pretext, scheme, pretence, ploy
ant. openness, honesty

subversive (adj)
syn. seditious, riotous, revolutionary, destructive
ant. loyal, trusty

succeeding (adj)
syn. coming, following, next, later, subsequent
ant. previous

succinct (adj)
syn. concise, condensed, laconic, brief, crisp, compact, summary, short
ant. prolix, wordy, verbose

succulent (adj)
syn. juicy, moist, tender, mouth-watering, delicious
ant. dry

succumb (v)
syn. submit, die, yield, fall victim, surrender
ant. overcome, resist

sue (v)
syn. prosecute, charge, litigate, take to court, summon
ant. defend

suffering (n)
syn. misery, torment, hardship, anguish, distress, affliction, anguish, pain
ant. pleasure, joy, ease

sulky (adj)
syn. sullen, petulant, resentful, moody, aloof, morose, unsociable
ant. cheerful, sociable

sullen (adj)
syn. sulky, cheerless, morose, gloomy, dull, sombre, moody, unsociable
ant. cheerful, sociable

sully (v)
(literary)
syn. dirty, pollute, blemish, spoil, disgrace, dishonour
ant. clean, cleanse

sultry[1] (adj)
syn. muggy, humid, oppressive, hot, sweltering
ant. cool, cold

sultry[2] (adj)
syn. sexy, attractive, erotic, passionate, voluptuous, seductive, alluring
ant. sexless, unattractive, repulsive

summary (n)
syn. synopsis, epitome, abstract, resume, review, outline, compendium, precis
ant. amplification, expansion

summit (n)
syn. peak, top, apex, pinnacle, acme, zenith, meeting, conference
ant. base, bottom, nadir

summon (v)
syn. call, invite, call for, convene, gather together, assemble
ant. dismiss

sumptuous (adj)
syn. luxurious, lavish, magnificent, opulent, expensive, rich, superb
ant. plain, poor, mean

sundry (adj)
syn. various, varied, many, several, miscellaneous, manifold, diverse
ant. similar, uniform

sunny (adj)
syn. cloudless, sunlit, bright, sunshiny, luminous, cheerful, jolly, optimistic, good-natured, happy
ant. dull, cloudy, gloomy, cheerless, sad

super (adj)
(informal/old-fashioned)
syn. excellent, wonderful, marvellous, superb, smashing, splendid
ant. poor, awful

superb (adj)
syn. excellent, wonderful, marvellous, awesome, great, super, fantastic, splendid
ant. poor, awful, unimpressive

supercilious (adj)
syn. arrogant, conceited, haughty, insolent, proud, scornful, contemptuous
ant. humble, modest, meek

superficial (adj)
syn. external, outer, casual, cursory, hurried, slapdash, apparent, shallow, trivial, silly, frivolous, empty-headed
ant. deep, thorough, detailed

superfluous (adj)
syn. excess, extra, unnecessary, surplus, unused, waste, remaining
ant. necessary, deficient

superhuman (adj)
syn. phenomenal, paranormal, supernatural, extraordinary, exceptional, prodigious, herculean
ant. natural, ordinary, average

superior (adj)
syn. senior, higher, better, top-quality, excellent, supercilious, haughty, high and mighty
ant. junior, inferior

superior (n)
syn. senior, chief, supervisor, boss
ant. junior, subordinate

supernatural (adj)
syn. paranormal, magical, psychic, mystic, ghostly, phantom

ant. natural, normal

supplicate (v)
(literary)
syn. plead, pray, petition, ask, implore, beg, beseech
ant. demand

supporter (n)
syn. backer, advocate, follower, defender, fan, ally, patron, well-wisher
ant. opponent, adversary, rival

supposition (n)
syn. belief, presumption, conjecture, assumption, feeling, idea, hypothesis
ant. knowledge, wisdom

suppress (v)
syn. crush, subdue, quell, repress, control, censor, hide, withhold
ant. encourage, incite, reveal

supremacy (n)
syn. superiority, authority, primacy, dominion, ascendancy, control
ant. subjection, subordination

supreme (adj)
syn. highest, top, principal, foremost, prime, exceptional, extraordinary, greatest, ultimate
ant. subordinate, lowest, lowly, poor

surfeit (n)
syn. excess, glut, plethora, surplus, superabundance
ant. lack, deficiency

surly (adj)
syn. sulky, morose, moody, sullen, unfriendly, unsmiling, grumpy, rude, bad-tempered, touchy
ant. affable, amicable, friendly, pleasant

surmise (n)
syn. assumption, guess, hypothesis, notion, idea, opinion
ant. certainty, knowledge

surmount (v)
syn. overcome, vanquish, beat, triumph, conquer
ant. succumb, submit

surplus (n)
syn. surfeit, glut, excess, remains, superfluity, plethora, superabundance
ant. dearth, deficit, lack

surreptitious (adj)
syn. furtive, secret, stealthy, secretive, fraudulent, sly, clandestine
ant. open, blatant
surveillance (n)
syn. watch, supervision, observation, espionage, spying, control, scrutiny
ant. freedom, privilege
sustenance (n)
syn. nourishment, nutrition, food, grub, livelihood
ant. starvation
swarm (v)
syn. throng, mob, flock, crowd, overrun
ant. scatter
swanky (adj)
(also *swank, informal*)
syn. expensive, lavish, fancy, fashionable, stylish, exclusive, posh, glamorous
ant. discreet, modest
swarthy (adj)
syn. dark, black, dark-skinned, dark-complexioned, brown
ant. fair, pale
sweltering (adj)
syn. hot, scorching, airless, sultry, suffocating, humid, oppressive
ant. breezy, airy, cool, fresh
swift (adj)
syn. rapid, fast, brisk, hurried, hasty, immediate, sudden
ant. slow, leisurely, tardy
swimmingly (adv)
(*informal*)
syn. easily, smoothly, successfully, effortlessly
ant. laboriously
swindle (n)
syn. fraud, deception, con, cheat, sharp practice, trickery
ant. honesty
swindler (n)
syn. fraudster, fraud, cheat, trickster, rogue, crook, scoundrel, imposter, charlatan, shark, con man
ant. gentleman, saint, worthy

swingeing (adj)
syn. excessive, oppressive, drastic, draconian, severe, harsh, punishing
ant. mild, moderate, soothing
swinging (adj)
(informal/old-fashioned)
syn. fashionable, lively, contemporary, trendy, modern, stylish, up-to-date
ant. old-fashioned, out-of-date
sybarite (n)
syn. hedonist, voluptuary, sensualist, epicure
ant. ascetic, hermit
sycophancy (n)
syn. flattery, fawning, adulation, servility, bootlicking, toadyism
ant. censure, criticism, abuse
sycophant (n)
syn. flatterer, fawner, yes-man, bootlicker, parasite, toady
ant. censure, critic, faultfinder
sylph-like (adj)
syn. graceful, elegant, slender, slim and attractive
ant. plump, bulky
symmetry (n)
syn. balance, harmony, proportion, correspondence, regularity, similarity
ant. asymmetry, irregularity
sympathetic (adj)
syn. compassionate, warm-hearted, kind-hearted, caring, empathetic, understanding, congenial, likeable, agreeable
ant. unsympathetic, harsh, antipathetic, indifferent
sympathiser (n)
syn. supporter, backer, adherent, fan, admirer, partisan
ant. opponent, enemy
sympathy (n)
syn. compassion, pity, empathy, condolence, commiseration, understanding, affinity, harmony
ant. indifference, antipathy, disharmony
synonymous (adj)
syn. identical, equal, similar, equivalent, the same
ant. opposite, dissimilar
synopsis (n)
syn. summary, resume, outline, precis, epitome, compendium, abridgement,

abstract, condensation
ant. expansion, amplification
systematic (adj)
syn. organized, planned, structured, coherent, methodical, orderly
ant. unsystematic, disorganized, disorderly

taboo (adj)

syn. banned, prohibited, forbidden, proscribed, unacceptable, unspeakable

ant. permitted, acceptable

tacit (adj)

syn. unsaid, implicit, understood, silent, unvoiced, unspoken, unexpressed

ant. explicit, spoken, avowed

taciturn (adj)

syn. uncommunicative, silent, tight-lipped, reserved, reticent, mum, quiet

ant. communicative, talkative, sociable

tactful (adj)

syn. diplomatic, politic, discreet, thoughtful, judicious, prudent

ant. tactless, untactful, undiplomatic

tailor-made (adj)

syn. bespoke, suited, ideal, made-to-measure, perfect

ant. unsuitable, ill-adapted

taint (v)

syn. pollute, spoil, contaminate, sully, damage, blot

ant. purify, cleanse

talent (n)

syn. aptitude, ability, flair, forte, genius, gift, skill

ant. ineptitude, inability

talented (adj)

syn. accomplished, able, skilful, expert, gifted, ace

ant. inept, clumsy

talkative (adj)

syn. garrulous, chatty, mouthy, communicative, long-tongued

ant. taciturn, reserved

talking-to (n)

(informal)

syn. reproach, rebuke, scolding, telling-off, criticism, reprimand

ant. commendation, praise

tall (adj)

syn. big, huge, large, gigantic, high

ant. short, low

tame (adj)

syn. docile, gentle, pet, mild, domesticated, unexciting, dull, uninteresting, boring

ant. wild, exciting, unmanageable

tangible (adj)

syn. actual, definite, real, perceptible, visible, palpable, substantial, evident

ant. intangible, abstract, theoretical

tantalize (v)

syn. tease, torment, torture, excite, entice, fascinate, beguile

an. satisfy

tantrum (n)

syn. outburst, frenzy, fury, rage, temper, paddy, paroxysm

ant. calm, composure, peace

tardy (adj)

syn. late, delayed, belated, leisurely, slow, sluggish

ant. punctual, prompt

tarnish (v)

syn. discolour, stain, rust, blemish, disgrace, ruin, harm, damage, sully

ant. polish, cleanse, clean

tart (adj)

syn. sour, tangy, acidic, hurtful, sarcastic, biting, scathing, sharp

ant. sweet, kind

tasty (adj)

syn. delicious, appetizing, palatable, mouth-watering, flavoursome, yummy

ant. tasteless, bland, insipid

tattered (adj)

syn. torn, tatty, ragged, ripped

ant. trim, neat

taunt (v)

syn. sneer, jeer, provoke, insult, mock, reproach, ridicule, tease

ant. respect, admire

taunt (n)

syn. jibe, jeer, sneer, barb, insult, dig, mockery, provocation, derision

ant. respect, admiration

tautology (n)

syn. repetition, reiteration, redundancy, verbosity

ant. conciseness
tawdry (adj)
syn. showy, flashy, gaudy, shabby, tasteless, vulgar
ant. tasteful, excellent
taxing (adj)
syn. demanding, difficult, tough, onerous, tiring, stressful, burdensome
ant. easy, effortless
tearful (adj)
syn. woeful, sorrowful, weepy, close to tears, emotional, poignant, pathetic
ant. cheerful, happy
tedious (adj)
syn. boring, uninteresting, dull, monotonous, lifeless, prosaic, tiresome
ant. interesting, exciting
teaming (adj)
syn. full, brimming, abundant, swarming, prolific, overflowing, packed, pregnant
ant. lacking, empty, sparse
telling (adj)
syn. effective, potent, powerful, cogent, striking, influential, significant
ant. weak, ineffective, insignificant
telling-off (n)
(informal)
syn. scolding, reprimand, rebuke, reproach, tongue-lashing
ant. commendation, praise
temerity (n)
syn. boldness, impudence, recklessness, rashness, audacity, daring, nerve
ant. caution, timidity
temperamental (adj)
syn. emotional, hot-headed, sensitive, moody, volatile, impatient, excitable, petulant, highly-strung, touchy
ant. placid, calm, composed, serene
temperance (n)
syn. abstinence, moderation, restraint, prohibition, self-control, sobriety, self-discipline
ant. intemperance, excess
temperate (adj)
syn. mild, calm, composed, moderate, self-controlled, sober, abstemious, self-restrained

ant. intemperate, excessive, extreme
tempest (n)
syn. typhoon, storm, commotion, disturbance, tumult, uproar, furore
ant. calm, peace
tempestuous (adj)
syn. violent, stormy, turbulent, intense, passionate, emotional, uncontrolled
ant. calm, peaceful, quiet
temporary (adj)
syn. brief, short-lived, impermanent, transitory, stopgap, provisional
ant. lasting, permanent
tempting (adj)
syn. alluring, attractive, appealing, seductive, enticing, beguiling
ant. repulsive
tenable (adj)
syn. defensible, supportable, justifiable, rational, sound, plausible, believable, reasonable
ant. untenable, indefensible, unreasonable, unsound
tenacious (adj)
syn. determined, resolute, untiring, persevering, firm, purposeful, stubborn, strong-willed, tough
ant. weak, loose, slack
tendency (n)
syn. inclination, leaning, bent, propensity, partiality
ant. aversion
tender-hearted (adj)
syn. kind-hearted, compassionate, kind, humane, merciful, sympathetic, soft-hearted, warm-hearted
ant. hard-hearted, cruel, callous
tenebrous (adj)
syn. dark, unlit, murky, gloomy, sombre
ant. light
tense (adj)
syn. strained, tight, anxious, stressed, nervous, restless, uneasy, worrying
ant. relaxed, calm
tension (n)
syn. tightness, strain, stress, anxiety, nervousness, apprehension
ant. relaxation, calm

tentative (adj)
syn. provisional, preliminary, unconfirmed, uncertain, timid, shaky, hesitating
ant. sure, definite, confident

tenuous (adj)
syn. insubstantial, slight, insignificant, doubtful, questionable, weak, vague
ant. substantial, convincing, significant

tepid (adj)
syn. lukewarm, half-hearted, unenthusiastic, indifferent, apathetic, uninterested
ant. hot, animated, passionate

terminate (v)
syn. end, finish, conclude, close, axe, abort, discontinue, wind up
ant. begin, start, initiate

termination (n)
syn. end, finish, conclusion, close, abortion, discontinuation, ending
ant. beginning, start, initiation

terrible (adj)
syn. awful, extreme, dreadful, terrifying, shocking, gruesome
ant. wonderful, superb

terrify (v)
syn. scare, terrorize, frighten, horrify, shock
ant. reassure

terror (n)
syn. horror, panic, fear, consternation, awe
ant. reassurance

terse (adj)
syn. brief, concise, crisp, to the point, short, laconic, blunt, curt
ant. prolix, long-winded, polite

testing (adj)
syn. tough, difficulty, demanding, challenging, stressful, hard
ant. easy, simple, effortless

testy (adj)
syn. irritable, peevish, touchy, quick-tempered, short-tempered, grumpy, quarrelsome
ant. genial, friendly, good-humoured

thankful (adj)
syn. grateful, glad, pleased, beholden, obliged

ant. thankless, ungrateful
thanks (n)
syn. gratitude, thankfulness, gratefulness, acknowledgement
ant. ingratitude
thaw (v)
syn. melt, dissolve, unfreeze, defrost
ant. freeze
theoretical (adj)
syn. hypothetical, impractical, conjectural, ideal, abstract
ant. practical, actual
theory (n)
syn. hypothesis, premise, thesis, proposition, belief, opinion, philosophy, ideology
ant. practice, certainty
therapeutic (adj)
syn. healing, remedial, curative, restorative, beneficial
ant. harmful, damaging
therefore (adv)
syn. hence, so, accordingly, then, thus
ant. because
thickhead (n)
(also *thicko, informal*)
syn. fool, idiot, blockhead, dimwit, imbecile, nitwit, dummy
ant. genius
thick-skinned (adj)
syn. insensitive, unfeeling, tough, callous, obdurate
ant. thin-skinned, sensitive
thief (n)
syn. robber, pickpocket, burglar, crook, embezzler, swindler
ant. saint, gentleman
thieve (v)
syn. steal, rob, pilfer, swindle, embezzle
ant. return
thin-skinned (adj)
syn. sensitive, hyper sensitive, touchy, irritable, soft, testy, peevish
ant. thick-skinned, insensitive
thorough (adj)
syn. comprehensive, detailed, in-depth, rigorous, complete, meticulous,

scrupulous, careful, perfect
ant. superficial, cursory, careless, partial
thoughtful (adj)
syn. pensive, musing, contemplative, introspective, philosophical, attentive, considerate, kind
ant. unthoughtful, thoughtless, unthinking, inattentive
thralldom (n)
(literary)
syn. slavery, servitude, captivity, enslavement
ant. freedom
threadbare (adj)
syn. worn, old, scruffy, ragged, tatty, moth-eaten, shabby
ant. new, fresh
threaten (v)
syn. browbeat, terrorize, bully, intimidate, endanger
ant. reassure, comfort
thrift (n)
syn. saving, frugality, parsimony, economy, prudence
ant. extravagance, waste
thrifty (adj)
syn. saving, frugal, parsimonious, economical, prudent, provident, careful, penny-pinching
ant. thriftless, extravagant, wasteful, prodigal
thrill (n)
syn. excitement, sensation, stimulation, kick, charge
ant. boredom
thrill (v)
syn. excite, rouse, arouse, intoxicate, electrify
ant. bore
thrilling (adj)
syn. exciting, rousing, moving, electrifying, stimulating, hair-raising
ant. boring, unexciting, uninteresting
thriving (adj)
syn. developing, prospering, flourishing, booming, going strong, blooming, successful
ant. declining, languishing, failing
thumping (adj)
syn. big, enormous, exorbitant, huge, great, immense, tremendous, massive

ant. petty, trivial, insignificant

thwart (v)
syn. stop, prevent, block, defeat, foil, frustrate
ant. aid, help

tidy (adj)
syn. neat, well kept, orderly, clean, meticulous, organized, methodical
ant. untidy, disorganized

tiff (n)
(informal)
syn. quarrel, argument, row, squabble, disagreement, tantrum
ant. harmony, amity, peace

tight-fisted (adj)
syn. parsimonious, mean, miserly, penny-pinching, niggardly
ant. generous, charitable

tight-lipped (adj)
syn. mum, uncommunicative, reticent, taciturn, quiet, silent
ant. talkative, garrulous

timely (adj)
syn. well-timed, appropriate, opportune, prompt, punctual, convenient
ant. ill-timed, unfavourable

timid (adj)
syn. frightened, shy, cowardly, fearful, afraid, apprehensive, pusillanimous
ant. bold, brave, audacious

timorous (adj)
(literary)
syn. timid, apprehensive, fearful, cowardly, nervous, pusillanimous, faint-hearted
ant. bold, brave, assertive

tiny (adj)
syn. small, minute, little, very small, dwarf, microscopic, mini
ant. enormous, huge, big

tirade (n)
syn. abuse, denunciation, outburst, invective, attack, blast, tongue-lashing
ant. eulogy, commendation, praise

tired (adj)
syn. exhausted, weary, drowsy, fagged, fatigued, bored overused, clichéd
ant. refreshed, energetic, fresh

tiresome (adj)
syn. wearisome, tedious, uninteresting, annoying, dull, boring, troublesome, irritating
ant. pleasant, interesting
titanic (adj)
syn. immense, gigantic, giant, huge, herculean, jumbo
ant. small, insignificant
titter (v)
syn. giggle, chuckle, laugh, snigger
ant. weep
toil (v)
syn. labour, work, drudge, slog, sweat, struggle
ant. relax, rest
toilsome (adj)
syn. laborious, tough, tiresome, arduous, difficult, hard
ant. easy, effortless, simple
tolerance (n)
syn. open-mindedness, acceptance, toleration, forbearance, understanding, patience, endurance
ant. intolerance, narrow-mindedness, bigotry, prejudice
tolerant (adj)
syn. open-minded, broad-minded, forbearing, patient, unprejudiced, easy-going, liberal
ant. intolerant, narrow-minded, bigoted, prejudiced
tomfoolery (n)
(old-fashioned)
syn. foolishness, folly, nonsense, silliness, stupidity, antics, skylarking
ant. sense, wisdom, prudence
tongue-tied (adj)
syn. speechless, dumb, silent, mute, inarticulate
ant. garrulous, talkative
toothsome (adj)
(humorous)
syn. tasty, delicious, appetizing, luscious, palatable
ant. insipid, nasty
topical (adj)
syn. contemporary, current, recent, up to date, relevant
ant. out of date

topmost (adj)
syn. highest, top, dominant, supreme, leading, uppermost, paramount
ant. lowest, bottom, subordinate

topsy-turvy (adj)
(informal)
syn. chaotic, disorderly, confused, disorganized, messy, untidy, jumbled
ant. ordered, tidy

torment (n)
syn. suffering, anguish, agony, trauma, distress, misery, pain, torture
ant. relief, happiness

tornado (n)
syn. hurricane, storm, cyclone, whirlwind, tempest, typhoon, twister
ant. calm, tranquillity

torpid (adj)
syn. lethargic, apathetic, lazy, sluggish, dull, lifeless, inert, indolent, inactive, slothful
ant. active, lively, vigorous

torpor (n)
syn. lethargy, sluggishness, apathy, inertia, torpidity, inactivity
ant. activity, vigour, animation

torrid (adj)
syn. hot, sultry, scorching, arid, tropical, passionate, lustful, erotic
ant. arctic, cold

tortuous (adj)
syn. twisting, zigzag, meandering, complex, complicated, labyrinthine, lengthy
ant. straight, direct

torture (n)
syn. abuse, persecution, cruelty, ill-treatment, suffering, torment, trauma
ant. ease, comfort

totalitarian (adj)
syn. autocratic, dictatorial, fascist, undemocratic, tyrannical
ant. democratic

totally (adv)
syn. completely, thoroughly, absolutely, entirely, wholly
ant. partly, partially

touchy (adj)
syn. sensitive, offended, easily, hypersensitive, irritable, peevish, petulant,

awkward, thin-skinned, grumpy
ant. calm, genial, imperturbable
toxic (adj)
syn. poisonous, deadly, polluting, harmful
ant. harmless
tractable (adj)
syn. amenable, docile, submissive, willing, manageable, complaisant
ant. intractable, stubborn
traduce (v)
syn. slander, defame, libel, vilify, misrepresent, malign, revile
ant. eulogize, praise, laud
tragedy (n)
syn. adversity, catastrophe, calamity, disaster, misfortune, affliction
ant. prosperity, success
tragic (adj)
syn. devastating, awful, disastrous, terrible, sad, pathetic, heart-rending
ant. comic, fortunate, happy
traitor (n)
syn. betrayer, back-stabber, defector, informer, rebel, deceiver
ant. loyalist, patriot
trammel (n)
syn. hindrance, restraint, bond, fetter, check
ant. freedom
trance (n)
syn. stupor, unconsciousness, daze, ecstasy, rapture, dream
ant. alertness
tranquil (adj)
syn. calm, peaceful, serene, undisturbed, quiet, placid, unruffled
ant. busy, agitated, excitable
tranquillity (n)
syn. calm, composure, peace, calmness, repose, quietness
ant. disturbance, agitation
transgress (v)
syn. disobey, exceed, violate, break, offend, go beyond
ant. obey
transgressor (n)
syn. offender, sinner, criminal, culprit, wrongdoer, felon
ant. saint, gentleman

transient (adj)
syn. temporary, transitory, short-lived, brief, short, momentary
ant. permanent

transition (n)
syn. change, transformation, alteration, shift, progress
ant. beginning, end

transitory (adj)
syn. temporary, short-lived, brief, momentary, transient
ant. permanent

transparent (adj)
syn. clear, crystal, sheer, obvious, apparent, manifest
ant. opaque, obscure, unclear

trash (n)
syn. nonsense, rubbish, waste, garbage, refuse
ant. sense

trauma (n)
syn. stress, anguish, shock, ordeal, suffering, injury
ant. healing, relaxation

travesty (n)
syn. parody, mockery, ridicule, burlesque, caricature
ant. respect, admiration

treacherous (adj)
syn. traitorous, unfaithful, untrustworthy, false, disloyal, two-faced, dangerous
ant. loyal, faithful

treachery (n)
syn. disloyalty, treason, infidelity, betrayal, unfaithfulness
ant. loyalty, faithfulness

treason (n)
syn. sedition, treachery, mutiny, disloyalty, betrayal, subversion
ant. loyalty, allegiance

tremendous (adj)
syn. immense, huge, colossal, excellent, marvellous, superb, fabulous, awesome, remarkable
ant. tiny, boring, run-of-the-mill, ordinary

tremulous (adj)
(literary)
syn. trembling, quivering, shivering, fearful, anxious, jittery, nervous, jumpy

ant. calm, composed, steady, firm
trenchant (adj)
syn. incisive, acid, acerbic, acidulous, caustic, bitter, sarcastic, strong, powerful, effective
ant. mild, ineffective, weak
trendy (adj)
(informal)
syn. fashionable, latest, funky, groovy, stylish
ant. unfashionable, dated
trepidation (n)
syn. fear, apprehension, alarm, nervousness, anxiety, fright, agitation
ant. calm, composure, unapprehensiveness
trespass (v)
syn. encroach, invade, intrude, enter without permission
ant. obey
tribulation (n)
syn. trouble, suffering, adversity, misery, distress, affliction, pain
ant. joy, happiness
tribute (n)
syn. homage, accolade, honour, praise, eulogy, compliments, commendation
ant. censure, criticism, blame
trickery (n)
syn. cheating, fraud, con, dishonesty, deceit, double-dealing
ant. honesty
trifling (adj)
syn. trivial, insignificant, unimportant, incidental, petty, silly
ant. important
trim (adj)
syn. neat, orderly, tidy, smart, well kept, well-dressed, slender, slim
ant. disorderly, untidy, scruffy
triumph (adj)
syn. victory, achievement, success, elation, jubilation, joy
ant. defeat, failure, disappointment
triumphant (adj)
syn. victorious, winning, successful, unbeaten, elated, jubilant, joyful, proud
ant. defeated, beaten, despondent, dejected

trivial (adj)
syn. petty, unimportant, insignificant, trifling
ant. significant, important
tropical (adj)
syn. sultry, humid, hot, sweltering, oppressive
ant. cold, arctic
troublemaker (n)
syn. mischief-maker, instigator, firebrand, meddler
ant. peace-maker
troublesome (adj)
syn. irksome, annoying, nagging, oppressive, difficult
ant. easy
truce (n)
syn. ceasefire, peace, lull, respite, pact, treaty
ant. war, hostilities
truculent (adj)
syn. aggressive, bellicose, hostile, antagonistic, ill-tempered, violent,
belligerent, savage
ant. gentle, good-natured, co-operative
true-blue (adj)
syn. loyal, faithful, trusty, dedicated, uncompromising
ant. superficial
trustworthy (adj)
syn. honest, ethical, true, reliable, authentic
ant. unreliable
truth (n)
syn. accuracy, authenticity, correctness, actuality, reality
ant. falsehood, fiction
truthful (adj)
syn. honest, sincere, trustworthy, candid, faithful, correct, true, realistic
ant. untruthful, deceitful, false
tubby (adj)
syn. chubby, plump, fat, stout
ant. slim
tumble (v)
syn. fall, collapse, slip, plunge, drop
ant. rise

tumbledown (adj)
syn. broken-down, ramshackle, shaky, dilapidated
ant. well-kept
tumult (n)
syn. pandemonium, uproar, commotion, noise, din, confusion, disorder, turmoil
ant. peace, calm, silence
turbulent (adj)
syn. chaotic, lawless, riotous, tempestuous, anarchic
ant. peaceful, calm
turmoil (n)
syn. confusion, bedlam, chaos, pandemonium, tumult, mayhem, violence
ant. calm, peace, order
turpitude (n)
syn. wickedness, sin, vice, baseness, iniquity, crime, corruption
ant. nobility, honour
twaddle (n)
(old-fashioned)
syn. nonsense, balderdash, rubbish, prattle
ant. sense
twit (n)
(informal)
syn. idiot, ass, halfwit, simpleton, fool
ant. genius, brain
two-faced (adj)
(informal)
syn. treacherous, deceitful, false, insincere, hypocritical
ant. honest, candid
tycoon (n)
syn. baron, mogul, magnate, industrialist, big shot
ant. nobody
tyrannical (adj)
syn. absolute, despotic, high-handed, oppressive, autocratic
ant. tolerant, liberal
tyranny (n)
syn. despotism, fascism, autocracy, injustice, dictatorship
ant. liberality, democracy

tyro (n)
syn. novice, learner, beginner, apprentice, student
ant. master

ubiquitous (adj)
syn. everywhere, all over, universal, global, common, worldwide, omnipresent
ant. rare

ugly (adj)
syn. unattractive, unlovely, repellent, horrible, unpleasant, nasty, dangerous, menacing
ant. beautiful, charming, pleasant

ultra (adj)
syn. immoderate, fanatical, radical, extreme, excessive
ant. moderate

unaccompanied (adj)
syn. alone, unescorted, solitary
ant. accompanied

unaccountable (adj)
syn. inexplicable, incomprehensible, unexplainable, strange, peculiar, odd, mysterious, astonishing
ant. explicable, explainable, understandable

unaccustomed (adj)
syn. unfamiliar, unusual, uncommon, strange, unused
ant. accustomed, familiar

unafraid (adj)
syn. fearless, daring, intrepid, confident
ant. afraid

unalterable (adj)
syn. inflexible, fixed, permanent, unchangeable, final
ant. alterable, flexible

ulterior (adj)
syn. hidden, covert, concealed, undisclosed, secret, underlying
ant. overt, declared

unabashed (adj)
syn. bold, blatant, confident, unembarrassed, unblushing, composed, unashamed, brazen

ant. abashed, sheepish

unanimity (n)

syn. accord, consensus, agreement, concord, harmony, unity, like-mindedness

ant. dissent, disagreement, disunity

unanimous (adj)

syn. agreed, united, harmonious, in accord, common, of one mind, in agreement

ant. split, disunited, disagreeing

unanswerable (adj)

syn. undeniable, irrefutable, indisputable, unarguable, absolute

ant. refutable

unappetising (adj)

syn. unappealing, unpleasant, unattractive, insipid, tasteless

ant. appetising, delicious

unapproachable (adj)

syn. aloof, withdrawn, unfriendly, unsociable, reserved, inaccessible, remote

ant. approachable, friendly, accessible

unarmed (adj)

syn. unguarded, defenceless, helpless, unprotected, open

ant. armed, protected

unashamed (adj)

syn. shameless, unrepentant, unabashed, impenitent, unconcealed, brazen

ant. ashamed, sheepish, abashed

unassuming (adj)

syn. modest, meek, humble, unostentatious, natural, self-effacing, unpretentious, simple

ant. ostentatious, pretentious, presumptuous

unattractive (adj)

syn. unappealing, ugly, plain, uninviting

ant. attractive

unauthorized (adj)

syn. unofficial, illegal, illicit, unlicensed, banned, prohibited, unapproved, unaccredited

ant. authorized, official, legal

unaware (adj)

syn. ignorant, uninformed, unconscious, oblivious, in the dark

ant. aware

unbearable (adj)
syn. unendurable, intolerable, unspeakable, too much
ant. bearable, acceptable
unbeaten (adj)
syn. undefeated, supreme, unbowed, winning
ant. defeated
unbiased (adj)
syn. disinterested, impartial, unprejudiced, unbigoted, fair
ant. biased
unblemished (adj)
syn. perfect, faultless, spotless, flawless, immaculate, pure
ant. imperfect, flawed
uncanny (adj)
syn. odd, strange, mysterious, weird, unnatural, ghostly, amazing,
remarkable, exceptional
ant. ordinary
uncertainty (n)
syn. confusion, perplexity, vagueness, insecurity, dilemma
ant. certainty
uncharitable (adj)
syn. unfeeling, unkind, selfish, mean, cruel
ant. charitable
unchaste (adj)
syn. impure, immoral, lewd, indecent, loose
ant. chaste, pure
uncivilized (adj)
syn. uncouth, uncultivated, uneducated, uncultured, vulgar, coarse
ant. civilized, cultured
uncommunicative (adj)
syn. taciturn, unsociable, reserved, withdrawn, tight-lipped, quiet, reticent
ant. communicative, garrulous, talkative
uncongenial (adj)
syn. antagonistic, unsympathetic, disagreeable, discordant, unpleasant,
uninviting
ant. congenial, agreeable, sympathetic
unconscionable (adj)
syn. unprincipled, unethical, unscrupulous, amoral, excessive, extreme,
unreasonable

ant. principled, reasonable
unconventional (adj)
syn. unorthodox, uncommon, eccentric, odd, unusual, peculiar
ant. conventional, orthodox, normal
uncouth (adj)
syn. uncivilized, coarse, crude, rude, disrespectful, uncultured, boorish, clumsy
ant. civilized, polite, refined
uncultured (adj)
syn. uncultivated, uncivilized, uncouth, unrefined, rustic, boorish, coarse
ant. cultured, civilized
undefiled (adj)
syn. chaste, pure, unblemished, uncontaminated, immaculate, clean
ant. defiled, impure
undeniable (adj)
syn. unquestionable, irrefutable, indisputable, definite, sure
ant. deniable, questionable
underestimate (v)
syn. misjudge, underrate, miscalculate, undervalue
ant. overestimate
underhand (adj)
syn. underhanded, secret, surreptitious, stealthy, unscrupulous, dishonest
ant. open, honest
undermine (v)
syn. reduce, spoil, weaken, threaten, shake, damage
ant. strengthen
underprivileged (adj)
syn. deprived, poor, impoverished, disadvantaged, destitute, needy
ant. affluent, wealthy
underrate (v)
syn. undervalue, underestimate, belittle, discount
ant. overrate, exaggerate
understanding (n)
syn. comprehension, awareness, grasp, intellect, brainpower, intuition, wisdom, perception, compassion, agreement
ant. ignorance
understate (v)
syn. minimize, underrate, make little of, trivialize, brush aside

ant. exaggerate
undervalue (v)
syn. underrate, underestimate, belittle, discount, misjudge, depreciate
ant. overrate, overestimate, exaggerate
undesirable (adj)
syn. unattractive, unwelcome, unpleasant, unsuitable, unwanted
ant. desirable
undignified (adj)
syn. improper, inappropriate, inelegant, indecorous, unseemly
ant. dignified
undisciplined (adj)
syn. unruly, uncontrolled, wild, unschooled, untrained
ant. disciplined
undisputed (adj)
syn. unquestionable, unchallenged, unquestioned, undoubted, sure, certain, indisputable
ant. uncertain, debatable, questionable
undistinguished (adj)
syn. unexceptional, mediocre, ordinary, so-so, commonplace, run-of-the-mill
ant. exceptional, remarkable
undo (v)
syn. unfasten, unhook, untie, unbolt, open, cancel, repeal, ruin, undermine, sabotage, blow
ant. fasten
undue (adj)
syn. immoderate, excessive, unreasonable, improper, unjustified, unnecessary, disproportionate
ant. appropriate, reasonable, moderate
unearth (v)
syn. disclose, discover, uncover, dig up, find, expose
ant. bury
uneasiness (n)
syn. anxiety, misgiving, apprehension, apprehensiveness, worry, agitation
ant. calm, composure
uneducated (adj)
syn. ignorant, uncultured, uncultivated, unread, unschooled, unlettered, illiterate

ant. educated, literate, lettered

unemotional (adj)

syn. apathetic, dispassionate, indifferent, passionless, unexcitable, unfeeling, cool, cold

ant. emotional, excitable, feeling

unemployed (adj)

syn. jobless, workless, unoccupied, laid off, resting

ant. employed

unending (adj)

syn. endless, never-ending, nonstop, constant, perpetual, everlasting, continual

ant. transient, brief, intermittent

unenthusiastic (adj)

syn. apathetic, half-hearted, unresponsive, indifferent, cool, bored, uninterested, nonchalant

ant. enthusiastic, ardent, whole-hearted, passionate

unequalled (adj)

syn. unparalleled, unmatched, peerless, matchless, incomparable, paramount, supreme

ant. ordinary, inferior

unequivocal (adj)

syn. unambiguous, unquestionable, undeniable, unmistakable, absolute, sure, clear, obvious, certain

ant. equivocal, ambiguous, vague, unclear

unerring (adj)

syn. perfect, infallible, sure, accurate, precise, exact, unfailing, impeccable

ant. erring, fallible, faulty, imperfect

unethical (adj)

syn. immoral, unprincipled, underhand, dishonest, improper

ant. ethical, moral

unexceptional (adj)

syn. mediocre, unremarkable, unimpressive, undistinguished, indifferent, average, ordinary

ant. exceptional, impressive, remarkable

unfair (adj)

syn. partisan, biased, unjust, one-sided, prejudiced, discriminatory, unjustified, undeserved, dishonest

ant. fair, just, justified, honest

unfaithful (adj)
syn. faithless, untrustworthy, disloyal, fickle, unreliable, imperfect, inaccurate, wrong
ant. faithful, loyal, accurate, perfect

unfamiliar (adj)
syn. odd, unusual, new, uncommon, inexperienced, unskilled, unversed
ant. familiar, customary, skilled

unfashionable (adj)
syn. outmoded, old hat, dated, old-fashioned
ant. fashioned

unfeeling (adj)
syn. unsympathetic, harsh, cold, cruel, callous, hard-hearted, inhuman, numb
ant. concerned, compassionate

unflappable (adj)
syn. imperturbable, calm, composed, unworried, unexcitable, unruffled, self-possessed
ant. nervous, excitable, temperamental

unflinching (adj)
syn. brave, bold, unwavering, resolute, firm, fearless, unshaken
ant. scared, cowed

unfold (v)
syn. open, disclose, show, reveal, expand, explain, display, describe
ant. fold, withhold, suppress

unforeseen (adj)
syn. unexpected, sudden, startling, unanticipated, unpredicted, accidental
ant. expected, predictable

unforgivable (adj)
syn. unpardonable, unjustifiable, inexcusable, deplorable, shameful
ant. forgivable, venial

unfounded (adj)
syn. baseless, unproven, groundless, unsubstantiated, unjustified, fabricated
ant. justified, reasonable

unfriendly (adj)
syn. antagonistic, hostile, uncongenial, unsociable, disagreeing, aloof, cold, cool
ant. friendly, amiable, agreeable

unfruitful (adj)
syn. fruitless, unprofitable, infertile, unproductive
ant. fruitful

ungenerous (adj)
syn. parsimonious, tight-fisted, selfish, mean, penurious, niggardly, stingy
ant. generous, charitable, benevolent

ungracious (adj)
syn. impolite, unmannerly, discourteous, rough, churlish, rude, bad-mannered
ant. gracious, polite, courteous

ungrateful (adj)
syn. unthankful, thankless, ungracious, ill-mannered, unmindful
ant. grateful, thankful

unheeded (adj)
syn. overlooked, unnoticed, ignored, disregarded
ant. heeded

unhurried (adj)
syn. slow, relaxed, leisurely
ant. haste

unification (n)
syn. combination, incorporation, amalgamation, coalition, union, alliance
ant. separation, split, partition

uniformity (n)
syn. similarity, regularity, monotony, sameness, invariability
ant. dissimilarity, difference

unify (v)
syn. combine, merge, unite, fuse, amalgamate, consolidate
ant. separate, split

unimpassioned (adj)
syn. unemotional, dispassionate, calm, cool, moderate, controlled, composed
ant. impassioned, passionate, excited

unimpeachable (adj)
syn. unquestionable, blameless, faultless, perfect, impeccable
ant. blameworthy, faulty

unintelligent (adj)
syn. slow, obtuse, foolish, stupid, brainless, dull
ant. intelligent

unintelligible (adj)
syn. incomprehensible, meaningless, incoherent, illegible, indistinct, muddled
ant. intelligible, understandable, clear

unintentional (adj)
syn. accidental, unpremeditated, unintended, unthinking
ant. intentional, deliberate

uninterested (adj)
syn. apathetic, bored, unconcerned, uninvolved, unenthusiastic, indifferent, unresponsive, incurious
ant. interested, concerned, enthusiastic, responsive

uninteresting (adj)
syn. boring, unexciting, bland, lifeless, insipid, dull
ant. interesting, exciting

unique (adj)
syn. specific, distinctive, matchless, exclusive, one-off, remarkable, incomparable
ant. common, commonplace, ordinary

unison (n)
syn. accord, concord, harmony, agreement, unanimity, unity
ant. disharmony, discord

unjust (adj)
syn. unfair, biased, one-sided, undue, partial, prejudiced, unmerited
ant. just, fair, impartial

unjustifiable (adj)
syn. unforgivable, wrong, inexcusable, indefensible, unacceptable
ant. justifiable

unkempt (adj)
syn. disordered, messy, shabby, ungroomed, untidy
ant. tidy, neat

unleash (v)
syn. unloose, free, untie, loose, release
ant. restrain

unlikely (adj)
syn. improbable, implausible, doubtful, unrealistic, questionable, slight
ant. likely, probable, plausible

unmannerly (adj)
syn. bad-mannered, impolite, rude, churlish, uncouth, discourteous, boorish

ant. well-mannered, polite, courteous

unmerciful (adj)

syn. merciless, heartless, ruthless, pitiless, inhuman, harsh, cruel, implacable, inexorable

ant. merciful, compassionate, humane

unmethodical (adj)

syn. unsystematic, immethodical, disorderly, unorganized, uncoordinated, illogical

ant. methodical, systematic, organized

unmindful (adj)

syn. mindless, careless, heedless, negligent, oblivious, unthinking, unaware, remiss

ant. mindful, heedful, careful, alert

unobtrusive (adj)

syn. unostentatious, unpretentious, inconspicuous, simple, modest, meek, humble, restrained

ant. ostentatious, pretentious, showy, mannered

unorthodox (adj)

syn. heterodox, unconventional, unusual, heretical

ant. orthodox, conventional

unperturbed (adj)

syn. calm, cool, composed, placid, self-possessed, untroubled, unruffled, unexcited, unworried

ant. perturbed, anxious, agitated

unpolished (adj)

syn. rude, crude, rough, unsophisticated, uncultured, uncivilized, coarse

ant. polished, civilized, elegant

unprejudiced (adj)

syn. unbiased, disinterested, fair, impartial, just, objective, open-minded

ant. prejudiced, narrow-minded

unprincipled (adj)

syn. unethical, dishonest, immoral, amoral, unscrupulous, deceitful, unprofessional

ant. principled, honest, ethical

unproductive (adj)

syn. unfruitful, fruitless, futile, ineffective, useless, barren, worthless

ant. productive, fertile

unprofessional (adj)
syn. amateur, unskilled, incompetent, inexperienced, untrained
ant. professional, skilful
unravel (v)
syn. explain, resolve, solve, figure out, undo, free
ant. complicate, entangle
unreal (adj)
syn. imaginary, false, fictitious, illusory, hypothetical, mythical, phoney, fanciful
ant. real, true, genuine
unrealistic (adj)
syn. impractical, idealistic, half-baked, theoretical, romantic
ant. realistic, pragmatic, truthful
unrelated (adj)
syn. different, unassociated, inapplicable, unlike, irrelevant
ant. related, similar
unreliable (adj)
syn. untrustworthy, changeable, undependable, fickle
ant. reliable
unrest (n)
syn. turmoil, chaos, protest, disturbance, rioting, anxiety, discord
ant. peace, calm
unripe (adj)
syn. immature, raw, undeveloped, green, unready
ant. ripe
unrivalled (adj)
syn. unsurpassed, unmatched, matchless, supreme, incomparable, peerless
ant. ordinary, inferior
unruffled (adj)
syn. self-possessed, placid, calm, cool, composed, unperturbed, undisturbed, peaceful
ant. ruffled, anxious, discomposed
unscathed (adj)
syn. unhurt, undamaged, unharmed, sound, safe
ant. hurt, harmed
unscrupulous (adj)
syn. dishonest, corrupt, unprincipled, unethical, shameless, deceitful, crooked

ant. scrupulous, honest
unseat (v)
syn. depose, overthrow, oust, remove, dethrone
ant. install, reinstate
unselfish (adj)
syn. selfless, generous, charitable, magnanimous, altruistic, disinterested
ant. selfish, self-centred, ungenerous
unsightly (adj)
syn. unattractive, unpleasant, repulsive, horrible, disagreeable
ant. attractive, beautiful
unskilful (adj)
syn. inept, incompetent, inexpert, clumsy
ant. skilful
unsolicited (adj)
syn. unasked, unrequested, unsought, unwanted, uninvited, unwelcome
ant. requested, invited
unsound (adj)
syn. weak, unwell, unhealthy, imperfect, fallacious, wrong, erroneous, unstable
ant. sound, perfect
unsung (adj)
syn. forgotten, unnamed, unhonoured, anonymous, uncelebrated, overlooked, neglected, unacknowledged
ant. famous, celebrated, renowned
unsure (adj)
syn. doubtful, uncertain, sceptical, irresolute
ant. sure
unsympathetic (adj)
syn. unkind, unfeeling, unmoved, callous, cold, heartless
ant. sympathetic, compassionate
untenable (adj)
syn. unsound, faulty, weak, illogical, unreasonable, indefensible
ant. tenable, sound
unthinkable (adj)
syn. inconceivable, unbelievable, unimaginable, absurd, impossible
ant. thinkable, conceivable
untimely (adj)
syn. early, premature, ill-timed, inconvenient

ant. timely

untoward (adj)

syn. unexpected, surprising, unfortunate, unfavourable, ill-timed, unlucky, adverse

ant. suitable, auspicious

untruthful (adj)

syn. untrue, insincere, dishonest, lying, deceitful, false

ant. truthful, honest

unveil (v)

syn. expose, uncover, bare, unfold, disclose, reveal

ant. veil, cover, hide

unwarranted (adj)

syn. unjustified, unforgivable, inexcusable, unjust, unfair, undeserved, unauthorized, illegal

ant. justified, excusable

unwise (adj)

syn. imprudent, senseless, injudicious, indiscreet, ill-considered, stupid, foolish

ant. wise, prudent, rational

unwitting (adj)

syn. unaware, unknowing, unconscious, unintentional, unthinking, ignorant

ant. conscious, knowing

unwonted (adj)

syn. unusual, unfamiliar, uncommon, peculiar, rare

ant. usual, common

unyielding (adj)

syn. inflexible, adamant, obstinate, stubborn, rigid, unbending

ant. flexible, amenable

upbeat (adj)

syn. optimistic, cheerful, hopeful, positive, bright

ant. downbeat, pessimistic

upbraid (v)

syn. reproach, rebuke, reprimand, scold, blame, condemn, criticize

ant. praise, commend

upheaval (n)

syn. turbulence, turmoil, disturbance, disorder, chaos

ant. order, calm

uphold (v)
syn. approve, endorse, confirm, support, maintain, keep, protect, keep going, justify
ant. oppose, counter

upright (adj)
syn. straight, vertical, honest, law-abiding, decent, principled
ant. flat, horizontal, dishonest

uprising (n)
syn. revolt, rebellion, mutiny, coup, insurgence, revolution
ant. loyalty, obedience

uproar (n)
syn. chaos, pandemonium, commotion, disorder, furore, outcry, rumpus
ant. calm, peace

upshot (n)
syn. outcome, conclusion, result, end, effect
ant. beginning

upstanding (adj)
syn. upright, ethical, moral, principled, honest, trustworthy, firm, sturdy, strong
ant. dishonest, untrustworthy, puny

uptight (adj)
syn. tense, anxious, uneasy, irritated, prickly
ant. calm, relaxed

up to date (adj)
syn. modern, advanced, familiar, current, stylish, trendy
ant. out of date, old, old-fashioned

upturn (n)
syn. increase, rise, advancement, improvement, boost, revival
ant. downturn, reduction

urban (adj)
syn. city, town, metropolitan
ant. rural

urbane (adj)
syn. civilized, courteous, debonair, refined, well-mannered, cultured
ant. uncivilized, uncouth

urge (v)
syn. encourage, implore, press, beg, plead, advocate, advise, counsel
ant. deter, discourage

urge (n)
syn. desire, wish, yearning, thirst, craving, itch
ant. disinclination, aversion

uselessness (n)
syn. hopelessness, ineffectiveness, idleness, futility, ineptitude
ant. usefulness, effectiveness

utility (n)
syn. benefit, value, usefulness, advantage, service
ant. futility, inutility

utmost (adj)
syn. greatest, maximum, highest, supreme, most
ant. minimum

utopian (adj)
syn. fanciful, imaginary, idealistic, romantic, wishful, fantastic, visionary, illusory
ant. realistic, pragmatic, sensible

Vv

vacate (v)
syn. evacuate, quit, leave
ant. occupy

vacillation (n)
syn. irresolution, indecision, inconstancy, wavering, shilly-shallying, hesitation
ant. resolution, firmness, decision

vagabond (n)
(old-fashioned)
syn. nomad, tramp, wanderer, vagrant, rogue
ant. gentleman, worthy

vague (adj)
syn. unclear, blurry, indistinct, indefinite, inexact, non-specific, forgetful, absent-minded
ant. clear, certain, definite

vain (adj)
syn. arrogant, immodest, proud, conceited, futile, failed, useless, unsuccessful, worthless, unimportant
ant. modest, successful, worthwhile

valediction (n)
syn. farewell, send-off, adieu, goodbye
ant. welcome, greeting

valiant (adj)
syn. bold, brave, heroic, intrepid, gallant, fearless
ant. timorous, cowardly

valour (n)
syn. boldness, gallantry, bravery, heroism, courage, mettle
ant. timorousness, cowardice

vandalism (n)
syn. destruction, mutilation, damage, ruin
ant. creation

vanity (n)
syn. conceit, pride, egotism, self-love, arrogance, narcissism,

self-admiration, cockiness
ant. modesty, humility, self-consciousness
vanquish (v)
syn. defeat, overthrow, subjugate, beat, conquer
ant. surrender
vapid (adj)
syn. flavourless, insipid, bland, dull, uninteresting, boring
ant. piquant, interesting
variable (adj)
syn. inconstant, changeable, fluctuating, unstable, up and down, inconsistent
ant. invariable, constant
variance (n)
syn. disagreement, dissent, discord, discrepancy, conflict, disparity
ant. agreement, harmony
varied (adj)
syn. miscellaneous, sundry, diverse, manifold, different
ant. uniform, similar
variety (n)
syn. difference, change, collection, sort, category, miscellany
ant. uniformity, monotony
vehement (adj)
syn. passionate, spirited, powerful, forceful, strong, zealous, enthusiastic
ant. subdued, mild
veil (v)
syn. cover, obscure, mask, conceal, hide
ant. expose, uncover
venal (adj)
syn. corrupt, bribable, sordid, corruptible
ant. incorruptible
vendetta (n)
syn. feud, enmity, bad blood, quarrel, hostility
ant. agreement, peace
veneration (n)
syn. adoration, reverence, devotion, respect, esteem, awe, worship
ant. contempt, scorn, disrespect
vengeance (n)
syn. revenge, reprisal, retribution, retaliation

ant. forgiveness
venial (adj)
syn. forgivable, excusable, pardonable, insignificant, trivial, slight
ant. unforgivable, inexcusable
venomous (adj)
syn. poisonous, deadly, toxic, malevolent, malicious, spiteful
ant. harmless, benevolent
venturesome (adj)
syn. adventurous, courageous, bold, daring, intrepid, spirited, fearless
ant. timorous, cowardly
veracious (adj)
syn. candid, honest, truthful, faithful, trustworthy, accurate, true
ant. untruthful, dishonest
veracity (n)
syn. honesty, truthfulness, credibility, accuracy, precision, truth
ant. untruthfulness, dishonesty
verbose (adj)
syn. phrasy, wordy, long-winded, garrulous, prolix, talkative, lengthy
ant. terse, succinct, short
verity (n)
syn. actuality, truthfulness, truth, soundness, veracity
ant. untruth, falsity
vernacular (adj)
syn. native, local, colloquial, indigenous, common, informal
ant. foreign
versatile (adj)
syn. multitalented, all-round, resourceful, many-sided, adjustable, flexible
ant. limited, inflexible
versed (adj)
syn. skilled, experienced, proficient, knowledgeable, experienced
ant. inexperienced, unskilled
verve (n)
syn. gusto, enthusiasm, liveliness, vigour, animation, spirit, vivacity
ant. apathy, unfeelingness, lethargy
veteran (n)
syn. old hand, old-timer, past master, old soldier, doyen
ant. novice, learner

veteran (adj)
syn. long-serving, experienced, old, practiced, professional, expert
ant. inexperienced, unpractised

veto (v)
syn. disallow, reject, rule out, turn down, prohibit, proscribe
ant. approve, consent, sanction

veto (n)
syn. rejection, embargo, ban, proscription, dismissal, prohibition
ant. approval, assent

vex (v)
(old fashioned)
syn. irritate, annoy, anger, irk, exasperate, harass, torment, pester, bug
ant. soothe, comfort, pacify

viable (adj)
syn. feasible, practical, workable, practicable, realistic, possible
ant. impracticable, unworkable, impossible

vibrant (adj)
syn. energetic, dynamic, lively, spirited, brilliant, glowing, bright, rich
ant. lifeless, pale

vice (n)
syn. wickedness, immorality, sin, misconduct, blemish, defect, fault
ant. virtue, goodness, morality

vicious (adj)
syn. violent, brutal, ruthless, inhuman, malicious, bitter, cruel
ant. gentle, kind

vicissitude (n)
syn. variation, fluctuation, change, shift
ant. stability

victor (n)
syn. champion, winner, hero, conqueror
ant. loser

victory (n)
syn. success, win, walkover, conquest
ant. defeat, loss

vigilant (adj)
syn. alert, observant, careful, watchful, eagle-eyed, attentive, cautious
ant. careless, inattentive, negligent

vigorous (adj)
syn. energetic, sturdy, tough, active, robust, strenuous, aggressive, powerful
ant. lethargic, weak, feeble
vigour (n)
syn. energy, robustness, health, passion, dynamism, strength, spirit
ant. lethargy, weakness, impotence
vile (adj)
syn. unpleasant, nasty, bad, foul, hateful, repulsive, disgusting, immoral, worthless
ant. pleasant, good
vilification (n)
syn. slander, abuse, criticism, defamation, aspersion, mud-slinging, calumny, scurrility
ant. commendation, compliment, praise
vilify (v)
syn. slander, abuse, criticize, defame, malign, denounce, decry, libel
ant. praise, compliment, adore, glorify
vindicate (v)
syn. exonerate, acquit, absolve, let off, confirm, justify, defend, prove, endorse
ant. incriminate, accuse, convict
vindictive (adj)
syn. revengeful, malicious, punitive, merciless, spiteful, venomous, unforgiving
ant. merciful, forgiving
violent (adj)
syn. aggressive, fierce, savage, brutal, forceful, powerful, extreme, uncontrollable
ant. gentle, mild, calm, peaceful
virile (adj)
syn. manly, strong, powerful, robust, masculine, vigorous, potent
ant. effeminate, unmanly, weak
virility (n)
syn. manliness, manhood, masculinity, huskiness, vigour
ant. effeminacy, weakness
virtual (adj)
syn. potential, practical, implicit, effective, implied
ant. actual

virtually (adv)
syn. practically, effectively, nearly, almost, close to
ant. actually
virtue (n)
syn. goodness, uprightness, morality, honour, good quality, forte, merit, worth, plus
ant. vice, wickedness, immorality
virulence (n)
syn. malevolence, acrimony, antagonism, hatred, hostility, malice, spite, toxicity, venom
ant. benevolence, love, compassion
visionary (adj)
syn. idealistic, unreal, utopian, romantic, fanciful, unrealistic, imaginary.
ant. realistic, pragmatic
visionary (n)
syn. idealist, theorist, dreamer, daydreamer, romantic
ant. pragmatist, cynic
vital (adj)
syn. important, crucial, essential, mandatory, active, lively, energetic, spirited
ant. unimportant, dead
vitality (n)
syn. vigour, vivacity, passion, spirit, life, liveliness, energy, dynamism
ant. weakness, sluggishness
vitiate (v)
syn. spoil, harm, impair, ruin, pollute, defile
ant. improve, purify
vituperation (n)
syn. vilification, abuse, reprimand, rebuke, scurrility, blame, reproach
ant. commendation, eulogy, praise
vivacious (adj)
syn. lively, cheerful, spirited, gay, animated, sportive, jolly, frolicsome
ant. languid, torpid, lethargic, lifeless
vociferous (adj)
syn. loud, clamorous, shouting, noisy, uproarious, thundering, loud-mouthed
ant. silent, quiet

void (adj)
syn. vacant, empty, free, invalid, ineffective, worthless, useless
ant. full, valid

volatile (adj)
syn. fickle, emotional, unpredictable, erratic, unstable, tense, uncomfortable
ant. stable, steady, constant

volition (n)
syn. choice, will, free will, decision, option, preference
ant. compulsion, force

voluble (adj)
syn. garrulous, talkative, fluent, loquacious
ant. taciturn, silent

voluntary (adj)
syn. optional, elective, unpaid, honorary, unforced, willing
ant. compulsory, forced

voluptuous (adj)
syn. sensual, licentious, carnal, hedonistic, erotic
ant. ascetic, self-denying

voracious (adj)
syn. avid, greedy, hungry, unquenchable, eager, devoted
ant. indifferent, apathetic

vulgarity (n)
syn. coarseness, indecency, crudeness, dirtiness, indecorum, ribaldry
ant. decency, politeness

vulnerable (adj)
syn. defenceless, helpless, in danger, weak, sensitive, tender
ant. invulnerable, strong, tough

Ww

waggish (adj)
(old-fashioned)
syn. funny, witty, sportive, jocular, mischievous, humorous, comical
ant. serious, pensive

wail (v)
syn. cry, weep, moan, howl, mourn
ant. rejoice, joy

waive (v)
syn. renounce, give up, surrender, turn down, abandon, ignore, disregard
ant. assert, claim, maintain

wane (v)
syn. decrease, decline, fade, weaken, lessen, diminish, dwindle, shrink
ant. increase, grow, wax

warfare (n)
syn. conflict, hostilities, combat, fighting, arms, war, struggle
ant. peace, harmony

warily (adv)
syn. cautiously, carefully, vigilantly, apprehensively, suspiciously
ant. unwarily, recklessly

warm-hearted (adj)
syn. kind, kind-hearted, compassionate, sympathetic, generous, loving, affectionate, cordial
ant. cold-hearted, unkind, cold, unsympathetic

warmth (n)
syn. cosiness, heat, geniality, friendliness, kindness, amiability, fondness
ant. coldness, unfriendliness

warrantable (adj)
syn. justifiable, lawful, permissible, defensible, right, allowable
ant. unwarrantable, unjustifiable

wary (adj)
syn. apprehensive, alert, careful, cautious, attentive, vigilant, suspicious, distrustful
ant. rash, inattentive, trustful, careless

waspish (adj)
syn. irritable, touchy, peevish, bad-tempered, peppery
ant. genial, friendly
wasteful (adj)
syn. imprudent, lavish, prodigal, thriftless, spendthrift, uneconomical
ant. frugal, thrifty, economical
watch (v)
syn. observe, track, guard
ant. ignore
watchful (adj)
syn. alert, cautious, vigilant, wary, heedful
ant. inattentive, heedless
wavering (adj)
syn. doubtful, dithering, doubting, hesitant, in two minds
ant. determined
wax (v)
syn. increase, grow, rise, expand, enlarge
ant. decrease, wane
wayward (adj)
syn. headstrong, obstinate, stubborn, unmanageable, refractory, self-willed
ant. complaisant, docile, submissive
weaken (adj)
syn. enfeeble, lessen, lower, enervate, undermine
ant. strengthen
wealthy (adj)
syn. rich, affluent, moneyed, loaded, well-to-do, well-off
ant. poor, penniless
weariness (n)
syn. drowsiness, lethargy, sleepiness, tiredness, prostration
ant. liveliness, freshness
weary (adj)
syn. tired, fatigued, shattered, tiring, exhausting, arduous
ant. energetic, fresh, refreshed
weedy (adj)
syn. feeble, insipid, frail, weak
ant. strong
weep (v)
syn. moan, sob, bemoan, cry

ant. rejoice
weird (adj)
syn. supernatural, ghostly, uncanny, strange, idiosyncratic, eccentric, unconventional
ant. normal, ordinary, conventional
well-bred (adj)
(old-fashioned)
syn. well-mannered, polite, cultivated, mannerly, courteous, genteel, refined
ant. ill-bred, ill-mannered, impolite
well-disposed (adj)
syn. friendly, amicable, well-minded, agreeable, sympathetic
ant. ill-disposed, unfriendly
well-known (adj)
syn. renowned, famous, popular, celebrated, eminent
ant. unknown
wheedle (v)
syn. coax, persuade, flatter, implore, cajole, entreat, butter up, soft-soap
ant. coerce, force, browbeat
whimper (v)
syn. cry, weep, sob, moan
ant. laugh
whimsical (adj)
syn. fanciful, idiosyncratic, eccentric, mischievous, unconventional, curious, weird
ant. sensible, realistic
wholehearted (adj)
syn. heartfelt, hearty, sincere, enthusiastic, unreserved, absolute
ant. half-hearted
wholesale (adj)
syn. total, wide-ranging, extensive, comprehensive, large-scale
ant. partial
wholesome (adj)
syn. healthy, good, nourishing, hygienic, clean, pure, ethical, uplifting, helpful
ant. unwholesome, deleterious, harmful
wholly (adv)
syn. totally, entirely, completely, absolutely, altogether

ant. partly
whopping (adj)
(informal)
syn. enormous, huge, big, tremendous, great, extraordinary
ant. small, tiny
wicked (adj)
syn. immoral, bad, evil, corrupt, crooked, mischievous, roguish
ant. virtuous, modest, good
wild (adj)
syn. ferocious, untamed, uncultivated, rough, turbulent, unruly, unrestrained, foolish, rash
ant. tame, cultivated, restrained, disciplined
wiles (n)
syn. tricks, artfulness, schemes, ploys, ruses, guile, stratagems, cunning
ant. artlessness, honesty
wilful (adj)
syn. planned, intentional, deliberate, obstinate, strong-willed, headstrong
ant. accidental, docile, meek
willing (adj)
syn. ready, minded, prepared, inclined, enthusiastic
ant. unwilling, reluctant
willingly (adv)
syn. readily, voluntarily, cheerfully, happily, eagerly
ant. unwillingly, reluctantly
willingness (n)
syn. readiness, desire, inclination, compliance
ant. unwillingness, reluctance
wilt (v)
syn. droop, flop, wither. languish, fade, weaken
ant. flourish, thrive
wily (adj)
syn. cunning, artful, foxy, crafty, shrewd, canny, clever
ant. naïve, artless, innocent
winsome (adj)
syn. winning, pleasing, engaging, attractive, enchanting, captivating
ant. unattractive, repulsive
wisdom (n)
syn. sense, shrewdness, understanding, prudence, common sense,

astuteness, rationale, knowledge
ant. folly, foolishness, nonsense, imprudence
wise (adj)
syn. clever, intelligent, astute, sage, perceptive, smart, prudent, canny
ant. unwise, foolish, imprudent
wit (n)
syn. astuteness, intelligence, insight, humour, jokes, joker, comedian, comic
ant. stupidity, seriousness
wither (v)
syn. wilt, perish, fade, shrivel, shrink, lessen, diminish
ant. thrive, flourish
withering (adj)
syn. scornful, scathing, contemptuous, humiliating, devastating
ant. respectful, supportive
withhold (v)
syn. retain, hide, hold back, repress, suppress, control
ant. release, give
withstand (v)
syn. confront, face, oppose, defy, resist, tolerate
ant. yield, surrender
witty (adj)
syn. amusing, humorous, comic, funny, scintillating, jocular, clever
ant. unwitting, unamusing, dull
wobbly (adj)
syn. unsteady, shaky, unsafe, unstable
ant. stable
woe (n)
syn. sorrow, sadness, misery, heartbreak, adversity, distress, trouble, tribulation
ant. ecstasy, joy, delight
woeful (adj)
syn. sorrowful, gloomy, sad, awful, deplorable, pathetic, appalling, rotten
ant. joyful, cheerful, excellent
womanizer (n)
syn. Casanova, philanderer, seducer, romeo, ladies' man
ant. puritan, moralist

wonderful (adj)
syn. marvellous, superb, magnificent, delightful, fantastic, great, awesome, smashing
ant. ordinary, common, awful
wordy (adj)
syn. verbose, long-winded, phrasy, lengthy, prolix, garrulous
ant. succinct, terse, concise
worldly (adj)
syn. earthly, mundane, human, material, experienced, sophisticated
ant. spiritual, naïve
worn (adj)
syn. ragged, shabby, scruffy, tatty, exhausted, moth-eaten
ant. new, fresh, smart
worry (n)
syn. anxiety, apprehension, tension, distress, fear, misgiving, trouble, problem
ant. delight, reassurance, comfort
worship (v)
syn. adore, exalt, honour, revere, glorify, venerate, pray, love
ant. despise, scorn, disregard, hate
worship (n)
syn. adoration, exaltation, honour, reverence, veneration, glorification, devotion, prayer
ant. vilification, contempt, mockery, scorn
worthless (adj)
syn. valueless, ineffective, pointless, senseless, useless, lousy, good-for-nothing
ant. worthy, valuable, useful
worthwhile (adj)
syn. valuable, worthy, beneficial, helpful, useful, effective, productive, profitable
ant. worthless, useless, valueless
worthy (adj)
syn. moral, righteous, upright, good, decent, respectable, principled, high-minded, virtuous, reputable
ant. unworthy, disreputable, unprincipled
wrangle (n)
syn. argument, clash, brawl, altercation, quarrel, tiff, controversy, dispute

ant. amity, agreement, harmony
wrath (n)
syn. fury, spleen, anger, temper, rage, ire, resentment
ant. calm, composure, happiness
wreck (v)
syn. destroy, ruin, break, demolish, smash, spoil, devastate
ant. build, repair, save
wretched (adj)
syn. sad, distressed, miserable, desolate, melancholy, dejected, harsh, hopeless, bleak
ant. cheerful, comfortable, fine, excellent
wrongful (adj)
syn. wrong, unfair, unjust, unlawful, unethical, immoral, improper
ant. rightful, fair, lawful

X Y Z

xenophobia (n)
syn. racialism, ethnocentrism, racism, prejudice, intolerance, bigotry, sexism
ant. xenomania, moderation, liberalism, tolerance

yearn (v)
(literary)
syn. long, desire, crave, want, hanker, thirst, itch
ant. dislike, hate

yell (v)
syn. shout, wail, roar, howl, scream
ant. whisper

yes-man (n)
syn. minion, crawler, sycophant, toady, bootlicker
ant. critic, rebel

yield (v)
syn. surrender, submit, give in, produce, provide, bear
ant. resist, withhold

yielding (adj)
syn. submissive, obliging, docile, obedient, complaint, flexible, elastic, soft
ant. unyielding, stubborn, obstinate, rigid

youngster (n)
syn. child, youth, adolescent, juvenile, teenager, kid, lad
ant. adult, oldie

youthful (adj)
syn. young, young-looking, boyish, girlish, active
ant. elderly, aged

yucky (adj)
(informal)
syn. unpleasant, disgusting, horrible, dirty, foul, messy
ant. nice, pleasant

zany (adj)
(informal)
syn. idiosyncratic, mad, eccentric, crazy, comic, unconventional, funny,

screwy, kooky
ant. serious, conventional, normal
zeal (n)
syn. passion, enthusiasm, vigour, eagerness, energy, devotion, spirit, fire
ant. apathy, indifference, lethargy
zealous (adj)
syn. passionate, enthusiastic, ardent, devoted, fervent, dedicated, committed, eager
ant. apathetic, indifferent, lethargic
zenith (n)
syn. apex, top, peak, high point, summit, acme, pinnacle
ant. nadir, bottom, base
zest (n)
syn. zeal, liveliness, enthusiasm, energy, passion, eagerness, gusto
ant. apathy, lethargy, sluggishness
zoom (v)
(informal)
syn. speed, rush, hurry, race, dash
ant. slow

Bibliography

Oxford Advanced Learner's Dictionary (UK: Oxford University press, Ninth Edition 2015).

Longman Dictionary of Contemporary English (England: Longman Group Ltd, First Indian reprint 1998).

Cambridge Advanced Learner's Dictionary (New Delhi: Cambridge University Press, Fourth Edition 2013).

Chambers Pocket Thesaurus (London: Hodder & Stoughton, 2002).

The Penguin Dictionary of English Synonyms and Antonyms (London: Penguin Books, 1992).

Oxford Dictionary of Synonyms and Antonyms (UK: Oxford University Press, Third Edition 2014).

The New Roget's Thesaurus (USA: Berkley Publishing, 1986).

S.M. Haseebuddin Quadri, *A Companion to Research Methodology in Humanities* (Hyderabad: Hi-tech Publishers, First Edition 2009).

Mohd Masood Ishaq, *Effective Spoken English and Grammar* (Hyderabad: Neelkamal Publishers, First Edition 2015).

Norman Lewis, *Word Power Made Easy* (New Delhi: Goyal Publishers, Second Edition 2013).

Terry O'Brien, *English Vocabulary Today* (New Delhi: Rupa Publishers 2011).

Abdul Hashem, *Improve Your Vocabulary* (New Delhi: Ramesh Publishing House, Twentieth Edition 2015).

Wilfred Funk, *Word Origins and Their Romantic Stories* (New Delhi: Goyal Publishers, Indian Edition 2013).

Chambers Twentieth Century Dictionary (London: Chambers, 1983).

The Merriam Webster Thesaurus (USA: Merriam-Webster INC Publishers, First Edition 2013).

Jennifer Seidl and W. McMordie, *English Idioms* (New Delhi: Oxford University Press, Fifth Edition 1989).

H.W. Fowler, *A Dictionary of Modern English Usage* (UK: Oxford University Press, 2010).

Acknowledgements

The first words of thanks must go to my wife, daughters and my students for their love and support towards the making of this book. They enhanced my confidence in all my efforts on this small project. Also, my thanks to Almighty God, who always looks after me and keeps me in high spirits.

I am deeply indebted to all my well-wishers for their invaluable suggestions and encouragement to read and publish books. Their advice always helps me to write more books in future.

I profusely thank Rupa Publications for accepting my manuscript and recognizing me as one in their family of authors. I'm extremely grateful to the editors for their painstaking work in making this book better.

I would be failing in my duty if I did not express my deep gratitude to my dear friend Mr Raju Chennoju, a well-known ELT expert, who was kind enough to evaluate this book and offer his valuable comments and suggestions. Despite his busy schedule, he helped me throughout the preparation of this project.

I am very much thankful to all the newspapers, magazines and writers for giving me worldly knowledge and motivating me to think and write more.

I am also grateful to my wife and my daughters Sara Kulsum and Maryam Fatima for their remarks and appreciation that allow me to take up meaningful work in my life. I owe a huge debt of gratitude to Sara Kulsum for her meticulous typing and proofreading of the manuscript.

I express my deep gratitude to Professor Syed Mohd Haseebuddin Quadri, Maulana Azad National Urdu University, Hyderabad. His style of hard work always inspired me and his book *A Companion to Research Methodology in Humanities* was also of great help in this project.

I would also like to express my sincere thanks to the great communicator and author Colonel Venugopalan Nair for his continuous encouragement and comments on this book.

Finally, I would like to thank all my friends, colleagues and all my well-wishers for their direct and indirect support that helped me complete this small project.